LIBRARY OF HEBREW BIBLE/ OLD TESTAMENT STUDIES

533

Formerly Journal for the Study of the Old Testament Supplement Series

T&T CLARK • LIBRARY OF BIBLICAL STUDIES •

MICHAL'S MORAL DILEMMA

A Literary, Anthropological and Ethical Interpretation

Jonathan Y. Rowe

t&t clark

Published by T & T Clark International
A Continuum imprint
80 Maiden Lane, New York, NY 10038
The Tower Building, 11 York Road, London SE1 7NX

www.continuumbooks.com

Visit the T & T Clark blog at www.tandtclarkblog.com

Library of Congress Cataloging-in-Publication Data
Rowe, Jonathan Y.
Michal's moral dilemma : a literary, anthropological, and ethical interpretation / Jonathan Y. Rowe.
p. cm. — (The library of Hebrew Bible/Old Testament studies ; #533)
Includes bibliographical references and index.
ISBN-13: 978-0-567-27179-2 (hardcover : alk. paper)
ISBN-10: 0-567-27179-X (hardcover : alk. paper) 1. Michal (Biblical figure) 2. Bible. O.T. Samuel, 1st, XIX, 10-18—Criticism, interpretation, etc. 3. Ethics in the Bible. I. Title.
BS580.M53R68 2011
222'.4306—dc22 2010009131

ISBN: HB:978-0-567-27179-2

Typeset by Pindar NZ, Auckland, New Zealand
Printed and bound in the United States of America by Thomson-Shore, Inc

TABLE OF CONTENTS

List of Figures

For

Hilary

and

Elizabeth and Benjamin

אנכי וביתי נעבד את־יהוה

– Joshua 24:15

Acknowledgements

My most profound thanks for the support and encouragement that have resulted in this book are due to Hilary. Our children, Elizabeth and Benjamin, have grown a lot since its inception; they are no longer bemused by Daddy's 'boring books' – ones without pictures.

In terms of academic stimulus, I am most indebted to Nathan MacDonald and Mario Aguilar and I gladly acknowledge their sage advice over a number of years. They are not alone, however, in sharing their erudition, and I should also like to thank Richard Cleaves, Philip Esler, Walter Houston, Andrew Mein, Nathan Moser, Sergio Rosell, Chris Wright and Pedro Zamora for pertinent and helpful observations at various stages of the book's gestation. Naturally, any inadequacies in the final text are mine.

I am also grateful to the Kirby Laing Institute for Christian Ethics and its director, Jonathan Chaplin, for a generous grant that helped finance the research contained in this book.

Finally, I thank Rowman & Littlefield Publishing Group for permission to reproduce Figure 4 on page 155 from Kathey-Lee Galvin, 'Schneider Revisited: Sharing and Ratification in the Construction of Kinship,' in *New Directions in Anthropological Kinship* (Lanham: Rowman & Littlefield, 2001), 109–24. © Rowman & Littlefield Publishers, Inc.

ABBREVIATIONS

AA	*American Anthropologist*
AAASP	American Anthropological Association Special Publication
AB	Anchor Bible
ABD	*Anchor Bible Dictionary*
AE	*American Ethnologist*
AJA	*Australian Journal of Anthropology*
AJS	*American Journal of Sociology*
ANE	Ancient Near East
Ant.	Josephus, *Antiquities of the Jews*
AOTC	Apollos Old Testament Commentary
ARA	*Annual Review of Anthropology*
ASAOSP	Association for Social Anthropology in Oceania Special Publications
ASR	*American Sociological Review*
AT	*Anthropological Theory*
BA	*Biblical Archaeologist*
Bd'A	La Bible d'Alexandrie
BASOR	*Bulletin of the American Schools of Oriental Research*
BBC	The Broadman Bible Commentary
BDB	F. Brown, S. R. Driver and C. A. Briggs, *A Hebrew and English Lexicon of the Old Testament*
BI	*Biblical Interpretation*
BJS	*British Journal of Sociology*
BR	Bucknell Review
BS	The Biblical Seminar
BT	*The Bible Translator*
BTB	*Biblical Theology Bulletin*
BW	*The Biblical World*
CA	*Cultural Anthropology*

CAT	Commentarie de L'Ancien Testament
CB	Cambridge Bible
CBQ	*Catholic Biblical Quarterly*
Civ.	Augustine, *De civitae Dei* [The City of God]
CH	Codex Hammurabi
C. mend.	Augustine, *Contra mendacium* [To Consentius: Against Lying]
CSCD	Cambridge Studies in Christian Doctrine
CSSA	Cambridge Studies in Social Anthropology
CSSCA	Cambridge Studies in Social and Cultural Anthropology
CSSH	*Comparative Studies in Society and History*
CT	Colección Teorema
Curr Anthropol	*Current Anthropology*
DBHE	*Diccionario Bíblico Hebreo-Español*
DCCS	*Diccionario Crítico de Ciencias Sociales*
DEFM	*Diccionario de Ética y de Filosofía Moral*
De mend.	Augustine, *De mendacio* [On Lying]
DJD	Discoveries in the Judean Desert
DTMAT	*Diccionario Teológico Manual del Antiguo Testamento*
EJST	*European Journal of Social Theory*
EN	Aristotle, *Nicomachean Ethics*
EP	*The Encyclopedia of Philosophy*
ER	*Encyclopedia of Religion*
ESCA	*Encyclopedia of Social and Cultural Anthropology*
EstBib	*Estudios Bíblicos*
FBD	Father's Brother's Daughter
FP	*Faith and Philosophy*
FZD	Father's Sister's Daughter
GBS	Guides to Biblical Scholarship
GKC	*Gesenius' Hebrew Grammar*, 2nd English Edition, Edited by E. Kautzsch, Translated by A. E. Cowley
HR	*History of Religions*
HumStud	*Human Studies*
HTR	*Harvard Theological Review*
IB	*The Interpreter's Bible*
ICC	International Critical Commentary

IEES	*International Encyclopedia of Economic Sociology*
IJMSS	*International Journal of Moral and Social Studies*
ISBE	*International Standard Bible Encyclopedia*
JASO	*Journal of the Anthropological Society of Oxford*
JBL	*Journal of Biblical Literature*
JBS	Jerusalem Biblical Studies
JCC	*Journal of Cognition and Culture*
JCS	*Journal of Cuneiform Studies*
JETS	*Journal of the Evangelical Theological Society*
JJS	*Journal of Jewish Studies*
JLR	*Journal of Law and Religion*
JLS	*Journal of Libertarian Studies*
JMF	*Journal of Marriage and the Family*
JP	*The Journal of Philosophy*
JPS	Jewish Publication Society
JPSP	*Journal of Personality and Social Psychology*
JR	*Journal of Religion*
JRAI	*Journal of the Royal Anthropological Institute*
JSNT	*Journal for the Study of the New Testament*
JSOT	*Journal for the Study of the Old Testament*
JSOTSup	Journal for the Study of the Old Testament Supplement Series
JSS	*Journal of Semitic Studies*
JTS	*Journal of Theological Studies*
JTSB	*Journal for the Theory of Social Behavior*
LAI	Library of Ancient Israel
LC	Lange's Commentary
LHB	Library of Hebrew Bible
LXX	Septuagint
LXX^{A}	Codex Alexandrinus of LXX
LXX^{B}	Codex Vaticanus of LXX
LXX^{L}	Lucianic manuscripts of LXX
MAQ	*Medical Anthropology Quarterly*
MBD	Mother's Brother's Daughter
MNK	C. H. J. van der Merwe, J. A. Naudé and J. H. Kroeze, *A Biblical Hebrew Reference Grammar*

MS	Manuscript
MT	Masoretic Text
NAC	New American Commentary
NCBC	New Century Bible Commentary
NDCEPT	*New Dictionary of Christian Ethics and Pastoral Theology*
NICOT	New International Commentary on the Old Testament
NIBC	New International Biblical Commentary
NIDOTTE	*New International Dictionary of Old Testament Theology and Exegesis*
NIV	New International Version
NLH	*New Literary History*
NLR	*New Left Review*
NRSV	New Revised Standard Version
NS	New Series
NSBT	New Studies in Biblical Theology
OBT	Overtures to Biblical Theology
OS	Oudtestamentische Studiën
OTL	Old Testament Library
OTS	Old Testament Studies
PBM	Paternoster Biblical Monographs
PC	Pulpit Commentary
PPR	*Philosophy and Phenomenological Research*
REP	*Routledge Encyclopedia of Philosophy*
RTR	*Reformed Theological Review*
SARASS	School of American Research Advanced Seminar Series
SBLit	Studies in Biblical Literature
SBLDS	Society of Biblical Literature Dissertation Series
SBLSP	Society of Biblical Literature Seminar Papers
SBTS	Sources for Biblical and Theological Study
SCE	*Studies in Christian Ethics*
SHBC	Smyth & Helwys Bible Commentary
SJT	*Scottish Journal of Theology*
SSH	*Social Science History*
SSN	Studia Semitica Neerlandica
Summa	Thomas Aquinas, *Summa Theologica*
TDOT	*Theological Dictionary of the Old Testament*

TOTC	Tyndale Old Testament Commentaries
TWOT	*Theological Wordbook of the Old Testament*
TynBul	*Tyndale Bulletin*
UCOP	University of Cambridge Oriental Publications
VT	*Vetus Testamentum*
VTSup	Vetus Testamentum Supplement Series
WBC	Word Biblical Commentary
WO'C	Bruce Waltke and M. O'Connor, *An Introduction to Biblical Hebrew Syntax*
ZAW	*Zeitschrift für die alttestamentliche Wissenschaft*

Introduction

Plaisante justice qu'une rivière borne!
Vérité au-deça des Pyrénées, erreur au-delà.

Blaise Pascal, *Pensées et opuscules*[1]

Blaise Pascal's polemical response to Michel de Montaigne's relativism asserts that universal moral standards exist, despite the fact of cultural plurality.[2] Although the cultural differences that spurred Montaigne's reflections are now more obvious than in his day, one could conclude that such diversity is unimportant, simply a reflection of the richness of human existence. While this may often be a perfectly satisfactory conclusion, there are good reasons for thinking that the matter cannot be left there. Since societies are not discrete but intimately connected, usually comprising people of disparate ethnic backgrounds, the experience of culturally divergent moralities is becoming commonplace. The global 'clash of civilizations', therefore, is experienced as the pressing parochial and personal issue of 'getting on with my neighbour', something that soon leads to ethical questions: how *should* one relate to 'the other'? In an essay on cultural diversity the eminent anthropologist Clifford Geertz argues that value conflicts due to cultural differences are 'one of the major moral challenges we these days face'.[3]

1 The epigraph is from B. Pascal, *Pensées et opuscules* (20th ed.; Paris: Librairie Hachette, n.d.), para. 294.

2 Gewirth distinguishes between positive morality (those rules for behaviour that exist) and normative morality (those rules for behaviour that should exist). Positive plurality does not imply normative plural*ism*, see A. Gewirth, 'Is cultural Pluralism Relevant to Moral Knowledge?', in *Moral Disagreements: Classic & Contemporary Readings* (ed. C. W. Gowans; London: Routledge, 2000), 181. I will follow the customary distinction between 'ethics' and 'morality' (and their variants): 'morality' is actual behaviour and standards; 'ethics' is reflection about these practices.

3 C. Geertz, *Available Light: Anthropological Reflections on Philosophical Topics*

When considering value conflict arising from cultural differences it is not necessary to refer only to extreme cases that have rather obvious answers to which virtually all people subscribe, for the matter is often not so much one of disagreement about what is good or evil, but about relative priorities. For example, people from different societies may well agree that both 'telling the truth' and 'being loyal to one's family' are good, indeed, since one *ought* to do them, that they are *moral* goods. Yet these individuals may disagree about which moral good takes precedence in situations when they cannot both be achieved. This particular difference of opinion concerns whether one has a greater obligation to an impersonal 'value' such as truth or a known individual.[4] It is important to realize that such conundrums are by no means merely hypothetical curiosities but that they constitute many people's daily dilemmas.

Cultural diversity is also observed within the community that shares one Lord and one faith: the Church. If a common life is a feature of the Church's mission, its common witness, an important question concerns the limits, if any, to acceptable moral diversity. Comprehensive Christian reflection about cross-cultural value conflict would marshal the gamut of biblical, theological, philosophical and social-scientific resources. This book, however, has more limited ambitions. I will investigate one particular value clash within 1 Samuel, for while ethical reflection must involve much more that an appeal to a selection of biblical verses, the Scriptures – as Scriptures not simply a particular interpretation of them – do constitute a tract of common ground upon which or from which one can consider the sort of differences annotated above. Moreover, because Old Testament texts hail from a very different cultural milieu to our own they may provide new perspectives upon contemporary value conflict, perhaps exposing weaknesses with some of our own presuppositions.

The 'cultural distance' between the biblical and modern worlds has led

(Princeton: Princeton University Press, 2000), 86.

4 Attwood objects to the use of 'value' as a term in ethical debate since it assumes that 'value' is a common denominator that allows 'values' to be compared and traded, thus excluding objective (i.e. reasoned rather than simply chosen) morality: 'non-negotiable values' are oxymoronic, see D. Attwood, *Changing Values: How to Find Moral Truth in Modern Times* (Carlisle: Paternoster, 1998), 12–16. While accepting his concerns I will continue to use 'value' as useful shorthand for moral goods. Note that while I have expressed the matter in terms of a conflict of priorities in a moment of 'decision', the issue is similar for those who would frame the question in terms of dispositions towards family loyalty or truth.

some commentators to highlight what one might call the moral problem *of* the Old Testament. Walter Kaiser, for example, observes a conflict between the behaviour of biblical characters and modern sensibilities.[5] He posits that God is changeable (Gen. 6:6), malevolent (Mal 1:2-3) and deceptive (1 Kgs 22:2-23), while Abraham lies (Gen. 12:10-20), David commits adultery (2 Sam. 11:2-5), and Ehud and Jael commit murder (Judg. 3:15-26; 4:17-20). He also highlights what he considers to be morally offensive laws and sanctions, for instance, the treatment of women, slavery and the death penalty. Kaiser seeks to exculpate actions that impugn God's character or that of important persons, an approach aptly criticized by John Rogerson for supposing that the standard of morality is *modern* moral sensitivity. Whether ancient biblical, modern Western or some other morality should be normative is not the concern of the present book. My focus will be upon moral conflict *within* the Old Testament and the text's own assessment of its resolution.

Rogerson identifies a number of passages in which conflicts occur, including 'Abraham's question' (Gen. 18:22-33), the Hebrew midwives' deception (Exod. 1:15-20), Jonathan and David's friendship (1 Sam. 20:1-34), and Elisha's lie (2 Kgs 8:7-15). Rogerson makes an obvious yet key observation, namely, that the 'moral dilemmas explored in these stories must have been credible to the presumed authors and readers'.[6] This is undoubtedly a challenge for those who live in societies distant in time and place from ancient Israel, both because the dilemmas are often not obvious and, even when they are, they are understood differently. A key purpose of this book, therefore, is to commend a particular approach to reading Old Testament narrative in order to appreciate what it has to say about ethics.

1. Michal's Moral Dilemma

John Barton proposes that conflicts of moral values in the books of Samuel might be especially illuminating because neither God nor a divine word is adduced as literary *deus ex machina*. He suggests that they 'could be read with

5 See W. Kaiser, *Toward Old Testament Ethics* (Grand Rapids: Zondervan, 1983), 247–304.

6 J. Rogerson, 'Old Testament Ethics', in *Text in Context: Essays by Members of the Society for Old Testament Study* (ed. A. D. H. Mayes; Oxford: OUP, 2000), 116–37, quote 126. See also the dilemma in 1 Macc. 2:32-41.

an eye to the complexity of human ethical dilemmas and to the need for ethical conduct even in the midst of far too many constraints on human freedom'.[7] Such is the situation in which Michal finds herself in the narrative of 1 Samuel.

At first blush the pericope in 1 Sam. 19:10-18a is a straightforward account of how Michal aided David's flight from a spear-wielding maniac and his henchmen. The moral questions touched upon by the text, though, are more complex. The prima facie problem concerns Michal's lie to facilitate David's escape. A number of commentators suggest that Michal ought to have had the strength of character exhibited by her brother Jonathan who, they maintain, unflinchingly declared the truth to Saul instead of dissembling (cf. 1 Sam. 20:32).[8] However, given that the passage's quest is David's escape from Saul's unambiguously murderous intentions most commentators excuse Michal's lie as the lesser of two evils.[9] In this book I will show that this is an inadequate interpretation and explain how modern readers can properly comprehend Michal's moral dilemma.

Before proceeding, however, it is necessary to address two important issues. The first concerns the version of 1 Samuel to be used. As is well known, there are many differences between the MT, the various versions of the LXX, and the fragments discovered at Qumran. There is a case for simply deciding which version one wishes to interpret and then proceeding to do so, a reading strategy that possesses the advantages of not needing to defend every variant followed. This does not seem to me to be entirely satisfactory, since it ignores the possibility that the single, coherent text originally authored is not extant in any of the versions now available. Nevertheless, because this book focuses upon the ethics of the narrative rather than textual criticism the latter will be discussed in the footnotes. Moreover, key historical-critical themes that have interested previous commentators will be discussed in detail only where issues of interpretation are at stake.

The second issue concerns the passage to be interpreted. I have chosen

7 J. Barton, 'Reading for Life: The Use of the Bible in Ethics', in *Understanding Old Testament Ethics: Approaches and Explorations* (Louisville: Westminster John Knox Press, 2003), 55–64, quote 61.

8 See D. Erdmann, *The Books of Samuel* (LC 5; trans. C. H. Toy and J. A. Broadus; New York: Scribner, Armstrong and Co., 1877), 255; Hugenberger, 'Michal', *ISBE* 3.348.

9 For discussion of narrative 'quest', in this passage highlighted in the *inclusio*, vv. 10 and 18, and vv. 12 and 17, see Jan P. Fokkelman, *Reading Biblical Narrative: An Introductory Guide* (trans. I. Smit; Louisville: Westminster John Knox, 1999), 73–96.

to study 1 Sam. 19:10c-18a, the limits of which are clearly indicated by the phrases ודוד נס וימלט and ודוד ברח וימלט.[10] It could be objected that David's fleeing should be understood with reference to its cause and, therefore, that one should commence interpretation at the beginning of v. 10, where we read that Saul sought to pin David to the wall with his spear. This reasoning, however, would drive us back yet further, for in v. 9 the author highlights that Saul's actions occur because 'an evil spirit from the LORD' came upon him. Far from indicating that Saul was merely a puppet unable to exercise individual agency I think this authorial note points to YHWH having ultimate control. But perhaps even going back to the start of v. 9 is inadequate, because v. 8 indicates the start of a new stage in the narrative with a refrain familiar to readers of the books of Samuel: 'there was war, and David went out to fight the Philistines' (cf. 1 Sam. 4:1; 7:10; 17:1; 28:1; 2 Sam. 3:1, 6; 11:1; 21:15). However, notwithstanding the importance of these start points for the interpretation of Michal's moral dilemma in its narrative and theological context, only vv. 10c-18a concern her actions. For this reason it is quite appropriate to restrict interpretation of Michal's dilemma to the self-contained passage delineated by the *inclusio*, and this is what I shall do.

A close analysis of the passage's structure reveals that it comprises three sections plus an introduction and conclusion. Each of the sections contains a self-contained narrative in which Michal interacts with different characters. The scene is set by the narrator describing Saul's cordoning of David's dwelling. In the first section Michal orchestrates David's escape then, in the second, she executes a ploy to deceive Saul's messengers. In the final section Saul confronts Michal, demanding a reason for her deception, in response to which she blames David. The conclusion re-emphasizes that David escaped Saul's clutches. The whole displays a chiastic structure, as in Figure 1.[11]

10 See H. Rouillard and J. Tropper, '*TRPYM*, Rituels de Guérison et Culte des Ancêtres d'après 1 Samuel XIX 11–17 et les Textes Parallèles d'Assur et de Nuzi', *VT* 37 (1987): 340–61, especially 342–43. LXX^{B} starts v. 11 with καὶ ἐγενήθη ἐν τῇ νυκτὶ ἐκείνῃ = ויהי בלילה ההוא, 'and it happened that night', while MT attaches the defective form בלילה הוא (also at Gen. 19:33; 32:23) to the end of v. 10, see K. McCarter, *1 Samuel*: *A New Translation with Introduction, Notes and Commentary* (AB 8; Garden City: Doubleday, 1980), 325; A. Campbell, *1 Samuel* (FOTL 7; Grand Rapids: Eerdmans, 2003), 203. Cross contends that one cannot argue from space requirements in 4QSam^{b} for either reading, see F. M. Cross, 'The Oldest Manuscripts from Qumran', *JBL* 74 (1955): 147–72, especially 167.

11 Few commentators propose detailed structures. Fokkelman is the only other exegete

Introduction

A David flees, but Saul corners him (10c-11a)

First Section

B Michal tells David he will be killed if he doesn't save himself (11b)

C David escapes (12)

D Michal disguises teraphim (13)

Second Section

E Saul sends messengers (14a)

F Michal says 'David is sick' (14b)

E' Saul sends the messengers (15a)

F' Saul says 'bring him to me in order to kill him' (15b)

Third Section

D' Teraphim's disguise is discovered (16)

C' Saul demands to know why Michal let his enemy escape (17a)

B' Michal says David threatened to kill her; she had to save herself (17b)

Conclusion

A' David flees, and escapes (18a)

Figure 1 The Structure of 1 Samuel 19:10-18a

If this structure is considered in terms of characters' moral choices a pattern contrasting truth and lying, loyalty and deception is observed, as in Figure 2.

It is clear that ethical behaviour is central to the interpretation of this text. There seem to be two voices offering distinct moral perspectives: Michal lies, but to save a life; Saul tells the truth, but with murderous intent.

It is my contention, however, that simply identifying that the passage is concerned with ethical issues does not ensure an adequate interpretation. Because biblical texts hail from temporally distant societies one can concur with Philip Esler that they 'need to be investigated using disciplines developed

to suggest 1 Sam. 19:11-17 is structured chiastically, dividing it into two sequences, deception (11-14) and discovery (15-17), see J. P. Fokkelman, *Narrative Art and Poetry in the Books for Samuel. A Full Interpretation Based on Stylistic and Structural Analyses. Vol. II: The Crossing Fates (I Sam 13–31 and II Sam 1)* (SSN 23; Assen: Van Gorcum, 1986), 266. Campbell proposes a two-fold framework: problem (11a) and solution (11b-17); the latter comprising three sections: the escape (11b-12), delaying tactics (13-16) and confrontation (17), see Campbell, *1 Samuel*, 203.

B True words to David: the situation as it is
  C Loyalty to David: aiding his escape
    F A lie: 'he is sick'
    F' The truth: 'in order to kill him'
  C' Deception of Saul: the reverse of her loyalty to David
B' Lying words to Saul: dissembling to portray her disloyalty as a last resort

Figure 2 Moral Choices in 1 Samuel 19:10-18a

specifically to comprehend the social dimensions of human experience'.[12] Only then can readers discern what loyalty, lying, telling the truth, or betrayal mean in context, and so be equipped to appreciate and evaluate the text's theological message.

2. Interpreting Michal's Dilemma

All readings of the Bible are interpretations. While there is no neutral standpoint from which one can judge interpretations this does not mean all readings are equally good interpretations *of the text*. People who read the Bible from different cultural backgrounds or holding divergent convictions can be expected to produce distinct interpretations. Nevertheless, if they are to be faithful to the original telling, they must not ride roughshod over it but must account both for what it says and the way in which it is said.

I observed above how their cultural distance from the Old Testament means that interpreters in modern Western societies must tread carefully in order to avoid imposing foreign ideas upon these ancient texts. But it is possible that an alternative movement may help: perhaps the way moral dilemmas are perceived in some contemporary societies may suggest ways of interpreting those found in the Old Testament. If so, then we need to find tools that sensitize us to these perspectives. In recent decades the academic discipline of anthropology has been employed by a number of exegetes to do just this. The present book learns from those who have travelled this particular road before, while also proposing new ways in which the journey should be made.

Within the field of Old Testament ethics some significant work has been

12 P. Esler, *The First Christians in their Social Worlds: Social-scientific Approaches to New Testament Interpretation* (London: Routledge, 1994), 2.

generated since the 1980s, some of which has attended to interpretative method. Nevertheless, many descriptions of the ethics of the Old Testament remain 'under-theorized'. *Michal's Moral Dilemma* seeks to fill this lacuna by carefully interpreting a single text and explicating the theoretical basis for this interpretation. To do so it brings Old Testament studies, anthropology and ethics into conversation – Figure 3 presents the interdisciplinary nature of the study graphically.

Although each discipline can inform the others, limitations of space preclude a systematic examination of, for example, how anthropology might interact with ethics – in the diagram such learning is shown by the uncapitalized letters. Instead, by maintaining a focus on the interpretation of a particular text, I seek conclusions that involve all three disciplines, represented by the central space labelled 'Michal'.

In the next chapter, I initiate the conversation by elucidating the Old Testament's own resources for addressing cases of conflicting moral values. I go beyond a simple appeal to Old Testament 'law', an obviously important

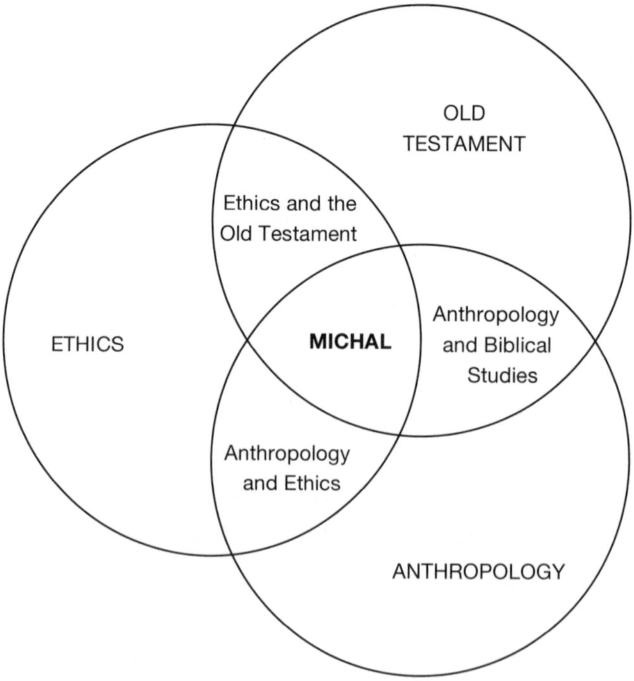

Figure 3 An Interdisciplinary Conversation

topic for Old Testament ethics, proposing that the questions at hand are best addressed by considering the moral goods in play.

Chapter 2 examines the nature of 'good' in more detail, along with the ways in which it has been related to 'the right'. Because this study is not an investigation in moral philosophy my aim is simply to show the contested nature of 'the good' and 'goods', and the implications of choosing a particular interpretation when seeking to comprehend Old Testament ethics. At this point one must take up the challenge of John Barton, who advocates using Martha Nussbaum's work to study biblical narrative. Nussbaum uses studies of Greek tragedy to argue that particular situations should take precedence over ethical rules; I shall argue that rather than think in terms of rules or situations it is better to proceed by assuming 'the priority of the good'.

Since the 'family' has been identified as one of the most significant Old Testament moral goods, Chapter 3 examines anthropological approaches to kinship and the ethics of kinship, concluding the 'family' is not so much an institution as a 'practice'. The analysis of 'practice' has typically been undertaken in terms of 'structure' and 'agency', and I examine how these categories are related to each other according to the school of thought labelled 'practice theory'. In addition, I advocate attention to the importance of ambiguity in interpersonal interaction.

The accounts of practice found in the Old Testament are to be *read*. Chapter 4 explains how a modified version of Mikhail Bakhtin's theory of heteroglossia enables readers to appreciate how authors present a moral vision by promoting some characters' narrative voices while undermining others. I then briefly discuss how I shall use anthropological resources in exegesis, before summarizing the methodology I employ to seek 'interpretative understanding' of characters' moral choices.

The discussion up to this point might be considered a methodological introduction. Although relatively extensive, I consider it essential to show that each of the elements that form part of my methodology are matters of dispute and debate, and that interpreters who tread unwarily, perhaps ignorant of the complexities of 'good', 'kinship', or 'practice', to name just some of the more important facets of this study, may produce explanations characterized more by their own context than that of the text's. Chapters 2–4, therefore, delineate an exegetical method and carefully position my approach vis-à-vis those of other commentators.

Chapter 5 examines the moral conundrum facing Michal as she lies to save her husband from her father, King Saul. I am interested in the moral goods presented or alluded to within the text, and what happens when they conflict. In order to justify my interpretation, particular attention is paid to violence, the implications of marriage for a woman's personal loyalties, and lying. I argue that each character within the narrative attempts to 'resolve' the conflict of moral values by acting in a certain way. Familiarity with the David tradition leads many commentators to assume that Michal's decision was straightforward – but I shall propose that it was not. Indeed, because her choice was startlingly unexpected I conclude the study by enquiring after the theological import of Michal's moral dilemma.

Chapter 1

Old Testament Morality and Value Conflict

חסד־ואמת נפגשו צדק ושלום נשקו

Psalm 85:10 [11]

So that we are less likely to impose upon the text our own preconceptions about the issues at hand, it is important to start thinking about conflicts of moral values in the Old Testament by using its own resources. This is the task of the first part of this chapter; in the second section I consider in more detail the moral goods mentioned in the text.

1. Old Testament Resources for Value Conflict

The most obvious resource within the Old Testament for addressing value conflict is 'law'. Facets of the legal corpus that may be particularly useful are the content of individual stipulations, and the sanctions and/or motivations attached to each decree. The law codes, however, are not the only sources of moral norms to be found in the Old Testament. Some writers have suggested that the Bible points to a 'natural law'. Similarly, the imitation of God has been considered a basis for ethics. Both or either of these may also provide resources for ethical reflection in situations of value conflict. In this section I shall examine each of these possible resources for clues that may help resolve value conflicts.

A. OLD TESTAMENT 'LAW'

Christian writers have traditionally emphasized law as a source for ethics and in cases of conflict have searched for a hierarchy of values. Norman Geisler calls his scheme 'graded absolutism'. It is based upon three premises: the fact of higher and lower moral laws; the existence of unavoidable moral conflicts; and the absence of guilt for the unavoidable. Using the analogy of two cars simultaneously approaching a junction Geisler suggests that 'when a person enters an ethical intersection where two laws come into unavoidable conflict, it is evident that one law must yield to the other'.[1] He offers three signposts: love of God over love for people; obedience to God before government; and mercy before veracity. Despite Geisler's assertion that this scale is divinely ordained, weaknesses include its very high level of abstraction, and the assumption that these pairings are themselves unproblematic, for example, that mercy and truth are mutually exclusive categories in situations of value conflict.

In terms of Old Testament ethics, Christopher Wright offers a more sophisticated proposal, arguing the law codes contain an implicit scale of values. According to Wright, the following ordering (in descending importance) is visible in the Decalogue: God, Sabbath for the good of the whole community, authority and integrity of the family, human life, sex and integrity of marriage, property and judicial integrity.[2] Although YHWH is obviously the foundation and most important 'value', this ordering is problematic. Wright himself recognizes that given the centrality of the 'father's house' in the Old Testament its

> strict sexual ethic must be seen in the context of [the] primary concern for preserving the stability of the larger family structure, since that in turn was an essential part of Israel's understanding and experience of the covenant relationship between the nation and Yahweh.[3]

Furthermore, judicial integrity is connected both to individual well-being and justice within the community; and while the individual appears to be inferior to the family and community in Wright's prioritization, there are laws protecting

1 N. Geisler, *Christian Ethics* (Leicester: Apollos, 1990), 113–32, quote 120.

2 See C. Wright, 'Ethics', *NIDOTTE* 4.585–94, especially 593; idem, *Living as the People of God: The Relevance of Old Testament Ethics* (Leicester: IVP, 1983), 163–68; idem, 'Old Testament Ethics', *NDCEPT* 48–55, especially 54; idem, *Old Testament Ethics for the People of God* (Downers Grove: IVP, 2004), 305–14. See also G. Wenham, 'Law and the Legal System in the Old Testament', in *Law, Morality and the Bible* (ed. B. N. Kaye and G. J. Wenham; Leicester: IVP, 1978), 24–52, especially 29.

3 Wright, 'Old Testament Ethics', 54.

the well-being of the individual from communal and familial tyranny (e.g. Deut. 19:15-21; 21:18-21).

Wright considers other laws also reveal a scale of values: life matters more than property, persons matter more than punishments and needs matter more than rights and claims. The justification of this ordering is based upon the fact that capital punishment is not prescribed for property crimes and could not, according to Wright, be commuted for murder;[4] an interpretation of the *lex talionis* as restricting punishment, along with limitations to judicial beating and the absence of bodily mutilation (with the single exception of Deut. 25:11); and the placing of human physical need above property rights (Deut. 23:24-5; 24:19-22). Although significantly more nuanced and textually founded than Geisler, Wright's scheme is insufficient for two reasons. First, on a technical level, although it is possible that Old Testament law reflects a scale of values, a finer tool is necessary to sketch it with sufficient precision for it to be useful in more than a handful of straightforward cases. Second, legal values are not the only relevant ones for Old Testament ethics – something Wright would not contest.[5] Gordon Wenham highlights the important, albeit not absolute, difference between law and ethics.

> In most societies what the law enforces is not the same as what upright members of that society feel is socially desirable, let alone ideal. There is a link between moral ideals and law, but law tends to be a pragmatic compromise between the legislators' ideals and what can be enforced in practice.[6]

Although Old Testament 'law' is frequently paraenetic, this difference means that even if were possible exactly to delineate the law's scale of values it may

4 On whether capital punishment was always executed see also W. Kaiser, *Toward Old Testament Ethics* (Grand Rapids: Zondervan, 1983), 297–99; H. McKeating, 'Sanctions against Adultery in Ancient Israelite Society, with Some Reflections on Methodology in the Study of Old Testament Ethics', *JSOT* 11 (1979): 57–72; G. Wenham, *Leviticus* (NICOT; Grand Rapids: Eerdmans, 1979), 281–86.

5 See also G. Wenham, *Story as Torah: Reading the Old Testament Ethically* (OTS; Edinburgh: T&T Clark, 2000), 2, where he criticizes Otto for an exclusive focus upon law, see E. Otto, *Theologische Ethik des Alten Testaments* (Stuttgart: Kohlhammer, 1994); idem, 'Of Aims and Methods in Hebrew Bible Ethics', *Semeia* 66 (1994): 161–72.

6 G. Wenham, 'The Gap between Law and Ethics in the Bible', *JJS* 48 (1997): 17–29, quote 18.

prove insufficient to resolve particular value conflicts. Wright himself observes that narratives might shed light on cases of moral conflict since 'actors in a story have to make choices according to some implicit prioritizing even of the Ten Commandments'.[7] This is suggestive, although I propose it is unnecessary to suppose either that law always precedes narrative, or that the matter need be restricted to the Decalogue.

Despite these cautions it is possible that law does assist the resolution of value clashes. Consider, for example, Exod. 22:2-3: 'If a thief is found breaking in, and is beaten to death, no bloodguilt is incurred; but if it happens after sunrise, bloodguilt is incurred'.[8] The law states that life is more important than belongings, refusing to exculpate the daytime killing of an intruder when, one assumes, the owners of the house could both see and overpower the thief. At night, however, the risk to the lives of household members is heightened, since a ruckus in the dark could easily lead to injury to the residents themselves, and so there is no culpability should the trespasser be bludgeoned to death. In both cases human life is preferred: during the day, life is preferred to property; during the night, the life of the innocent to that of a guilty intruder. Three observations are in order. First, I propose that human life and property are considered as 'goods', and their elimination or removal as 'evils'. Further, because the author assumes that people *ought* to promote goods and avoid evils, human life and property are *moral* goods. The fundamental issue at stake in law, therefore, is the desirability of a moral good or evil vis-à-vis other moral goods or evils. Second, laws sometimes indicate the prioritization of goods to be adopted in particular cases. Third, the prioritization reflected in these laws may depend upon the circumstances of a situation. This is obviously so with casuistic laws describing what to do in certain cases, but even unexplained or unelaborated apodictic decrees must be employed in concrete circumstances. In this respect, it is important to observe that Old Testament codes were not used in the same way as modern laws, which are applied by a judge to specific cases. If a similar approach is taken to Old Testament law it can lead to questions like: 'What if a son is rebellious but not a drunkard?' (see Deut. 21:18-20).[9] Bernard

7 C. Wright, *Walking in the Ways of the Lord: The Ethical Authority of the Old Testament* (Leicester: Apollos, 1995), 143.

8 All English language biblical quotes NRSV unless otherwise indicated.

9 For discussion see J. Burnside, *The Signs of Sin: Seriousness of Offence in Biblical*

Jackson argues that the 'modern model of law, based upon the "application" of statutes in court, is not applicable to the ancient Near East. The "codes" have a different purpose – didactic, sapiential, monumental'.[10] 'Law', therefore, had a similar function to the wisdom literature, but in a different environment: the wisdom sayings provided guidance for the young while the law codes were to educate adults, perhaps especially elders.[11] In neither case were either wisdom or legal stipulations 'applied', but used to inform individuals' judgments in particular situations.

It seems Old Testament legal texts may provide some help in the resolution of value conflicts, but that they do not tell the whole story.

B. OLD TESTAMENT LEGAL MOTIVATIONS

The Old Testament is very realistic concerning people's propensity to observe its commandments and carefully attaches reasons for keeping them to many individual stipulations. I shall first consider positive motivations, leaving their obverse, negative sanctions, until the next section.

John Barton proposes a helpful typology of Old Testament legal motivations as past, present and future.[12] Many scholars note that prime among past motivations is the exodus. In Deut. 15:13-15, for example, Israel is instructed to treat captives justly since having 'experienced God's justice and compassion themselves, the Israelites could only properly express their gratitude by showing a similar concern for the weak and underprivileged in their midst'.[13]

Law (JSOTSup 364; Sheffield: Sheffield Academic Press, 2003), 16.

10 B. Jackson, 'Ideas of Law and Legal Administration: a Semiotic Approach', in *The World of Ancient Israel: Sociological, Anthropological and Political Perspectives* (ed. R. E. Clements; Cambridge: CUP, 1989), 185–202, quote 186. For a more extensive justification of this thesis see idem, 'Models in Legal History: The Case of Biblical Law', *JLR* 18 (2002–2003): 1–30; idem, *Wisdom – Laws: The Mishpatim of Exodus 21:1-22:16* (Oxford: OUP, 2007), 3–76.

11 Cf. Jackson, 'Ideas of Law'; J. Crenshaw, *Old Testament Wisdom: An Introduction* (London: SCM, 1982). For the Old Testament's own presentation of the use of law see James Watts, *Reading Law: The Rhetorical Shaping of the Pentateuch* (BS 59; Sheffield: Sheffield Academic Press, 1999), 15–31.

12 J. Barton, *Ethics and the Old Testament* (London: SCM, 1998), 82–95.

13 E. Davies, 'Walking in God's Ways: The Concept of *Imitatio Dei* in the Old Testament', in *In Search of True Wisdom* (JSOTSup 300; ed. E. Ball; Sheffield: Sheffield University Press, 1999), 99–115, quote 103.

Covenant relationship as the motivation for ethical behaviour is highlighted by James Muilenburg.

> [The Israelite] knew perfectly well that he had not been confronted with ethical abstractions, but rather had been addressed by One who had spoken to him in the events of the great tradition of which he was a part, to which he inwardly belonged, and which described him as a person.[14]

Indeed, ingratitude and indifference to the covenant are two reasons why the prophets railed against Israel's rebellion (Mic. 6:3-4; Isa. 63:7-64:12). Present motivation includes the reward for keeping the laws intrinsic to the regulations themselves: keeping them should be a delight (Deut. 4:5-8; Pss. 19; 119). Barton notes that the law was conceived as revealing God, which 'implies a very high evaluation of the expressed will of God as the way by which people are meant to live, and which will be their whole and only good, whatever consequences may or may not follow'.[15] Future motivations are the most frequent, comprising conditional promises and threats against disobedience. The intertwining of act and consequence means that to desire the one is to will the other. This perspective is so pervasive that Barton suggests the Old Testament is not the paradigmatic case of deontological ethics is it usually presumed to be.

> A teleological element in ethics seemed simply common sense to ancient Israelites, who acted so as to obey God, of course, but in the belief that he had promised good things to those who did obey him and threatened with misfortune those who left his ways. To say that we should be moral,. but not for the sake of gaining anything, would have struck them as an unrealistic refinement of piety.[16]

Motivations for moral living are particularly visible in biblical motive clauses. In an early, influential study Berend Gemser defined motive clauses as 'grammatically subordinate sentences in which the motivation for the commandment

14 J. Muilenburg, *The Way of Israel: Biblical Faith and Ethics* (New York: Harper & Row, 1961), 15.

15 Barton, *Ethics*, 96. See also Cyril Rodd, *Glimpses of a Strange Land: Studies in Old Testament Ethics* (OTS; Edinburgh: T&T Clark, 2001), 120.

16 Barton, *Ethics*, 90.

is given'.[17] Rifat Sonsino distinguishes between exhortations independent of the legal codes, and motive clauses proper attached to individual commands, which he classifies.[18] On the basis of this classification, could one seek a hierarchy of motivations? Perhaps, for example, motivations linked to God are more pressing than the promise of well-being? Taking the goods of honour, truth and loyalty one observes that commands relating to these values are variously motivated (if they are motivated at all: compare Exod. 20:12 with Lev. 19:3; and Exod. 20:16 with Lev. 19:11). 'Honour' features in Exod. 20:12: 'Honour your father and mother, so that your days may be long in the land that the LORD your God is giving you' (see also Deut. 5:16, where the motivation is similar). Leaving to one side what 'honour' might mean, the injunction is motivated by reference to YHWH's acts and the eudaemonistic incentive of longevity. This is conceivably a baser motive than that attached to Exod. 23:8: 'You shall take no bribe, for a bribe . . . subverts the cause of those who are in the right'. Should someone need to decide between honouring parents and not taking a bribe, perhaps the latter duty should trump the former? Matters are complicated by Lev. 19:3. The command 'You shall each revere your mother and father, and you shall keep my sabbaths' is immediately preceded by the phrase 'You shall be holy, for I the LORD your God am holy', and succeeded by the refrain 'I am the LORD your God'. Thus *both* of these commands are unequivocally tied to the deity, which is more important? Furthermore, Deut. 25:13-16 contains two motivations for transacting honest commerce: 'so that your days may be long in the land that the LORD your God is giving you' *and* 'all who act dishonestly, are abhorrent to the LORD your God'. A further, prominent example is the Sabbath command in Exodus and Deuteronomy, which are motivated by creation and Egyptian slavery, respectively (Exod. 20:8-11; Deut. 5:12-15). One observes, therefore, that different texts supply disparate motives for very similar commands, and that the same law can be

17 B. Gemser, 'The Importance of the Motive Clause in Old Testament Law', in *Congress Volume: Copenhagen 1952* (VTSup 1; ed. G. W. Anderson *et al.*; Leiden: Brill, 1953), 50–66, quote 50.

18 R. Sonsino, *Motive Clauses in Hebrew Law: Biblical Forms and Near Eastern Parallels* (SBLDS 45; Chico: Scholars Press, 1980), 66–69. For summaries of five alternative classificatory schemes and a comparative summary of motive clauses in other ANE texts see Rodd, *Glimpses*, 110–13.

variously motivated. Furthermore, Sonsino remarks that the motivations actually attached to individual laws are not the only ones that could have been used.

> The same law could very well have been motivated by another kind of motive clause (e.g., Exod. 20:9-11 and Deut. 5:12-15) or, if it does not already have it, by a multiple motive clause. Probably the intention was not to provide a motivation that would justify the law from all perspectives but to select from among all the possible rationales the one that would denote best the law's appropriateness in the eyes of the people to whom it was addressed.[19]

It would seem that comparison of motivations as the basis for addressing value conflicts is a stony and unfruitful path. This approach, however, does not exhaust the usefulness of motive clauses. Sonsino observes that the choice of motive clauses reveals a particular mode of thinking. This may be clear from the clause, or it may be necessary to understand some of the context to know why an action is considered wrong. For example, a series of prohibitions of sexual relations simply state that the action is forbidden because it is *that* relation. Lev. 18:14 is illustrative: 'You shall not uncover the nakedness of your father's brother, that is, you shall not approach his wife; she is your aunt' (Lev. 18:3, 8, 16). To discern the force of the motivation, it is necessary to understand relevant cultural assumptions. Even in the case where the motive is ostensively transparent, knowing the cultural outlook can add richness to one's reading. For example, Deut. 25:3 deals with flogging: 'Forty lashes may be given but not more; if more lashes than these are given, your neighbour will be degraded in your sight'. Most commentators talk of 'protection of human dignity' and the like,[20] but comprehending the place of 'shame' in ancient Near Eastern culture enables readers to perceive an added dimension to the law's concern.[21] In fact, motive clauses can be important clues to key moral goods.

19 Sonsino, *Motive Clauses*, 116.

20 E.g. G. von Rad, *Deuteronomy: A Commentary* (OTL; trans. D. Barton; London: SCM, 1966), 154; G. Millar, *Now Choose Life: Theology and ethics in Deuteronomy* (NSBT; Leicester: Apollos, 1998), 141; G. McConville, *Deuteronomy* (AOTC 5; Leicester: Apollos, 2002), 368.

21 Craigie speaks of the fellow Israelite not being 'publicly humiliated' but does not mention 'shame' as a cultural value; see Peter Craigie, *Deuteronomy* (NICOT; Grand Rapids: Eerdmans, 1976), 312. Wright notes *both* the covenant and human dignity as reasons for the limit of 40 strokes, observing that קלל is the verb used for dishonouring parents in Deut.

In Lev. 18:14 knowing something of ancient Near Eastern family structure enables readers to appreciate that the good of harmonious internal family relations is in view; while Deut. 25:3 attests to the goods of personal honour and appropriate punishment for misdemeanour, conceiving of situations in which they might be in conflict by setting a limit to the number of lashes that can be administered. Thus while it is impossible to deduce a hierarchy of motives, and thus ethical obligations, from biblical motive clauses, they may yet serve, in conjunction with other data, to address our problem.

C. OLD TESTAMENT LEGAL SANCTIONS

Having considered the carrot of positive motivation for ethical living, I turn to the stick of sanction. Gordon Wenham discerns five principles of punishment within Old Testament law: the offender must receive his legal desert, which is not equal to revenge; to purge guilt from the land and its inhabitants; deterrence; atonement for the offender, with no subsequent loss of civil rights; and recompense by the offender to the injured party.[22] There are three main types of penalty: capital punishment (as a maximum penalty); 'cutting off'[23] and restitution. One approach to value conflicts might be to examine the punishments that accrue to individual commands, and order 'crimes' accordingly. Appendix A contains a table of 'Crime and Punishment' in the Book of the Covenant. Supposing that death is the most severe penalty it is clear that murder, for example, is more serious than assault. This level of detail, however, is not especially useful in most cases. Furthermore, given that capital punishment is stipulated for murder, kidnap, bestiality, sorcery and striking

27:16, see C. Wright, *Deuteronomy* (NIBC 4; Carlisle: Paternoster, 1995), 264–65. Only Lyn Betchel points to the importance of 'honour and shame' for understanding the text, see L. Betchel 'Shame as a Sanction of Social Control in Biblical Israel: Judicial, Political, and Social Shaming', in *Social-Scientific Old Testament Criticism: A Sheffield Reader* (BS 47; ed. D. J. Chalcraft; Sheffield: Sheffield University Press, 1997), 232–58; repr. from *JSOT* 49 (1991): 47–76; for a summary see Rodd, *Glimpses*, 19–27.

22 Wenham, *Leviticus*, 282–84.

23 Although sometimes synonymous with the death penalty (see, e.g. Exod. 12:15, 19; Lev. 7:20-27; 17:4; 18:29; 19:8; Num. 15:30-31) in Lev. 20:2-5 'cutting off' is contrasted with execution. However, since both Lev. 13:45-46 and Num. 5:1-4 refer to animals it probably does not mean 'excommunication'. Wenham concludes it speaks of premature death by divine intervention, Wenham, *Leviticus*, 285; Rodd agrees, listing proponents of alternative views, Rodd, *Glimpses*, 127.

or cursing parents, the method does not even prioritize these crimes (even though it is difficult to imagine situations in which this might be problematic). Appendices B and C contain similar tables for the Holiness and Deuteronomic Codes, respectively.

Two issues are worthy of mention. First, the slight differences between the codes, for example, Exod. 22:18 prescribes death for the female sorcerer while the sanction in Lev. 20:27 applies to mediums of both sexes, point to the need for interpretation of the laws: they cannot be applied automatically. The need for interpretation is evident also from a comparison of Lev. 18:16 and Deut. 25:5 (cf. Lev. 20:21). In the Holiness Code sexual relations between a man and his brother's wife are prohibited on pain of being 'cut off' from the people, while in Deuteronomy *not* having sexual relations with the same woman is sanctioned by 'shaming'. The juxtaposition of these laws within the canon raises issues of possible contradiction. S. R. Driver thought that the Leviticus text was the general rule and the Deuteronomic an exception.[24] It is better, however, to interpret them both with respect to the moral goods they have in view rather than as a qualification of the other. This reveals that both laws, although differently motivated, strive to protect the same thing. The Leviticus text seeks intrafamilial harmony, expressed in terms of taboo, while the Deuteronomic teaching aims to protect the patrimony of the 'father's house'. Both have in mind the good of family continuity (conceived as male heirs farming their own land), but this is expressed and motivated differently according to the specific context in mind.

The second issue is which punishments were considered more severe. While modern people might not think that 'shaming' is especially severe, Lyn Betchel's analysis of the function of 'shame' reaches the opposite conclusion, arguing that this lies behind the seriousness of the offence in Deut. 25:5-10. Thus, regardless of whether this punishment was ever applied, the *threat* of shame will have added to the persuasive power of the sanction. In a similar vein, Henry McKeating argues that law can still affect behaviour even though transgressed in the same way that a 30 mph sign (and related sanction) will induce few to drive at that speed, but will prevent many from accelerating to 50 mph. In this way Old Testament sanctions can illuminate ethical dilemmas,

24 S. R. Driver, *Deuteronomy* (3rd ed.; ICC; Edinburgh: T&T Clark, 1901), 285.

even though they do not provide sufficient evidence on their own to enable prioritization of moral values.

In addition to legal sanctions the wisdom literature points to a natural order of penalties. For example, regarding adultery, Prov. 6:27-35 'has a whole battery of discouragements to offer', from general hints of consequences, such as 'can one walk on hot coals without scorching one's feet?', to intimations of more specific ramifications, like 'for jealousy arouses a husband's fury, and he shows no restraint when he takes revenge'.[25] Although by examining the cultural background of these 'natural sanctions' one could conceivably present them in rough order of perceived severity, the same problems are faced as with legal sanctions.

To conclude, while prioritizing ethical obligations on the basis of sanctions' severity alone is insufficient to resolve value conflicts in most cases, sanctions are an important element of the overall picture of Old Testament ethics because they provide information about moral goods.

D. NATURAL MORALITY IN THE OLD TESTAMENT

When the prophet Amos asks the rhetorical questions 'Do horses run on rocks? Does one plough the sea with oxen?' (Amos 6:12), he assumes the answer is obvious. This is what gives the following phrase its force: 'But you have turned justice into poison and the fruit of righteousness into wormwood'. The sins enumerated by Amos are presented as *obviously* unnatural, and the rejection of justice and righteousness as simply perverse, a 'cosmic nonsense' or 'reversal of a sane way of viewing the world'.[26] The right 'order of things' might be called 'natural morality': 'the view that there are certain precepts or norms of right conduct, discernible by all men'.[27] One must look quite closely

25 See McKeating, 'Sanctions', 59. McKeating opines that the text means the offended spouse may press for the most severe legal punishment, even if it did not happen frequently; I think it is more likely the text speaks of the risk of being murdered as vengeance for dishonouring the husband.

26 J. Barton, 'Natural Law and Poetic Justice in the Old Testament', in *Understanding Old Testament Ethics: Approaches and Explorations* (Louisville: Westminster John Knox Press, 2003), 32–44, quote 38.

27 Barton, 'Natural Law', 33, quoting V. J. Bourke, 'Natural Law', in *Dictionary of Christian Ethics* (ed. J. Macquarrie; London: SCM, 1967). Barton originally used the term 'natural law' but in the reprint accepts John Rogerson's 'natural morality'. See Rogerson,

for evidence of natural morality in the Old Testament.[28] Nevertheless, there is no necessary conflict between it and the obligations of revealed law. As Jon Levenson notes, the

> sovereignty of God is larger than his suzerainty . . . biblical Israel believed the will of God to be known not only through history, but also through what we moderns call nature, and not only through the word proclaimed, but also through thought and cognition.[29]

Indeed, James Barr, observing that biblical law shares affinities with other ancient Near Eastern law codes, even suggests Old Testament 'revealed' law has a 'natural' basis.[30]

What could natural morality contribute to the resolution of value conflicts? Three observations are possible. First, the essence of natural morality concerns 'goods' and 'evils'. In general, it is a good thing that justice abounds; it is an evil thing that people exploit others. Thus when Isaiah pronounces 'Woe to those who join house to house' (Isa. 5:8-12) he specifies the goods in peril as a result of avaricious property speculation, viz., agricultural productivity and 'fairness' with respect to the enjoyment of the fruit of the land. Second, this text presents a view of the prioritization of goods, asserting that 'large and beautiful

'Old Testament Ethics', 128; Barton, *Understanding*, 179, n.16. For other definitions of 'natural law' see Alan Johnson, 'Is There a Biblical Warrant for Natural-Law Theories?', *JETS* 25 (1982): 185–99, especially 198–99.

28 Lists of texts can be found, e.g. in J. Barton, 'Amos's Oracles Against the Nations', in *Understanding Old Testament Ethics: Approaches and Explorations* (Louisville: Westminster John Knox Press, 2003), 77–129; Rodd, *Glimpses*, 59–64; M. Bockmuehl, 'Natural Law in Second Temple Judaism', *VT* 45 (1995): 17–44. For the debate about whether the wisdom literature is natural morality or merely accumulated experience see J. Levenson, 'The Theologies of Commandment in Biblical Israel', *HTR* 73 (1980): 17–33, especially 26. On 'natural theology' in the Old Testament see J. Barr, *Biblical Faith and Natural Theology – The Gifford Lectures for 1991* (Oxford: OUP, 1994), 81–101.

29 Levenson, 'Theologies of Commandment', 32. See also Barton, *Ethics*, 72–76; T. Fretheim, *God and the World in the Old Testament: A Relational Theology of Creation* (Nashville: Abingdon, 2005), especially 140–44; J. Bruckner, *Implied Law in the Abraham Narrative: A Literary and Theological Analysis* (JSOTSup 335; London: Sheffield, 2001), 44–50.

30 Cf. Barr, *Biblical Faith*, 97–98; Exod. 18; Hos. 4:1-3, a text usually associated closely with the Decalogue. Levenson notes the 'easy juxtaposition of Torah and creation' in Psalm 119, see Levenson, 'Theologies of Commandment', 28.

houses' or feasting should be less important than justice to the Judahites. Third, the identification of things as goods or evils, and their prioritization, is either not always obvious or, if it is, people do not behave as they should.[31] In this regard, Daniel Carroll R. cautions that one must take into account the difference between the existence of a consensus regarding moral convictions and natural law as philosophical or theological category. This is an important point, although for appeal to 'natural morality' to be successful it must be widely recognized as an objective norm. Accepting Carroll's distinction means the opposite may also be true: moral consensus can err – something with which Old Testament prophets would have concurred. Indeed, perhaps it was the opacity of natural morality that led the biblical writers to specify in more detail what sort of comportment was appropriate.

E. IMITATION OF GOD IN THE OLD TESTAMENT

Several scholars suggest that imitation of God is a vital premise of Old Testament ethics.[32] Cyril Rodd, however, is sharply critical, branding the concept of *imitatio Dei* 'a scholarly wish'.[33] The clearest indication of *imitatio Dei* is usually thought to be Lev. 19:2: 'You shall be holy, for I the LORD your God am holy'.[34] Wenham considers this not merely the levitical motto, 'but the key to biblical ethical theory'.[35] According to Wright, the text declares that Israel's 'quality of life . . . must reflect the very heart of God's character'.[36] Waldemar Janzen disagrees. He opines that 'holiness' speaks of 'otherness' and questions

31 See D. Carroll R., *Contexts for Amos: Prophetic Poetics in Latin American Perspective* (JSOTSup 132; Sheffield: JSOT Press, 1992), 131.

32 See especially J. Barton, 'The Basis of Ethics in the Hebrew Bible', in *Understanding Old Testament Ethics: Approaches and Explorations* (Louisville: Westminster John Knox Press, 2003), 45–54, especially 50–54; V. Fletcher, 'The Shape of Old Testament Ethics', *SJT* 24 (1959): 47–73, especially 57–61; Davies, 'Walking', 100–101, where he notes the importance of 'imitating God' within the rabbinic tradition. Barton is more cautious in his subsequent article, J. Barton, 'Imitation of God in the Old Testament', in *The God of Israel* (UCOP 64; ed. R. P. Gordon; Cambridge: CUP, 2007), 35–46. For a thorough survey of the evidence and measured discussion see Walter Houston, 'The Character of YHWH and the Ethics of the Old Testament: Is *Imitatio Dei* Appropriate?', *JTS* 58 (2007): 1–25.

33 Rodd, *Glimpses*, 73.

34 Cf. Lev. 11:44; 20:7, 26; 21:8.

35 Wenham, 'Gap', 27.

36 Wright, *Living*, 27; cf. Matt 5:48.

whether the same standard of perfection can be applied to Creator and created, before concluding that it is impossible for humans to imitate *God's* perfection.[37] He allows a formal comparison only: God perfectly fulfils his expectations of himself; humans should do perfectly what God expects *them* to do. Rodd asserts that the imitation of God 'rests ultimately on the belief in a God who has been brought down to the human level, and this God is never found in the Old Testament'.[38] In other words, the fact that God is holy precludes imitative human holiness. This is problematic for two reasons. First, Janzen appears to depend upon Rudolf Otto's attenuated concept of the holy as the numinous other.[39] Second, excluding imitation on these grounds thereby disallows all talk of God, since if the deity's ways are so far beyond human comprehension no theological reflection can occur, and even the affirmation that God's ways are far above human ways would be impossible – hence, Isa. 55:8-9 does *not* support Rodd's case. A key issue is the nature of holiness.[40] Mary Douglas argues holiness signifies completeness and the normal order of things.[41] Given that God is 'normally' holy, Isaiah describes God as the 'Holy One of Israel' and Hosea uses the title 'Holy One' (Isa. 1:4; 10:20; 17:7; 30:12; 40:25; 43:14-15; 45:11; 50:5; cf. 2 Kgs 19:22; Jer. 50:29; 52:5; Ezek. 39:7. Note also the description of God as holy without using this phrase in Isa. 6:3-5; Hos. 11:9; 11:12

37 W. Janzen, *Old Testament Ethics: A Paradigmatic Approach* (Louisville: Westminster John Knox, 1994), 115–16.

38 Rodd, *Glimpses*, 76.

39 See Rudolf Otto, *The Idea of the Holy: An Inquiry into the Non-Rational Factor in the Idea of the Divine and its Relation to the Rational* (2nd ed.; trans. J. W. Harvey; New York: OUP, 1950), especially, 25–30; for a critique see, *inter alia*, W. Moberly, *Bible, Theology and Faith* (CSCD; Cambridge: CUP, 2000), 88–96.

40 For a survey of views see P. Jenson, 'Holiness in the Priestly Writings of the Old Testament', in *Holiness: Past & Present* (ed. S. C. Barton; London: Continuum, 2003), 93–121.

41 M. Douglas, *Purity and Danger* (London: Routledge & Kegan Paul, 1966), 53–54: 'Holiness requires that individuals shall conform to the class to which they belong. And holiness requires that different classes of things shall not be confused'. For a critical summary of Douglas see Walter Houston, *Purity and Monotheism: Clean and Unclean Animals in Biblical Law* (JSOTSup 140; Sheffield: Sheffield Academic Press, 1993), 93–114, 120–22. Wenham observes that movement between classes is sometimes possible, subject to ritual restrictions, especially sacrifice, Wenham, *Leviticus*, 18–29. Naudé notes that 'there is a dynamism associated with those objects typified by the adj. . . . all possess the ability to move things or people into, or at least toward, the realm of the divine', J. Naudé, 'קדשׁ', *NIDOTTE* 3.877–87, quote 881.

[12:1]; cf. 1 Sam. 2:2; 6:19-20; Pss. 22:3 [4]; 99:3; Hab. 1:12). However, while Isaiah employs some of the Old Testament's most exalted language to describe God, he also proclaims that 'holiness calls'.[42]

Although we may say that God's holiness should evoke human holiness, is this the same as imitation? Rodd asserts that to 'imitate God is to attempt to recreate in the life of Israel and the activities of the individual the virtues and actions of God'.[43] He claims that this is distinct from merely 'mirroring' God by obeying commands or natural law. Rodd overreacts, first, because God's character is frequently linked to human conduct. In Deuteronomy, for example, the attributes of love, mercy, compassion and justice are highlighted, and the authors expect these virtues to be evident in his people (Deut. 4:31; 6:5; 7:7-8; 14:28-29; 16:19-20; 30:3; 32:4). A similar perspective is found in the prophetic literature, where God's will is related to his character as well as the law. As Eryl Davies comments, '[s]ince the ethical behaviour of the people was to flow naturally from the apprehension of God's character, it was clearly a matter of grave concern for the prophets that there appeared to be no "knowledge of God" in the land' (Mic. 6:8; Hos. 4:1; 5:4; 6:6; Jer. 4:22; 5:4-5; 9:3, 6).[44] Similarly, mention of moral virtues in the Psalms was 'designed to inculcate the same ethical values in the worshipper' (Pss. 25:6; 33:5; 37:28; 119:156; 146:6-9).[45] The parallel acrostic Psalms 111 and 112 are especially illustrative: the righteousness of both God and the upright endures forever (Pss. 111:3; 112:3), both are gracious and merciful (Pss. 111:4; 112:4); God gives food to his worshippers the godly give to the needy (Pss. 111:5; 112:9) and both act justly (Pss. 111:7; 112:5). Thus there is no reason to limit moral action by 'those who fear the LORD', the subjects of Psalm 112, to 'mirroring' divine attributes, perhaps by obeying the law. This is one way of doing so but, *pace* Rodd, deliberate imitation is another. Indeed, this appears to be enjoined by the juxtaposition of the psalms. Narratives are more problematic, however, because the deity sometimes acts in ways that are thought inappropriate for imitation.[46] The second reason for thinking Rodd overreacts is that the behaviour demanded

42 J. Gammie, *Holiness in Israel* (OBT; Minneapolis: Fortress Press, 1989), 96.

43 Rodd, *Glimpses*, 73.

44 Davies, 'Walking', 106.

45 Davies, 'Walking', 106. See also Houston, 'Character of YHWH', 13–14; Wright, *Living*, 28; Wright, *Walking*, 139–40; Gammie, *Holiness*, 129–33.

46 On 1 Sam. 26:19 Barton comments that 'God may persecute David if God chooses,

of Israelites emulates God's actions. Deut. 10:12-19 exhorts imitation of God by Israel based upon the paradigmatic event of the exodus, but Wright astutely observes that while God's 'action for Israel was paradigmatic *for them* . . . it was also paradigmatic *of God*', that is, it revealed what God was like.[47] In Ze'ev Falk's words, 'God is not only the commander but also the paradigm of all moral conduct'.[48] The fact that the response demanded of Israel is not labelled 'imitation' is beside the point. Barton concludes that the 'sense of community of moral perception between God and humanity, which seems inherent in the idea of imitating God, takes us well beyond the few texts which in so many words tell their readers to behave as God does'.[49]

To conclude, although imitation of God *is* a facet of the Old Testament's moral programme, its importance can be over-pressed. In terms of resolution of value conflicts it does not seem to offer anything distinctive. The laws that comprise the literary context of Lev. 19:2, for example, are elsewhere enjoined (compare Lev. 19:3 and Deut. 5:16 [filial respect]; Lev. 19:9-10 and Deut. 10:19 [generosity]; Lev. 19:5 and Deut. 19:15-21 [judicial integrity]; and Lev. 19:35-36 and Deut. 5:19-20 [honesty]). This assessment is not entirely negative, however, for if laws are statements about moral goods, as suggested above, then the link to God's character might give these goods a degree of objectivity. The next section investigates moral goods in more detail.

even through the agency of Saul; humans following their own volition may not', Barton, 'Basis', 51. See also Houston, 'Character of YHWH', 42–45; Barton, 'Imitation', 20–25.

47 Wright, *Deuteronomy*, 150. Emphasis original. Rodd accepts that Deut. 10:12-19 might support *imitatio Dei*, but correctly denies other instances of 'walking in God's ways' endorse the concept since they speak more of obedience than imitation, see Rodd, *Glimpses*, 330–33.

48 Ze'ev Falk, 'Law and Ethics in the Hebrew Bible', in *Justice and Righteousness: Biblical Themes and their Influence* (JSOTSup 137; ed. H. G. Reventlow and Y. Hoffman; Sheffield: JSOT Press, 1992), 83.

49 Barton, 'Basis', 52. Barton argues the vocation of particular individuals also witnesses to 'the possibility of the divine life and human life running in parallel', Barton, 'Basis', 53. Whether this is, as Barton claims, a special sort of imitation demanded only of selected individuals is debateable; it is equally possible that these characters are notable for living the life to which all should aspire. In terms of methodology, Rodd demands too much when he requires the biblical text to offer a 'clear and categorical' statement of Old Testament ethics as imitation of God, *Glimpses*, 72. A better standard is adequate evidence, which should, of course, be properly grounded, so Barton, 'Imitation', 39.

2. Moral Goods in the Old Testament

The Old Testament declares God to be unambiguously good.[50] It is unsurprising, therefore, that Kaiser should assert the 'standard of the good, the right, the just, and the acceptable is nothing less than the person of the living God'.[51] Despite the promise that an imitative ethic coupled with the goodness of God might appear to offer, few scholars have considered 'being good' an important focus for the study of Old Testament ethics.[52] On the contrary, commentators are often more impressed by mundane 'goods'. Note, for example, the remarks of Newman Smyth:

> the idea of the highest good which is to be derived from the prophetic literature of the Old Testament is the summation . . . of all those material goods – such as plentiful harvests, springs of water, increase of cattle, a vine and fig tree for every man, peace and prosperity within all the borders of a land flowing with milk and honey, – which make a people contented and prosperous.[53]

In this section I will ask what is 'good' according to the Old Testament, and how an understanding of goods might aid resolution of value conflicts.

50 See H. J. Stoebe, 'טוֹב *ṭôb Bueno*', *DTMAT* 1.902–918. Apart from bold statements to this effect (e.g. Pss. 31:19; 86:5; 100:5; 106:1; 107:1; 118:1, 29; 145:7, 9; 1 Chron. 16:34; Ezra 3:11; Jer. 33:11: Nah. 1:7; cf. Mk 10:18), note the parallelism of seeking God and seeking good in Amos 5:4, 6, 14-15 and the rejection of good as rejection of God in Hos. 8:3. God's name is good in Ps. 52:9 [11]; and he is 'good to Israel' in Ps. 73:1. Further, in Exod. 33:19 God tells Moses that he will make his goodness pass before him, cf. Exod. 31:6-7.

51 Kaiser, *Toward*, 6.

52 Two exceptions are Wright, *Old Testament Ethics*, 368–74; B. Birch, 'Moral Agency, Community, and the Character of God in the Hebrew Bible', *Semeia* 66 (1994): 23–41; idem, 'Divine Character and the Formation of Moral Community in the Book of Exodus', in *The Bible in Ethics: The Second Sheffield Colloquium* (ed. J. W. Rogerson, M. Davies and D. Carroll R.; JSOTSup 207; Sheffield: Sheffield Academic Press, 1995), 119–135. Note also the recent interest in virtue ethics in the Old Testament: J. Barton, 'Virtue in the Bible', in *Understanding Old Testament Ethics: Approaches and Explorations* (Louisville: Westminster John Knox Press, 2003), 65–74; D. Carroll R. and J. E. Lapsely (eds.), *Character Ethics and the Old Testament* (Louisville: Westminster John Knox, 2007); D. Carroll R., 'La ética de los profetas y su relevancia para América Latina hoy: La contribución de la ética filosófica', *Kairós* 35 (2005): 7–30.

53 N. Smyth, *Christian Ethics* (3rd ed.; Edinburgh: T&T Clark, 1892), 92. Cf. G. Berry, 'The Ethical Teaching of the Old Testament', *BW* 21 (1903): 108–18, especially 111–12.

A. GOOD IN THE OLD TESTAMENT

In a canonical context the first thing described as 'good' is creation itself (Gen 1:4, 10, 12, 18, 21, 25, 31). Gerhard von Rad thinks that טוב 'contains less an aesthetic judgment than the designation of purpose, correspondence'.[54] According to Norman Whybray it is creation's usefulness to people that is in view.[55] This coheres with the general usage of 'good' identified by Robert Gordon: 'a state or function appropriate to genre, purpose, or situation'.[56] Thus it is 'not good' that animals are unable to be a companion for Adam, that is, they cannot serve this function. Christopher Wright, however, sees in the creation narratives a description of 'a place of order, system and structure. We live in a cosmos, not a chaos . . . [which] provides an objective basis and authority for the exercise of moral freedom and sets limits to moral relativism'.[57] He continues

> There is a basic shape to that world which we did not invent, and therefore a corresponding shape to the moral response required of us if we are to live within it with the kind of freedom which, by God's so ordering, it authorizes. Morality, in

54 G. von Rad, *Genesis: A Commentary* (OTL; trans. J. H. Marks; Philadelphia: Westminster Press, 1961), 50. Moral goods are not always described using טוב, which is used as both verb and adjective, the difference not always easily distinguishable, see R. Gordon, 'טוב', *NIDOTTE* 2.353. See also I. Höver-Johag, 'טוֹב *ṭôb*; טוּב *ṭûb*; יטב *yṭb*', *TDOT* 5.296–317; Luis Alonso Schökel, 'טוֹב', *DBHE* 291–93; Stoebe, 'טוֹב *ṭôb Bueno*', 902–918; BDB 373–75. I take the כי in Gen. 1:4 *et passim* to be emphatic, so V. Hamilton, *The Book of Genesis: Chapters 1–17* (NICOT 1; Grand Rapids: Eerdmans, 1990), 118; J. G. Janzen, 'Kugel's Adverbial *kî ṭôb*: An Assessment', *JBL* 102 (1983): 99–106; *pace* J. Kugel, 'The Adverbial Use of *KÎ ṬÔB*', *JBL* 99 (1980): 433–35.

55 N. Whybray, 'Genesis', in *The Oxford Bible Commentary* (ed. J. Barton and J. Muddiman; Oxford: OUP, 2001), 38–66, especially 42. Contrast Whybray's view with translations like 'God was pleased with what he saw' (Speiser) or 'God saw how beautiful it was' (Hamilton), which point to some sort of intrinsic goodness, see E. A. Speiser, *Genesis* (AB 1; New York: Doubleday, 1964), 3, 5; Hamilton, *Genesis*, 118, 124. Wenham thinks that both 'fitness for purpose' and a reflection of the goodness of God in his works are meant, see G. Wenham, *Genesis 1–15* (WBC 1; Waco: Word, 1987), 18.

56 Gordon, 'טוב', 353; cf. Höver-Johag, 'טוֹב *ṭôb*', 304. The Old Testament frequently highlights instrumental, rather than intrinsic, goodness with the construction טוב ל, 'good for' or 'good to', see A. Schökel, 'טוֹב', 291–93.

57 Wright, 'Old Testament Ethics', 49. Cf. O. O'Donovan, *Resurrection and Moral Order: An Outline for Evangelical Ethics* (2nd ed.; Leicester: Apollos, 1994), 31–52.

biblical terms, therefore, is preconditioned by the given shape of creation, which underlies the relativity of cultural responses to it within history.[58]

Similarly, Walter Houston argues that if the Old Testament writers 'perceive that they do not live in a just society, at least they live in a just world. The world, or to put it in theological terms, God's creation, is ordered and therefore exhibits justice'.[59] That Wright and Houston are correct to identify an ethical and not merely functional created order is confirmed by the biblical author's evaluation of the immoral behaviour of humankind in Gen. 6:5, which mirrors God's initial positive appraisal. While 'God saw everything that he had made, and indeed, it was very good', post-fall, 'The LORD saw that the wickedness of humankind was great in the earth, and that every inclination of the thoughts of their hearts was only evil continually' (Gen. 1:31; 6:5). Furthermore, it is unnecessary to drive a wedge between creation as instrumentally good and creation as good because it possesses a moral order, for one aspect of this ordering is teleological.[60]

Genesis 3 attributes the fall to the primeval couple's consumption of fruit of the tree of the knowledge of good and evil (cf. Gen. 2:9, 17). Scholars debate whether this knowledge is moral awareness or a totality of knowledge inappropriate for humans.[61] The important aspect of this phrase for our purposes, however, is that good and evil are a contrasting pair. Indeed, Gordon calls the need to choose between good and evil a 'two-way theology'.[62] The impossibility of achieving both at the same time explains Amos' injunction to

58 Wright, 'Old Testament Ethics', 49. On the priestly vision of natural order in the first chapters of Genesis see W. Brown, *Structure, Role, and Ideology in the Hebrew and Greek Texts of Genesis 1:1-2:3* (SBLDS 132; Atlanta: Scholars Press, 1993), 214–29.

59 W. Houston, *Contending for Justice: Ideologies and Theologies of Social Justice in the Old Testament* (LHB/OTS 428; London: T&T Clark, 2006), 15.

60 The other is generic. On whether a Platonic (A ordered to serve B) or Aristotelian (A ordered to flourish as A) conception of teleological ordering is to be preferred see O'Donovan, *Resurrection*, 34.

61 For a summary of the debate see Gordon, 'טוב', 354–55. A moral interpretation of the idiom 'good and evil' is suggested by 1 Kgs 3:9; Isa. 7:15, 17; Deut. 1:39, but it does not fit 2 Sam. 19:35 [36], see Speiser, *Genesis*, 26. von Rad is unequivocal when he states that 'good and evil' is 'a formal way of saying what we mean by our colorless "everything"', von Rad, *Genesis*, 86–87. 'Everything' could, of course, include a moral evaluation, and it is certain that some instances of the expression do refer to ethical discernment; for references and discussion see Höver-Johag, 'טוֹב *ṭôb*', 309–11.

62 Gordon, 'טוב', 354; cf. Deut. 30:15; Jer. 21:8.

'seek good and not evil', a text that has a clear covenantal matrix.[63] Amos rails against Israel's unjust practices on the understanding that the reconciliation of justice and other goods is straightforward. In other places, however, the Old Testament is aware that moral living is more complicated. For example, Ps. 85:10 [11], this chapter's epigraph, envisages a time when 'faithfulness and truth meet; justice and well-being kiss'.[64] These goods are often difficult to achieve simultaneously because, for instance, being loyal to one person can mean deceiving another, therefore concurrent realization of loyalty and truth or justice and peace is God's gift. For this reason the psalmist sums up his vision of people acting morally with the phrase 'the LORD will give the good'.[65] This ample conception of the good is juxtaposed with a productive land. Kirkpatrick offers a pithy summary: 'Material prosperity will go hand in hand with moral progress. Earth responds to the divine blessing'.[66] Psalm 85, therefore, presents a vision not only of individual goods, but recognizes that

63 Amos 5:12. 'The good' is occasionally a synonym for the covenant, see A. González Lamadrid, 'Pax et Bonum: «*Shalôm*» y «*ṭôb*» en relación con «*berit*»', *EstBib* 28 (1969): 61–77; idem, 'Apuntes sobre טוב/יטב y su traducción en las Biblias modernas', *EstBib* 50 (1992): 443–56; M. Fox, 'Tôb as Covenant Terminology', *BASOR* 209 (1973): 41–42; M. Barré, 'The Formulaic Pair טוב (ו)חסד in the Psalter', *ZAW* 98 (1986): 100–5. On the dynamics of good and evil, i.e. whether good always produces good, etc., see M. Jacobs, 'The Conceptual Dynamics of Good and Evil in the Joseph Story: An Exegetical and Hermeneutical Inquiry', *JSOT* 27 (2003): 309–38.

64 JPS Tanakh (1985); MT נָשָׁקוּ (qal), without object, although many translations read נִשָּׁקוּ (niphal), 'kiss *each other*'; Kraus argues נָשַׁקוּ (niphal of שקק, 'rush together') would be a better emendation, thus 'embrace each other', see Hans-Joachim Kraus, *Los Salmos II: Salmos 60–150* (trans. C. Ruiz-Garrido; Salamanca: Sígueme, 1995), 262; also A. Anderson, *Psalms (73–150)* (NCBC; London: Marshal, Morgan & Scott, 1972), 612. Notwithstanding emendations the meaning is clear: these goods will be realized together, regardless of the usual difficulties of doing so. Kidner expresses it thus: 'The prevailing concept . . . is that of concord: vast, unspoilt and rich with life', D. Kidner, *Psalms 73–150* (TOTC; Leceister: IVP, 1975), 309 (although without accepting his view that v. 10 speaks of atonement); *pace* Tate who sees no conflict between the goods, Marvin Tate, *Psalms 51–100* (WBC 20; Waco: Word, 1990), 366. Kirkpatrick asks whether these are divine attributes or human virtues, concluding, with many commentators, that these goods are personifications of YHWH's agency in the world. He recognizes, however, that there is no need to exclude human virtue, indeed, this is the prominent thought in the next verses, see A. F. Kirkpatrick, *The Book of Psalms* (Cambridge: CUP, 1902), 513–14; Tate, *Psalms*, 371; Kraus, *Salmos II*, 268–69; Prov. 3:3; Isa. 32:16.

65 My translation.

66 Kirkpatrick, *Psalms*, 514.

they are often difficult to achieve at the same time and that only with divine blessing can a conflict of moral values be overcome.[67]

Many other things are considered 'good' in the Old Testament. Furthermore, the comparative construction טוב מן points to a suggested prioritization of goods, although many of the sayings are general.[68] Norman Whybray, in the only sustained study of goods in the Old Testament, collates them into twelve categories, suggesting that together they comprise a vision of 'the good life'.[69] It is instructive to examine his work in more detail.

B. THE 'GOOD LIFE'

Whybray defines the good life as 'a desirable state of happiness and prosperity' and 'a life of entire contentment with things as they are'.[70] He reviews the elements that comprise this ideal state by biblical book.[71] What each good signifies depends upon the text being examined, or even the development of the plot within a book. For example, within the Old Testament canon, possession of the land is presented first as a promise, then a reality, and then as a 'paradise lost'; and within the former prophets there is relative insecurity under Saul, security under David and Solomon, and eventual exile. Despite these vicissitudes the *land*, the first element of the good life described by Whybray, is an integral part of the vision of the ideal.[72] It is a place of *security*, which, he

67 Verse 13 [14] frames the question in terms of walking in God's ways, i.e. obedience to the law.

68 Especially in Prov. 12:9; 15:16-17; 21:9, 19; 25:7; 27:5, 10; Eccl. 4:6, 9; 5:4 [5]; 7:10. See also the goods listed in reply to the question 'what is good?' in Eccl. 1:3; 2:3, 22; 3:9; 5:15 [16]; 6:8, 12; 10:10-11; for comprehensive lists see Gordon, 'טוֹב'; Höver-Johag, 'טוֹב *ṭôb*'. There are similar rhetorical statements in prose, e.g. 1 Sam. 1:8; 15:28. For other frequent constructions with טוֹב see Alonso Schökel, 'טוֹב', 291–93.

69 N. Whybray, *The Good Life in the Old Testament* (Edinburgh: T&T Clark, 2002).

70 Whybray, *Good Life*, 4. He acknowledges that 'the good life' is not a biblical expression.

71 Excepting Obadiah, Nahum, Zephaniah and Habakkuk, which, Whybray maintains, do not contain information about the good life, see Whybray, *Good Life*, xi. In the following discussion I will illustrate, where necessary, by reference to the books of Samuel, since the moral conflict I examine later in the book is found in 1 Samuel.

72 On the land as *good* gift see N. Lohfink, 'God the Creator and the Stability of Heaven and Earth', in *Theology of the Pentateuch: Themes of the Priestly Narrative and Deuteronomy* (trans. L. M. Maloney; Minneapolis: Fortress, 1994), 116–35, especially 126–27.

posits, is 'the most fundamental of human goods'.[73] He argues that it is the good of *power* that enables secure possession of the land. Who exercises power is a theme of 1 Samuel 8. The prophet cautions that the pressing need for national restoration should not lead to precipitate decisions, painting a picture of 'the bad life' under an ancient Near Eastern monarch as a reversal of what YHWH had given Israel.[74] Note that injustice forms a key part of this portrayal: the king would enjoy the good life, but at the expense of his subjects. Apart from the very worst times, however, Israel is presented as benefiting from strong leaders possessing divinely endowed authority as they attempt to obtain peace and security for the people. One benefit of a securely held land is the produce or *food* it yields. 'A land flowing with milk and honey' is the epitome of this aspect of the vision of the good life (Exod. 3:8, 17; 13:5; 33:3; Lev. 20:24; Num. 16:13; Deut. 6:3; 11:9; 26:9, 15; 27:3; Josh. 5:6; Jer. 11:5; 32:22; Ezek. 20:6, 15). In the face of the danger of famine regular harvests are a blessing from God and the Old Testament asserts that the rains necessary for the land's fecundity are under his control.[75] A *long life* is a further characteristic of the blessed good life. Whybray summarizes

> The precariousness of life with the possibility of serious illness or death by violence led the Israelites also to place great emphasis on *long life*, and especially on the ideal of a 'good old age' – a long life lived to the full in peace and prosperity.[76]

In the books of Samuel, for example, David and Barzillai are credited with advanced years. Old age is not unambiguous, however, since Eli is old, but enfeebled (1 Sam. 4:15; compare David's final state 1 Kgs 1:1-4). Nevertheless, a prophetic anticipation of premature death can signify divine judgment (2 Sam. 12:13-19. Note the contrary activity of prophetic healing in 1 Kgs 17:17-24;

73 Whybray, *Good Life*, 4.

74 Cf. Whybray, *Good Life*, 72–77. On the religious justification for social stratification in the ANE see N. Gottwald, *The Tribes of Yahweh: A Sociology of the Religion of Liberated Israel 1250–1050 B.C.E.* (London: SCM, 1979), 498–554.

75 טוב is sometimes a euphemism for 'rain', cf. Höver-Johag, 'טֹוב *ṭôb*', 305; but not, in my view, in Ps. 85:12 [13], *pace* Gordon, 'טֹוב', 356. On the theological importance of YHWH's control of the elements see Iain Provan, *1 and 2 Kings* (NIBC 7; Peabody: Hendrickson, 1995), 132–34.

76 Whybray, *Good Life*, 5. Emphasis original. For example, 1 Kgs 3:11; 2 Chron. 1:11; Ps. 91:16; Prov. 3:16; 28:16.

2 Kgs 4:18-37; 5:1-19; 20:1-7). *Material prosperity* is regarded as a natural consequence of these goods. Although riches are associated with wickedness, especially in the latter prophets, wealth is not intrinsically evil but is more often associated with divine blessing. Indeed, poverty is viewed negatively, for example, David's conventional description of himself as 'poor and insignificant' (1 Sam. 18:23), the poor shepherd in Nathan's parable (2 Sam. 12:1-6), and the risk of debt slavery for a poor woman's child (2 Kgs 4:1-7). Furthermore, the misery caused by Philistine aggression is portrayed as a negation of the good life (1 Sam. 13:6, 19-22). The *family* is the arena in which food and material goods are enjoyed, and throughout the Old Testament the continuity of the kin group, conceived in terms of male heirs to inherit patrimony and continue the 'family line', is a prominent preoccupation. Harmonious family and communal living is summed up by Whybray under the rubric of *justice*, for which end many of the Old Testament's *laws* are formulated. *Wisdom* is another aspect of the good life he identifies, as is the good of *pleasure*. Finally, Whybray finds that living with reference to *God* himself is a key component of the Old Testament's view of the good life. He contends that the 'idea that people could enjoy the good life without reference to the gods would have been unthinkable in the ancient world'.[77]

Are the broad categories of goods that comprise the good life prioritized in the text? A preliminary observation is that the answer to this question will depend upon the passage being examined and, therefore, the context of the authors and their theological concerns. Overall, Whybray plumps for security expressed as possession of the land as the chief good.[78] In the books of Samuel, however, he thinks the principle of family continuity is especially prominent, echoing Smyth's conclusion (under the subtitle of 'The Old Testament conception of the supreme good', here a synonym of 'highest') that 'family life and its blessing came first in the divine order of blessing'.[79] Perhaps the crux of the matter is the definition of each good. Whybray defines 'family life' as 'the sense of an intimate community in which husband and wife, parents and

77 Whybray, *Good Life*, 6.

78 See Whybray, *Good Life*, 288.

79 Smyth, *Christian Ethics*, 89. Although Smyth contends that this later became a national good, and then a vision of 'social welfare to be realized in righteousness in the reign of the Holy One of Israel', Smyth, *Christian Ethics*, 92. It is not necessary, of course, to think that family and national concerns are mutually exclusive.

children and brothers lived together', so it is unsurprising that he thinks it 'is depicted only comparatively rarely'.[80] I propose that a different understanding of this good may lead interpreters to perceive it as more widespread, and thus more influential in terms of the moral actions portrayed in the text. Understanding Old Testament ethics, therefore, necessitates an adequate comprehension of the nature of the moral goods presented in the text.

3. Conclusion: Conflicting Moral Goods

In this chapter we have examined what the Old Testament itself might contribute to the resolution of value conflicts. Several conclusions are possible. First, it is important to recognize the great variety of resources for moral reflection in the Old Testament. At times this may result in prima facie contradictions, but in place of over-precipitous attempts at harmonization it is necessary to understand moral injunctions and so on on their own terms in the first instance.

A second conclusion is that while moral norms (either natural or revealed law) and motivations can provide useful information about Old Testament morality they are not themselves foundational. Instead, we have seen that legal stipulations or sapiential aphorisms, for example, can be considered to be statements about configurations of particular moral goods. Approaching Old Testament morality in this way provides new possibilities for understanding its view of value conflicts, for rather than centring upon apparently incompatible laws, the task becomes one of understanding the moral goods that they seek to protect.

Third, there are indications that moral goods *are* prioritized within the Old Testament. Slightly different orderings are discernable depending upon whether one examines moral norms, goods, or motivations, and, indeed, within these categories. These scales of values, however, are rather general and do not work at the level of detail necessary to inform value conflicts that people might ordinarily face. This is not to say that the biblical text could not provide this guidance, but that looking at resources other than those surveyed will be necessary. A lacuna in the field of Old Testament ethics is evidenced by the paucity of extant studies attending to narrative. Recently, some scholars

80 Whybray, *Good Life*, 290.

have suggested biblical story be mined for its ethical import.[81] I propose that researching clashes of moral goods in narrative could be especially fruitful and shall do so by focusing upon one particular value conflict in 1 Samuel.

Finally, when considering moral goods a proper understanding of their nature is required. Thus, for example, while there is some evidence that the family is near the top of the Old Testament's scale of values further work is necessary to define this 'institution' before any definitive evaluation of its importance is possible. This task must wait until Chapter 3; in the following chapter I examine the nature of 'good' in more detail.

81 See Barton, 'Reading', 55–64; idem, 'Disclosing Human Possibilities: Revelation and Biblical Stories', in *Revelation and Story: Narrative Theology and the Centrality of Story* (ed. J. Barton and G. Saute; Burlington: Ashgate, 2000), 53–60; Wenham, *Story*; B. Birch, 'Old Testament Narrative and Moral Address', in *Canon, Theology and Old Testament Interpretation* (ed. G. M. Tucker, D. L. Petersen and R. R. Wilson; Philadelphia: Fortress, 1988), 75–95; R. Parry, *Old Testament Story and Christian Ethics: The Rape of Dinah as a Case Study* (PBM; Milton Keynes: Paternoster, 2004). On the relationship between law and narrative see the typology in P. Barmash, 'The Narrative Quandary Cases of Law in Literature', *VT* 54 (2004): 1–16.

Chapter 2

The Priority of the Good

> [The] question, how 'good' is to be defined,
> is the most fundamental question in all Ethics . . .
> a mistake with regard to it entails a far larger number of
> erroneous ethical judgements than any other.
>
> George Moore, *Principia Ethica*[1]

A danger of investigating biblical texts for their 'ethics' is that one may force a modern concept upon documents to which systems of rules or right action are foreign, and potentially in opposition.[2] The previous chapter concluded that a focus upon moral goods as they are presented in narrative may be a fruitful approach to investigating value conflicts within the Old Testament. This chapter's epigraph, though, suggests that a particular conception of 'good' has far-reaching consequences and it is the task of the following pages to delineate a view in harmony with the Old Testament's own.

1. Moral Goods

I commence with a brief discussion of the nature of moral good and the relationship between good and right, before then examining how moral goods could relate to moral rules and the moral order. Finally, I refute the contention that attempting to resolve 'moral dilemmas' is futile.

1 The epigraph is from G. Moore, *Principia Ethica* (Cambridge: CUP, 1959 [1907]), 5.
2 Paraphrase of P. Esler, 'Social Identity, the Virtues, and the Good Life: A New Approach to Romans 12:1-15:13', *BTB* 33 (2003): 51–63, especially 52. See also P. Paris, 'An Ethicist's Concerns about Biblical Ethics', *Semeia* 66 (1995): 173–79.

A. THE NATURE OF MORAL GOODS

The study of 'the good' has a long history, although perhaps the most influential analysis remains Aristotle's.[3] He uses ἀγαθός in three ways. First, 'the good rationally aimed at'. Since there are many rational aims there are many goods, although there can also be a rational balance of multiple goods. Second, goods that are 'good for' something else, for example, exercise as good for health.[4] Third, 'a good something', for example, 'a good horse' as a good specimen of horses, where goodness is determined by the function of horses. These uses are related:

> What makes a knife a good knife (3), depends on what good (1) we want the knife to achieve, and that will depend on what the knife is good (2) for. Similarly a good (3) person will be able to achieve goods (1) that depend on what is good (2) for a person – his final good or happiness.[5]

Goods have been classified either as being means or ends, or as having intrinsic or extrinsic value. Aristotle thought that the attributes of intrinsic goodness were completeness and self-sufficiency, proposing that εὐδαιμονία was the highest good, since it is chosen only for itself.[6] The centrality of intrinsic good was maintained by Aquinas, who argued that the 'very nature of good is that something flows from it, but not that it flows from something else'.[7] Thus the

3 See Aristotle, *Nicomachean Ethics* (2nd ed.; trans. T. Irwin; Indianapolis: Hackett, 1999), 1094a17–24, 1097a24–37. For surveys of philosophical thought concerning 'the good' see R. Olson, 'Good, The', *EP* 3.367–70; A. MacIntyre, *A Short History of Ethics: A History of Moral Philosophy from the Homeric Age to the Twentieth Century* (2nd ed.; London: Routledge, 1998), especially 5–13, 42–44, 57–63, 249–66.

4 There is also a contrast between unqualified goods that are good for everyone and those goods 'for someone' in a specific situation, cf. *EN* 1113a22, 1129b2, 1152b26, 1155b24, 1157b26.

5 T. Irwin, Introduction, Notes and Glossary to *Nicomahcean Ethics* by Aristotle (2nd ed.; trans. T. Irwin; Indianapolis: Hackett, 1999), 332. Without original emphasis. Cf. *EN* 1098a8–12, 1106a15.

6 *EN* 1097a15–b21. εὐδαιμονία is often rendered 'happiness', but MacIntyre cautions that to change the language is to alter the concept, see MacIntyre, *Short History*, 59; I leave it untranslated.

7 *Summa Theologica* (2nd ed.; trans. Fathers of the English Dominican Province; London: Burns, Oates and Washbourne, 1920), I–II q.1 a.4 r.1. On Aquinas' general theory of good see *Summa* I q.5 a.1–6; Jean Porter, *The Recovery of Virtue: The Relevance of Aquinas for Christian Ethics* (Louisville: Westminster John Knox Press, 1990), 34–68.

good for a thing depends upon the nature of that thing: the human moral good is behaviour in accordance with human nature.[8]

The modern era saw a break with claims for the natural basis of goodness. George Moore, for example, argued that 'good' is simply an evaluative expression that cannot be defined with descriptors; it 'is incapable of any definition', but is known intuitively.[9] R. M. Hare, on the other hand, considered that the problem is not that the good cannot be defined but that in different contexts it is used in different ways.[10] So although 'good' means 'better' than others in a class of things this set is not fixed but dependent upon context, and statements about the good are simply commendations according to a person's chosen criteria.[11] Alasdair MacIntyre criticizes both Moore's intuitionism and Hare's prescriptivism, arguing it is insufficient to think of 'good' as merely evaluative, 'a status symbol for expression of choice'.[12] MacIntyre asks,

> why should it carry this type of prestige? The answer can only be that it carries with it a distinction derived from its past, that it carries a connection between the speaker's individual choices and preference and what *anyone* would choose, between *my* choice and the choice which the relevant criteria dictate.[13]

These 'relevant criteria' are learnt and, therefore, conceptions of 'the good' change through time.[14] Traditional aristocratic values, for example, considered thrift a vice and conspicuous consumption a virtue, while Puritanism thought the opposite was true. MacIntyre uses the example of Homeric ἀγαθός, with its ideal of warrior bravery, to question whether it is necessary or possible to distinguish between evaluative and descriptive uses of 'good'.

8 On Aquinas' theory of the human good see *Summa* I–II q.1; Porter, *Recovery*, 69–99. Perfect happiness, according to Aquinas, is contemplation of God, *Summa* I–II q.1 a.8.

9 Moore, *Principia Ethica*, 9. Note that Moore did not say that the good was unknowable or obscure, only indefinable: it is itself the ultimate term of reference by which other things must be defined, see Moore, *Principia Ethica*, 10–12, 35.

10 R. M. Hare, *The Language of Morals* (2nd ed.; Oxford: OUP, 1964), 137–50.

11 Cf. Hare, *Language*, 183.

12 MacIntyre, *Short History*, 254–62, quote 92.

13 MacIntyre, *Short History*, 92.

14 Cf. MacIntyre, *Short History*, 266.

> [T]hat a man has behaved in certain ways is sufficient to entitle him to be called ἀγαθός. Now, assertions as to how a man has behaved are certainly in the ordinary sense factual; and the Homeric use of ἀγαθός is certainly in the ordinary sense evaluative. The alleged gulf between fact and appraisal is not so much one that has been bridged in Homer. It has never been dug. Nor is it clear that there is any ground in which to dig.[15]

The descriptive basis of evaluation is taken further by Philippa Foot. She argues that calling someone 'daughter' or 'father' indicates what 'goodness' in each case means, and that the variety of cultural practice must occur within certain limits for it to be described as 'good'.

> If it were expected, as in Nazi Germany, that a daughter (like a son) should denounce disloyal parents to the police, this still could not be part of being a good *daughter*; a word which combined with 'good' to give this result would be closer to our word 'citizen' or 'patriot'.[16]

According to Foot, the 'nature of things' determines the range of permissible meanings of 'good', however, as the Puritan and aristocratic attitudes to money demonstrate, such appeals to nature do not mean people from different historical or cultural contexts agree about goods; indeed, they may be incompatible.[17] Although this is conceivably an epistemological problem, the difficulty of determining a cross-culturally valid content to the category 'good' remains one of the greatest challenges facing those who would employ nature in ethics.

For those who do accept natural foundations there arises the question of how the multiplicity of goods may be prioritized. John Finnis wrestles with this question, identifying seven basic human goods, but arguing that they are

15 MacIntyre, *Short History*, 7. See Philippa Foot's discussion of rudeness: if 'rude' is a lack of respect, this can be conventional (e.g. a man keeping his hat on indoors) or naturally disrespectful (e.g. pushing someone out of the way); the point is that it is possible for a descriptive term to be evaluative, P. Foot, *Virtues and Vices – And Other Essays in Moral Philosophy* (Oxford: OUP, 2002), 133–35.

16 Foot, *Virtues and Vices*, 137. Emphasis original.

17 In fact, Foot rather vitiates her argument when she continues the quote above with: 'Only in the context of a belief that denunciation would lead to regeneration could this be seen as one of the things by which the goodness of a daughter could be judged'.

equally fundamental and cannot be ordered.[18] This contrasts with Aquinas' contention that goods do possess a hierarchical ordering, viz. self preservation, procreation, life in society and knowledge of the truth about God.[19] He states that living things incline to goods desired by lower creatures as well as to goods appropriate to their own nature. This raises the question of why some people do not seek the highest goods. Porter, in conversation with Aquinas, makes two observations. First, a person's prioritization of lower goods may exclude the possibility of achieving higher ones because human life is limited by time and place.[20] Second, that something is a higher good may not be obvious. Indeed, the contested nature of goods – occasionally people need to be convinced that some things *are* good – demonstrates that their relative desirability is not always self-evident.[21]

In the light of these observations and the discussion in Chapter 1 it is possible to make four points about the Old Testament's view of the nature of the good. First, although the functional usage is prominent, all three of Aristotle's uses of good can be identified in the biblical text: one must not opt exclusively for any single one. In addition to the discussion above the following examples might be provided from 1 Samuel: good aim – 1 Sam. 15:22; 20:12; 25:15, 30, 36; functional good – 1 Sam. 1:8; 16:16, 23; 19:4; 27:1; good specimen – 1 Sam. 8:14, 16; 15:28; 16:12; 25:8 (note also the contrasting pairs 1 Sam. 24:18; 25:21 and the comparative forms 1 Sam. 15:22, 28). Second, while it is clear that the ethical concerns of Old Testament writers changed over the centuries, several texts appeal to the 'nature of things' as the basis for right behaviour. In other words, they do not seem to have conceived a breach between descriptive and evaluative uses of good. Third, contrary to a simple view that would categorize each good as a member of a species and then subspecies, Old Testament goods can pertain to more than one category.[22] Finally,

18 J. Finnis, *Fundamentals of Ethics* (Washington, DC: Georgetown University Press, 1983), 51. Finnis' basic goods are: life, knowledge, play, aesthetic experience, sociability, practical reasonableness and religion. For other lists of basic goods and discussion see S. Alkire, 'The Basic Dimensions of Human Flourishing: A Comparison of Accounts', in *The Revival of Natural Law: Philosophical, Theological and Ethical Responses to the Finnis-Grisez School* (ed. N. Biggar and R. Black; Aldershot: Ashgate, 2001), 73–110.

19 *Summa* I–II q.94 a.2.

20 See Porter, *Recovery*, 90; *Summa* I–II q.10 a.1, 3; q.94 a.2.

21 See Porter, *Recovery*, 88.

22 Cf. O. O'Donovan, *Resurrection and Moral Order: An Outline for Evangelical Ethics*

it is very obvious, especially in the prophets, that some configurations of goods are considered better than others; indeed, some are condemned as sinful.

Though our analysis of the Old Testament's resources for resolving value conflicts revealed that there were few detailed 'scales of values' there was an assumption that one ought to seek higher goods. It is usually thought that there is difference between a theory of obligation, concerning right and wrong, and a theory of value, of good and evil. Charles Larmore affirms that the 'idea of right refers to what is obligatory, to a prescription to which we ought to conform . . . The idea of good, by contrast, refers to what is desirable; it applies to whatever is worth having or doing and enhances the life of which it is a part'.[23] This is a very neat division. The relationship between the good and the right, however, is normally considered to be rather more complicated.

B. GOOD AND RIGHT

Any attempt to illuminate good and right must account for the radical change in the way their relationship has been perceived over the centuries. Henry Sidgwick warns that ancient ethical controversy employed a generic notion of the good, in contradistinction to the more specific judgements of action found in modern ethics.[24] Sidgwick contends that it is not simply that *what* is thought of as good has altered, but that there has been a transformation from an attractive view of the good to an imperative one. Ancient ethics, therefore,

> can scarcely be understood by us unless with a certain effort we throw the quasi-jural notions of modern ethics aside, and ask (as they did) not 'What is Duty and what is its ground?' but 'Which of the objects that men think good is truly Good or the Highest Good?'[25]

(2nd ed.; Leicester: Apollos, 1994), 34.

23 Larmore, 'Right and good', *REP*.

24 Paraphrase of H. Sidgwick, *Methods of Ethics* (7th ed.; London: MacMillan, 1907), 105. On the relationship of the right and good see also R. Kraut, *What is Good and Why: The Ethics of Well-Being* (Cambridge: Harvard University Press, 2007), 21–28.

25 Sidgwick, *Methods*, 106. Cf. the thesis of MacIntyre, *Short History*. With respect to the good and the right Plato is *not* a precursor to Kant. Plato thought that the basis of obligation was conformity to an ideal Form, which is the criterion for right action. Thus the ideal governor is 'occupied with the sight of things which are organized, permanent, and unchanging, where wronging and being wronged don't exist, where all is orderly and

Although 'ancient' in this context is normally understood to mean Greek and Roman, it is suggestive to consider whether it could also include the Old Testament. If so, modern (Western) readings that take its numerous rules as evidence for the primacy of the right over good would misrepresent the order assumed by original authors and readers.

The issues can be broached with a very brief statement of three common views of the relationship between good and right. I start with the position expounded by deontological theories, viz. 'there are some basic moral principles and rules in terms of which acts can be judged right and wrong and which can be justified independently of any developed idea of the good'.[26] To give an example of such reasoning: I should keep my promises because it is an act of fidelity, even if fidelity is not efficiently produced, that is, my keeping a promise causes others to break theirs. The deontological approach is typically exemplified by Immanuel Kant, who argues that the right can be deduced from a formal primordial 'ought', the categorical imperative, and that the only unqualified good is a 'good will' that chooses the right. 'A good will is not good because of what it effects or accomplishes – because of its fitness for attaining some proposed end: it is good through its willing alone – that is, good in itself'.[27] MacIntyre observes that Kant's imperative, being solely formal, can be given content by any moral tradition. Problematically, however, because

> it detaches the notion of duty from the notions of ends, purposes, wants, and needs it suggests that, given a proposed course of action, I may only ask whether, in doing it, I can consistently will that it shall be universally done, and not ask what ends or purposes it serves.[28]

rational; and he makes this realm the model for his behaviour, and assimilates himself to it as much as is feasible', Plato, *Republic* (trans. R. Waterfield; Oxford: OUP, 1993), 500c.

26 P. Byrne, *The Philosophical and Theological Foundations of Ethics: An Introduction to Moral Theory and its Relation to Religious Beliefs* (2nd ed.; Basingstoke: MacMillan, 1999), 86. Hursthouse, in a nuanced discussion of the issues, argues against the bold proposition that deontological theories presume the priority of the right while utilitarian and aretaic theories the priority of the good, see R. Hursthouse, *On Virtue Ethics* (Oxford: OUP, 1999), especially 25–31. For our purposes, however, the contrast is clear.

27 I. Kant, *Groundwork of the Metaphysics of Morals* (New York: Harper & Row, 1948 [1785]), 61–62. He compares this to talents or gifts of fortune, which may be directed to bad ends.

28 MacIntyre, *Short History*, 198. MacIntyre highlights the ease with which people can be educated into conforming to malevolent authority.

In contrast to the construction of good and right in deontological ethics, consequentialist moral theories make the ends of action the criteria of the right. For classic utilitarianism, right actions are those that maximize social well-being, and other goods are good to the extent that they promote such happiness. Although the simplicity of consequentialism is attractive, it has been criticized on three main fronts. First, it fails to allow questions of justice or, indeed, of any other consideration apart from outcomes of action. Second, it is impossible to know in advance all the consequences of an action.[29] Third, the incommensurability of goods precludes execution of the required calculations.[30] A final approach, aretaic moral theory, is not consequentialist in the traditional sense because right action does not merely lead to the good, it manifests it: acts are 'constitutive means' to good. However, the right *is* predicated on the good, and in this respect it differs from deontology. The essential insight is that right acts are those that are good for something: aretaic moral theories allow for actions that are wrong 'by reason of their object'.[31] A prominent representative of the approach asserts that 'the basic goodness of a moral act is provided by the befitting objective in which it is set: hence some moralists refer to an act as being "good of its kind" '.[32] In this scheme the object of an act leads to classification of species of acts, for example, charity, lying or killing. Peter Byrne summarizes that

> Aquinas' general teaching is that such classification begins the work of deciding whether individual acts are choiceworthy. If an act falls into a good species by

29 Foot raises another epistemological problem, viz. whether it is possible to evaluate the final 'states of affairs' produced by consequences apart from some other measure of good, see P. Foot, 'Utilitarianism and the Virtues', *Mind* NS 94 (1985): 196–209.

30 Thus, even if J. S. Mill's principle of justice is used to soften Bentham's original proposal, utilitarianism in particular, and consequentialism in general, cannot provide an adequate view of the right. For a helpful, if trenchant, critique of consequentialism that also highlights the dangers of exegetes unwittingly assuming its precepts see M. Banner, *Christian Ethics and Contemporary Moral Problems* (Cambridge: CUP, 1999), 272–78.

31 Virtue ethics has usually considered moral motivation decisive, but recent approaches have attempted to avoid positing right as solely determined by 'inner properties of a virtuous agent', C. Swanton, 'A Virtue Ethical Account of Right Action', *Ethics* 112 (2001): 32–52, quote 32. On virtue ethics in general see S. Darwall (ed.), *Virtue Ethics* (Oxford: Blackwell, 2003); C. Swanton, *Virtue Ethics: A Pluralistic View* (Oxford: OUP, 2003); Hursthouse, *On Virtue Ethics*.

32 Aquinas, *Summa* I–II q.18 a.2 as translated by Byrne, *Foundations*, 44. He follows Aristotle, who maintained that the criterion of right is the good of human εὐδαιμονία, see *EN* 1122b29.

> virtue of its objective, consideration of its end and circumstance will establish whether it is finally good.[33]

Objects are also the basis of moral rules that sum up the rationale for the classification of acts into good and bad, for example, 'do not kill'.[34] Moral rules, therefore, are adduced to protect moral goods, thus saving agents the effort of reinventing morality in every situation they face, since it is necessary only to identify the object of action.[35]

How might the Old Testament's view of the relationship between right and good be informed by these schemes? Three aspects of the discussion in Chapter 1 may be highlighted. First, it was clear that the basis of many affirmations of what is good or right is God. So, for example, because he is good, both the things he has created and those that he commands share this characteristic.[36] Second, although divine commands are prominent I have argued that they should be considered statements of how to configure particular goods, that is, commands themselves do not make something good, but arise from the need to prescribe or proscribe the seeking of specific goods or evils, often in particular situations. Furthermore, appeals to 'natural morality' reveal that the Old Testament indicates certain things are wrong because they are 'not good'. Third, discussion of the goodness of the created order highlighted not only its functional goodness but also that the structure of creation invites a morally good response from its inhabitants. In short, although opting for any one deontologic, teleologic or aretaic theory would be reductionist, when considering Old Testament ethics it does appear wise to heed Sidgwick's advice and, contrary to much modern ethical thinking, posit 'the priority of the good'.

33 Byrne, *Foundations*, 45.

34 The difference between moral rules and principles in Aquinas is that moral rules relate to species of act.

35 So also Kraut, *What is Good*, 29–34. Note that rules can favour particular groups and are thus not ideologically neutral, see Friedrich Nietzsche's first thesis in F. Nietzsche, *On the Genealogy of Morality: A Polemic* (trans. M. Clark and A. J. Swensen; Indianapolis: Hackett, 1998 [1887]), 9–33.

36 Some modern divine command theorists also attempt to push the start point back beyond the command itself to the nature of God, see, e.g. P. Quinn, 'Divine Command Theory', in *The Blackwell Guide to Ethical Theory* (ed. H. LaFollette; Oxford: Blackwell, 1999), 53–73.

Accepting this stance, however, does not exhaust the discussion. Even if one acknowledges the existence of a moral order of goods this is distinct to knowledge of that order.[37] It is obvious people can configure goods differently; in some cases to such an extent that one person can consider another's arrangement not good, but evil. In any case, the complexity of circumstances means that conflicts between goods, or the rules that describe them, are ubiquitous. Sidgwick is correct, therefore, to observe that simply identifying goods is insufficient, for even 'when we have judged conduct to be good, it is not yet clear that we ought to prefer this kind of good to all other good things: some standard for estimating the relative values of different "good" has still to be sought'.[38] Martha Nussbaum, a philosopher in the Aristotelian tradition, has suggested that the grounds for deciding between goods can be found in the particular situations in which they are in view, and maintains that it is necessary to attend to the particularity of each case. Since John Barton has invited biblical scholars to consider Nussbaum's studies of Greek tragedy as suggestive for Old Testament ethics it is important to examine her proposal in more detail.[39]

C. MORAL GOODS, MORAL RULES AND MORAL ORDER

Nussbaum's thesis is that the form of Greek tragedy is intrinsic to its message. 'Conception and form are bound together . . . Certain truths about human life can only be fittingly and accurately stated in the language and forms characteristic of the narrative artist'.[40] Nussbaum contrasts the ethics of narrative and that of moral rules. In *The Fragility of Goodness* she frames this distinction in terms of Platonic deductive philosophy, which operates from first

37 That is, questions of ontology are different to those of epistemology, cf. O'Donovan, *Resurrection*, 76–97.

38 Sidgwick, *Methods*, 106.

39 J. Barton, 'Reading for Life: The Use of the Bible in Ethics', in *Understanding Old Testament Ethics: Approaches and Explorations* (Louisville: Westminster John Knox Press, 2003), 55–64. Barton refers to two of Nussbaum's books: *The Fragility of Goodness: Luck and Ethics in Greek Tragedy and Philosophy* (2nd ed.; Cambridge: CUP, 2001) and *Love's Knowledge: Essays on Philosophy and Literature* (Oxford: OUP, 1990). See also her 'Non-Relative Virtues: An Aristotelian Approach', in *The Quality of Life* (ed. M. Nussbaum and A. Sen; Oxford: Clarendon Press, 1993), 242–269.

40 Nussbaum, *Love's Knowledge*, 4–5.

principles, and Aristotelian inductive empiricism.[41] Nussbaum observes that at the beginning of the *Nicomachean Ethics* Aristotle asserts that 'the educated person seeks exactness in each area to the extent that the nature of the subject allows' (1094b24). Nussbaum takes this proposition and argues that moral principles 'fail to capture the fine detail of the concrete particular, which is the subject matter of ethical choice'.[42] Narrative, in contrast, can explore moral problems in more depth than aphorism or legal stipulation. It is 'unlikely to conceal from view the vulnerability of human lives to fortune, the mutability of our circumstances and our passions, [and] the existence of conflicts among our commitments'.[43] For Nussbaum it is the idiosyncrasy of every moment that renders prefabricated rules inadequate. Instead, she contends, moral reasoning must attend first to the particular situation, and then see what rules might contribute, not vice versa.

Nussbaum argues that it is *always* impossible to give a general account of moral action that can be encapsulated in a set of laws, since rules can *never* become sufficiently detailed to accommodate all situations. This, she claims, is due to three features of practical situations: mutability, indeterminacy and particularity.[44] The mutability of the practical derives from its historical rootedness. Even justice is mutable, thus, she claims, 'a kind of improvisatory conjectural use of reason' is required rather than a thoughtless application of rules.[45] Indeterminacy derives from the fact that different people find different things attractive or repellent. The example she gives is of humour, concluding that 'excellent choice cannot be captured in universal rules, because it is a matter of fitting one's choice to the complex requirements of a concrete situation'.[46] Finally, particularity or non-repeatability is an inherent feature of many situations, above all personal relationships.

Despite her view of the limitations of general rules Nussbaum does allow them *a* role in moral deliberation as part of the perception of a situation: 'Perception, we might say, is a process of loving conversation between rules and concrete responses, general conceptions and unique cases, in which the

41 In *Love's Knowledge* Nussbaum extends her insights to modern literature.
42 Nussbaum, *Fragility*, 301.
43 Nussbaum, *Fragility*, 13.
44 Nussbaum, *Fragility*, 302–4.
45 Nussbaum, *Fragility*, 303. Cf. *EN* 1109a23, 30; 1106b15, 28; 1134b18–33.
46 Nussbaum, *Fragility*, 303. Cf. *EN* 1128a27.

general articulates the particular and is in turn further articulated by it'.[47] It is important to realize what Nussbaum means by 'rule'. She rejects the idea of rules as ultimate authorities against which to judge the particular. Instead, she views principles as summaries or rules of thumb derived from previous 'good' decisions. 'Principles are perspicuous descriptive summaries of good judgments, valid only to the extent to which they correctly describe such judgments'.[48] Even so, their strength, their simplicity, is also their weakness, they cannot adapt to complex cases. Rules, therefore, may be guidelines for growth in moral perception for those not yet fully equipped with practical wisdom, but they are not the culmination of moral understanding: the rule is a falling away from fully-fledged practical reason, not its fulfilment. Regarding the authority of rules Nussbaum states:

> Rules are authoritative only insofar as they are correct; but they are correct only insofar as they do not err with regard to the particulars. And it is not possible for a simple universal formulation intended to cover many different particulars to achieve a high degree of correctness.[49]

In other words, rules are not prior to practical perception but subject to it. In this way she aims to avoid the 'ethical crudeness' of morality based exclusively upon general rules.[50] Rules, in summary, are only prima facie obligations.[51]

Nussbaum commends Aristotle's depiction of the rule used by the builders at Lesbos as encapsulating her vision of rules in ethics. The Lesbian rule 'does not assume that the form of the rule *governs* the appearances; it allows the appearances to govern themselves and to be normative for correctness of rule'.[52] Aristotle thought that laws could not be formulated to apply to every situation, and that occasionally a decree addressed to a particular situation should be issued. 'For the standard applied to the indefinite is itself indefinite,

47 Nussbaum, *Love's Knowledge*, 95.

48 Nussbaum, *Fragility*, 299; cf. *Love's Knowledge*, 69.

49 Nussbaum, *Fragility*, 301; cf. *Love's Knowledge*, 69, where 'principles' replace 'rules' in the same quotation.

50 Nussbaum, *Love's Knowledge*, 37.

51 Nussbuam, *Love's Knowledge*, 156. Although Nussbaum is no intuitionist see Ross' claim that his prima facie duties rest on definite circumstances, W. Ross, *The Right and the Good* (ed. P. Stratton-Lake; Oxford: OUP, 2002), 21.

52 Nussbaum, *Fragility*, 301.

as the lead standard is in Lesbian building, where it is not fixed, but adapts itself to the shape of the stone; similarly a decree is adapted to fit its objects' (*EN* 1137b30). What, exactly, does this mean? The Oxford English Dictionary defines a Lesbian rule as 'a mason's rule made of lead, which could be bent to fit the curves of a moulding', and thus, figuratively, 'a principle of judgement that is pliant and accommodating'. This encompasses two attributes of the rule, its descriptive role and its prescriptive function. I suggest that the difference between these attributes is at the heart of a significant confusion regarding Nussbaum's (rhetorical) appropriation of the Lesbian rule. Irwin, in notes to his translation of the *Nicomachean Ethics*, comments that

> Aristotle refers to a flexible lead ruler that could be made to fit the shape of an irregular stone, and hence could be used to find a second stone to fit next to the first in a dry stone wall. For this purpose, having a rigid ruler would be useless for building. The point is that the rule or standard should be adaptable to fit the specific circumstances.[53]

It is essential to recognize that here the situation determines the 'rule': the rule is a *description* of the situation. But description is not prescription. If the former is meant it would be better to say 'measure', one function of the rule, rather than 'rule'. However, Nussbaum treats 'rule' and 'principle' as synonyms, thus demonstrating that she has in mind the latter, prescriptive function of the rule. This creates some fundamental problems for her position, above all with respect to the authority of the (prescriptive) rule. When employed to 'get the measure' of a new stone, it is not the rule that is 'authoritative', but the shape of the original stone, for which the Lesbian rule is merely a proxy. The Lesbian rule, having *described* one stone, is *not* then used to *describe* another stone in all its marvellous complexity, but *prescribe* which stone should be selected to adjoin the first. By analogy, therefore, it would not be a flexible rule that is authoritative when confronted by a new moral situation but *another* particular situation. In short, the proposal that a Lesbian rule be governed by the situation refers to the descriptive moment and not its prescriptive use, for which the rule is *not* governed by appearances. Nussbaum's appeal to the Lesbian rule,

53 Irwin, 'Introduction', 238.

therefore, performs a solely rhetorical function and does not illuminate how rules, in the prescriptive sense, can aid ethical reflection.[54]

Hilary Putnam has chided Nussbaum for her 'derogatory attitude towards rules' and suggested that her ethics veer towards 'an absolutely empty "situation ethics"', in which everything is a 'matter of trade-offs'.[55] Although she protests that she allows rules an important place in her ethics, Nussbaum has attempted to assuage some of this criticism by appealing to Aristotle's idea of 'spheres of experience', each of which possesses a corresponding virtue.[56] This, she avers, means one can speak of non-relative virtues. She is careful to distinguish between the formal definitions of each virtue and a more complete 'thick' description, asserting that 'we can understand progress in ethics, like progress in scientific understanding, to be progress in finding the correct fuller specification of a virtue, isolated by its thin or nominal definition'.[57] Nussbaum adopts this approach because she, like Aristotle, wishes to ground her ethics in experience rather than deducing it from first principles. Nevertheless, by appealing to 'grounding experiences'[58] as the basis for fixed spheres of experience she appears to be implying some sort of foundational order. Is this the case?

Despite Nussbaum's explicit rejection of a teleological moral order,[59] she seems to depend upon it in other places. At one point, discussing relations between the particular and general, she asserts that the general should be governed by the particular. However, 'particular human contexts are never, if seen well, sui generis in all of their elements, nor divorced from a past full of obligations. And fidelity to those, as a *mark of humanity*, is one of the most essential values of perception'.[60] But what is a 'mark of humanity' except a description

54 This criticism can be levelled as much at Aristotle as Nussbaum.

55 H. Putnam, 'Taking Rules Seriously: A Response to Martha Nussbaum', *NLH* 15 (1983): 193–200, quote 193.

56 Cf. *EN* Book VI; Nussbaum, 'Non-Relative Virtues', 263–64. She suggests the following features of common humanity as spheres: morality, body, pleasure and pain, cognitive capability, practical reason, early infant development, affiliation and humour.

57 Nussbaum, 'Non-Relative Virtues', 248, cf. 249–50.

58 Nussbaum, 'Non-Relative Virtues', 262.

59 Cf. *Fragility*, xv.

60 Nussbaum, *Love's Knowledge*, 95. My emphasis. Barton makes a similar move, promoting particularity but also appealing to 'human affinities', see Barton, 'Reading', 59.

of a generic order?[61] And one that would seem to have *some* authority over the particular. In fact, she makes this very point, but does not reconcile her different statements:

> Aristotelian particularism is fully compatible with the view that what perception aims to see is (in some sense) the way things are . . . surely the use of the concept 'human being' will play an important role in suiting the conception to make cross-cultural judgments.[62]

Nussbaum also argues that moral agents come to situations with a history of ethical predispositions and obligations, perhaps expressed in rules of thumb, and that they have to be faithful to both these and the particulars of the situation. This does not mean that agents can do anything as long as they wrestle sufficiently with the situation. Instead, they must improvise, which may be difficult.[63] 'An improvising actress, if she is improvising well, does not feel that she can say just anything at all. She must suit her choice to the *evolving story*,

61 Note that Nussbaum rejects a *teleological* ordering, but I identify her references to a *generic* ordering. O'Donovan explains why the created order must possess both; see *Resurrection*, 31–54; thus my discussion of Nussbaum is not capricious.

62 Nussbaum, *Love's Knowledge*, 96.

63 Nussbaum follows Aristotle, who asks regarding anger with respect to his concept of the golden mean: 'How far, then, and in what way must someone deviate to be open to blame?' His answer is that it 'is not easy to answer in a [general] account; for the judgment depends on particular cases, and [we make it] by perception', *EN* 1126b3–4. Nussbaum defines perception as 'the ability to discern, acutely and responsively, the salient features of one's particular situation', Nussbaum, *Love's Knowledge*, 37; cf. her other definition: 'seeing a complex, concrete reality in a highly lucid and richly responsive way; it is taking in what is there, with imagination and feeling', Nussbaum, *Love's Knowledge*, 152. Nussbaum recognizes that different people perceive things differently, although she may have an overly 'thin' account of the process of perception. Blum, for example, describes a process of moral deliberation comprising seven stages: accurate recognition of a situation's features, to recognize these features as morally significant, the raising of the question as to whether one should act in this situation, then judging whether one should in fact take action, the selection of a rule that one takes to be applicable to the situation, determining the act that best instantiates the selected principle, and performing this action, see L. Blum, *Moral Perception and Particularity* (Cambridge: CUP, 1994), 57–59. Thus an observer of a situation must perceive that it involves promise-keeping, not just taking a walk, to be able to begin the process of moral judgment. Blum argues that because different people perceive differently and see, or don't see, the moral significance of situations to varying degrees it is obvious that perception is not a unified, intuitive capacity, and may be more difficult for some than others, see Blum, *Moral Perception*, 5, 30.

which has its own form and continuity'.[64] But what is the 'evolving story' if everything is particular? It is necessary to have a stage as well as the individual acts, and it is the context (in the metaphor the play, in reality the moral order) that both authorizes particular acts and constitutes the grounds for typifying other acts as 'unethical'.

In the previous chapter I observed that the Old Testament, both in its appeal to a 'natural morality' and within the creation narratives, assumes a moral order. It is necessary, therefore, to ask how this order relates to particulars. O'Donovan's analysis of the relationship is compelling.

> Even unlike things can be seen as part of the same universe if there is an order which embraces them in a relation to one another. The *plurality* of situations and events which characterizes the experience of history, the fact that every event is 'new' and different from every other, can be seen as a *pluriformity* in the world-order, which is a capacity for different things to transpire and succeed one another within a total framework of intelligibility which allows for their generic relationships to be understood. Without a generic order new things would indeed be incomprehensible, for they would be absolutely particular, which is beyond the power of human thought to grasp.[65]

Thus people see things within the framework of what they already know. This applies to knowledge in general and moral knowledge in particular. So an individual has already learnt what is good, because she has an understanding of the moral order, before she appraises X in order to understand whether X is morally desirable. What role should rules play in this evaluation?

Since agents must know *before* they take a decision about a particular case whether X is right or wrong, pondering the particular concrete situation confronting the agent does *not* add to knowledge about whether X is morally good, only whether *this* is a situation in which X is at issue, that is, whether rules concerning X are at all relevant. I have suggested that rules should be considered as descriptions of aspects of the moral order. The multitude of biblical moral rules, therefore, can be viewed as attempts to grasp something of the proper order of moral goods. 'Do no steal', for example, places limits upon

64 Nussbaum, *Love's Knowledge*, 94. My emphasis.
65 O'Donovan, *Resurrection*, 189. Emphasis original.

the achievement of other goods because people have learnt that the protection of a person's possessions is fundamental for socially harmonious existence. In other words, the moral order, as they perceive it, demands this rule, and the relevant question in any particular situation is whether an action is 'stealing'. If it is, then the rule applies. Of course, this is not quite the whole story since comprehension and application occur simultaneously: the perception of the particular situation and the application of the rule are two processes that take place in conversation with each other. O'Donovan concludes his discussion of a particular case by observing that the 'engagement with the case showed up a measure of haziness and ill-definition in our understanding of the moral principle; the particular acted as a kind of magnifying glass through which the generic appeared with more clarity'.[66] However, neither this dialectic nor the a priori force of moral rules as descriptions of a moral order is what Nussbaum has in mind.

A further observation concerning the priority of the particular and moral rules can be made. Aristotle thought that because the mean was a fine-edged ridge, falling away on both sides to ever greater depths of error, there were numerous ways of doing something wrongly, but few right ways. Using the idea of hitting a target, he maintained that 'there are many ways of missing to be in error . . . But there is only one way to be correct. That is why error is easy and correctness is difficult' (*EN* 1106b30–32). If one accepts a created moral order of the type envisaged by the Old Testament, however, Aristotle's stance cannot be accepted. Instead, there will be many possible ways of responding well to the moral order, including in situations of moral conflict. The contrast between Aristotle and this notion could be illustrated by pinnacled mountains and Table Mountain, South Africa.[67] Just as Grotius suggested that justice cannot be defined, but that just ways could be known only *via negativa*, by observing injustice, so a negative decree, for example 'do not murder', sets a limit but leaves plenty of scope for perfectly moral human behaviour that values the good protected by the rule.[68]

66 O'Donovan, *Resurrection*, 195.

67 See also the discussion of 'good' dilemmas in Hursthouse, *On Virtue Ethics*, 66–67.

68 T. Grotius, *On the Law of War and Peace* (trans. A. C. Campbell; Kitchener: Batoche Books, 2001), 7. It might be objected that 'do not murder' is also positive law, but one would expect important features of the moral order, like protection of human life, to be codified.

To conclude, Nussbaum argues for the priority of the particular but, for the reasons I have outlined, her thesis cannot be accepted without qualification and Barton is overly enthusiastic about the potential contribution of her approach. A better strategy is to approach Old Testament ethics thinking of the 'priority of the good', where rules reflect an understanding of goods in their generic and teleological relations. Thus although rules are not final – that status belongs to the moral order – neither are they rootless 'rules of thumb', and must have a fuller authority than allowed by Nussbaum. Nevertheless, because moral rules must remain provisional for epistemological reasons attention to the particular *can* produce greater moral understanding, especially by illuminating how moral rules, and the goods that they protect or promote, are to be understood.[69] With respect to the interpretation of the ethics of the Old Testament such a view allows one to take seriously both law and narrative without collapsing the one into the other.

Particular goods, however, may clash, indeed, may be expected to clash. Before proceeding further it is necessary to consider whether such conflicts are sometimes irresolvable.

D. INCOMMENSURABILITY AND MORAL GOODS

In *The Fragility of Goodness* Nussbaum describes two very different approaches to 'luck', conceived as the vicissitudes of human existence. Plato argued *technē* could form a bulwark against luck, proposing a system of commensurable values in which differences between goods were quantitative, not of kind.[70] According to Nussbaum, the basic assumptions underpinning this scheme are: metricity, that there is a measurable value common to all goods; singleness, that only one metric exists; and consequentialism, that choices and actions have no intrinsic value but are purely instrumental means for procuring good consequences. Combining metricity and consequentialism produces the idea of

69 On the epistemological question see G. Outka, *Agape: An Ethical Analysis* (New Haven: Yale University Press, 1972), 96–97; O'Donovan, *Resurrection*, 76–97. Outka observes that it is one thing to say that there *are* laws that cohere with a moral order but another to claim that (1) they are adequately *known*, or (2) given that they are known they have been formulated in sufficient detail so that they are binding *as stated*, and (3) that the rules or laws that fulfil (2) may be indisputably identified. It is obvious that we do not possess a complete and infallible knowledge of the rules corresponding to the moral order.

70 Cf. Nussbaum, *Fragility*, 108, 110; *Love's Knowledge*, 106–24.

maximization. This, when combined with singleness, produces the idea of one value that is the point of rational choice.[71] Nussbaum rejects this calculus in its entirety. Following Aristotle, she asserts that the good life consists of various elements, each separate from the others and with its own intrinsic worth. To

> effect the commensurability of [these] values is to do away with them all as they currently are, creating some new value that is not identical to any of them. The question will then be whether his single-valued world can possibly have the richness and inclusiveness of the current world. A world in which wealth, courage, size, birth, justice are all put into the same scale and weighed together, made in their nature functions of a single thing, will turn out to be a world without any of these items, as now understood.[72]

This does not mean that non-metric choice must be arbitrary: Nussbaum rejects the opposition of quantitative versus ignorant choice as false. The alternative is

> qualitative and not quantitative, and rational just because it is qualitative, and based upon a grasp of the special nature of each of the items in question. We choose this way all the time; and there is no reason for us to let the rhetoric of weighing and measuring bully us into being on the defensive here, or supposing that we must, if we are rational, be proceeding according to some hidden metric.[73]

Incommensurability, however, leaves open the door for insoluble 'moral dilemmas', situations in which it is not just *difficult* to give reasons for choosing between competing obligations, but impossible.[74] It is inappropriate to say that one ought is not relevant because one of the grounds for action trumps the other; nor can one affirm that both obligations are oughts, but that in this

71 Cf. Nussbaum, *Love's Knowledge*, 56. In *Fragility* Nussbaum traces the development of Plato's thought concerning commensurability, noting that his later work seems to move away from the advocacy of *technē* found in *Protagoras* and *The Republic*.

72 Nussbaum, *Fragility*, 296.

73 Nussbaum, *Love's Knowledge*, 61. For an argument for this approach in Christian ethics see Banner, *Contemporary Moral Problems*, 136–203.

74 'A moral dilemma is a situation in which an agent *S* morally ought to do *A* and morally ought to do *B* but cannot do both, either because *B* is just not-doing-*A* or because some contingent feature of the world prevents doing both', C. Gowans, 'The Debate on Moral Dilemmas', in *Moral Dilemmas* (ed. C. W. Gowans; New York: OUP, 1987), 3.

situation one takes precedence,[75] which seems to be the solution Nussbaum herself envisages.

Thomas Nagel identifies five types of values between which there can be such a conflict,[76] and is unwilling to prioritize these values for theoretical reasons.

> I do not believe that the source of value is unitary – displaying apparent multiplicity only in its application to the world. I believe that value has fundamentally different kinds of sources, and that they are reflected in the classification of values into types. Not all values represent the pursuit of some single good into a variety of settings.[77]

Nagel sees the fundamental conflict as that between personal and impersonal values.

> Conflicts between personal and impersonal claims are ubiquitous. They cannot, in my view, be resolved by subsuming either of the points of view under the other, or both under a third. Nor can we simply abandon any of them. There is no reason why we should. The capacity to view the world simultaneously from the point of view of one's relations to others, from the point of view of one's life extended through time, from the point of view of everyone at once, and finally from the detached viewpoint often described as the view sub specie aeternitatis is one of the marks of humanity. This complex capacity is an obstacle to simplification.[78]

75 Cf. Gowans, 'Debate', 17–18. The second strategy may produce feelings of guilt, which are the basis of one argument for the existence of moral dilemmas: guilt shows that the obligation remained even though the agent was not able to fulfil it. See P. Foot, 'Moral Realism and Moral Dilemma', in *Moral Dilemmas* (ed. C. W. Gowans; New York: OUP, 1987), 250–70; C. Trappolet, 'Dilemas Morales', *DEFM* 1.437–42; A. MacIntyre, 'Moral Dilemmas', *PPR* 50 (1990): 367–82, especially 370.

76 T. Nagel, 'The Fragmentation of Value', in *Moral Dilemmas* (ed. C. W. Gowans; New York: OUP, 1987), 175–76. They are: (1) specific obligations to other people, institutions or community; (2) constraints on action deriving from universal rights, e.g. not to assault or coerce; (3) utility: the effects of one's actions upon the welfare of all; (4) perfectionist ends or values – those things with intrinsic value rather than utility; and (5) commitment to one's own undertakings, regardless of initial motives.

77 Nagel, 'Fragmentation of Value', 178.

78 Nagel, 'Fragmentation of Value', 180.

Thus, argues Nagel, while people still need to make decisions, the fact that action must be unitary does not mean that the justification for action can be similarly distilled.

While concurring that there can be good action without total justification there are several problems with Nagel's thesis. First, it is not certain that there are multiple sources of value. The biblical tradition claims a single source, God, and it is usually assumed that although there are different ethical obligations ultimately there are ways of resolving apparent contradictions between them because they are related to one, internally consistent, deity.[79] Whether this stance can be maintained with respect to the Old Testament is an empirical question and not to be decided a priori, although diversity of perspective per se may not be a problem.[80] O'Donovan suggests that uncertainly about moral judgments arises not because of multiple sources of value but 'because the moral field is pluriform'.[81] Only a moral code with one principle could avoid conflicting demands, but that would be of insufficient use to moral agents because the moral field is complex. In his scheme individual moral injunctions are to the created moral order as bricks to a building. Ethical thinking, therefore, should seek a comprehensive moral perspective, a view of the whole edifice. While not automatically solving the problem of conflicts in moral perspectives, O'Donovan does point to a way of accommodating different moral values without the need to posit multiple sources of value.[82]

79 Other traditions also look to this sort of resolution. Aristotle's doctrine of the unity of the virtues implies there can be no conflict between them, and Gowans notes that both Kantian and utilitarian theories of obligation are monist, see Gowans, 'Debate', 10.

80 Note Keck's suggestion that the perspectives of individual books are to 'New Testament ethics' as archipelagos to the submerged mountain ranges to which they attest, L. Keck, 'Rethinking "New Testament Ethics"', *JBL* 115 (1996): 3–16.

81 O'Donovan, *Resurrection*, 199.

82 Hebblethwaite raises a slightly different objection from a Christian perspective in B. Hebblethwaite, *Ethics and Religion in a Pluralistic Age* (Edinburgh: T&T Clark, 1997), 49–63. He argues that despite God being one, there are varieties of goodness because people relate to God in various ways. One can agree that relationship to God is morally important, but this does not preclude, as part of the relationship, behaviour that conforms to some divine standard(s) and/or some divinely ordained end(s), themselves part of the created moral order. In fact, O'Donovan reaches the opposite conclusion to Hebblethwaite: there is a unity behind the many ways of being good based on the fulfilment of the moral law. 'That is what makes these differentiations of character good: they are true interpretations, each within a unique vocational matrix, of the one moral life, the life which is given to all men to live', O'Donovan, *Resurrection*, 223.

The second problem with Nagel's position is that it assumes people's epistemological limitations vitiate arguments for a coherent moral order.[83] Although I have argued such an order may provide resources to resolve moral conundrums, it does not mean one can avoid moral indeterminacy. Paul Ramsey acknowledges that while moral goods are occasionally commensurable, in other instances moral choices involve incommensurable conflicting values, either because there is no common scale, or because there are gaps in the hierarchy of values. This means it is impossible to compute morality, although it remains possible

> that values are in some sense *comparable*, that some are higher than others. Values may be comparable qualitatively, yet there may be no way to measure addition to the one against subtraction from the other. Higher and lower values, more worthy and less worthy goods, may be known to us while still there may be gaps – incommensurability – in the scale, or perhaps there may be no clear single scale on which to measure the lesser or greater good or evil.[84]

In such a situation proportionate rather than commensurable reason is required. However, when 'human goods or evils differ from one another qualitatively *and differ qualitatively in such fashion that they are incommensurate on any single scale*, then choice is irreducibly ambiguous'.[85] Are personal and impersonal values so separated? Is it, for example, impossible to decide between 'truth' and friendship with a particular individual? Even if no rule can be devised to determine this question, it is unnecessary to conclude with Nagel that a conflict of these or similar values constitutes an unsolvable moral dilemma. In the case of the Old Testament, for example, such conundrums are presented in narrative contexts that may offer clues to their resolution.[86] That there may be some moral loss in making the decision is obvious from genres

83 Cf. O'Donovan, *Resurrection*, 19. This could be expressed in terms of Nagel's non-realism, cf. Foot, 'Moral Realism', 269; O'Donovan, *Resurrection*, 76–103; MacIntyre, 'Moral Dilemmas'.

84 P. Ramsey, 'Incommensurability and Indeterminacy in Moral Choice', in *Doing Evil to Achieve Good: Moral Choice in Conflict Situations* (ed. R. McCormick and P. Ramsey; Chicago: Loyola University Press, 1978), 69–145, quote 71. Emphasis original.

85 Ramsey, 'Incommensurability', 88. Emphasis original.

86 While Nussbaum's emphasis upon narrative as a source of moral guidance is apt, Pamela Hall suggests her predilection for tragedy and Henry James obscures the fact that

such as tragedy, but that is the significance of the moral distinction between desiring and unwillingly permitting a particular outcome.[87]

A final criticism of Nagel is that he supposes the possession by a single individual of myriad points of view means that people can view the world from places other than where they are. Despite the fact people may have multiple perspectives, this is simply impossible.[88] One advantage of cross-cultural moral reflection is that it may stimulate more accurate knowledge of the moral order since '[t]ruth may be one, but our apprehension of it is limited and perspectival'.[89]

To conclude, while it appears that insoluble moral dilemmas are a spectre, knowing how to choose rightly in some situations remains difficult and may be indeterminate. In everyday situations, however, people do not seem to struggle to juggle moral goods, but exhibit a fairly clear idea of which ones are more important. Douglas Davies' distinction between systematic and clustered convictions is helpful here.[90] The systemization of thought is typical of academic discourse, in which ideas are organized and presented in an orderly fashion. Real life, however, is not like this, but a farrago of complex and frequently conflicting convictions about varied aspects of living. Because temporal constraints militate against people systematizing all their thought about life, Davies observes that everyday thinking and practice centre around dominant clusters of issues. In terms of lived morality and ethical reflection this means that certain selections of moral goods are considered especially important, and value clashes connected to this nexus are viewed as more significant than those that are not. The variety of moral goods and their relationship to socially important clusters are important factors to consider in cross-cultural comparisons and, because the social world depicted by the Old Testament is so distinct from our own, the next section moves from theoretical considerations

ethical solutions may be more readily available than she would care to admit. See P. Hall, 'Limits of the Story: Tragedy in Recent Virtue Ethics', *SCE* 17 (2004): 8–9.

87 Cf. Ramsey, 'Incommensurability', 78.

88 O'Donovan, *Resurrection*, 80–81.

89 J. M. Soskice, 'The Truth Looks Different from Here or On Seeking the Unity of Truth from a Diversity of Perspectives', in *Christ and Context: The Confrontation between Gospel and Culture* (ed. H. D. Regan and A. J. Torrance with A. Wood; Edinburgh: T&T Clark, 1993), 43–59, quote 57.

90 Cf. D. Davies, *Anthropology and Theology* (Oxford: Berg, 2002), 19–26.

of the good and right to how kinship has been considered a central feature of Old Testament morality.

2. Kinship as a Moral Good

In the discussion in Chapter 1, I outlined a number of goods that feature in the text of the Old Testament, and how some scholars have identified the family as among the most significant. Although the family is a ubiquitous social phenomenon Patricia Dutcher-Walls observes that 50 years ago 'one would have looked in vain for much understanding or information about the family in ancient Israel'.[91] She traces scholarly interest in the subject since then, noting a shift towards using sociological and anthropological models of families to explicate texts. Dutcher-Walls shows how the focus upon a mundane institution rather than a political history characterized by kingly genealogies has enabled interpreters to get under the skin of apparently innocuous texts and perceive previously ignored dynamics. The reason for this becomes clear when one understands the marked differences between the structure of contemporary Western and ancient families.

It is a commonplace among commentators to note the hierarchy שבט (tribe) – משפחה (kin-group) – בית (house).[92] Many suppose the basic family unit in the Old Testament to be the בית אב, 'all the descendants of a single living ancestor (the head, *rō'š-bêt-'āb*) in a single lineage, excluding married

91 P. Dutcher-Walls, 'The Clarity of Double Vision: Seeing the Family in Sociological and Archaeological Perspective', in *The Family in Life and in Death: The Family in Ancient Israel* (LHB/OTS 504; ed. P. Dutcher-Walls; New York: T & T Clark, 2009), 1–15.

92 I follow Wright in translating משפחה as 'kin-group', C. Wright, *God's People in God's Land: Family, Land and Property in the Old Testament* (Grand Rapids: Eerdmans, 1990), 48; N. Gottwald, *The Tribes of Yahweh: A Sociology of the Religion of Liberated Israel 1250–1050 B.C.E.* (London: SCM, 1979), 301–5. Note Meyers' suggestion that בית אב should be translated 'father's household', C. Meyers, 'The Family in Early Israel', in *Families in Ancient Israel* (ed. L. G. Perdue *et al.*; Louisville: Westminster John Knox, 1997), 1–47, quote 19. For discussion of the relationship between these three groupings see also F. Andersen, 'Israelite Kinship Terminology and Social Structure', *BT* 20 (1969): 29–39; S. Bendor, *The Social Structure in Ancient Israel: The Institution of the Family (*Beit 'ab*) from the Settlement to the End of the Monarchy* (JBS 7; Jerusalem: Simor, 1996), 67–86; P. McNutt, *Reconstructing the Society of Ancient Israel* (LAI; London: SPCK, 1999), 66–70, 87–94; K. van der Toorn, *Family Religion in Babylonia, Syria and Israel: Continuity and Change in the Forms of the Religious Life* (Leiden: Brill, 1996), 183–205; C.Wright, 'Family', *ABD* 2.761–9.

daughters (who entered their husbands' *bêt-'āb*) along with their families'.[93] However, while it may have been 'the smallest, viably self-sufficient unit within Israel's system of land division and tenure', it was probably not the smallest discrete unit, which was the individual household.[94] Archaeological evidence reveals that the four-roomed pillared house with an average of four inhabitants was typical of highland dwellings.[95] In many cases these were arranged around a common courtyard, and it is supposed that several, related nuclear families residing in close proximity comprised the בית אב.[96] A number of these, in turn, constituted a village.[97] Membership of the בית אב is suggested by Judges 17–18 where Micah, upon the death of his father, becomes head of a household comprising himself, his widowed mother, his sons (and possibly their families), and a Levite responsible for the family shrine.[98] If, as Blenkinsopp proposes, the forbidden degrees of consanguinity in Leviticus 18 are motivated by the need to preserve order within the household these

93 Wright, 'Family', 762. Although generally applicable note Lemche's discussion showing בית אב is used for the nuclear family, extended family and lineage, N. Lemche, *Early Israel: Anthropological and Historical Studies on the Israelite Society Before the Monarchy* (VTSup 37; Leiden: Brill, 1985), 251–59.

94 Wright, *God's People*, 1. See also van der Toorn, *Family Religion*, 194–99.

95 L. Stager, 'The Archaeology of the Family in Ancient Israel', *BASOR* 260 (1985): 1–35. Further archaeological evidence is summarized in F. Deist, *The Material Culture of the Bible: An Introduction* (BS 70; ed. R. P. Carroll; London: Sheffield Academic Press, 2000), 195–209; A. Mazar, 'Three Israelite Sites in the Hills of Judah and Ephraim', *BA* 45 (1982): 167–78; R. Miller II, *Chieftains of the Highland Clans: A History of Israel in the Twelfth and Eleventh Centuries B.C.* (Grand Rapids: Eerdmans, 2005); J. Zorn, 'Estimating the Population Size of Ancient Settlements: Methods, Problems, Solutions, and a Case Study', *BASOR* 295 (1994): 31–38.

96 Cf. Judg. 18:22: והאנשים אשר בבתים אשר עם־בית מיכה, which NRSV translates as 'the men who were in the houses near Micah's house'; but Gottwald is to be preferred: 'the men who were in the houses comprising the household of Micah', Gottwald, *Tribes*, 291.

97 According to Bendor this configuration of dwellings continues to exist in the more densely populated settlements of IA II, leading him to conclude that the 'structure absorbed the pressure of the monarchy and its machinery, and adapted to it just as it adapted to other factors that determined its struggle for existence', Bendor, *Social Structure*, 32. See also N. Lemche, 'From Patronage Society to Patronage Society', in *The Origins of the Ancient Israelite States* (JSOTSup 228; ed. V. Fritz and P. R. Davies; Sheffield: Sheffield Academic Press, 1996), 106–20. However, see the recent study highlighting differences in house size by Bruce Routledge, 'Average Families? House Size Variability in the Southern Levantine Iron Age', in *The Family in Life and in Death: The Family in Ancient Israel* (LHB/OTS 504; ed. P. Dutcher-Walls; New York: T&T Clark, 2009), 42–60.

98 A priest is allowed to defile himself for a similar range of kin (Lev. 21:1-4).

prohibitions also point to the structure of the בית אב.[99] Stager uses models of birth and death rates alongside building size to calculate that each 'joint family' comprised 10–30 people.[100] Meyers concludes that over 80 per cent of the Iron Age I population inhabited villages of less than 100 people.[101]

Appreciation of ancient Israelite family structures has led several commentators to posit a central place for the family in Old Testament ethics. Chief among these have been Norman Gottwald's sociological reconstruction of the role of the family in the society of ancient Israel, and Christopher Wright's theological interpretation that places the family in the centre of a triangle of concerns encompassing God, the people of Israel and the land.[102] Two scholars in particular, however, have proposed roles for the family that serve as a useful stepping-off point for my study. Erhard Gerstenberger proposes that kinship is the matrix or context of the morality we find in the text of Old Testament, while

99 Cf. J. Blenkinsopp, 'The Family in First Temple Israel', in *Families in Ancient Israel* (ed. L. G. Perdue *et al.*; Louisville: Westminster John Knox, 1997), 48–103, especially 59; Bendor, *Social Structure*, 57–66; Blenkinsopp also thinks economic concerns are important. Bendor suggests Leviticus 18 was composed during a period of settled agricultural society similar to the transition to monarchy described in 1 Samuel; for a similar view see Meyers, 'Family', 17–18. Although this is plausible, if the structure of the בית אב remained constant through the monarchy it is not possible to provide such a firm date. On the omission of the daughter from Leviticus 18 see Wenham: 'it was already accepted that such a union was illicit (Gen. 19:31ff). It is expressly forbidden both in the laws of Hammurabi (LH 154) and in the Hittite laws (HL 195)', Wenham, *Leviticus*, 254. In any case simultaneous relations between a man and a *living* mother and her daughter *are* excluded (Lev. 18:17). This rather cuts the ground from under I. Rashkow, 'Daughters and Fathers in Genesis . . . Or, What is Wrong with This Picture?', in *A Feminist Companion to Exodus to Deuteronomy* (ed. A. Brenner; Sheffield: Sheffield Academic Press, 1994), 22–36.

100 Stager, 'Archaeology', 18–21. Meyers estimates that average size rarely exceeded 15 people, Meyers, 'Family', 18. Explicit mention of בית אב in Samuel indicates that it included sons and parents and could be numerous – Ziba's included 15 sons and 20 slaves, presumably with their families, and Doeg the Edomite kills 85 priests of Nob (2 Sam. 9:10-12). van der Toorn thinks that the 85 priests comprised the entire adult male population of the settlement, and it is possible that they did not pertain to the same father's house but to the kin-group that occupied a village, see van der Toorn, *Family Religion*, 191; 1 Sam. 22:19, which reads נב עיר־הכהנים, although note 1 Sam. 22:11: את־אחימלך בן־אחיטוב הכהן ואת כל־בית אביו הכהנים אשר בנב.

101 Meyers, 'Family', 12. See also Gunnar Lehmann, 'Reconstructing the Social Landscape of Early Israel: Rural Marriage Alliances in the Central Hill Country', *Tel Aviv* 31 (2004): 141–93.

102 See Gottwald, *Tribes*; Wright, *God's People*.

Waldemar Janzen suggests that all Old Testament ethics is under-girded by an overarching 'familial paradigm'. I will consider each of these proposals in turn.

A. KINSHIP AS THE MATRIX OF OLD TESTAMENT MORALITY

Gerstenberger argues that Old Testament morality was profoundly affected by social location.[103] He asserts that, 'everything that we learn in the Old Testament about interpersonal 'loyalty to the community' (*ḥesed*) and 'trust-worthiness' ('*ᵉmūnāh*) has its original setting in . . . family existence, orientated on mutuality'.[104] In other words, what one might call the cluster of kinship forms the matrix of Old Testament morality.

Gerstenberger defines the family as a community in which all members shared both work and possessions.[105] He argues that disputes were resolved within the family according to ancestral custom, postulating that the biblical records show special cases concerning inheritance and power (Gen. 27; Num. 27:1-11; Judg. 9:1-6; 2 Sam. 13), rebellious sons (Deut. 21:18-21), complaints about wives (Num. 5:11-13), sexual violence (2 Sam. 13), and conversion to an alien cult (Deut. 13:7-12). A key assumption is that families' theological horizons are restricted by the need for survival and that wider concerns are irrelevant. The dream is self-sufficiency (Mic. 4:4; 1 Kgs 5:5; Zech. 3:10). Internal relationships necessary for survival of families came to be viewed as protected by deities, with attendant taboos. Thus the precedence of parents over children is viewed as divinely ordained – part of the natural order (Prov. 15:20; 17:25; 19:26; 20:20; 23:25; 28:24; 30:17; Lev. 19:3. Note also the role of the older brother in 1 Sam. 20:29).

In terms of a specific family morality Gerstenberger looks to narrative sources, wisdom, and legal prohibitions (Exod. 20:12-17; 23:1-9; Lev. 19:13-18).[106] He proposes that these reveal the content of unconscious socialization. Regarding prohibitions, Exod. 21:13-17 twice forbids cursing parents (vv. 15,

103 E. Gerstenberger, *Theologies in the Old Testament* (trans. J. Bowden; Edinburgh: T&T Clark, 2002). He analyses the following social locations: family and clan; the village and small town; tribal alliances; monarchical state and exilic parochial communities.

104 Gerstenberger, *Theologies*, 31.

105 Cf. Gerstenberger, *Theologies*, 19–20.

106 Cf. Amadi's view that the notion of the good in Nigeria is captured in proverbs, E. Amadi, *Ethics in Nigerian Culture* (Ibadan: Heinemann, 1982), 50–64.

17; cf. Deut. 27:16), and restrictions on sexual activity among those who live under same roof, but who are not married, are prominent (Lev. 18:6-16). Jokes, anecdotes and proverbial sayings reinforce conceptions of proper behaviour whose *telos* is intra-familial harmony.[107] For example, the need to participate in agricultural tasks essential to family wellbeing is reinforced by proverbial comments concerning the sluggard (Prov. 26:13-16). Loyalty to the family is an important value and behaviour to 'outsiders' (probably people from the same clan rather than non-Israelites) has to be learnt.[108] Gerstenberger concludes that, 'the core of the matter is family solidarity'.[109] It is instructive, therefore, that Micah's vision of disaster portrays dysfunction at this foundational level.

> Put no trust in a neighbour, have no confidence in a friend; guard the doors of your mouth from her who lies in your bosom; for the son treats the father with contempt, the daughter rises up against her mother, the daughter-in-law against her mother-in-law; a man's enemies are the men of his house (Mic. 7.5–6; compare the positive vision of Ps. 133:1b–3a).

Gerstenberger discusses other social locations, but in the ethical realm each builds upon this base.[110] Overall, he presents a cogent case for the centrality of the family for understanding Old Testament ethics. Given that the family was central to Old Testament life, alienation from it was an extreme recourse (although see 1 Sam. 23:13), and being apart from the family exposed one to danger and uncertainty (Psalm 120). Whether this necessitates Gerstenberger's

107 Gerstenberger, *Theologies*, 64, 71.

108 Gerstenberger, *Theologies*, 65, 74. The 'one for all, and all for one' attitude is apparent in Jacob's dismay at his son's actions yet unwillingness to publicly distance himself from them (Gen. 34); cf. Saul's expectation of loyalty from his son in 1 Sam. 20:27-34.

109 Gerstenberger, *Theologies*, 75.

110 In the village setting, with a wider body of neighbours, issues of property come to the fore but, overall, he proposes that village morality is an extension of the family ethic. At the level of the tribal alliance Gerstenberger claims little can be said, save the possible existence of norms for fighting males for the duration of hostilities, for example, sexual abstinence and fasting. Despite an extended discussion of the history and theology of the monarchy he does not highlight novel ethical developments, although there were new ethical *issues*, e.g. hereditary succession and the status of the king. Gerstenberger argues differentiation from other nations is the key to understanding exilic and post-exilic ethics, and although family metaphors are used to describe exilic Israel, moral concerns go beyond the family since the horizons of faith were survival and being an 'ecumenical community under the one God Yahweh', Gerstenberger, *Theologies*, 271.

conclusion that moral goods were restricted to those that fostered survival is moot. Such goods may have been important, but this does not require an entirely pragmatic 'survival of the strongest', since the text highlights others (e.g. at the most basic level, 'do not kill'). Furthermore, any account that requires different moral standards according to situation possesses an intrinsic instability. It is more plausible to suppose that virtues were virtues and moral acts were moral regardless of social location, and then explain why the good of 'family solidarity', an obviously important factor, might demand ostensively amoral action. *How* this might be explained is a separate question. In terms of socialization, what needs to be learnt is not behaviour to outsiders per se but all moral conduct, including when *not*, for example, to be loyal or to tell the truth. The normative evaluation of these decisions requires their identification within the text.

B. A 'FAMILIAL PARADIGM'

Instead of attempting a historical reconstruction of lived morality, Waldemar Janzen identifies several theological-ethical paradigms within the Old Testament, all under-girded by an overarching 'familial paradigm'. For Janzen, a paradigm is, 'a personally and holistically conceived image of a model (e.g. a wise person, good king) that imprints itself immediately and non-conceptually on the characters and actions of those who hold it'.[111] With this definition Janzen seeks both to steer a path between Old Testament ethics as law and as principle, and to appropriate stories about individual characters in ways that do not assume they are always exemplary.[112] For example, 1 Samuel 24 relates how David and Saul meet in a cave. In what sense did David act morally? Was it simply returning good for evil? Janzen suggests there is a deeper dimension. David's men remind him of God's promise to judge Saul, and tempt him to realize the promise himself: 'David's greatest claim to ethical modeling here

111 W. Janzen, *Old Testament Ethics: A Paradigmatic Approach* (Louisville: Westminster John Knox, 1994), 28.

112 Janzen, *Old Testament Ethics*, 8–9, notes that the tendency to view characters as exemplary has led in two alternative directions: on the one hand the view that real ethical models are the prophets – earlier characters were ethically ambiguous; and, on the other, the 'Salvation History' view – the texts deal with *God's* dealings with imperfect people, none of whom are necessarily role models.

... is his refusal to diminish the sovereignty of God through his own autonomous action'.[113] David, according to Janzen, models a royal paradigm. Similarly, Phinehas, Abigail and Elijah model priestly, wisdom and prophetic paradigms of ethical behaviour.[114] It is not, in the case of wisdom, that the paradigmatic figure is equal to Abigail (or Job, Joseph, or the woman of Proverbs 31), rather 'ethical model stories flow together directly to form such a paradigm before the mental eye, as the pieces of a jigsaw puzzle fit together to yield a picture'.[115] This occurs in much the same way as people picture a 'good driver'.

Janzen maintains these four paradigms feed into and are nourished by a familial paradigm.[116] He accepts that changing social contexts will have meant the familial paradigm will not have been the same in, for example, semi-nomadic times and the late monarchy, but argues that the ANE concern for family *shalom* is given special literary-theological importance in biblical texts. Three stories exemplify the familial paradigm. Genesis 13 considers family harmony the key moral good.[117] The book of Ruth points to other family orientated virtues, viz., care for the stranger and widow (Lev. 19:9-10; Deut. 24:19-22), redemption of a kin's inheritance (Lev. 25:25) and observance of levirate laws (Deut. 25:5-10). Judges 19 speaks of models (the concubine's father and old man)[118] and counter-models (the men of Gibeah) of hospitality. Janzen contends that the differences between the stories of Abraham, Ruth and Judges do not derive from laws or general principles, but the various understandings (or lack thereof) of the kinship context. Taken together he claims that they witness to a three-pronged familial paradigm which is concerned for life (understood as progeny), land and hospitality.[119]

113 Janzen, *Old Testament Ethics*, 16.

114 Janzen, *Old Testament Ethics*, 9–20. Cf. Numbers 25; 1 Samuel 25; 1 Kings 21.

115 Janzen, *Old Testament Ethics*, 27.

116 Janzen denies that the others can be subsumed into the familial paradigm, but does postulate that they complete its 'sub-structure'. If so, his criticism of Wright's scheme is misplaced, since Janzen's proposal is also based upon a single paradigm, but with a life-land-hospitality matrix instead of Wright's God-Israel-land. My main problem with the non-familial paradigms is that they seem to describe literary *form* rather than moral content, cf. Janzen, *Old Testament Ethics*, 85–86, 100.

117 The story has other functions in the context of the wider narrative, especially the promise of Gen. 12:1-3.

118 Feminist scholars have severely criticized this interpretation, most convincingly Phyllis Trible, *Texts of Terror* (OBT; Minneapolis: Fortress, 1984).

119 See Janzen, *Old Testament Ethics*, 43.

Janzen's paradigmatic approach is potentially fruitful. It is not afraid of narrative texts, nor of prima facie amoral behaviour like Phinehas'. Especially important is his emphasis upon the family as the context and end of moral action. Three important criticisms, however, can be levelled. First, paradigms are a step away from the actual stories. Despite Janzen's avowed aversion to abstractions his paradigms are exactly that, being deduced from model behaviour. Second, while the analogy of the 'good driver' is suggestive, the idea that people piece together a mental image is problematic since we need something to guide our puzzle construction; something prior to the puzzle. Christian ethics has often appealed to rules, in the form of either revealed or natural law. Janzen demurs on this point, but at the very least a wider (meta)narrative that gives appropriate signals as to the meaning of the stories is necessary to identify the import of individual elements. Third, Janzen does not allow space for conflict between familial values. This is especially important since ultimately he includes all moral action within this paradigm.

3. Conclusion: The Priority of Kinship

This chapter started with a discussion of the nature of the good, observing that it has several possible meanings, including instrumental and intrinsic. Although intrinsic goodness can be conceived as having a natural basis, what this might mean in practice is difficult to identify. On the contrary, different historical and cultural understandings of the good point to the varieties of goodness, and the need to delineate any particular definition with care. I have particularly highlighted that this process must account for the important change between ancient and modern ethics with respect to the relationship between the good and the right. This raises questions about the nature of moral rules, apparently prominent within the Old Testament, and in conversation with Martha Nussbaum I examined the relationship between moral rules, moral order, moral goods and particular situations. This analysis has demonstrated that an exclusive focus upon either rules or the particularity of individual situations is theoretically problematic. I have argued that it is better to focus upon moral goods, which must be understood with reference to their generic and teleological relations to other goods, that is, to the moral order. While this order may be partly delineated by rules, such description is not exhaustive, so that studying the peculiarities of particular situations may lead to a fuller understanding of goods themselves.

The primary observation regarding moral goods is that they are legion, which means cases of conflict between them are inevitable. The 'family' has been identified as a key nexus of moral goods within the Old Testament. Gerstenberger observes that many rules and much moral guidance concern family activities, proposing that the family was the matrix of Old Testament morality. Janzen, on the other hand, argues that a 'familial paradigm' was the foundational conception of Old Testament ethics. Notwithstanding several criticisms, I judge the focus on kin relations of these authors to be extremely suggestive and agree that the moral good of 'family' is fundamental for understanding Old Testament ethics. The task of the following chapter, therefore, will be to examine kinship in more detail.

Chapter 3

Anthropological Approaches to Kinship

Kinship is to anthropology
what logic is to philosophy
or the nude is to art.

Robin Fox, *Kinship and Marriage*[1]

The epigraph indicates that 'the family' has been a traditional focus of anthropology, a discipline that seeks to comprehend the lives of 'others'. I have already mentioned the 'otherness' of the world of the Old Testament and in this chapter I will examine anthropological approaches to kinship to identify how its findings might orientate the present study.

The need to undertake this task is immediately obvious if one thinks of Michal, who is obliged to make choices about whether to lie to or protect different members of her family. Moreover, the author not only has to present Michal credibly but, in order that readers interpret correctly, also portray the reactions of other characters according to socially accepted ways of negotiating these relationships. It is significant, therefore, that Michal's choice is between her 'father' and 'husband'. Ferdinand Deist argues that 'different kinship terms imply meaning derived from the social system, they "stand for" more than their mere translation "equivalents" '.[2] On such a view, an examination of the relationships between characters must attend to the social roles implied by each expression. Here, however, the waters turn murky. Consider, the technical term for a person's father's brother, דוד. According to Deist, the fact that there is a

1 The epigraph is from R. Fox, *Kinship and Marriage* (London: Penguin, 1967), 10.

2 F. Deist, *The Material Culture of the Bible: An Introduction* (BS 70; ed. R. P. Carroll; London: Sheffield Academic Press, 2000), 247.

special word to refer to this particular group of individuals probably 'indicates their relative importance in the *lineage* system'.[3] The word, therefore, is evidence of a way of social organization based upon inheritance through the male line. If we were to interpret 1 Sam. 19:10-18a using this idea we might enquire into the implications of inheritance for women, or ask after Michal's interests vis-à-vis Saul and David in such a society. Perhaps, though, it is not so much inheritance that is in view but practical family life involving such things as presiding at the family sacrificial meal, directing family burials or deciding whether to redeem a kinsman. This is the view of Karel van der Toorn, who states that דוד is not merely equivalent to אחי אב, 'but a designation of the oldest brother of the father having the status of paterfamilias'.[4] Taking our cue from this understanding would mean asking less about 'family structure' and more about 'family living', and so attempting to account for Michal's choice of David in the context of the exercise of authority in the families portrayed in the text.

Anthropology has been attentive to these sorts of issues since the inception of the discipline, and an awareness of the different approaches it has taken to the 'institution' of the family will prevent readers imposing modern, alien, understandings of kinship upon the Old Testament. Note, though, that there is more than one anthropological perspective upon kinship and family. It is important, therefore, that those who employ anthropology in exegesis do so with an awareness of the theoretical basis of the resources that they utilize so that they avoid importing unevaluated assumptions into their readings. For this reason this chapter examines the main schools of anthropological thought concerning kinship and the ethics of kinship. It will become clear that I think 'practice theories' offer the most fruitful ways of understanding family relations and, in the third section of the chapter, I examine the assumptions that underpin this approach. Although some readers may find the focus upon anthropology novel, one of the premises of my interdisciplinary approach is that each discipline should be considered on its own terms before being brought into conversation with others.[5] A further advantage of this proced-

3 Deist, *Material Culture*, 246. Emphasis original.

4 K. van der Toorn, *Family Religion in Babylonia, Syria and Israel: Continuity and Change in the Forms of the Religious Life* (Leiden: Brill, 1996), 198.

5 Cf. the interactionist paradigm for interdisciplinary work (as opposed to exclusivist

ure will become apparent in Chapter 4 where, because I have outlined my understanding of human interaction in this chapter, I can simply affirm how anthropology should be used in exegesis rather than reconsidering foundational issues all over again. To anticipate the argument of this chapter, I shall contend that one must account for both 'social context' – in more technical terminology the way that the acting subject's environment is 'structured' – *and* the ability of people consciously to act innovatively or counter-culturally. In addition, I propose that it is important to account for ambiguity in human interaction. All these facets of how people relate to each other are essential for the interpretation of Michal's moral dilemma. First, though, we examine anthropological approaches to kinship.

1. Kinship

In the following brief discussion, I outline four anthropological approaches to the family – classificatory or descent theories, alliance theories, culturalist theories and practice theories – before summarizing how each might inform the interpretation of characters' interactions in 1 Samuel.

From the publication of L. H. Morgan's *Systems of Consanguinity and Affinity of the Human Family* in 1871 until the 1960s the study of kinship could be described as the basic discipline of anthropology, its 'hard core'.[6] Alan Barnard eulogizes Morgan's classificatory system of relationship terminology as 'the single most significant ethnographic breakthrough of all time'.[7] The key distinction made by Morgan is between a descriptive terminology, in which a term applies to a single individual in a genealogy, and classificatory system, in which a term applies to a number of individuals. This difference is significant because Morgan offered reasons for kinship classification, claiming that it is

or inclusivist approaches) proposed by T. Lawson and R. McCauley, *Rethinking Religion: Connecting Cognition and Culture* (Cambridge: CUP, 1990), 14–31, 170–72.

6 E. Leach, 'Brain Teaser', *NY Review of Books*, Oct (1967): 10; cited in M. G. Peletz, 'Kinship Studies in Late Twentieth-Century Anthropology', *ARA* 24 (1995): 343–72, see 344. A particularly useful survey of kinship studies is P. Schweitzer, 'Introduction', in *Dividends of Kinship: Meanings and Uses of Social Relatedness* (ed. P. P. Schweitzer; London: Routledge, 2000), 1–32.

7 A. Barnard, 'Rules and Prohibitions: The Form and Content of Human Kinship', in *Companion Encyclopedia of Anthropology* (ed. T. Ingold; 2nd ed.; London: Routledge, 2002), 783–812, quote 803.

a cipher for acceptable behaviour towards a particular group of relatives.[8] So, for example, many societies distinguish between parallel and cross-cousins, and marriage 'rules' reflect this distinction.[9] One such 'rule' would be that a man 'must' marry his 'Father's Brother's Daughter'. It is important to understand that the central problem that concerned early anthropologists was how 'primitive' societies could maintain stable political interaction without the apparatus of the Western state. Classificatory theories of kinship, it was thought, explain how an individual's relations with others are not anarchic or unpredictable, but proceed according to his or her place in the family as indicated by the names used by people as they refer to others. Although later theorists modified Morgan's thesis, proposing that descent *groups* or kinship *networks* functioned to achieve the same purpose,[10] all these concepts take as the 'atom of kinship'[11] the nuclear family and descent from mother, father, or both. If one were to undertake ethnographic 'fieldwork' in the Old Testament the concern with descent would quickly become apparent. But one would also observe the many stories of marriages and attempts to marry, a focus that is central to anthropological 'alliance theories' of kinship.

Claude Lévi-Strauss argues that the fundamental relationships are not 'parent – child', but 'brother – sister – sister's husband'. Starting from the observation that the incest taboo is universal he contends that the 'prohibition of incest is less a rule prohibiting marriage with the mother, sister or daughter, than a rule obliging the mother, sister or daughter to be given to others'.[12]

8 The significance of terminology has been debated from the genesis of kinship studies – for a convenient list of views see D. Parkin, 'Introduction: Terminology and Affinal Alliance', in *Kinship and Family: An Anthropological Reader* (ed. R. Parkin and L. Stone; Oxford: Blackwell, 2004), 121–35, especially 121–22.

9 A parallel cousin is one's father's brother's son or daughter, or mother's sister's son or daughter; a cross cousin is one's father's sister's son or daughter, or mother's brother's son or daughter.

10 See A. Radcliffe-Brown, 'Introduction', in *African Systems of Kinship and Marriage* (ed. A. R. Radcliffe-Brown and D. Forde; Oxford: OUP, 1950), 1–85; E. Evans-Pritchard, *The Nuer: A Description of the Modes of Livelihood and Political Institutions of a Nilotic People* (Oxford: Clarendon Press, 1963); M. Fortes, *The Web of Kinship Among the Tallensi* (Oxford: OUP, 1949).

11 F. Zonabend, 'An Anthropological Perspective on Kinship and the Family', *A History of the Family: Volume One: Distant Worlds, Ancient Worlds* (ed. A. Burguière *et al.*; trans S. H. Tenison, R. Morris and A. Wilson; London: Polity Press, 1996), 8–68, quote 24.

12 C. Lévi-Strauss, *The Elementary Structures of Kinship* (London: Eyre & Spottiswoode, 1969), 481, cf. 12–25.

Note that Lévi-Strauss' work refers to elementary marriage systems, that is, those with positive marriage 'rules' that someone 'must' marry another from a certain category of individual. Complex systems have only negative rules prohibiting who one can marry, for example, proscribing marriage between siblings.[13] The point is that alliance theory shifts the focus from group formation through descent to links formed by marriage. Using the illustration of European royal houses Robin Fox expresses the distinction thus: 'One sees marriage as useful in providing royal heirs: the other sees royal heirs as useful in that they can be used in dynastic marriages'.[14] The fundamental question, then, is similar to that which drove initial anthropological investigation, namely, that of social cohesion. Lévi-Strauss explains that

> the value of exchange is not simply that of the goods exchanged. Exchange – and consequently the rule of exogamy which expresses it – has in itself a social value. It provides the means of binding men together, and of superimposing upon the natural links of kinship the henceforth artificial links . . . of alliance governed by rule.[15]

Modern anthropologists do not, of course, attempt to define 'others' in terms of the *absence* of something in their own society, for example, European institutions of government. But this does not mean that they are aware of all their suppositions, something that is highlighted by the third anthropological approach to kinship, 'culturalist theories'. Lévi-Strauss talks of overcoming 'the natural links of kinship', but it is precisely these that are the target of David Schneider's iconoclastic analysis, which exposes the ethnocentric assumptions of anthropologists themselves. Schneider focuses upon the commonly held supposition that 'blood is thicker than water', arguing that it is not actually held by people in the societies studied by anthropologists. In fact, he claims that even the whole idea of 'kinship' is a Euro-American cultural construction. It is, declares Schneider, 'a non-subject. It exists in the minds of anthropologists but not in the cultures they study'.[16] Instead, he contends, it is necessary

13 Some complex systems encompass so many people that they appear almost elementary, famously the Crow-Omaha system.

14 Fox, *Kinship and Marriage*, 23.

15 Lévi-Strauss, *Elementary Structures*, 480.

16 D. M. Schneider, 'What is kinship all about?', in *Kinship and Family: An*

to seek the insider's (or *emic*) perspective. 'One must take the native's own categories, the native's units, the native's organization, and articulation of those categories and follow their definitions, their symbolic and meaningful divisions wherever they may lead'.[17]

Schneider's thesis was like a large rock dropped into a still pond, creating ripples that continue to generate debate about how to approach kinship studies. These discussions have been echoed in work in the humanities in general and in biblical studies by feminist scholarship. Although one might initially suppose that Schneider is correct to propose that 'the native point of view' is something to be sought, it is necessary to unpack his proposal in a little more detail. In doing so it will become clear why culturalist theories of kinship are inadequate, and that practice theories should be preferred.

In *American Kinship* Schneider states there 'are biological facts . . . There is also a system of constructs in American culture about those biological facts',[18] and in *A Critique of the Study of Kinship* he argues that 'culture, even were it to do no more than recognize biological facts, still adds something to those facts'.[19] It is clear that Schneider actually maintains the very distinction against which he argues, namely the existence of natural facts apart from cultural constructions of them.[20] The more thoroughgoing work of feminist anthropologists, on the other hand, posits no universal biological given called 'sex', which is subsequently interpreted in culturally distinct ways as 'gender'.[21] Instead, 'sex' itself is viewed as a construction formulated in the context of competing hier-

Anthropological Reader (ed. R. Parkin and L. Stone; Oxford: Blackwell, 2004), 257–74; repr. from *Kinship Studies in the Morgan Centennial Year* (ed. P. Reining; Washington DC: Anthropological Society of Washington, 1972), 32–63, quote 269. On problems with 'Euro-American' as a term of reference see L. Stone, 'Introduction: The Demise and Revival of Kinship', in *Kinship and Family: An Anthropological Reader* (ed. R. Parkin and L. Stone; Oxford: Blackwell, 2004), 241–56, especially 253.

17 Schneider, 'What is kinship all about?', 270.

18 D. M. Schneider, *American Kinship* (Englewood Cliffs: Prentice Hall, 1968), 80.

19 D. M. Schneider, *A Critique of the Study of Kinship* (Ann Arbor: University of Michigan Press, 1984), 199.

20 See J. Carsten, 'Introduction: cultures of relatedness', in *Cultures of Relatedness: New Approaches to the Study of Kinship* (ed. J. Carsten; Cambridge: CUP, 2000), 1–36, especially 5.

21 For example, S. Yanagisako and J. Collier, 'Towards a Unified Analysis of Gender and Kinship', in *Gender and Kinship: Essays towards a Unified Analysis* (Stanford: Stanford University Press, 1987), 14–50. See also S. Yanagisako and C. Delaney, 'Naturalizing Power', in *Naturalizing Power: Essays in Feminist Cultural Analysis* (ed. S. Yanagisako

archies of power. This enables the door to be shut more firmly on biological determinism in relation to gender, that is, the claim that certain roles pertain 'naturally' to men or women. Similar work involving the anthropological study of non-traditional family structures and new reproductive technologies has also been used to destabilize the natural basis for gender roles and kinship relations. The thesis of many studies in this area is that biology is *used* to justify *choices*.[22] This work focuses on individuals rather than 'cultures', attending in rich detail to personal aspirations and frustrations instead of amorphous generalizations. It leads to a critique of culturalist approaches to kinship that assume any given 'culture' is bounded and homogeneous, or which divorce 'culture' from actual social relations. One commentator observes that culturalist ethnographers 'tend to escape the muddle that a plurality of perspectives poses by being highly selective as to *which* "native point of view" they listen to'.[23] Indeed, even the grounds for comparison between cultures are determined by which point of view is preferred. For example, Schneider, perhaps betraying his American roots, uses individuals rather than families; but people from other societies might prefer to take the latter.[24]

Nevertheless, differences of kinship organization between societies are clearly visible, and one must be careful not to throw out the baby with the bathwater. Although individuals can and do construct 'family' in a great variety of ways these are often justified or contested on the basis of what is 'natural'. This leads Janet Carsten to propose that instead of abandoning the nature – culture distinction,

and C. Delany; London: Routledge, 1995), 1–22; S. Franklin, 'Re-thinking Nature-Culture: Anthropology and the New Genetics', *AT* 3 (2003): 65–85.

22 See L. Stone, ed., *New Directions in Anthropological Kinship* (Lanham: Rowman & Littlefield, 2001); C. Hayden, 'Gender, Genetics, and Generation: Reformulating Biology in Lesbian Kinship', *CA* 10 (1995): 41–63. A strong biological base for kinship has not been abandoned by all anthropologists, e.g. M. Bloch and D. Sperber, 'Kinship and Evolved Psychological Dispositions: the Mother's Brother Controversy Reconsidered', *Curr Anthropol* 43 (2002): 723–48.

23 M. Trawick, *Notes on Love in a Tamil Family* (Berkeley: University of California Press, 1990), 132. Emphasis original.

24 See S. Yanagisako, 'Variance in American Kinship: Implications for Cultural Analysis', *AE* 5 (1978): 15–29.

> it is precisely the ways in which people in different cultures distinguish between what is given and what is made, what might be called biological and what might be called social, and the points at which they make such distinctions, that, without preconceptions, should be at the center of the comparative anthropological analysis of kinship.[25]

Indeed, the preoccupation with sex and gender in recent scholarship has been challenged by Helle Rydstrøm. She observes that while there is indubitably a natural basis for human existence, the irreducible element is not sex but the human body; sex is merely one facet of embodied existence.[26] Rydstrøm proposes that anthropology should focus upon the whole person, which will include, but not be limited to, sex and gender. In doing so she advocates taking into account the fourth major movement in kinship theory, which examines how kinship is constructed through everyday practice, rather than definitions.

'Practice theories' of kinship consider family relations to be constructed by individuals seeking to satisfy their material and symbolic interests. It is especially attentive to the social *uses* of kinship and the fact that kinship requires *work*. Regarding affinal relationships, for example, Pierre Bourdieu comments that 'it is only when one records them as a *fait accompli*, as the anthropologist does when he establishes a genealogy, that one can forget that they are the product of strategies oriented towards the satisfaction of material and symbolic interests'.[27] In the process of accruing symbolic capital and wealth it is

25 J. Carsten, *After Kinship* (Cambridge: CUP, 2004), 189.

26 H. Rydstrøm, *Embodying Morality: Growing Up in Rural Vietnam* (Honolulu: University of Hawai'i Press, 2003). See also N. Rapport and J. Overing, *Social and Cultural Anthropology: The Key Concepts* (London: Routledge, 2000), 227–28; J. Carsten, 'The Substance of Kinship and the Heat of the Hearth: Feeding, Personhood, and Relatedness among Malyans in Pulau Langkawi', *AE* 22 (1995): 223–42; H. Scheffler, 'Sexism and Naturalism in the Study of Kinship', in *Gender at the Crossroads of Knowledge: Feminist Anthropology in the Postmodern Era* (ed. M. di Leonardo; Berkeley: University of California Press, 1991), 361–82. Scheffler argues that the kinship universal is not biology but genealogy. Biology does play a part – it is women who have children and form primary bonds with them – but it is the various uses of these givens to construct genealogical relations that are important, regardless of any biological link between persons.

27 P. Bourdieu, *The Logic of Practice* (trans. R. Nice; Stanford: Stanford University Press, 1990), 167. These strategies do not have to follow any 'rules' of kinship. Note also the distinction between prescription (formal relations between idealized categories of kin), preference (recognized jural rules) and practice (actual social behaviour) in R. Needham, 'Prescription', *Oceania* 42 (1973): 166–81.

important to remember that not all kinship relations are the same. Bourdieu refers to a 'privileged network of practical relationships' in contradistinction to official kin.[28] The respective roles of each sort of relationship are especially clear in marriages: 'Practical kin make marriages; official kin celebrate them'.[29] A similar emphasis upon the importance of non-biological kin is found in the work on 'house societies', that is, groupings of corporate estates or 'houses' perpetuated through property, names, and real or fictive descent.[30] These studies have found that the insiders' understanding of themselves and their relationship with others is in terms of their 'house' and not simply as discrete individuals.[31] It is significant, however, that this identification does not always signify harmony but frequently disguises tensions, for example, between brothers. In fact, relationships require constant work to maintain solidarity.[32]

This discussion of anthropological understandings of kinship has several important implications for readings of the Michal narratives. First, since the author invites consideration of Michal's kin relations by including the phrase 'David's wife Michal' at the beginning of the narrative (1 Sam. 19:11), it is probably significant that Michal lies to her 'father' and is loyal to her 'husband'. Yet, beyond this observation a classificatory understanding of kinship does not offer much interpretative insight, because we do not know to which of the two men Michal *ought* to have been loyal. Of course, a consideration of the social roles of fathers and husbands in the Old Testament might help, but what would one then do with a situation in which Michal did not act in line with these? Classificatory theories of kinship cannot answer such questions and, on their own, are insufficient as interpretative tools. Considering the key ethical questions surrounding Michal in terms of alliance theory would focus attention upon her marriage as a feature of the relationship between Saul and David. This approach, however, also strips Michal of her agency. Although

28 Bourdieu, *Logic*, 168.

29 Bourdieu, *Logic*, 168, cf. the case study 168–69.

30 J. Carsten and S. Hugh-Jones, 'Introduction: About the House – Lévi-Strauss and Beyond', in *About the House: Lévi-Strauss and Beyond* (ed. J. Carsten and S. Hugh-Jones; Cambridge: CUP, 1995), 1–46; C. Lévi-Strauss, *The Way of Masks* (trans. S. Modelski; London: Jonathan Cape, 1983).

31 Stone, 'Introduction', 247.

32 See also the view that constructing relatedness is 'hard work' in Carsten, 'Introduction', 26; I. Lepri, 'The Meanings of Kinship among the Ese Ejja of Northern Bolivia', *JRAI* 11 (2005): 703–24.

some commentators think this is indeed what happens, I strongly disagree with such interpretations (for reasons I discuss in Chapter 5). Viewing the morality of kinship solely through the lens of alliance theory, therefore, does not offer readers sufficient grip upon *Michal's* choice. This is not to deny that her marriage to David is conceived by Saul for his own ends or that ancient marriage practices are important for the interpretation of the relevant texts, simply that the men's manoeuvrings are only one ingredient in the narrative mix. Rather than a focus upon descent or alliance, culturalist theories of kinship direct attention to the context of individuals' actions, that is, the culture of the society in which people act. Such a view is very helpful when it comes to interpretation of the Bible because individual biblical characters exist in narratives that were written and read in societies where people possessed particular attitudes and expectations. In the case of Michal, for example, we might enquire into how she might have been expected to act towards other kin, including her father and husband. Yet, as feminist critiques of Schneider demonstrate, this sort of question alone is inadequate, for it can ignore the acting subject herself. While the culture of context must not be ignored, neither can one assume that social context is identical to individual agency, a point made forcefully by those who advocate the view that kinship is a choice. In contrast to classificatory, alliance and culturalist theories, practices theories of kinship invite interpreters to consider how Michal will 'work' to maintain family relationships in the context of her insider's understanding of what constitutes her 'family'. And, similarly, how Saul and David utilize the opportunity of Michal's marriage for their own idiosyncratic ends. Such a concern with agency takes us a long way from the 'bastard algebra'[33] of early kinship studies with its preoccupation with terminology, to the practice of becoming and staying 'related'.

Second, although practice theories of kinship encourage interpreters to focus upon individual agency, one must also account for the fact that action occurs in a particular time and place. It is important, therefore, to account for the 'cultural context' of Michal's choice, especially with respect to established attitudes regarding a daughter's obligations to both husband and father and their responsibilities to her. In other words, in order to know if something is 'counter-cultural' one must first discern what is 'cultural'.

33 B. Malinowski, 'Kinship', *Man* 30 (1939): 19–29, quote 19.

The third implication of anthropological understandings of kinship for this study is the general point that interpreters who utilize other social-sciences to explicate the biblical text must be cognizant of trends within the discipline employed and not simply select a particular approach 'off the peg' without considering its intrinsic strengths and weaknesses. Thus although I have stated a preference for practice theories of kinship it is necessary to investigate 'practice' in more detail. I shall undertake this task later in the chapter, but since this book concerns not simply kinship but the 'ethics of kinship' I look first at how the latter has been broached by anthropologists.

2. The Ethics of Kinship

The discussion commences rather inauspiciously with James Laidlaw's claim that 'the anthropology of ethics' is non-existent. He avers that there 'is no connected history we can tell ourselves about the study of morality in anthropology, as we do for a range of topics such as kinship'.[34] Thus despite some of the anthropological 'classics' attending to ethical issues D. Pocock can quip that '"Morals", "morality", "ethics" are not words commonly found in the indices of anthropological monographs and, if they are found, they are not commonly followed by many page references'.[35] Indeed, most anthropological studies refrain from defining 'morality', either because they think it is constantly changing,[36] or because they view such imprecision as something positive.[37] Laidlaw laments that a Durkheimian view holding morality is the product of social interaction is so pervasive that it has tended to exclude work on 'morals' per se.[38] Laidlaw's judgment, however, is overly pessimistic for, although relatively limited, there *is* a corpus of anthropological reflection about

34 J. Laidlaw, 'For an Anthropology of Ethics and Freedom', *JRAI* 8 (2002): 311–32, quote 311.

35 D. Pocock, 'The Ethnography of Morals', *IJMSS* 1 (1986): 3–20, quote 7.

36 See J. Rasanayagam and M. Heintz, 'An Anthropology of Morality', in *Max Plank Institute for Social Anthropology Report 2004–2005* (Halle: Max Plank Institute for Social Anthropology, 2005), 51–60.

37 David Parkin considers the wide scope of the word 'evil' an advantage, asserting that it is 'precisely because the term has been so loose analytically that it has been able to reveal so much empirically', D. Parkin, 'Introduction', in *The Anthropology of Evil* (ed. D. Parkin; Oxford: Basil Blackwell, 1985), 1–25, quote 2.

38 See the critical exposition of Durkheim in S. Wolfram, 'Anthropology and Morality', *JASO* 13 (1982): 262–74.

ethics.[39] There are two main foci. One concerns the morality of the anthropological endeavour itself. Issues include the discipline's colonial heritage, power relations between anthropological observer and the people studied, and matters of confidentiality and disclosure.[40] While these concerns are important, it is the second focus, the study of the 'moralities' of others, which is of direct interest to this study. Several distinct emphases may be discerned, each mirroring trends in the discipline as a whole. Early research, as in kinship studies, examined the vocabulary of moral appraisal, an approach that has not been entirely abandoned.[41] It is the 'culturalist' approach to morality, however, that has been most prevalent. The first monograph on the anthropology of ethics defined the task as seeking to identify patterns or systems of moral behaviour, and much anthropological investigation aims to uncover and explain culturally distinct moralities.[42] Such an approach, though, raises questions about ostensibly incompatible moral systems. Is there any basis for a cross-cultural comparison based upon universal moral standards, or does the key anthropological working assumption of cultural relativity lead inexorably to an affirmation of ethical relativity?[43] These sorts of questions cannot

39 For surveys of 'the anthropology of ethics' see Pocock, 'Ethnography of Morals'; K. Hoeyer, 'Ethics Wars: Reflections on the Antagonism between Bioethicists and Social Science Observers of Biomedicine', *HumStud* 29 (2006): 203–27; S. Howell, 'Introduction', in *The Ethnography of Moralities* (ed. S. Howell; London: Routledge, 1997), 1–22; J. Zigon, 'Moral Breakdown and the Ethical Demand: A Theoretical Framework for an Anthropology of Moralities', *AT* 7 (2007): 131–50; idem, *Morality: An Anthropological Perspective* (Oxford: Berg, 2008).

40 For a survey of anthropologists' moral questioning of their task and the development of professional ethical standards see P. Caplan, 'Introduction: Anthropology and Ethics', in *Ethics and Anthropology: Debates and Dilemmas* (ed. P. Caplan; London: Routledge, 2003), 1–33; D. Mills, '"Like a Horse in Blinkers?" A Political History of Anthropology's Research Ethics', in *Ethics and Anthropology: Debates and Dilemmas* (ed. P. Caplan; London: Routledge, 2003), 35–55.

41 E.g. C. Kluckhohn, 'Some Navaho Value Terms in Behavioural Context', *Language* 32 (1956): 140–45. Boehm contends that the advantage of semantic analyses is that they are anchored to observable data, C. Boehm, 'Exposing the Moral Self in Montenegro: The Use of Natural Definitions to Keep Ethnography Descriptive', *AE* 7 (1980): 1–26.

42 See M. Edel and A. Edel, *Anthropology & Ethics: The Quest for Moral Understanding* (1968; repr. New Brunswick: Transaction Press, 2000), 9, 108–47.

43 See Edel and Edel, *Anthropology and Ethics*, 19–33; C. Kluckhohn, 'Ethical Relativity: Sic et Non', *JP* 52 (1955): 663–77; B. Shore, 'Human Ambivalence and the Structuring of Moral Values', *Ethos* 18 (1990): 165–79, especially 166–67; R. Shweder, 'Ethical Relativism: Is There a Defensible Version?', *Ethos* 18 (1990): 205–18. Pocock

be considered in depth here, but the remarks of one commentator are important. Bradd Shore observes that debate about this question has used terms that have tended to hide complexity within both societies and individuals. At the level of society, generalizations about morality, exemplified in work directed at identifying 'moral systems', can point only to different emphases vis-à-vis other societies and cannot explain how particular people behave, since they do not *have* to act according to 'cultural norms'. At the level of the individual, if people are merely vehicles for 'the simple mobilization of values' there is no theoretical space for those who, sometimes, at least, view ethics in terms of moral dilemmas.[44] In fact, Shore argues something very pertinent for the investigation of Michal's moral dilemma, contending that ethical discourse is a means of justifying action in the light of conflicting moral imperatives. For this reason he maintains that generalizations 'squeeze life out of . . . reality . . . by treating human action as if it proceeds from a simple activation of cultural values rather than from the problematical and always partial resolution of dilemmas'.[45] This is important, for it recognizes that people are confronted by moral choices, and that they do not always choose according to culturally accepted ways of resolving dilemmas. Indeed, these socially endorsed pathways through the moral maze are themselves a particular configuration of moral values or goods.[46] We might draw two conclusions. First, any attempt to interpret a moral dilemma such as that faced by Michal must attend not only to 'cultural context' but also an individual's choice. Second, interpreters must be alert to the nature of the dilemma itself and not just the socially acceptable 'solution' or 'answer'. In other words, one must investigate the moral goods in play not simply, for example, the moral rule or moral virtue that seeks to express the desired selection of goods.

provocatively suggests that claims for ethical relativity hide a proposal for the normativity of subjectivism, Pocock, 'Ethnography of Morals', 9. Note the rejection of ethical relativity as an inappropriate response to injustice, and the call for a politically committed and morally engaged anthropology of the 'other' in N. Scheper-Hughes, 'The Primacy of the Ethical: Propositions for a Militant Anthropology', *Curr Anthropol* 36 (1995): 409–40. Rapport develops a liberal ethic by maintaining a focus upon the individual human agent in N. Rapport, *Transcendent Individual: Towards a Literary and Liberal Anthropology* (London: Routledge, 1997), 180–201.

44 Shore, 'Human Ambivalence', 168.

45 Shore, 'Human Ambivalence', 172. Without original emphasis.

46 See Shore, 'Human Ambivalence', 174–76.

In this light, it is instructive to note the specifically ethical categories (as practised in Western ethics) used by anthropologists. Julian Pitt-Rivers argues that '[m]oral values are best examined through the sanctions that operate against their violation'.[47] He attends to the 'norms' of honour and shame, observing that sanctions are often informal, for example, gossip about infractions of socially expected behaviour. Although much Western ethical discourse conceives of moral norms as universal, among the Gahuku-Gama of New Guinea compliance is not even expected of everyone within society, for a person's moral obligations depend upon relationships with particular individuals. 'Stated as sharply as possible, moral obligations are primarily contingent on the social positioning of individuals'.[48] Because duties are established by personal relationships the public and private are not discrete domains. This means that practices often glossed as 'corruption' are conceived as morally acceptable or socially desirable configurations of goods. Nevertheless, because people recognize simultaneous obligations to known people and more abstract ideas such as 'honesty' they can feel ambivalent about the practices in which they are morally obliged to engage.[49] The very idea of 'norms', however, may itself be culturally specific. In her ethnography of Mongolia, Caroline Humphrey proposes that an 'ethics of exemplars' is a better description of Mongolian morality. She observes that while exemplars are selected by each individual, there are commonalities in different people's choices because they originate from the same societies: Genghis Khan, for example, is a popular exemplar in Mongolia.[50]

47 J. Pitt-Rivers, 'The Moral Foundations of the Family', in *The Fate of Shechem, or the Politics of Sex: Essays in the Anthropology of the Mediterranean* (CSSA 19; Cambridge: CUP, 1977), 71–93, quote 83.

48 K. E. Read, 'Morality and the Concept of the Person Among the Gahuku-Gama', *Oceania* 25 (1955): 233–82, quote 260. Note that Read, as might be expected from the date of his study, seeks to uncover 'moral systems'. A 'person orientated' morality is also identified by D. Rosengren, 'Matsigenka Myth and Morality: Notions of the Social and the Asocial', *Ethnos* 63 (1998): 249–72.

49 See D. Smith, 'Kinship and Corruption in Contemporary Nigeria', *Ethnos* 66 (2001): 344–64.

50 C. Humphrey, 'Exemplars and Rules: Aspects of the Discourse of Moralities in Mongolia', in *The Ethnography of Moralities* (ed. S. Howell; London: Routledge, 1997), 25–47, especially 34–38. Yet another challenge to assuming the applicability of Western notions of moral reasoning comes from Signe Howell, who questions whether choices are inevitably reflexive, advocating comparative study of the processes of moral choice, see

In contrast to a focus upon norms, sanctions, or even exemplars, Thomas Widlock advocates concentrating upon moral virtue, asserting that 'ethos' in anthropology 'relates above all to everyday customs and to practical needs, and not to aloof concepts of right or wrong and good or bad'.[51] The anthropology of ethics, says Widlock, should attend to how basic human goods feature in moral practices, claiming that a focus on how societies conceive of 'virtuous agency' would enable anthropologists both to account for the particularity of moral practices and to engage in cross-cultural comparison. Like Shore, therefore, Widlock highlights the multiplicity of goods and goals, affirming that moral decisions take place in a complex environment.

A growing awareness of the limitations of Western categories of ethical reflection, in particular of the emphasis upon rules, has led the recent major monographs on the anthropology of ethics to focus upon the *practice* of morality. Although few authors describe their work as 'the anthropology of the ethics of kinship', their focus upon individuals in family contexts means that this is, *de facto*, what they produce.[52] Each, naturally, has its own emphasis, but the common features of these practice focused ethnographies are that the authors seek to avoid assuming both that 'culture' is equivalent to 'morality', and that social context is irrelevant for personal action. It is noteworthy that they achieve this objective only by focusing upon individuals in concrete social contexts: rather than seeking generalizations these anthropologists are highly

Howell, 'Introduction', 14–15. Jarrett Zigon is to be commended for explicitly delineating the philosophical underpinnings of his proposal that 'a distinction must be made between the unreflective moral dispositions or everyday life and the conscious ethical tactics performed in the ethical moment', Zigon, 'Moral Breakdown', 148. He claims that an anthropology of morality is only possible to the extent to which attention is paid to the moment of 'moral breakdown' when habitual solutions do not work, thus demanding ethical reflection. However, this seems unnecessarily restrictive; and in the following section it will become clear why I think it is important to attend to both reflexive and un-reflexive moral action.

51 T. Widlock, 'Sharing by Default?: Outline of an Anthropology of Virtue', *AT* 4 (2004): 53–70, quote 57. James Faubion also proposes that the anthropology of ethics should focus upon virtue, although, following Foucault, his scheme pays more attention to the unmasking of power relations, see J. Faubion, 'Toward an Anthropology of Ethics: Foucault and the Pedagogies of Autopoiesis', *Representations* 74 (2001): 83–104.

52 Although Faubion's subtitle, 'Toward an Anthropology of the Ethics of Kinship', entitles a section of his article, he simply summarizes the methodology he proposes in J. Faubion, 'Introduction: Toward an Anthropology of the Ethics of Kinship', in *The Ethics of Kinship: Ethnographic Inquiries* (ed. J. D. Faubion; Lanham: Rowman & Littlefield, 2001), 1–28. Other authors actually produce ethnographies of family morality.

responsive to both patterns and idiosyncrasies.[53] This is not to forget that an individual's personal freedom is constrained by power relations in the context in which they act or, more positively, that the need to make choices in the context of multiple responsibilities can stimulate creativity.[54] But it does recognize that people continually face situations in which it is impossible to secure all (moral) goods, that there is often a variety of ways in which goods can be configured, and that there are various justifications for these arrangements even though they are rarely free of problems or fail to create other conflicts.[55]

This discussion of the anthropology of ethics has two implications for the study of Michal's moral dilemma in addition to the observations above. First, we are confirmed in the view that considering moral issues in terms of moral goods is a profitable way of approaching the matter. It both offers more interpretative possibilities than an evaluation of, for example, moral norms or laws, and avoids the potential imposition of Western categories of ethical thinking upon the very different society in which the books of Samuel were first written and read. Second, we observe that a particular configuration of moral goods (and evils) can be socially endorsed, even if it is not always or even often the selection actually chosen by individuals. Of course, individuals' choices bring consequences in their wake, for their actions do not occur in isolation but in a

53 Margaret Trawick writes a 'thick description' of the dynamics of a single Tamil family in *Notes on Love*; Unni Wikan describes in fine detail the life and choices of a single individual called 'Suriati' in *Managing Turbulent Hearts: A Balinese Formula for Living* (Chicago: University of Chicago Press, 1990); Laura Ahearn's longitudinal study of love letters tells how this innovative practice affects selected couples in Nepal in *Invitations to Love: Literacy, Love Letters, & Social Change in Nepal* (Ann Arbor: University of Michigan Press, 2001); Italo Pardo investigates how people negotiate paths through conflicting obligations and desires in the context of multiple relationships with family and friends in inner city Naples in *Managing Existence in Naples: Morality, action and structure* (CSSCA 104; Cambridge: CUP, 1996); Steven Parish illuminates moral formation through both everyday and ritual practices in the Kathmandu Valley in *Moral Knowing in a Hindu Sacred City: An Exploration of Mind, Emotion, and Self* (New York: Columbia University Press, 1994); and Helle Rydstrøm examines practices of moral socialization, highlighting gender differences in socially acceptable behaviour in 'Like a White Piece of Paper. Embodiment and the Moral Upbringing of Vietnamese Children', *Ethnos* 66 (2001): 394–413; idem, *Embodying Morality*.

54 See Rasanayagam and Heintz, 'An Anthropology of Morality', 56; A. Walsh, 'Responsibility, Taboos and 'The Freedom to do otherwise' in Ankarana, Northern Madagascar', *JRAI* 8 (2002): 451–68, especially 465.

55 See C. Lisón-Tolosana, 'The Ethics of Inheritance', in *Mediterranean Family Structures* (CSSA 13; ed. J. Peristiany; Cambridge: CUP, 1976), 305–15.

particular social context where other people also choose moral goods according to their own preferences. For this reason it is important to attend to both individual action and 'cultural context'.

The survey of the anthropology of kinship with which I commenced this chapter outlined how anthropologists have theorized kinship relations, concluding that 'the family' was not essentially a matter of descent, nor marriage alliance, nor even cultural understandings of gender, but rather a constellation of practices. Similarly, it is apparent that studies of the anthropology of ethics have been most fruitful when they have analysed morality in terms of practice. But what is 'practice'? How does one person's practice relate to that of others? And how can patterns of practice be explained alongside the observation that people do new things? These are the questions I will address in the following section.

3. The Practice of the Ethics of Kinship

In the anthropological and sociological literature the debate about practice is usually framed in terms of 'structure' and 'agency'. Indeed, the tension between them has been called 'a leitmotiv in the history of the social sciences'.[56] What is at issue is the nature of the source or prompt for action. Is it social structure, that is, the context of action? Or is it agency, that is, the acting subject, the individual who decides to act? Or is it a mixture of the two?

One school of thought that attempts to hold structure and agency together is 'practice theory'.[57] Sherry Ortner notes that this is not really a theory, since

56 C. B. Brettell, 'The Individual/Agent and Culture/Structure in the History of the Social Sciences', *SSH* 26 (2002): 429–45, quote 442.

57 One cannot strictly speak of the singular 'practice theory' since there are various versions. The foundational texts are Bourdieu, *Logic*; idem, *Outline of a Theory of Practice* (Cambridge: CUP, 1977); A. Giddens, *Central Problems in Social Theory: Action, Structure and Contradiction in Social Analysis* (Berkeley: University of Los Angeles Press, 1979); M. Sahlins, *Historical Metaphors and Mythical Realities: Structure in the Early History of the Sandwich Islands Kingdom* (ASAOSP 1; Ann Arbor: University of Michigan Press, 1981); M. de Certeau, *The Practice of Everyday Life* (trans. S. Rendall; Berkley: University of California Press, 1984); and Sherry Ortner, *High Religion: A Cultural and Political History of Sherpa Buddhism* (Princeton: Princeton University Press, 1989). Andreas Reckwitz explains that they have in common a dismissal of the 'blind spot' of both rational choice and norm-orientated theories of social action, namely the implicit knowledge 'which enables symbolic organization of reality', A. Reckwitz, 'Toward a Theory of Social Practices: A Development in Culturalist Theorizing', *EJST* 5 (2005): 243–63, quote 246.

it lacks an underlying conception of the social order. 'There is only as it were an argument – that human action is made by "structure", and at the same time always makes and potentially unmakes it'.[58] Perhaps the best known advocate of practice theory is Pierre Bourdieu. In *Outline of the Theory of Practice* and *The Logic of Practice*, he seeks to bridge the 'ruinous divide' between objectivism and subjectivism. Objectivism argues social practices derive from social structure. It cannot, however, account adequately for different acting subjects making distinct choices in identical situations: the charge is that objectivism is too deterministic. Subjectivism explains social practices as the aggregate of individual choice. But it cannot account adequately for regularity of behaviour: the charge is that subjectivism is too voluntaristic. Attempting to overcome the dichotomy between objectivism and subjectivism Bourdieu argues that *both* acting subjects, themselves the product of past practices, *and* social structure, which is (re)produced by actors, are necessary to explain practice. One of Bourdieu's key concepts is *habitus*, which he defines in *The Logic of Practice* as:

> systems of durable, transposable dispositions, structured structures predisposed to function as structuring structures, that is, as principles which generate and organize practices and representations that can be objectively adapted to their outcomes without presupposing a conscious aiming at ends or an express mastery of the operations necessary in order to attain them.[59]

Bourdieu's rather dense prose requires some explication. The essence of the concept of *habitus* is found in the juxtaposition of 'structured structures' and 'structuring structures'. In principle, 'structure' is something distinct from and 'beyond' individuals' voluntary dispositions and actions. By describing the *habitus* as a 'structured structure' Bourdieu affirms that structure is a 'given',

58 S. Ortner, *Making Gender: The Politics and Erotics of Culture* (Boston: Beacon Press, 1996), 2. Shilling explains that practice theory avoids giving either structure or agency 'explanatory priority' since this fails to examine the interplay between them, see C. Shilling, 'Towards an embodied understanding of the structure / agency relationship', *BJS* 50 (1999): 543–62, quote 544.

59 Bourdieu, *Logic*, 53. For a summary of Bourdieu's *habitus* see D. Robbins, *Bourdieu and Culture* (London: SAGE, 2000), 26–29. On the etymology of the term from Aristolian *hexis*, through Thomistic *habitus*, to Bourdieu's usage see L. Wacquant, 'Habitus', *IEES* 315–19.

not open to manipulation. In other words, the consequences of a subject's prior actions have crystallized, thus giving the *habitus* a definite shape or form. Yet, the point of the concept of *habitus* is that 'structure' is not only 'beyond' but also 'within' the individual. In other words, although the *habitus* is something external it is internalized by individuals and so affects their action. In contradistinction to voluntarism, therefore, Bourdieu can affirm that individuals' actions are not *de novo* but are constrained (in both senses of the word) by structure. This is what he means by the *habitus* being a 'structuring structure'. Yet, because the whole process is circular any particular action affects the context of future action; its structuring function does not mean the *habitus* fails to remain a 'structured structure'. Bourdieu claims he avoids a mechanistic derivation of practice from *habitus*, allowing for strategic or novel responses to *habitus*, however, even these are defined with reference to the possibilities inherent in the *habitus* itself.

The orchestration provided by the *habitus* produces a commonsense world that individuals think is 'objective'. Thus even though there may be vigorous debate about many issues, the shared assumptions of this worldview are not questioned. Bourdieu remarks that '[b]ecause the subjective necessity and self-evidence of the commonsense world are validated by the objective consensus on the sense of the world, what is essential *goes without saying because it comes without saying*'.[60] This is significant, for it means that those who share a *habitus*, for example those of the same class, understand each other's practices intuitively. The result is that acting subjects are unaware of the influence of structure on their actions. Bourdieu notes that if 'agents are possessed by their habitus more than they possess it, this is because it acts within them as the organizing principle of their actions, and because this *modus operandi* [motive] informing all thought and action (including thought of action) reveals itself only in the *opus operatum* [practice]'.[61] For this reason Loïc Wacquant proposes that the *habitus* is analogous to 'generative grammar', which enables proficient speakers to use a language unthinkingly 'in inventive yet predictable ways'.[62]

60 Bourdieu, *Outline*, 167. Emphasis original. See also the diagram in Bourdieu, *Outline*, 80.

61 Bourdieu, *Outline*, 18.

62 Wacquant, 'Habitus', 316.

Bourdieu's theory of practice attempts to hold together individual agency and 'cultural context' in a way that does not subsume the one into the other, yet also does not separate them from each other. His synthesis, however, has been challenged on a number of fronts, both by those who wish to overthrow the whole edifice and, more constructively, by fellow practice theorists who wish to hone the explanatory possibilities afforded by his basic insight. In order to elucidate an adequate understanding of practice, in the following section I will probe the strengths and weaknesses of practice theory listening, in particular, to the criticisms and proposals of Nigel Rapport and Sherry Ortner.

A. STRUCTURE AND AGENCY

We have seen that practice theory, as conceived by Bourdieu, seeks to understand human agency in terms that recognize that people internalize their environment. Yet even when action is in some sense habitual, agency can also be the result of conscious resolution, a fact that leads some to argue that practice theory fails to account for an individual's consciously perceived goals. Nigel Rapport is especially critical of the idea of *habitus* because if people are aware of what they are doing then the potential consciously to manipulate or manage responses is real. He declares that

> Durable, transposable, cognitive, and behavioural, *habituses* [*sic*] function to generate an homogenous social conventionality, while subjects remain unconscious of the consequences of the actions and 'misrecognize' the objectivity of the social relations that these reproduce.[63]

Rapport's argument is that socialization does not lead to patterns of behaviour becoming 'things-in-themselves'. The *habitus*, therefore, can never become a verbal subject: *it* has no agency. Interpretation remains the task of individuals, and although people may use learned conventions, these 'will be animated by purposes that are individual and ultimately', claims Rapport, 'indeterminate'.[64] Given his insistence that social relations are an aggregation of individuals'

63 N. Rapport, 'Envisioned, Intentioned: A Painter Informs an Anthropologist about Social Relations', *JRAI* 10 (2004): 861–81, quote 862. See also J. Throop and K. Murphy, 'Bourdieu and Phenomenology', *AT* 2 (2002): 185–207.

64 Rapport, 'Envisioned, Intentioned', 864.

purposes he objects to the analytical separation of intention and action, asserting that simply because 'the consequences of individual's actions are not always (or even not often) as intended does not make those consequences any less personal or individual in their nature'.[65] To illustrate his thesis, Rapport compares the art and letters of Stanley Spencer. He opines it is not possible to understand Spencer's relations with others without appreciating the artist's own, at times contradictory, understandings of those same relationships, because Spencer himself claimed that 'all I am wishing to do is to enable anyone to stand on the exact spot in my mind and see what I see'.[66] Rapport conceives an elevated role for individual creativity, which he defines as 'the novel individual use of collective cultural forms'.[67] This is because

> the world is not organized into neat pieces of information merely waiting for human retrieval, what the brain is doing in interacting with an environment is actually structuring its life-world. The environments in which human beings find themselves are open-ended and ambiguous, and their order, their codification into distinct, bounded and labelled things and relations, derives from human organisms engaged in acts of perceiving.[68]

Rapport's concern is to rescue individual agency and avoid an image of people as passive victims of historical, social and cultural vicissitudes. Indeed, although there is truth in the assertions of some that the emphasis upon individual agency is itself a cultural phenomenon, individual agency *is* an essential analytical category, if only because human beings are singularly embodied: Rapport's concern with agency is not an inherent weakness of his argument. Yet, overall I think that the thesis that conscious individual action is the source

65 Rapport, 'Envisioned, Intentioned', 877.

66 Quoted in Rapport, 'Envisioned, Intentioned', 871.

67 N. Rapport, *The Prose and the Passion: Anthropology, Literature and the Writing of E. M. Forster* (Manchester: Manchester University Press, 1994), 260. The novel use could be novel combinations, novel constitution of forms or novel meanings. His vision of creative agency is 'breaking the teacup of conventional experience', which can be done in five ways: composition and decomposition – division and re-building of old forms; weighting – accentuating certain elements of culture; reordering; deletion and supplementation – exclusion of some elements; and deformation – distorting or elaborating certain cultural elements, see Rapport, *Prose*, 261.

68 N. Rapport, 'Random Mind: Towards an Appreciation of Openness in Individual, Society and Anthropology', *AJA* 12 (2001): 190–208, quote 194.

of all practice is too bold. First, 'agency' as a category is only a potential capacity, which must take concrete form in specific situations. In other words, there is no 'a-cultural' agency, and its shape will depend upon an agent's position in a particular society, including her power.[69] Declan Quigley astutely remarks that 'not all individuals live in historical conditions where their opportunities to express their individuality bear much resemblance to each other . . . no individual lives in a society where s/he can express his or her individuality in any way s/he pleases' – the latter only exists in fiction or fairy-tales.[70] Individuals' creativities, therefore, are only formally, not substantially, the same. This is not necessarily a negative thing, for social constraint is not always wrong and can prevent or stop evil as well as curtail legitimate individuality. Second, it may be impossible to know about an individual's intentions; indeed this knowledge may be unavailable even to the acting subject. What is observable, however, is socialized behaviour. This means that an account of practice must include social context, even if it is not a personal subject in itself. Third, individualistic approaches over-emphasize individuals' predilection for change while downplaying how personal psychology is organized by culture.[71]

Because Rapport's attempt to rectify the overly deterministic nature of Bourdieu's *habitus* swings the pendulum too far in the direction of individual, conscious agency, it is preferable to follow Ortner's more nuanced position. She proposes that it is important 'to articulate a position in which there is some distance between actor and culture, and yet which does not postulate a culturally unconstrained actor rationally manipulating cultural imagery and options'.[72] She proposes a 'loosely structured' actor

> who is prepared – but not more than that – to find most of his or her culture intelligible and meaningful, but who does not necessarily find all parts of it equally meaningful in all times and places. The distance between culture and actor is there, but so too is the capacity to find meaning, in more than a manipulative way, in one's own cultural repertoire.[73]

69 See C. Ratner, 'Agency and Culture', *JTSB* 30 (2000): 413–34.

70 D. Quigley, 'Anthropology in Disneyworld: Rapport, Gardner, and the 'Discipline' of Social Anthropology', *AJA* 12 (2001): 182–89, especially 184–85; cf. Bourdieu, *Logic*, 64.

71 See G. Obeyesekere, *Medusa's Hair* (Chicago: University of Chicago Press, 1981).

72 Ortner, *High Religion*, 198.

73 Ortner, *High Religion*, 198.

The proposed 'distance' between structure and actor means that action is not produced simply by some combination of things received. This means that, at the point of decision, the structuring aspect of *habitus* is *not* the only determinate of action. This insight enables Ortner to propose a version of practice theory that not only emphasizes structural reproduction but also innovation. She argues that Bourdieu conceives practice as a loop, thus neglecting instances of 'slippage', that is, times when agents do not reproduce patterns.[74] Ortner, however, proposes that 'slippage' is important and that one must account for instances when the *habitus* is not reproduced but challenged or changed. It is unimportant whether these 'slippages' are intentional or unintentional, only that they can and do occur. Ortner's, then, is a 'version of practice theory, with everything slightly – but not completely – tilted toward incompleteness, instability, and change'.[75] She makes this proposal because of a fundamental insight. Ortner observes that structures, *habitus*, and 'cultures' are not monolithic but contain many elements, some of which contradict each other. This forces actors to choose between cultural goods or aspects of the *habitus*. 'The point here is that structure does not just sit there, constraining actors by its formal characteristics, but recurrently poses problems to actors, to which they must respond'.[76] Ortner complements this observation with a second concept of structure, that of a 'cultural schema', a standard, socially acceptable, even laudable, way of resolving the structure's inherent contradictions. These moves provide Ortner with the theoretical space to account for subversions of the dominant paradigm from within, and thus to explain why individual actors sometimes choose to act outside the schema, for example, by eloping to marry for love, or forgiving a slight to honour. Thus 'structure is practiced, it is lived, it is enacted, but it is also challenged, defended, renewed, changed'.[77] Ortner develops the resultant possibilities into a typology of practice, each with a different relation to 'structure'. 'Ordinary practice' is repetitive or everyday action, which leads to internalization of structure. 'Intentional action' concerns the pursuit of individual goals and desires. An important question is how structure constitutes

74 Ortner, *Making Gender*, 17.

75 Ortner, *Making Gender*, 18. Ortner labels her vision a 'subaltern practice theory'. On changes to the *habitus* in Bourdieu's theory see P. Bourdieu, *Pascalian Meditations* (trans. R. Nice; Cambridge: Polity, 2000), 159–63.

76 Ortner, *High Religion*, 196.

77 Ortner, *High Religion*, 196.

these desires, and in her study of Sherpa Buddhist monasteries Ortner argues that various historical factors pushed individuals in certain directions because of extant cultural structures and that, concurrently, actors used historical circumstances in ways that made sense given their cultural milieu. The third type of practice is 'extraordinary praxis', that is, sustained activity based upon a culturally alternative logic.

Ortner's important modifications to Bourdieu's practice theory, which partly recognize the force of arguments for a prominent role for individual agency, have obvious implications for the study of Michal's moral dilemma. Before proceeding to summarize them, however, I highlight a frequently overlooked feature of human interaction: its ambiguity.

B. AMBIGUITY

Ambiguity arises because of differences of perception between people, not only between those from different cultural backgrounds, although they are often more pronounced when this is the case, but also among those who share cultural understandings. Nigel Rapport's ethnographic research in the English village of 'Wanet' highlights the ubiquity of varying interpretations and, consequently, the ambiguity of social interaction. Reflecting upon his fieldwork experience Rapport submits that social life could not be neatly classified. Rather, it was 'farcical, chaotic, multiple, contradictory; it was a muddling-through, which turned on the paradoxical distinction between appearance and actuality'.[78] He contends the picture of Wanet as 'rural idyll' represented the town as a homogenous and uniform culture, so obscuring diversity. In fact, he argues, whatever social structure there may have been was manifest in various ways; hence the necessity of examining particular examples.[79]

> In a compendium of such cases, moreover, one should not expect a gluey coherence or neat integration (any more than an assemblage of unique isolates). Rather,

78 N. Rapport, *Diverse World-Views in an English Village* (Edinburgh: Edinburgh University Press, 1993), ix. Contrast Rapport's *use* of 'chaos' and Malinowski's *imposition* of an ordered functional scheme, see B. Malinowski, *Argonauts of the Western Pacific* (London: Routledge, 1922); idem, *A Diary in the Strict Sense of the Term* (New York: Harcourt, 1967).

79 Rapport, *Diverse*, 40.

> from case to case there will be an overlapping of behavioural samenesses and differences . . . In short, far from simple dichotomies and continua, from generalisable categories of behaviour in village community or town, a compendium of cases of social life in Britain will consist of an aggregation of partially (polythetically) connected behaviours.[80]

Rapport observed the relationships between two farming families, the Rowlands and Whitehouses. A number of considerations affected their interaction, including familial, occupational, neighbourly, economic and spiritual, but none of these was of consistently overriding importance. It was 'individual interpretation of the relations of the moment which determine[d] which consideration [was] pertinent, and which construction [was] salient, when'.[81] A further observation complicates matters even more: individual interpretation is contradictory, changing according to the moment. Rapport claims that some anthropological thought represents contradiction as a problem and equates social order to the eradication of 'symbolic contrarieties'.[82] In contrast, he argues that social order 'is predicated not upon the absence of contradiction but upon its co-presence: the cognitive co-presence of the contradictory, of both/and, together with the classificatory order of either/or'.[83] Rapport asserts that 'both/and', as well as being a cognitive norm, is the cognitive reality behind the social reality of either/or classifications. Although he errs in placing all his eggs in the cognitive basket, one can concur that Rapport correctly highlights the inherent contradictions ordered (and ordering) cultural schemata seek to resolve in either/or terms.

Rapport uses three informants to investigate *when* contradictions surface: Rachel, in Mitzpe Ramon, Israel, and Sid and Doris, in Wanet. Rachel admitted and even celebrated contradiction within moments, describing herself as 'a bit schizo'.[84] Doris and Sid, though, experienced no contradiction *within* any *one* moment, just between moments.

80 Rapport, *Diverse*, 41.

81 Rapport, *Diverse*, 51.

82 N. Rapport, 'The "Contrarieties" of Israel: An Essay on the Cognitive Importance and the Creative Promise of Both/And', *JRAI* 3 (1997): 653–72, quote 657.

83 Rapport, 'Contrarieties', 657–58. Without original emphasis.

84 Rapport, 'Contrarieties', 665.

> Being for Doris, Sid, *et al.*, turned on momentary thoughts, feelings, apprehensions, emotions, on discrete experiential units of time and place, of self, of individuality. And while the momentariness of their lives formed a constant, while their moments were 'for ever', between moments there was need for no consistent cognitive connexion.[85]

It is important to assess these distinct observations of when contradiction occurs. Although I do not wish to re-evaluate Rapport's field notes it is significant that Rachel recognized her experience of simultaneous 'contradictory cognitions'[86] as problematic: schizophrenia is not culturally 'normal'. Thus although people's ability to generate multifaceted perspectives is part and parcel of life, the inability to select or perceive as dominant a single perspective at any one time is not, and the observation does not advance our discussion significantly.[87] Rapport's observations regarding Doris and Sid are more pertinent for social-scientific study of biblical characters' interactions since they underscore the potential for actors to behave differently according to the person with whom they are interacting, not just some amorphous 'cultural context'.

In his article comparing the art and letters of Stanley Spencer, Rapport asks how and why an actor's conception of his or her social relations affects those relations.[88] He asserts that a 'routine and shared form to social life, an apparent patterning to social-relational habitude, actually disguises depths and diversities of articulate consciousness', and his analysis of Spencer evinces that individuals both participate in and manipulate routine discourse for their own ends, claiming that 'discursive exchange is never unmediated by a creative individual improvisation of its forms and conventions'.[89] Although a radical voluntarism – perhaps indicated by the categorical 'never' – is untenable, Rapport does demonstrate there may be a gulf between shared discourse and shared understanding. The point is that different people do not inhabit the same 'world-views', and even when there are shared views they only partially

85 Rapport, 'Contrarieties', 667.

86 Rapport, 'Contrarieties', 665.

87 Rapport advocates Rachel's schizophrenic sort of contrariety as an anthropological project, but I think it falls foul of Quigley's objections noted above.

88 In contrast to Rapport, I am not concerned about why different perceptions arise, only how they affect relations.

89 Rapport, 'Envisioned, Intentioned', 865.

overlap. Rapport suggests that people construct identities in relation to a range of other people, objects and events.[90] Doris and Sid assumed different *personae* according to the various social interactions in which they were involved. Nine *personae* are enumerated for Doris: farmer, English, wife, villager, middle class, a neighbour, a friend, as aggrieved, and as a mother. Sid has seven *personae*: craftsman, a local, husband, pal, father, a man, and English. The views expressed by each different *persona* were both contradictory and predictable. Thus 'diversity and inconstancy of opinion was swallowed up by the regularity of moving from one habitual interactional routine to another and the habituality once one was ensconced in each'.[91] The different *personae* derive 'from individuals defining their own stimuli in a social situation and constructing their own responses'.[92] In each discourse the actor affirms some identities and negates other potential *personae*. Although people seek 'the security of habitual meanings',[93] this does not mean that when two people converse they use the same conventions. 'The words they exchange prove ambiguous enough for each to impart to them their own meanings, for each to aggregate them together as part of different associational sets to form different cognitive contexts'.[94] Thus although individuals do acquire an ability to read others' behaviour this is not by learning a communal cognitive map of the world, but by coming to appreciate that under certain circumstances others' actions are predictable, and thus able to be correlated with one's own.[95]

90 Rapport, *Diverse*, 152. See also his 'Context as an Act of Personal Externalisation: Gregory Bateson and the Harvey Family in the English Village of Wanet', in *The Problem of Context* (ed. R. Dilley; New York: Berghahn Books, 1999), 187–211.

91 Rapport, *Diverse*, 123. It is significant that only strangers have to deal with 'the incoherence, partiality and contradictoriness inherent in the assumptions of people's everyday commonsensical knowledge'. Rapport further argues that by representing themselves as different *personae* they thereby *realize* these identities, see Rapport, *Diverse*, 152. In the light of the discussion of structure and agency, above, one can accept that this will be partially true.

92 Rapport, *Diverse*, 152.

93 Rapport, *Diverse*, 153.

94 Rapport, *Diverse*, 155. Rapport recognizes that he highlights the differences in perspective between Sid and Doris, not their shared grammar, but, he argues, the latter is mere form, not meaning. Rapport further notes that standardized communication on acceptable topics can limit personal and uncommon information, see Rapport, *Diverse*, 164.

95 See Rapport, *Diverse*, 184. I would dispute whether these constructions are random, as proposed by Rapport, 'Random Mind', 198. In reducing *all* perception and the *entirety* of justification for action to the cognitive he minimizes the role of both cultural structure (the

Rapport's work highlighting the ubiquity of ambiguity in human interaction is an important contribution to the understanding of practice, and hence the interpretation of family relations like those portrayed in the text of 1 Samuel. In the concluding section of this chapter I draw together the most pertinent elements of this chapter's discussion and highlight their relevance for the interpretation of Michal's moral dilemma.

4. Conclusion: Choosing Kin

So far this study has examined whether the Old Testament contains resources necessary to address moral dilemmas, proposing a focus upon moral goods. Given that 'the family' is a central moral good within the Old Testament it proceeded to examine anthropological perspectives upon the family and the ethics of kinship. Because both have been approached using the categories provided by practice theory, I have briefly analysed important aspects of the theorizing of practice. Two observations are now required. First, my aim has not been to present a definitive genealogy of practice, nor to defend all versions of practice theory from the gamut of possible criticisms, only to commend it as a way of understanding social action with sufficient subtlety that it does not ride roughshod over the essential components of situated individual agency. In addition, I have highlighted a frequently overlooked feature of social interaction, its ambiguity. Second, I have not proposed that practice theory is more 'true' than other potential ways of explaining human action. Andreas Reckwitz explains that social theories are underdetermined by empirical data and that the key questions are ones of utility.[96] This does not mean that important consequences do not follow from choosing one sort of social theory rather than another; or that my choice has been arbitrary. Practice theory invites interpretations of embodied practices rather than mental maps or spheres of discourse. Just as anthropologists have found it to be a profitable means of understanding their data about 'others' in more nuanced and compelling ways than a focus upon forms of thought or patterns of behaviour only occasionally reproduced on

existence of which he denies) and (culturally, not merely personally, perceived) physical constraints and stimuli. Thus his astute observation that Doris construes situations in ways that relate more to her perceptions and preoccupations than any 'objective' reading of life in Wanet does not necessitate his assertion that these conceptions are random.

96 Reckwitz, 'Toward', 257.

the ground, so I propose that it will aid this investigation by maintaining open the possibility of a variety of possible reactions to particular stimuli. Having made these observations it is now possible to enumerate three features of how goods and practices may be related as the basis for entering the world of my chosen text.

First, the context for practice includes *the existence of multiple, contradicting and potentially mutually exclusive moral goods*. Following Rapport's lead we may suppose that clashes and contradictions are 'normal' and that order is as much constructed as observed. In terms of moral goods I have already insisted upon actors continually facing a plurality of moral goods, and upon the inevitability of value clashes. But alongside this observation one can follow Ortner in proposing that there are also culturally acceptable ways of resolving putative dilemmas so that moral choices in favour of some goods seem natural or commonsensical. Note, however, that '[c]ommon sense is the world-classifying face of power; the social dramas of everyday life forever oscillate between reproducing and disputing its authority'.[97] Thus there is no *automatic* preference for cultural schemata: the possibility remains that *another* choice of moral goods be realized.

Second, *the variety of perception of any particular situation or action in which moral goods are in play*. One consequence is that stimuli can be variously interpreted, producing idiosyncratic responses, thus even though there may be culturally informed norms, including moral standards, it cannot be assumed that these are perceived in the same way by all actors. Bourdieu noted different perceptions and justifications of the same event in relation to parallel cousin marriage among the Kabyle. He observed that it could be viewed *simultaneously* as an ideal, rarely achieved, an ethical norm (derived from a duty of honour), which can be broken, and a pragmatic move.[98] The polysemous nature of this particular type of union means it is a good example of how interpretation of practice is open to manipulation despite being constrained. Constraints in general include both physical limitations and social expectations that place limits

97 M. Herzfeld, *Anthropology: Theoretical Practice in Culture and Society* (Oxford: Blackwell, 2001), 72.

98 Bourdieu, *Outline*, 43. Note that there is nothing mutually exclusive about these interpretations: I am not contradicting my observations regarding Rachel's 'schizophrenia', above.

upon the attainability of moral goods.[99] In cases of value conflict, therefore, not all choices are equally possible, although variety of perception may mean that people view constraints differently – some might even fail to see a problem that vexes another: David and Michal themselves would be a good example.

A related issue is the perception of action that does not fit the cultural schema. Signe Howell concludes her ethnography of Lio ritual with two important observations. On the one hand, 'it is possible to identify certain general patterns of maleness and femaleness without thereby applying these to all men and to all women, to the corresponding sexes, to all contexts and to all socialities'.[100] On the other hand, the 'fact that kin, affinal or ritual status may, in some instances, overshadow the simple duality of men and women does not necessarily mean that maleness and femaleness are not conceptualized'.[101] In other words, there are both general norms and individual acts, yet from the fact that norms are not always followed one cannot deduce that they fail to influence behaviour. I submit that although acts may not cohere with the norms, for example, of maleness or femaleness, the *interpretation* of them by other actors *will* be guided by the socially accepted standards. We shall see that this has important implications for the interpretation of biblical characters' actions.

Third, *the necessarily personal, and thus open, nature of practice, which nevertheless can exhibit regularity*. Because the acts of practice are personal the selection of moral goods can be variously classified. It could be quasi reflexive, for example, the removal of one's hand from a flame to avoid pain. Or it could simply cohere with learnt behaviour, for example, someone offers a handshake simply because he 'always' does. Or, because one person finds another odious, he consciously decides not to offer a handshake in order to offend by slight. The point is that not all acts of practice are the same. Because practice is personal and people can act and react in a great variety of ways there is a similarly wide range of possible actions involving moral goods. Yet, because people learn which selections of moral goods are acceptable

99 Goffman proposes that the very fact of face-to-face interaction is a limiting factor, E. Goffman, 'The Interaction Order', *ASR* 48 (1983): 1–17.

100 S. Howell, 'Many Contexts, Many Meanings? Gendered Values among the Northern Lio of Flores, Indonesia', *JRAI* 2 (1996): 253–69, quote 256.

101 Howell, 'Many Contexts', 261.

within the society in which they find themselves, practice can also exhibit regularity.

I have related Ortner's typology of practice to the ideas of multiple cultural goods and dominant cultural schemata in conversation with Louise Lawrence.[102] She discusses shame and desire in the Song of Songs, arguing that the 'shameful' behaviour envisaged by the lyricist reinforces the honour paradigm. It is unnecessary, however, to say cultural values negate their opposites, since the goods of romantic love and duty, modesty and desire are perceived simultaneously.[103] The dominant cultural schema encapsulated in the modesty code provides *one* way of ordering these goods that 'works'. Ordinary practice, routine responses to situations, would include adherence to this schema. This is not much in evidence in the Song of Songs, which is better considered as envisaged extraordinary praxis, action that changes the ordering of these cultural goods: a vision of love unencumbered by duty.[104] Returning to the importance of kinship, ordinary practice in this context means habitually 'choosing kin', that is, prioritizing their interests over that of others, including, at times, one's own desires. Yet the frequency of this 'pattern' of practice, which gives an aura of normality and naturalness to, for example, family loyalty as a moral good, should not hide the fact that this ordering of goods is a personal *choice*. Thus although people habitually choose kin, it is their status as *choosing* subjects that leaves open the possibility they may not, a prospect that means cold draughts of ambiguity continually threaten family cosiness.

The Old Testament text I have chosen to examine concerns Saul's daughter, who chooses in the context, one may suppose, of others who often choose kin. Understanding kinship and the ethics of kinship as the practice of choosing moral goods, including loyalty to kin itself, enables new interpretations of her

102 My correspondence is cited in L. Lawrence, *Reading with Anthropology: Exhibiting Aspects of New Testament Religion* (Carlisle: Paternoster, 2005), 182.

103 And are in conflict, both in the story world of the Bible (e.g. 1 Sam. 18:20, 28) and societies studied by anthropologists. I ignore the issue of whether binary opposition is always the best way to present these conflicts – the relationships between goods are probably more complex.

104 It is noteworthy *who* subverts the cultural schema. Although older women will not have had comparable status to men, they would normally have attained an interest in the cultural schema, i.e. support from appropriately married sons. I maintained, therefore, that it would be the young who would be more likely to envisage an alternative world, one in which their concerns take precedence, see Lawrence, *Reading*, 182.

choice. Yet, Michal is a literary character in a narrative that makes theological assertions. Before turning to an interpretation of the stories it is necessary to examine *how* one might understand the account of her practice contained in 1 Samuel. This is the task of the next chapter.

Chapter 4

UNDERSTANDING MORAL CHOICE IN 1 SAMUEL

Good general diagnosticians are rare,
not because most doctors lack medical knowledge,
but because most are incapable of taking in all the possible relevant facts –
emotional, historical, environmental as well as physical.
They are searching for specific conditions
instead of the truth about a man
which may then suggest various conditions

John Berger, *A Fortunate Man*[1]

Since Robert Alter's *The Art of Biblical Narrative* many scholars have used literary theory to elucidate how biblical narratives can be understood and to expose the theoretical issues behind the reading strategies they propose. However, despite its preponderance the relevance of narrative for ethics has received surprisingly little attention until recent years.[2] In this chapter, I will

1 The epigraph is from J. Berger, *A Fortunate Man: The Story of a Country Doctor* (New York: Holt, Rinehart and Winston, 1967), 72.

2 I take as axiomatic that narrative *can* contribute to moral understanding. This is because human existence has a narrative quality, so S. Crites, 'The Narrative Quality of Experience', *JAAR* 39 (1971): 291–319. And because it is situated in an ongoing communal narrative: MacIntyre asserts that 'I can only answer the question, "What am I to do?" if I can answer the prior question, "Of what story or stories do I find my self a part?" ', A. MacIntyre, *After Virtue: A Study in Moral Theory* (3rd ed.; London: Duckworth, 2007), 216. Of course, any particular narrative can function ideologically to reinforce or subvert the original community narrative: I will argue that Old Testament texts do just that, cf. W. Houston, *Contending for Justice: Ideologies and Theologies of Social Justice in the Old Testament* (LHB/OTS 428; London: T&T Clark, 2006). For a detailed discussion of how Paul Ricoeur's work can provide the foundations for a narrative hermeneutic see R. Parry,

explain how I will approach the interpretation of Old Testament narrative with respect to how it presents its author's vision of ethics.

The most obvious way in which stories, inevitably bound to particular characters, settings and moments, provide a guide to behaviour is by exemplifying virtues or general principles. Lawrence Blum's discussion of moral exemplars enables exegetes to avoid a superficial evaluation of the merits of 'model morality'.[3] Blum identifies two sorts of moral models, the moral hero, who acts rightly in a specific, risky situation, and the moral 'saint', who exhibits a virtuous character over time. At times these categories may be mutually exclusive: referring to Oskar Schindler he observes that although 'even paragons of honesty ought to lie to Nazis if this is necessary to save lives, only certain kinds of personalities could have pulled off the sort of vast and intimately maintained deception that Schindler did; and a person considered to be devoted to truthfulness would probably not have been such a one'.[4] Even if this is not normally the case, only three of the five criteria for a moral hero are shared by the moral 'saint'.[5] Blum argues it 'is the greater absence of unworthy or suspect elements of consciousness, not a greater remoteness from the world, which distinguishes the saint from the hero'.[6] Within each of these categories agents may be idealists or responders. An idealist has a prior ideal to which he aspires and that guides his actions; a successful idealist can be a moral exemplar. A responder does not choose an ideal that she wishes to actualize, but responds to situations as they present themselves to her.[7] Blum

Old Testament Story and Christian Ethics: The Rape of Dinah as a Case Study (PBM; Milton Keynes: Paternoster, 2004), 4–27.

3 Parry's phrase. L. Blum, *Moral Perception and Particularity* (Cambridge: CUP, 1994), 65–97.

4 Blum, *Moral Perception*, 72.

5 The criteria are: (1) bringing a great good (or preventing a great evil); (2) acting to a great extent from morally worthy motives; (3) substantial embeddedness of those motives in the agent's psychology; (4) carrying out one's moral project in the face of risk or danger; and (5) relative 'faultlessness', or absence of unworthy desires, dispositions, sentiments, attitudes. Of which the saint shares attributes 2, 3 and 5. Blum, *Moral Perception*, 75–77.

6 Blum, *Moral Perception*, 77.

7 The gender of the pronouns in the last two sentences has been chosen to reflect a further debate about whether there are peculiarly male and female modes of moral reasoning. Part 3 of Blum's book explores these issues; for a critical evaluation see P. Byrne, *The Philosophical and Theological Foundations of Ethics: An Introduction to Moral Theory and its Relation to Religious Beliefs* (2nd ed.; Basingstoke: MacMillan, 1999), 163–90.

asserts that to be '*morally excellent*, both idealists and responders must act from dispositions, sentiments, and [character] traits'.[8] Looking at moral exemplars in this way means that interpreters need not be fazed by what Birch terms 'the ambiguities of righteousness'.[9]

Parry, for example, finds the following difficulties with biblical 'model morality'. First, it only works well with clear-cut goodness or evil, but many biblical characters are ambiguous. Second, models do not comprise the totality of biblical ethical behaviour, and concentrating solely on them is reductionist, oversimplifying the complexity of moral living. Third, there is a danger of extracting too strong a principle from a story, since '[a]bsolute rules cannot be inferred from particular narratives even if general principles can'.[10] Fourth, a reader may identify with the 'wrong' character traits, or only partially, in some of his roles but not others. I sense that the problem lies in Parry's conception of model. He posits that to 'function well as a prescriptive model an act must be fairly clear-cut as far as its morality is concerned. The more ambiguous acts complicate the judgment of the reader and make simple imitation or avoidance impossible'.[11] In other words, Parry is looking for a clear-cut exemplar. However, his first assertion is only true if moral exemplars *must* be 'clear cut' and patently either wholly good or bad in order to be understood. Blum's typology shows that such simplification is not necessary, and I would argue that moral ambiguity can be a means of drawing readers into a narrative so that the moral lessons it wishes to impart are more completely appropriated by readers. The second and third assertions are uncontentious, but hardly problematic for those who would engage with the whole Old Testament corpus. And the fourth assertion has to do with readerly competence rather than any problem with the model as such. Nevertheless, I concur with Parry that the value for moral instruction of any individual narrative calls for attention to its particularity.

In this light, it does not take a reader long to appreciate that the Bible describes 'a world where there are few perfect saints and few unredeemable sinners: most of its heroes and heroines have both virtues and vices, they mix

8 Blum, *Moral Perception*, 85. Emphasis original.

9 B. Birch, *Let Justice Roll Down: The Old Testament, Ethics, and the Christian Life* (Louisville: Westminster John Knox Press, 1991), 64.

10 Parry, *Story*, 33

11 Parry, *Story*, 32.

obedience and unbelief'.[12] In fact, this might be part of their pedagogical value. 'Their stories reflect all the ambiguities and complexities of human experience and the struggle to find and live out faith relationships to God in the midst of life'.[13] Readers *have* to think and reflect upon the stories, rather than consume the 'moral lesson' and dispose with the narrative wrapper.[14] In this way stories come to have 'an existential force'.[15]

Wenham argues that despite the ostensive didactic handicap of morally ambiguous characters, biblical narratives, like all literary works, possess an ethical point of view, and that authors attempt, explicitly or implicitly, to convince readers of its merits.[16] Although a narrative may not appear to moralize, for readers to understand the implied author's tale they have to share her perspectives and values; to use Wayne Booth's metaphor, the author and reader must be 'friends'.[17] Characters' complexities are then a challenge to avoid arbitrary or mundane readings. Wenham seeks to acknowledge both diversity and unity of presentation by proposing biblical narrative is 'scenic', dramatising the action like a film and thus allowing presentation of different points of view.[18] This is different from the dialogical perspective of Mikhail Bakhtin, the twentieth-century Russian literary philosopher whose ideas have enjoyed considerable currency in biblical and theological studies since the 1980s, hav-

12 G. Wenham, *Story as Torah: Reading the Old Testament Ethically* (OTS; Edinburgh: T&T Clark, 2000), 15. On the character of David, for example, see R. Bowman, 'The Complexity of Character and the Ethics of Complexity: The Case of King David', in *Character and Scripture: Moral Formation, Community and Biblical Interpretation* (ed. W. P. Brown; Grand Rapids: Eerdmans, 2002), 73–97.

13 B. Birch, *Let Justice Roll Down: The Old Testament, Ethics, and the Christian Life* (Louisville: Westminster John Knox Press, 1991), 53.

14 Cf. J. Barton, *Ethics and the Old Testament* (London: SCM, 1998), 20. Cultural distance may mean that stories are more obtuse to modern Western readers that to the implied readers – hence the value of social-scientific criticism.

15 Barton, *Ethics*, 32.

16 Cf. Wenham, *Story*, 11–13.

17 W. Booth, *The Company We Keep: An Ethics of Fiction* (Berkley: University of California Press, 1988), 169–224.

18 Wenham, *Story*, 15, cf. Gen. 27. Bruckner argues that although the terms 'ought' and 'ought not' are rarely used for references to right or wrong behaviour, narratives use such devices as dialogue and plot development to indicate ethical requirements, J. Bruckner, *Implied Law in the Abraham Narrative: A Literary and Theological Analysis* (JSOTSup 335; London: Sheffield, 2001), 11. Bruckner overemphasizes law (he looks for judicial language and contexts in the Abraham narrative), which is not the only sort of ought, although as a project within a wider examination of narrative and ethics his study is extremely valuable.

ing been appropriated for Old Testament studies, in the field of ethics and by one scholar who combines both a literary and social-scientific approach to the text.[19] Moreover, two recent monographs by Barbara Green read 1 Samuel through the lens of Bakhtin's ideas concerning dialogism.[20] It is necessary to consider his approach in more detail.

1. Understanding Dialogical Voices

Clark and Holquist offer a helpful characterization of Bakhtin's view of the location of meaning.[21] In contradistinction to both personalists, who maintain that *I* hold meaning, and to deconstructionalists, who hold that *no one* owns meaning, Bakhtin argues *we* possess meaning. The underlying philosophical justification for his position is the denial of absolute truth, a denial made in the totalitarian political context of Stalinist Russia. Even if one is unprepared, for example, on theological grounds, to accept this starting point it is possible, on the same grounds, to maintain that knowledge of truth is partial and, therefore, that Bakhtin's argument concerning dialogism has potential merit.

There are three key components to Bakhtin's thesis: heteroglossia, dialogism and polyphony. Bakhtin identifies several elements of language, the most basic of which are words and utterances. An utterance pertains to a peculiar 'language', a form of discourse shaped by the social reality of the speaker at that moment, for example, a male peasant dealing with a state bureaucrat. Given the fact of social stratification various socially positioned 'languages' exist simultaneously, even though there is only one national language. This

19 See, respectively, R. Polzin, *Moses and the Deuteronomist* (Bloomington: Indiana University Press, 1980), 20–24; E. Reed, *The Genesis of Ethics: On the Authority of God as the Origin of Christian Ethics* (London: Darton, Longman & Todd, 2000); L. Lawrence, *An Ethnography of the Gospel of Matthew: A Critical Assessment of the Use of the Honour and Shame Model in New Testament Studies* (Tübingen: Mohr Siebeck, 2003).

20 B. Green, *Mikhail Bakhtin and Biblical Scholarship: An Introduction* (Atlanta: Society of Biblical Literature Press, 2000); idem, *How Are the Mighty Fallen? A Dialogical Study of King Saul in 1 Samuel* (JSOTSup 365; Sheffield: Sheffield Academic Press, 2003).

21 K. Clark and M. Holquist, *Mikhail Bakhtin* (London: Belknap, 1984), 11–12, 348. See the critical introductions for full bibliographies of Bakhtin's work. The essay that deals most directly with my concerns is M. Bakhtin, 'Discourse in the Novel', in *The Dialogic Imagination: Four Essays* (ed. M. Holquist; trans. C. Emerson and M. Holquist; Austin: Texas University Press, 1981), 259–401.

is heteroglossia.[22] Heteroglot 'languages' take different perspectives on the world, abut and clash, interact and, affirms Bakhtin, 'dialogue'. He asserts that

> all languages of heteroglossia, whatever the principle underlying them and making each unique, are specific points of view on the world, forms for conceptualizing the world in words . . . As such they all may be juxtaposed to one another, mutually supplement one another, contradict one another and be interrelated dialogically.[23]

The environment into which a particular utterance is projected is thus 'dialogized heteroglossia'.[24] The meaning of the utterance is not objectively fixed, but evolves in dialogue with its heteroglossic context, 'negotiating' its meaning. Without this process words 'will not sound'.[25] Bakhtin offers a suggestive metaphor for such dialogism.

> If we imagine the *intention* of such a word, that is, its *directionality toward the object*, in the form of a ray of light, then the living and unrepeatable play of colors and light on the facets of the image that it constructs can be explained as the spectral dispersion of the ray-word, not within the object itself . . . but rather as its spectral dispersion in an atmosphere filled with alien words, value judgments and accents through which the ray passes on its way toward the object; the social atmosphere of the word, the atmosphere that surrounds the object, makes the facets of the image sparkle.[26]

Bakhtin further contends that words are directed towards an answer, that is, the involvement of the interlocutor. 'Understanding and response are dialectically merged and mutually condition each other; one is impossible without the other'.[27] Dialogism is thus an essential process in a world of heteroglossia, and

22 Polyglossia is the obverse of heteroglossia, i.e, two or more national languages interacting in a single cultural system, see the glossary prepared by M. Holquist in Bakhtin, *The Dialogic Imagination* (ed. M. Holquist; trans. C. Emerson and M. Holquist; Austin: Texas University Press, 1981), 428.

23 Bakhtin, 'Discourse in the Novel', 291–92.

24 Bakhtin, 'Discourse in the Novel', 272.

25 Bakhtin, 'Discourse in the Novel', 278.

26 Bakhtin, 'Discourse in the Novel', 277. Emphasis original.

27 Bakhtin, 'Discourse in the Novel', 282.

dialogue, conceived as an exchange between simultaneous differences, is the context of all socially derived 'languages'.

Bakhtin theorized about the novel employing these insights, positing two sorts of novelistic works, the sophistic and dialogic.[28] The former is essentially monologic. Although it may reflect heteroglossia the voices are not equally significant. Instead, the non-authorial 'language' 'appears, in essence, as a *thing*, it does not lie on the *same* plane with the real language of the work: it is the depicted gesture of one of the characters and does not appear as an aspect of the word doing the depicting'.[29] This is the case, for example, with the rhetorical genre, which instead of accepting dialogism intents 'to outwit possible retorts to itself'.[30] The dialogic novel, in contrast, lets all voices be heard not solely the author's. The plot, for example, 'serves to represent speaking persons and their ideological worlds. What is realized in the novel is the process of coming to know one's own language as it is perceived in someone else's language'.[31] It is fallacious to suppose that this variety of literature is

> just chaotically multi-voiced; it is art, and its special artistic province is *dialogized* heteroglossia: different points of view embodied in 'voice zones' and intentional hybridizations that test one another and question each other's boundaries and authority.[32]

Bakhtin labelled this authorial strategy 'polyphony'. Polyphony is not heteroglossia, rather

> polyphony is a way of realizing heteroglossia in the novel, without being identical to heteroglossia. 'Polyphony' means 'multi-voicedness,' while 'heteroglossia' means 'multi-languaged-ness,' and this apparently small difference in meaning

28 Bakhtin used the terms First Line and Second Line. He used the epithet 'sophistic' of the former, I supply 'dialogic' for the latter. Bakhtin enquires after the sociological preconditions for the dialogic novel, observing that its advent occurred at the same time as the monologic shackles of medievalism were being challenged by the Renaissance and Protestantism, see Bakhtin, 'Discourse in the Novel', 414–15.

29 Bakhtin, 'Discourse in the Novel', 287. Emphasis original.

30 Bakhtin, 'Discourse in the Novel', 353.

31 Bakhtin, 'Discourse in the Novel', 365.

32 Caryl Emerson, 'Theory', in *The Cambridge Companion to the Classic Russian Novel* (ed. M. V. Jones and R. F. Miller; Cambridge: CUP, 1998), 271–92, quote 286–87. Emphasis original.

> is very significant. Polyphony refers to the arrangement of heteroglot variety into an aesthetic pattern. One of the principal ways of ensuring the presence of the different voices of heteroglossia in the novel is the creation of fictional characters.[33]

Thus polyphony concerns the relationship of the author to the text. In the polyphonic novel she does not have the final word, but is a participant who lets herself be guided by dialogues that emerge from her characters. Bakhtin does not thereby negate authorial activity, for the 'authorial emphasis is present, of course, in all these orchestrating and distanced elements of language, and in the final analysis all these elements are determined by the author's artistic will – they are totally the author's responsibility – but they do not belong to the author's *language*'.[34]

It is necessary to consider several criticisms of Bakhtin's thesis before concluding what he can contribute to this study. First, he restricts himself to spoken discourse. Only thus can he assert that Adam alone, who 'approached a virginal and as yet verbally unqualified world with the first word, could really have escaped from start to finish this dialogic inter-orientation with the alien word that occurs in the object'.[35] Even allowing that Bakhtin uses the creation accounts rhetorically, a pertinent observation is that both Genesis 1:28 and

33 S. Vice, *Introducing Bakhtin* (Manchester: Manchester University Press, 1997), 113. Bakhtin's imprecision concerning nomenclature has generated debate around this issue. Polyphony and heteroglossia are treated as synonyms by Clark and Holquist who declare that the 'phenomenon that Bakhtin calls "polyphony" is simply another name for dialogism', Clark and Holquist, *Bakhtin*, 242, cf. 129, citing in support Mikhail Bakhtin, *Problems of Dostoevsky's Poetics* (trans. C. Emerson; Minneapolis: University of Minnesota Press, 1984), 32: 'Every thought of Dostoevsky's heroes . . . senses itself to be from the very beginning a *rejoinder* in an unfinalized dialogue . . . It lives a tense life on the borders of someone else's thought, someone else's consciousness'. Yet, at another point they assert that 'Dostoevsky's polyphony must be conceived against the larger meaning of dialogue in human existence', seeming to indicate that the two are not synonyms, see Clark and Holquist, *Bakhtin*, 251. Although the words are different in the Russian, not all translators render them consistently. Zappen sounds a realistic note arguing that polyphony, heteroglossia and carnival are all 'dialogic interrelations', but that Bakhtin uses each in different places. 'Each of these terms captures, though each with a different emphasis, the dialogic interrelationship of utterances as a complex unity of differences', J. Zappen, 'Mikhail Bakhtin (1895–1975)', in *Twentieth-Century Rhetoric and Rhetoricians: Critical Studies and Sources* (ed. M. G. Moran and M. Ballif; Westport: Greenwood Press, 2000), 7–20, quote 11. In any case it is clear that polyphony can be linked to the polyphonic novel.

34 Bakhtin, 'Discourse in the Novel', 416. Emphasis original.

35 Bakhtin, 'Discourse in the Novel', 279.

2:18-20 conceive human action as a response to God's prior communication, which includes both word ('be fruitful and multiply') and act (creation, bringing the animals to Adam), and are not necessarily limited to the verbal. Emerson argues this has implications for Bakhtin's interpretation of Dostoevsky. 'The possibility that verbal dialogue might actually drain away value or flatten out a subtlety or be so subject to terror and constraint that it depreciates into outright fraud is not for Bakhtin a theoretically serious issue'.[36] Second, it is not certain that polyphony is an adequate description of Dostoevsky's authorial strategy because he patently intended to transmit Christian truth. Indeed, heteroglossia in the novel is actually dependent upon a specific historical situation, viz. the printed work. Furthermore, the idea of heteroglossia is attractive in a particular historical period: Ken Hirschkop caustically comments that '[t]o stumble upon a theorist who claims that language itself is inherently "dialogical" and that "a living utterance cannot avoid becoming a participant in social dialogue" is . . . an irresistible windfall for the liberal consciousness'.[37] Third, dialogue may be 'unnatural', not the way utterances actually work in practice, since it usually takes a considerable effort to effect real dialogue. Fourth, Natalia Reed argues dialogism is inherently hostile to others. 'It might welcome them for a moment, as a temporary stimulus or trigger, but it rarely has the patience to orient outwardly toward another person's words and acts *over time*'.[38] The charge is that dialogism is attractive because it resonates with the values of Western liberalism rather than being derived from the 'fact' of social heteroglossia. Fifth, the language of characters, especially major characters, has an effect upon other actors in the narrative. In other words, the space surrounding them is dialogized, but not neutrally. And it is plain that dialogue can be coercive, not only by itself but also in tandem with forms of non-verbal communication. Finally, it is intuitively true that a single person can create a novel with two or more voices, but not that she can possess two consciousnesses.[39]

If his thesis must be modified, how far can Bakhtin be appropriated for a study of Old Testament ethics? One issue is whether the Bible is polyphonic

36 C. Emerson, *The First Hundred Years of Mikhail Bakhtin* (Princeton: Princeton University Press, 1997), 132–33.

37 K. Hirschkop, *Mikhail Bakhtin: An Aesthetic for Democracy* (Oxford: OUP, 1999), 9.

38 Emerson, *First Hundred Years*, 139. Emphasis original. Emerson summarizes the unpublished work of Reed, which she discusses on pages 132–52.

39 K. Hirschkop, 'Bakhtin, Discourse and Democracy', *NLR* 160 (1986): 92–111.

literature. Green answers in the negative, opining that 'polyphony as Bakhtin develops it does not really function substantially in 1 Samuel and that Saul cannot accurately or fairly be called a polyphonic hero'.[40] But the two issues are separate. Even if biblical heroes are not polyphonic, they are multifaceted, complicated moral agents. And the biblical text could well juxtapose differing perspectives 'pseudo-polyphonically' and without explicit evaluation, which readers are then invited to appraise for themselves in the light of other biblical texts and cultural expectations. In such a case it will be profitable to read with an eye for multi-voicedness, not merely the narrator's tune. In fact, while Bakhtin argues in the first chapter of *Dostoevsky's Poetics* that a polyphonic narrative can be misread as monologic, Green helpfully suggests that inverting the concept may mean 'a monologic work may flower a bit if we read it with some awareness of polyphonic strategies'.[41]

Esther Reed has drawn upon Bakhtin to expound a particular view of authority in ethics. She argues that (Christian) ethics is not monologic, but is a polyphonic, free response to God's Word that avoids ready-made answers. She cautions that one should '[b]eware of identifying authority with monologism and polyphony with relativism'.[42] This coheres with my argument above that there are many ways of responding morally well to situations, including moral dilemmas. In this regard Bakhtin's observations concerning the hero of a novel

40 Green, *Mighty*, 273.

41 Green, *Mighty*, 275. Compare Newsom's more definite claim that Job and Genesis – 2 Kings are polyphonic literature, Carol Newsom, 'Bakhtin, the Bible, and Dialogic Truth', *JR* 76 (1996): 290–306, especially 297–304.

42 Reed, *Genesis*, 133. She proceeds to contrast an ethic of polyphony and an ethic of heteroglossia, asserting that the former relates to the truth of a person and the latter to individualism: the Tower of Babel depicts the punishment upon sin as forced mutation of polyphony into heteroglossia, see Reed, *Genesis*, 152–53. It seems to me, however, that the equations 'polyphony = acceptable difference = good' and 'heteroglossia = relativism = bad', although decidedly more elegant and heuristically helpful than Bakhtin himself, are rhetorical. Although Bakhtin thought that all Dostoevsky's polyphonic voices were valid (see Bakhtin, *Dostoevsky's Poetics*, 6) the fact that characters hailed from distinct social milieu meant that they spoke different 'languages': polyphonic voices within the novel are also heteroglossic voices. Thus the neat distinction she offers cannot be derived from Bakhtin. Reed may acknowledge this in her qualification of the definition of polyphony: 'Polyphony – in the particular sense of different voices speaking a single language and using the same words', Reed, *Genesis*, 152. A separate, although fundamental issue, is whether *all* (polyphonic) voices are of equal moral value, which could be implied from Bakhtin, but not, in my view, from Dostoevsky.

may have particular relevance for my investigation. He claims that the testing of a character is a fundamental means of organizing the narrative, because it provides an arena in which to examine that actor's discourse.[43]

To conclude, although 1 Samuel is probably not polyphonic literature in Bakhtin's sense, it is quite possible that the author employs different voices as vehicles for presenting different perspectives upon the moral conflicts presented in the text. An important step in my exegesis, therefore, is the identification of these voices, the discernment of what they are saying – both verbally and by their actions – and the evaluation of them found in the text itself, in order to ascertain how action by the narrative's 'heroes' is viewed.

Discerning what voices say is complicated by the cultural distance between text and modern-day readers. Proponents of social-scientific criticism in biblical studies argue that the breach entailed by temporal distance can be traversed by studying contemporary, spatially separate, pre-industrial societies.[44] Before advancing to summarize my exegetical methodology, I defend an anthropologically informed interpretative understanding of the text.

43 Bakhtin, 'Discourse in the Novel', 388–96.

44 Social-scientific study of the Old Testament has a long pedigree. Carter and Meyers date its *terminus a quo* to W. Robertson Smith's *Lectures on the Religion of the Semites*, published in 1889, see S. Carter and C. Meyers, editors' preface to *Community, Identity and Ideology: Social Science Approaches to the Hebrew Bible* (SBTS 6; ed. S. Carter and C. Meyers; Winona Lake: Eisenbrauns, 1996), xiii. For an up-to-date survey of social-scientific study of the Old Testament see P. Esler and A. Hagedorn, 'Social-Scientific Analysis of the Old Testament: A Brief History and Overview', in *Ancient Israel: The Old Testament in Its Social Context* (ed. P. F. Esler; Minneapolis: Fortress, 2006), 15–32. It is important to note that most social-scientific work has focused on the society of 'ancient Israel' rather than its culture. That is, rather look at how individuals might have reacted in everyday situations, scholars have investigated social structure and institutions, and their historical development, or, for example, the roles of prophets and priests. 'Culture' has been investigated from relatively early on, but it is only recently that a concern with behaviour has gained prominence, see J. Pedersen, *Israel: Its Life and Culture* (4 vols.; Oxford: OUP, 1926); L. Betchel, 'Shame as a Sanction of Social Control in Biblical Israel: Judicial, Political, and Social Shaming', in *Social-Scientific Old Testament Criticism: A Sheffield Reader* (BS 47; ed. D. J. Chalcraft; Sheffield: Sheffield University Press, 1997), 232–58; repr. from *JSOT* 49 (1991); K. Stone, *Sex, Honor, and Power in the Deuteronomistic History* (JSOTSup 234; Sheffield: Sheffield Academic Press, 1996). Works of this type have generated some reflection concerning methodology in 'culture' orientated social-scientific criticism of the Old Testament, e.g. J. Stiebert, *The Construction of Shame in the Hebrew Bible: The Prophetic Contribution* (JSOTSup 346; Sheffield: Sheffield Academic Press, 2002).

2. Interpretative Understanding

The discussion from Chapter 2 onwards has not only served to present the material I believe is necessary to perform an adequate exegesis of my chosen texts, but also to situate my approach vis-à-vis that of other commentators. This section will make patent what until now has been only implicit. The epigraph alludes to two ways in which the interpretative task can be undertaken. The first is to have in mind a model of behaviour, then seek to confirm the presence of this particular pathology. The second is to appreciate the whole, which might then suggest a particular interpretation. They could be termed, respectively, 'scientific' and 'interpretative' approaches.

A prominent advocate of social-scientific criticism, John Elliott, defines it as 'that phase of the exegetical task which analyzes the social and cultural dimensions of the text and of its environmental context through the utilization of the perspectives, theory, models and research of the social sciences'.[45] Starting from the observation that all knowledge is culturally conditioned he argues that exegetes must clarify differences between the social locations of authors and contemporary readers. This is because

> the meanings communicated by the author(s) of these texts to their intended hearers or readers and the texts' persuasive power are determined by the social and cultural systems that author(s) and audiences inhabited and that enabled meaningful communication in the first place.[46]

Several critics, however, argue that it is anachronistic to assume models developed during the twentieth century can be applied to the social world of people living millennia previously. There is a danger that 'the data from antiquity, while they are becoming intelligible and accessible to the modern reader, are also becoming fundamentally distorted into just another instance of what we know about already'.[47] In a similar vein, Edmund Leach argues that there is 'no case for reading biblical texts as if they were a record of remote

45 J. Elliott, *What is Social-Scientific Criticism?* (GBS; Minneapolis: Fortress, 1993), 7.

46 Elliott, *Social-Scientific Criticism*, 50.

47 S. Barton, 'Historical Criticism and Social-Scientific Perspectives in New Testament Study', in *Hearing the New Testament: Strategies for Interpretation* (ed. J. B. Green; Grand Rapids: Eerdmans, 1995), 74.

history which, by some happy accident, becomes more intelligible if referred to the present!'[48] A straightforward response to the charge of anachronism, as one manifestation of incommensurability, is to admit its potential ubiquity, yet observe that it is not a problem with social-scientific criticism per se but all historical investigation. Furthermore, the danger of anachronism should not delude interpreters into thinking that they themselves possess some neutral vantage point – a historical version of cross-cultural superiority. Another general criticism of social-scientific criticism of the Bible is that more context is read back into the biblical texts than is justified by them. According to one sceptic there is 'too much theory chasing too little data'.[49] By justifying their readings with detailed appeals to theory exegetes can certainly give the impression that explicit conceptual schemes dominate texts, but this may be a necessary corrective to the use of unrecognized, implicit perspectives. Whether the theory coheres with the data is a separate matter, which must be tested empirically. I concur with Esler, therefore, that explicit assumptions are to be preferred to implicit suppositions, for they enable other interpreters more accurately to assess the fruits of one's exegetical labours.[50]

The impossibility of an impartial perspective means that *all* exegesis comprises interpretative, rather than 'scientific', understanding of the text. The latter – like Berger's doctor seeking a specific condition – purports to make an explicit attempt to verify that behaviour suggested by modern social-scientific resources is also exhibited in the Bible. An interpretative approach, however, supposes both ancient and modern texts describe an 'ethnographic present',[51]

48 E. Leach, 'Anthropological Approaches to the Study of the Bible During the Twentieth Century', in *Structuralist Interpretations of Biblical Myth* (ed. E. Leach and D. A. Aycock; Cambridge: CUP, 1983), 20.

49 R. P. Carroll, 'Prophecy and Society', in *The World of Ancient Israel: Sociological, Anthropological and Political Perspectives* (ed. R. E. Clements; Cambridge: CUP, 1989), 219; cf. Cyril Rodd, 'On Applying a Sociological Theory to Biblical Studies', in *Social-Scientific Old Testament Criticism: A Sheffield Reader* (BS 47; ed. D. J. Chalcraft; Sheffield: Sheffield University Press, 1997; repr. from *JSOT* 19 (1981): 95–106), 22–33.

50 See P. Esler, 'Review of D. G. Horrell, *The Social Ethos of the Corinthian Correspondence*', *JTS* 49 (1998), 253–60, especially 254.

51 'A hypothetical time frame, characterized by the use of the present tense, employed in ethnographic writing. Normally it coincides with the time of fieldwork, which is not necessarily the time of writing, or indeed of reading', A. Barnard and J. Spencer, *Encyclopedia of Cultural and Social Anthropology* (3rd ed.; ed. J. Spencer and A. Barnard; London: Routledge, 2002), 604.

and maintains that the interpretative objective is not verification but plausible suggestion. In the words of Mario Aguilar 'there are no discoveries but insights, no explanations but interpretations, and an absence of hypotheses but the presence of argumentations'.[52]

By adopting this position I have plunged into a sometimes vitriolic debate about the use of anthropology in biblical studies and, in particular, whether 'models' of behaviour are appropriate exegetical tools. Although it is unnecessary to rehearse the arguments in detail I do need to justify my methodology. The advantage of having already outlined an understanding of social practices is that I can do so positively by affirming my stance in relation to those of others.

My first affirmation is that human practice often exhibits regularity amenable to summary in models of typical action. Bruce Malina, the foremost advocate of the use of models in biblical interpretation, offers the following definition:

> A model is an abstract, simplified representation of some real world object, event, or interaction constructed for the purpose of understanding, control, or prediction. A model is a scheme or pattern that derives from the process of abstracting similarities from a range of instances in order to comprehend.[53]

In ethnographic research a model comprises 'a researcher's attempt to simplify, generalise or abstract their *findings*'.[54] It looks backwards, offering, for example, a statistical summary of behaviour patterns or a descriptive framework. This is different from the proactive use of models envisaged by Malina. He contends that people 'cannot make sense of their experiences and their

52 M. Aguilar, 'Changing Models and the Death of Culture', in *Anthropology and Biblical Studies: Avenues of Approach* (ed. L. J. Lawrence and M. I. Aguilar; Leiden: Deo Publishing, 2004), 299–313, quote 307.

53 B. Malina, 'The Social Sciences and Biblical Interpretation', *Interpretation* 36 (1981): 229–42, quote 231.

54 D. Horrell, *The Social Ethos of the Corinthian Correspondence: Interests and Ideology from 1 Corinthians to 1 Clement* (Edinburgh: T&T Clark, 1996), 11. My emphasis. See also S. Barrett, *Anthropology: A Student's Guide to Theory and Method* (Toronto: University of Toronto Press, 1996), 216: 'The model is neither valid nor invalid; it is useful or not, in the sense of providing an overall picture of the central features of a research project'.

world without making models of it, without thinking in terms of abstract representations of it'.[55] In Malina's view, therefore, the task of biblical scholars is to offer potential domains of reference, that is, models of the biblical social world. The difference between the two sorts of models has been the subject of a debate concerning terminology; but in my view which meaning of 'model' is intended is usually clear from the context of its use.[56] The key question is *what* models are assumed to describe when they are employed in exegesis. There are several possibilities: models could purport to be predictions of actors' behaviour, they could describe a necessary action in a given situation, or they could outline typical behaviour. I perceive no difficulty with models as a description of typical observed behaviour, and thus an explication of the social context of any particular action. However, they can only 'predict' actors' choices in a statistical sense, and given that the Old Testament does not provide sufficient information to develop such mathematical constructs 'predictive' modelling is inappropriate. In any case, with regard to biblical interpretation, all one can say is whether the behaviour 'predicted' by the model is found, or not. But this tells us nothing about the *text*, which already contains the 'results' of actions.

The second affirmation is that models of typical action can be compared. The paucity of biblical ethnographic data leads Esler to contend that the comparative use of models is essential to highlight the different assumptions of modern readers and ancient authors and their implied audiences.[57] Although there is a risk that models will lead researchers to assume patterns of conduct are present even when they are not, once assumptions are made explicit whether this has occurred can become a matter of debate.[58] Crucially, however, one must be cognizant that comparison of models does *not* mean 'cultures' are being compared. Aguilar is correctly unequivocal: 'Cultures do not exist.

55 Malina, 'Social Sciences', 232.

56 See Esler, 'Review of Horrell', 254; David Horrell, 'Models and Methods in Social-Scientific Interpretation: A Response to Philip Esler', *JNTS* 78 (2000), 85–105; P. Esler, 'Models in New Testament Interpretation: A Reply to David Horrell', *JSNT* 78 (2000): 107–13, especially 108–12. For a recent defence of 'modelling' see P. Esler, 'Social-Scientific Models in Biblical Interpretation', in *Ancient Israel: The Old Testament in Its Social Context* (ed. P. F. Esler; Minneapolis: Fortress, 2006), 3–14. Despite their differences both Horrell and Esler seek a corrective to ethnocentric theological or ecclesiastical readings centred upon ideas unconnected to social context.

57 Esler, 'Review', 254.

58 Cf. this objection to 'modelling' in Horrell, 'Models and Methods', 91.

Instead, groups of human beings that share some common understanding, but also fight for their own identity . . . interact within larger contested worlds'.[59] When an exegete employs a model, therefore, she does not utilize a proxy for 'culture' but merely a summary description of typical behaviour. For this reason, there is no need for the model to be 'true'. Esler remarks that they are 'heuristic tools, not ontological statements. Accordingly, they are either useful or not, and it is meaningless to ask whether they are "true" or "false"'.[60] Although this pragmatic test might appear to beg certain questions, there is no way of avoiding this situation – that is why one can only achieve interpretative, not scientific, understandings. Whether any particular model is adequate even for this purpose is an empirical matter; but it can never be a description of 'culture'.

Third, human action is personal and open, that is, it does not *have* to cohere with that summarized in a model. According to Herzfeld's ethnography, any one society, village or family possesses '[e]mbarrasments of ambiguity'[61] so that even between conventional interpretations there is 'an expressive play of opposition'.[62] Herzfeld labels this 'disemia', claiming it speaks not of contradiction but tension. He offers the example of the diabolical and virginal aspects of women's sexuality in Greek and Indian contexts where 'the sweetness of domestic intimacy and the fear men have of their wives' and daughters' defilement by other men' are simultaneous concerns.[63] As I have already affirmed, the plurality of moral goods is a fundamental social reality, and any adequate interpretive method must be able to account for this variety, in part because agency will never completely mirror generalized abstractions; it may have very little to do with them.

Fourth, human action is ambiguous. Bourdieu shows why this affirmation is important. Highlighting the distinction between observers and observed, he

59 Aguilar, 'Changing Models', 307

60 P. Esler, 'Introduction: Models, Context and Kerygma in New Testament Interpretation', in *Modelling Early Christianity: Social-scientific studies of the New Testament in its context* (ed. P. F. Esler; London: Routledge, 1995), 1–20, quote 4.

61 M. Herzfeld, *Anthropology through the Looking-glass: Critical Ethnography in the Margins of Europe* (Cambridge: CUP, 1987), 104.

62 Herzfeld, *Looking-glass*, 114.

63 Herzfeld, *Looking-glass*, 99. Both of which, of course, are 'models'. See also M. Herzfeld, 'Disemia', in *Semiotics* (ed. M. Herzfeld and M. D. Lenhart; New York: Plenum, 1980), 205–15.

argues that observers, lacking an insider's (*emic*) mastery of situations, 'provide themselves with an explicit and at least semi-formalized substitute for it in the form of a *repertoire of rules*'.[64] The problem is that observers frequently forget this is an outsider's (*etic*), summary, view of behaviour.

> To slip from *regularity*, i.e. from what recurs with a certain statistically measurable frequency and from the formula which describes, to a consciously laid down and consciously respected *ruling* (*règlement*), or to unconscious *regulating* by a mysterious cerebral or social mechanism, are the two commonest ways of sliding from the model of reality to the reality of the model.[65]

Thus, even when a series of actions and reactions are predictable *from outside*, the subjective view remains uncertain. Bourdieu claims reification of practice by ignoring temporality 'is never more pernicious than when exerted on practices defined by the fact that their temporal structure, direction, and rhythm are *constitutive* of their meaning'.[66] Illustrating this contention by reference to gift-giving he notes that what from the outside, and *post factum*, might appear to be an ordered cycle of reciprocity, can be interrupted at any stage, and thus lose its intended meaning.[67] In fact, the difference between the observed and subjective appreciation of gift giving is essential to the essence of this practice:

> even if reciprocity is the 'objective' truth of the discrete acts that ordinary experience knows in discrete form and associates with the idea of a gift, it is perhaps not the whole truth of a practice that could not exist if its subjective truth coincided perfectly with its 'objective' truth.[68]

'Objective' models, by turning observers' *de facto* exclusion into a methodological preference, can mask both the reality of practice and interpreters' assumptions.

My final affirmation is that dominant constructions of power relations can

64 P. Bourdieu, *Outline of a Theory of Practice* (Cambridge: CUP, 1977), 2. Emphasis original.

65 P. Bourdieu, *The Logic of Practice* (trans. R. Nice; Stanford: Stanford University Press), 39. Emphasis original.

66 Bourdieu, *Outline*, 9. Emphasis original.

67 Bourdieu, *Logic*, 105.

68 Bourdieu, *Logic*, 105.

be both contested and accepted. Herzfeld explains that the 'honour-shame' model of male–female relations suppresses alternative views, 'not simply *of the women*, but *of most villagers when discussing intimate situations with those whom they regard as intimate friends*'.[69] That is, the situation affects behaviour. If dirt, in this case inappropriate deportment, is 'matter out of place', then what changes is not the matter but the place: what is acceptable in one situation is not in another, and vice versa. Thus

> in speaking of *the* symbolism of a given community, we too easily play into the hands of the dominant groups, those who *define* propriety. What we are then discussing is an official praxis; we ignore interpretations that may reverse the system by redefining, not matter, but place.[70]

It is necessary, therefore, to attend to the distribution of power and resources and the manipulation of symbolic meanings by individuals as they seek their own advantage.[71]

These five affirmations summarize the theoretical underpinnings of my approach to the use of anthropology in exegesis. They enable use of ethnographic and anthropological resources in creative ways to suggest understandings of the context of biblical characters' practices while allowing theoretical space for consideration of idiosyncratic acts that do not cohere with cultural schemata, acts which may contest dominant relations of power yet remain ambiguous. It is now possible to summarize my interpretative methodology.

3. Conclusion: Interpreting Voices

I commenced this book by examining the Old Testament's own resources for resolving value conflicts, arguing that moral goods are more foundational than

69 Herzfeld, *Looking-glass*, 99. Emphasis original.

70 Herzfeld, *Looking-glass*, 99. Emphasis original.

71 See Horrell, 'Models and Methods', 96. Esler agrees that power relations are important, 'Reply to Horrell', 107. Horrell also contends that the implicit assumptions entailed in using models comprise a second important issue relating to power because models are not merely heuristic, but shape observers' perceptions; they do not simply make explicit interpreters' perspectives, but reflect and contain their own implicit suppositions. This means that 'goodness of fit' of data is an insufficient test of a model's validity. It is also necessary to enquire 'how the model has *shaped*, prioritised and interpreted the evidence', Horrell, *Social Ethos*, 15–16. Emphasis original.

laws or their motivations. Within the biblical text the 'family' is prominent both as the matrix and end of moral action. An investigation of kinship as variously understood by anthropologists revealed that it is most appropriately considered a field of practices. Within anthropological theorizing, indeed the social-sciences in general, 'practice' has been conceived as arising from structure and/or agency. Rather than elucidate a genealogy of practice I sought to expose important questions of interpretation, identifying three key issues. Given that the ambiguity of social interaction is reflected in the Old Testament, especially its characterization of 'heroes', I have proposed that reading narrative with an ear to a text's 'voices' might reveal how the author uses value conflicts to establish a debate between different perspectives; and that by affirming some voices while undermining others the biblical writers present a view of moral goods and their prioritization for consideration by readers.

The following chapter contains an interpretation of the voices in 1 Samuel 19:10-18a. The first step, naturally, is to identify the voices. There appear to be two: those of Michal and Saul. The next move is to identify the moral goods in view and the perspective upon them presented by each voice. To do this I identify themes that feature prominently in the narrative, viz. violence, marriage and lying. My method then comprises three elements. First, I highlight how the Old Testament exhibits a variety of perspectives upon the theme to alert interpreters to the complexities facing them in this particular narrative. Second, I present anthropological perspectives upon the theme. Rather than simply describing models, which would ignore the fact that anthropology (the supposed source of such models) is itself an arena of contested meanings, I follow Aguilar who suggests that 'the use of a social author within a biblical paper needs always to be supported by some discussion on the author's context of writing', that is, the wider anthropological work relating to a particular theme.[72] Third, I employ these materials to suggest new interpretations of relevant aspects of the passage. Having interpreted the voices, I then assess how they are either subverted or approved. This is important in order to be able to

72 Aguilar, 'Changing models', 310. A problem with model use occurs when the model substitutes for anthropological or sociological data: cognizance of first hand studies, not merely secondary-level theorizing, is required. This is one difficulty with the 'abductive' use of models proposed by Elliott, *Social-Scientific Criticism*, 48–49. While it is true that there must be movement between text and anthropological resource, confining the latter to 'models' is inadequate.

identify the theological import of the chosen texts and their value for readers' ethical reflection. For the present it is sufficient to say that the complexity of the narrative points to the author's desire that readers should become involved with its characters. This is an essential didactic move, since he wishes to propose a novel solution to the moral dilemma he describes, one that implied readers would have found counter-intuitive, even shocking.

Chapter 5

MICHAL: LYING THROUGH HER *TERAPHIM*

I wished to tell the truth,
for truth always conveys its own moral
to those who are able to receive it.

Anne Brontë, *The Tenant of Wildfell Hall*[1]

In the introduction to this book I outlined how 1 Sam. 19:10-18a was structured to highlight the ethical questions faced by Saul, David and Michal. Thinking in Bakhtinian terms we can consider each character to be a 'voice' offering a vision of the world that readers are invited to assess. Although there is no explicit evaluation of these voices one cannot talk of polyphony, for the writer leaves plenty of clues as to which voice he prefers. Instead, readers hear heteroglot voices, one of which receives the author's approbation.

1. The Voices: Michal and Saul

The first 'voice' is Saul's. I argued above that it is necessary to go beyond Bakhtin's restriction to the spoken word and include behaviour when considering a character's 'voice'. Thus although Saul only speaks in v. 17, he is also heard in vv. 11, 14 and 15, where his actions, which truly speak louder than words, are revealed by the narrator. His first deed responds to David's successful evasion and return to his house.[2] Saul sends, שלח, messengers to watch the

1 The epigraph is from A. Brontë, *The Tenant of Wildfell Hall* (2nd ed.; Harmondsworth: Penguin, 1979 [1848]), 29.

2 Which night בלילה הוא refers to has been the subject of some speculation. According to George Caird 'that night' cannot be the night of the spear throwing in vv. 8-10 'since there David is said to have fled and escaped, which must mean more than that he

house, presumably to ensure that David does not evade him again, and to kill him the following morning.

The scene set, readers hear Michal's voice, which warns David of mortal danger and urges him to flee. David remains mute throughout this passage, an object acted upon by Michal and whose escapades are noted by the narrator; his only role is acquiescence. Michal, however, speaks loudly and clearly, not only facilitating his descent through the window but preparing a dummy using *teraphim* to replace David's prone frame.[3]

went home to his wife', G. Caird, 'The First and Second Books of Samuel', *IB* 2.986–87. He concludes (pp. 858, 986) that this text speaks of the wedding night and follows directly from 1 Sam.18:27. So also R. de Vaux, *Les Livres de Samuel* (2nd ed.; Paris: Les Éditions du Cerf, 1961), 102; R. W. Klein, *1 Samuel* (WBC 10; Waco: Word Books, 1983), 194; K. McCarter, *1 Samuel: A New Translation with Introduction, Notes and Commentary* (AB 8; Garden City: Doubleday, 1980), 325; S. R. Driver, *Notes of the Hebrew Text and the Topography of the Books of Samuel* (2nd ed.; Oxford: OUP, 1913), 156; Henry Smith, *Samuel* (ICC; Edinburgh: T & T Clark, 1899), 178–79. However, 'from that time' in 1 Sam. 18:29 is against such an interpretation and Campbell calls the assumption that the reference is to the wedding night 'unsupported', A. Campbell, *1 Samuel* (FOTL 7; Grand Rapids: Eerdmans, 2003), 203. Gordon notes it 'has the curious side-effect of making Michal pretend that David is ill on his wedding night!', R. Gordon, *1 and 2 Samuel* (Exeter: IVP, 1986), 164. Bressan thinks that David could well have returned home thinking that Saul's anger would blow over, as on previous occasions, G. Bressan, *Samuele* (Rome: Marietti, 1960), 317. See also 1 Sam. 20:33, where there is no indication Jonathan left court. I concur that the night in question follows the spear throwing incident.

3 There is unanimity among commentators that the plural represents a single image, cf. de Vaux, *Samuel*, 102, who compares the plural with אורים and תמים, and, more cautiously, with אלהים. As to size Keil and Delitzsch argue their dimensions must have been appropriate to serve as a human dummy, see C. F. Keil and F. Delitzsch, *Joshua, Judges, Ruth, I & II Samuel* (trans. J. Martin; Grand Rapids, Eerdmans, 1980), 195. Apart from the lack of archaeological evidence for objects of this size, however, the *teraphim* in Judges 18 are associated with the *ephod* and could be carried by priests, and those of Gen. 31:34 were hidden in a camel saddle. Gordon cautions that they 'were not invariably large', Gordon, *1 Samuel*, 164. Regarding use McCarter suggests *teraphim* had a role in divination 'and can perhaps be identified with the "gods" which adjudicate in clan or household law', McCarter, *1 Samuel*, 326; cf. Ezek. 21:21 [26]; Zech. 10:2. Gordon proposes they were possibly figurines venerated in the manner of Roman *lares* and *penates*, Gordon, *1 Samuel*, 164. Rouillard and Tropper, however, contend that *teraphim* were used in ancestor worship and in magical healing rituals, H. Rouillard and J. Tropper, '*TRPYM*, Rituels de guérison et Culte des Ancêtres d'après 1 Samuel XIX 11–17 et les Textes Parallèles d'Assur et de Nuzi', *VT* 37 (1987): 340–61. Kirkpatrick speculates that healing properties explain their surreptitious use by the barren Michal, A. F. Kirkpatrick, *The First Book of Samuel with Map, Notes and Introduction* (CB; Cambridge: CUP, 1890), 172; also Keil and Delitzsch, *Samuel*, 195. Finally, although this does not exhaust the suggestions, von Rad thinks *teraphim* could have been a cultic mask, G. von Rad, *Old Testament Theology* (trans. D. M. G.

In v. 14 Saul's voice is heard in refrain: he sends, שלח,[4] messengers, this time to take David prisoner. Michal's lie[5] delays the action for a single line before Saul is heard once more: he sends, שלח,[6] so that his emissaries can verify Michal's excuse for themselves.[7] Not satisfied with a mere report he continues by instructing them to bring David to him from his bed.[8] On discovering Michal's ploy Saul confronts her with a question, to which Michal, uttering the passage's final word, responds with a counter question.

One can imagine that characters in a situation like that of this passage

Stalker; New York: Harper & Row, 1962–65), 1.216. Obviously, translation of '*teraphim*' is problematic. Smith suggests that the LXX's κενοτάφια implies ancestral images, Smith, *Samuel*, 180; in Erdmann's phrase, 'a contemptuous designation of the vanity of the idols', D. Erdmann, *The Books of Samuel* (LC 5; trans. C. H. Toy and J. A. Broadus; New York: Scribner, Armstrong & Co., 1877), 249. NRSV has 'household gods' in Genesis 31, but opts for transliteration in Judg. 17:5; 18; Kgs 23:24; Ezk 21:21 [26]; Hos. 3:4, Zech. 10:2, and 'idol'/'idolatry' in 1 Samuel. Given the difficulties of defining *teraphim* and that they are described both positively (Hos. 3:4) and negatively, the more neutral rendering 'image' would appear most satisfactory, although I have chosen to transliterate.

4 In fact, the whole phrase is identical: וישלח שאול מלאכים.

5 Wellhausen follows LXX, which states that when Saul sent messengers to take David, λέγουσιν ἐνοχλεῖσθαι αὐτόν, and reads ויאמרו for the MT's ותאמר. He concludes that 'Die Worte „er ist krank" sind nicht Worte der Michal – die *sagt* nichts, sondern *zeigt* den Boten ihre Puppe –, sondern sie sind der Bescheid', J. Wellhausen, *Der Text der Bücher Samuelis* (Göttingen: Vandenhoeck und Ruprecht, 1871), 113. Emphasis original. Cross *et al.* posit that the *lectio difficilior* fits the space in 4QSam^b well and that Jerome may refer to a correct Old Latin understanding (*et responsum est*), F. M. Cross *et al.*, *Qumran Cave 4.XII: 1–2 Samuel* (DJD 17; Oxford: Clarendon, 2005), 229. Accepting this reading would create a problem for my interpretation of this passage – although not an insuperable one given the wider issues of deception I will discuss. However, apart from Cross and Smith (*Samuel*, 180 – on the basis that otherwise the dummy is unnecessary, a claim I will refute below) I have found no other commentator or Bible version that follows Wellhausen on this point, probably for the good reason that the majority of authorities support the MT, see Cross for a comprehensive list. Indeed, the parallelism of vv. 14-15, 'Saul sent . . . she said'/'Saul sent . . . he said', counts against such an emendation.

6 This time וישלח שאול את־המלאכים, which may indicate a different sort of messenger.

7 There is no need to follow LXX^B here since by omitting את־המלאכים לראות. Cross argues the Greek text exhibits 'a transparent haplography by *homoioarkton* (את . . . את)', and that space requirements in 4QSam^b are evidence for the originality of the longer reading, F. M. Cross, 'The Oldest Manuscripts from Qumran', *JBL* 74 (1955): 147–72, quote 167. 'He' would replace 'Saul' if one preferred LXX^B on text critical grounds as the shorter reading, despite the overwhelming majority reading, see McCarter, *1 Samuel*, 325; Klein, *1 Samuel*, 193; DJD 17.229.

8 McCarter argues English idiom requires 'from' for ב with verbs of motion, thus 'from the bed', McCarter, *1 Samuel*, 326.

would question each other extensively. This text, however, contains only two questions, both in v. 17. Each is introduced by למה. 'Why?' is an ethical interrogative enquiring after motive and reason. It is important for my argument to observe that Michal's למה is different from Saul's. Michal's is a rhetorical question justifying her action.[9] Saul's question, however, arises from a perceived slight. I propose that studying it *as a question* allows us to delve behind Saul's protest to the nature of the ethical dilemma facing Michal. The text is clear that Saul considered Michal's wrong her preference of David, believing himself to have been deceived. At this point modern readers, perhaps overfamiliar with hoary conundrums about whether one should lie when a would-be murderer knocks on the door, are prone to skate over the *moral* significance of Saul's protest. That is, what grounds could Saul have had for supposing Michal should *not* deceive him? Why should she *not* have 'let his enemy go'? Given that both Saul *and* Michal seem to accept that she should not have acted as she did – Michal lies again to defend her action – what ethical mores might lie behind their supposition? To answer these questions requires investigation of the practice of violence against enemies, the relationship between Michal and Saul as father and daughter, and the ethics of truth-telling. Only then will it be possible to discern what each voice is actually saying, and thus perceive how the author of Samuel simultaneously approves one and undermines the other.

2. Violence Against Enemies

Neil Whitehead observes that '[v]iolent actions, no less than any other kind of behavioral expression, are deeply infused with cultural meaning and are the moment for individual agency within historically embedded patterns of behaviour'.[10] Throughout 1 Sam. 19:10-18a Saul attempts to kill David; and in

9 For discussion and classification of interrogative clauses see also WO'C 315–16; J. Barr, 'Why? in Biblical Hebrew', *JTS* 36 (1985): 1–33. Not all questions require interrogative markers, see GKC 150 for examples in Samuel. On whether Michal's למה does in fact indicate a question see Driver who argues the 'use of למה is thoroughly idiomatic', meaning 'lest', Driver, *Notes*, 158. He is followed by van der Merwe, Naudé and Kroeze who provide Michal's riposte as an example of when למה '[f]unctions as an introduction to an alternative posed with a negative tenor: otherwise, or else', MNK 325. Without original emphasis. Regardless of the translation the point here is that Michal attempts to justify her behaviour.

10 N. L. Whitehead, 'Introduction', in *Violence* (SARASS; ed. N. L. Whitehead; Oxford: James Curry, 2004), 3–24, quote 10–11.

the climatic confrontation with Michal, angry that his machinations had come to naught, he wants to know why she has 'let my enemy go'. In this section I use these textual data as clues to start investigating Saul's stance, particularly asking how his actions might relate to a dominant cultural schema regarding violence towards enemies.

A. ENEMIES IN THE BOOKS OF SAMUEL

Enemies play a significant role in the Samuel narrative, not merely in terms of lexical occurrences (of the 283 occurrences of the root איב in the MT, 36 are found in Samuel; only the Psalms, with 74, have more), but their theological importance. Fokkelman argues that the songs of Hannah and David are key structural devices with thematic links. Their preoccupation with enemies is noteworthy: Hannah commences her praise with an affirmation that because of YHWH's intervention she can deride her enemies, and the theme of YHWH's deliverance from enemies echoes through David's hymns.[11]

Both national and personal enemies are identified. Throughout Samuel the Philistines are the national foe (1 Sam. 4:3; 12:10-11; 2 Sam. 3:18; 5:19-20; 19:9), although the author occasionally adds others including Moab, Ammonites, Edom, kings of Zobah (1 Sam. 14:47) and the Amalekites (1 Sam. 30:26).[12] Matters are more pointed, however, when individuals' enemies are identified. In the midst of battle Saul rashly curses all those who eat food before he has been avenged on his enemies, in this case the Philistines (1 Sam. 14:24, 30). They are also the enemy when Saul stipulates a bride price of a hundred foreskins (1 Sam. 18:25). As the narrative progresses one particular individual replaces this amorphous mass of foreigners as Saul's *bête noire*: David. He is called Saul's enemy, איב, for the first time in 1 Sam. 18:29. The author makes it clear that David has done nothing to provoke Saul's evaluation, since it is that fact that *God* is with him and that *Michal* loves him that causes Saul's reaction.

11 Cf. J. P. Fokkelman, *Reading Biblical Narrative: An Introductory Guide* (Leiderdorp: Deo, 1999), 160; 1 Sam. 2:1-10; 2 Sam. 1:19-27; 22:2-51. For a compelling social-scientific reading of Hannah's story see P. Esler, 'The Role of Hannah in 1 Samuel 1:1-2:21: Understanding a Biblical Narrative in its Ancient Context', in *Kontexte der Schrift. Band II: Kultur, Politik, Religion, Sprache. Festschrift fur Wolfgang Stegemann* (ed. C. Strecker; Stuttgart: Kohlhammer, 2005), 15–36.

12 The Amalekites are at least enemies of David having plundered his camp at Ziglag, although he describes them as איבי יהוה, cf. 1 Sam. 15:2.

Although the narrative avoids attributing the blame for his condition to David himself it does not follow that Saul's actions towards him as his enemy are incoherent. In fact, the books' account of attitudes towards *David's* enemies reveals that Saul behaves according to shared assumptions.

David's enemies are sometimes unspecified (2 Sam. 18:19, 32), but in two cases their referent is unambiguous. When Jonathan makes a covenant with David he asks that 'the LORD seek out the enemies of David', cutting them off from the face of the earth, but pleads that David should not show enmity towards Jonathan's descendants, since he is aware that this will mean their elimination (1 Sam. 20:15-16). The books of Samuel present David as (un)scrupulously compliant to this covenant, to the 'benefit' of Mephibosheth and detriment of the unfortunate sons of Rizpah and Merab (2 Sam. 21:7-8).[13] Saul is David's other enemy. While the text carefully avoids portraying David himself describing Saul as such, other characters do so vicariously. David's men describe Saul as David's enemy, and provide evidence of the expectation that enemies should be killed (1 Sam. 24:4). Indeed, Saul's own incredulity that David should not do so points in the same direction: 'For who has ever found an enemy, and sent the enemy safely away?' (1 Sam. 24:19). David justifies his magnanimity by arguing Saul continued to be YHWH's anointed (1 Sam. 24:6). Abishai also describes Saul as David's enemy (1 Sam. 26:8). Contrary to Abishai's expectations, David refuses to countenance Saul's death – with the very spear he threw at David? – on the basis that no one can 'raise a hand' against the Lord's anointed and remain guiltless. Obviously, this text wishes to make a political point regarding the inviolability of the Davidic dynasty, but for that very reason it evinces the 'normality' of killing one's enemies. This is the perspective of Rechab and Baanah, sons of Rimmon and erstwhile lieutenants to Saul's son, Ishbaal. Wishing to curry favour with the new regime they decapitate Ishbaal while he reposes in his house. Arriving at David's court they say 'Here is the head of Ishbaal, son of Saul, your enemy, who sought your life' (2 Sam. 4:8). It is inconceivable that they foresaw David's violent response, which can be interpreted as both principled and pragmatic: killing Rechab and Baanah both served as punishment for their assassination of Saul, thus demonstrating *his*

13 Following LXX^{L}; most MS read Michal, a *lapsus calami* for Merab according to Driver, *Notes*, 352; cf. Smith, *Samuel*, 376; A. Anderson, *2 Samuel* (WBC 11; Dallas: Word Books, 1989), 247.

virtue in this respect, and eliminated his opponent's potential military leaders in the case that they decided to turncoat once again (2 Sam 4:9-12). To summarize, all of these cases confirm the logic of Saul's protest to Michal in 1 Sam. 19:17.

Despite the indubitably mundane means by which enemies are deposed throughout Samuel, the books' theology is clear: it is God who vindicates, or does not vindicate, people in confrontations with their foes. This is the force of Abigail's invocation that David's enemies be like Nabal, and her contrast between God protecting David and 'slinging out' the lives of his enemies (1 Sam. 25:26, 29). Indeed, rest from enemies forms part of God's promise to David (2 Sam 7:1, 9, 11. Note that this comes immediately after the report that Michal remained childless until her death and may well allude to the house of Saul as David's adversary). In this connection Pedersen's observations concerning שלום are pertinent. 'In the olden time peace is not in itself the opposite of war. There are friends and there are enemies; peace consists in complete harmony between friends and victory in war against enemies'.[14] Thus peace does not follow war, for then the losers would also have peace, but victory. Niditch correctly summarizes Pedersen's view of peace *with enemies* as 'virtually equivalent to domination'.[15] Thus it is possible to assert that שלום 'expresses every form of happiness and free expansion, but the kernel in it is the community with others, the foundation of life',[16] because it is precisely who forms a part of that community that is at stake: the classification of 'the other' has practical relevance for behaviour.

Most contemporary readers of 1 Samuel do not think that receiving favour from God and love from Michal justify Saul's extreme measures. Above, I defended the use of social-scientific resources to aid interpretation and I now consider whether the anthropology of war and violence can offer clues for biblical exegetes.

14 J. Pedersen, *Israel: Its Life and Culture* (4 vols; Oxford: OUP, 1926), I–II.311.

15 S. Niditch, *War in the Hebrew Bible: A Study in the Ethics of Violence* (Oxford: OUP, 1993), 135. She tries to argue against this, but all her counter examples are from within Israel, see C. Rodd, *Glimpses of a Strange Land: Studies in Old Testament Ethics* (OTS; Edinburgh: T & T Clark, 2001), 197.

16 Pedersen, *Israel*, I–II.313.

B. ENEMIES AND VIOLENCE – ANTHROPOLOGICAL PERSPECTIVES

The definitions of violence and war are disputed; but the focus of anthropological study of these topics has centred on their social reality rather than semantics.[17] Early studies were unambiguously functionalist. Max Gluckman, for example, highlighted the integrating and differentiating function of conflict.[18] His thesis was that conflicts between a person's cross-cutting loyalties are the basis for societal stability. So, for example, while members of a family who find themselves in different tribes may be estranged, their kinship ties, although stretched, can ameliorate clan violence as women, who reside with their husband's family following marriage, pressurize men to resolve conflict through compensation rather than warfare. Structuralists have contrasted war and exchange. For Lévi-Strauss war was the opposite of exchange, a means of establishing peaceful sociality; each was mutually exclusive.[19] Brian Ferguson summarizes Lévi-Straus thus: 'war is the other side of exchange within a structure of relations – war is an exchange gone bad, and exchange is a war averted'.[20] Klaus -F. Koch attributed war to the belligerence inculcated into children who, when grown, encounter no political institutions to restrain them.[21] Based on this premise Napoleon Chagnon argues that war is the natural state for tribal groups.[22] Ferguson points out, however, that there is a logical error in this proposition for 'it equates the lack of *formal* institutions of conflict resolution with the absence of *any* means of regulating conflicts other than the unstable ties of reciprocal exchange'.[23] Furthermore, this explains only the

17 For a survey of definitions see G. Pontara, 'Violencia', *DEFM* 2.1659–64; for reviews of the anthropological literature on war see A. Simons, 'War: Back to the Future', *ARA* 28 (1999): 73–108; J. Spencer, 'Violence', *ESCA* 559–60; S. Harrison, 'Warfare', *ESCA* 561–62; I. Schröder and B. Schmidt, 'Introduction: Violent Imaginaries and Violent Practices', in *Anthropology of Violence and Conflict* (ed. B. Schmidt and I. Schröder; London: Routledge, 2001), 1–24.

18 M. Gluckman, *Custom and Conflict in Africa* (Oxford: Blackwell, 1959).

19 Cf. C. Lévi-Strauss, 'Guerre et commerce chez les Indiens de l'Amérique du Sud', *Renaissance* 1 (1943): 122–39.

20 B. Ferguson, 'Introduction: Studying War', in *Warfare, Culture and Environment* (ed. B. Ferguson; London: Academic Press, 1984), 1–79, quote 17.

21 K.-F. Koch, *War and Peace in Jalemo* (Cambridge: Harvard University Press, 1974).

22 N. Chagnon, 'Life Histories, Blood Revenge, and Warfare in a Tribal Population', *Science* 239 (1988): 985–92.

23 Ferguson, 'Studying War', 20.

potential for war, not its actual occurrence. Chagnon's study of the Yanomamo portrays men striving to dominate females for reproductive purposes.[24] Socio-biological interpretations of war as the product of innate drives, however, are peculiarly culture specific. William Golding's *Lord of the Flies*, for example, presents people as merely animals, whose innate proclivity for violence must be contained by external authority.[25] Signe Howell and Roy Willis remark that it is a 'particular view of human nature . . . not one shared by many other societies. They may attribute unattractive and negatively valued characteristics to their enemies or neighbours, but most certainly not to themselves'.[26] Furthermore, the assumption that conflict is the 'natural' state has been challenged by Simon Harrison. Writing about the Avatip of the Sepik River, he contends that the natural state of social relations is peaceful.[27] Ferguson adopts an ecological approach to communal violence, explaining conflict as competition for scarce resources such as land and food.[28] Howell and Willis, however, argue that none of the above approaches account sufficiently for context. 'Violent behaviour, in the most general sense, can only be understood in association with other behaviour within the same society. Behaviour is never culturally neutral, but always embedded within a shared set of meanings'.[29] Nigel Rapport and Joanna Overing concur that 'violence must be seen in the context of socio-cultural interaction, and defined in terms of all the complexities of particular situations'.[30] Paul Richards is also sceptical about ecological factors, cultural or political explanations for war, because they cannot explain 'peaceful' wars, e.g. Gandhi's resistance to the British Empire. 'In other words, war does not break out because conditions happen to be "right", but because

24 N. Chagnon, *Yanomamo: The Fierce People* (New York: Holt, Reinhardt and Winston, 1977).

25 W. Golding, *Lord of the Flies* (London: Faber & Faber, 1954).

26 S. Howell and R. Willis, 'Introduction', in *Societies at Peace: Anthropological Perspectives* (ed. S. Howell and R. Willis; London: Routledge, 1989), 1–28, quote 10.

27 S. Harrison, 'The Symbolic Construction of Aggression and War in a Sepik River Society', *Man* NS 24 (1989): 583–99. One consequence is that violence has to be created and sustained by ritual action. See also Howell and Willis, 'Introduction'.

28 B. Ferguson, *Warfare, Culture and Environment* (New York: Academic Press, 1984). In more recent work he attempts a synthesis of various materialist factors, see B. Ferguson, 'Explaining War', in *The Anthropology of War* (ed. J. Haas; Cambridge: CUP, 1990), 26–55.

29 Howell and Willis, 'Introduction', 7.

30 N. Rapport and J. Overing, *Social and Cultural Anthropology: The Key Concepts* (London: Routledge, 2000), 382.

it is organised'.[31] The need, therefore, is to examine violence in the context of everyday practice rather than as a discrete type of activity.[32]

This brief survey of anthropological perspectives upon violence enables us to situate a debate that is particularly pertinent to Saul's actions, that is, the grounds upon which boundaries between enemies and friends are drawn. Gluckman argued that violent conflict is a factor of greater social distance. 'Feud is waged and vengeance taken when the parties live sufficiently far apart, or are too weakly related by diverse ties'.[33] Evans-Pritchard, *pace* Gluckman, argued that the logic of segmentation means conflict increases with proximity.[34] Harrison agrees, but contends social distance is not a scale of 'peace, amity and security' versus 'war, hostility and danger', but rather one of 'alternating extremes of amity and enmity' versus 'uninvolvement, neutrality or dissociation'. Harrison questions not that feuds are rare in societies with cross-cutting ties, but that they are lower than would be the case in their absence. '[I]n arguing that the interpersonal ties between groups serve to limit conflict, Gluckman is of course assuming that the fundamental structures of tribal society are groups, and that these groups *could imaginably exist without their interrelations*'.[35] Harrison observes that in Melanesian societies the a priori is interrelationships, upon which groups are contingent.

31 P. Richards, 'New War: An Ethnographic Approach', in *No Peace No War: An Anthropology of Contemporary Armed Conflicts* (ed. P. Richards; Oxford: James Curry, 2005), 1–21, quote 4.

32 Riches distinguishes between operational and representational models of violence, see D. Riches, 'Aggression, War, Violence: Space/Time and Paradigm', *Man* NS 26 (1991): 281–97. Operational models refer to the tacit meaning of violence at the moment it occurs, where responsibility for the violent act lies with the acting agent. Representational models refer to judgments or commentaries about violence; they are removed in space and time from the event, and responsibility is attributed to others. Riches posits a universal experience of 'contestably rendering physical hurt' at the operational level, but highlights multiple, distinct interpretations of war, aggression and so on at representational levels. I find Riches exclusion of so-called symbolic and structural violence as violence problematic because these forms can be as prejudicial at a representational level as physical hurt. Riches' concern is to *define* violence; my focus is the role of violence in relations with enemies.

33 Gluckman, *Custom and Conflict*, 18.

34 E. Evans-Pritchard, *The Nuer: A Description of the Modes of Livelihood and Political Institutions of a Nilotic People* (Oxford: Clarendon Press, 1940), 150. Segmentation is 'a tendency to segment into opposed segments, and also for these segments to fuse in relation to other units', Evans-Pritchard, *Nuer*, 190.

35 S. Harrison, *The Mask of War: Violence, Ritual and Self in Melanesia* (Manchester: Manchester University Press, 1993), 13–14. Emphasis original.

> A group is a provisional entity, its existence having constantly to be accomplished against the claims which outsiders exercise upon its members and which threaten perpetually to dissolve it. The interrelations between groups, on the other hand, can never be abrogated. They are the very conditions upon which it is possible for groups to come into existence.[36]

That is, the fundamental problem is not ties between people but boundaries. Sociality is a given, but division into groups needs to be accomplished by prioritization of particular ties over the claims of others: 'groups of men acting *as if* the only social relationships they had were those that link them to each other'.[37] Thus, in contrast to Gluckman's argument that violence reflects the existence of extant boundaries, Harrison maintains that 'violence is one of a range of symbolic practices by means of which groups act to constitute themselves within the system of relationships encompassing them'.[38] The Gebusi tribe, for example, kills a suspected witch to redraw the community's moral boundaries as part of a continuous identification and expulsion of 'the evil other' in their midst.[39]

Herzfeld proposes that the definition of 'the other' fluctuates according to situation. That is, the 'terms "outsider" and "one of us", are signs whose meaning depends both on the perspective of the speaker and on that of the people whose actions are described'.[40] Herzfeld points to the importance of defining 'outsider' and how perspective affects this definition disemically. He claims it is characteristic of state authority to fix the definition of 'the other', in Canutian defiance of the reality of segmentation in which people constantly construct

36 Harrison, *Mask*, 9.

37 Harrison, *Mask*, 10. Emphasis original. Harrison concludes that in Melanesian war '[w]hat a group is fighting for is not the biological survival of its members but the survival of its socio-political identity', Harrison, *Mask*, 12.

38 Harrison, *Mask*, 14.

39 Cf. Harrison, *Mask*, 17; B. M. Knauft, 'Reconsidering Violence in Simple Human Societies: Homicide among the Gebusi of New Guinea', *CA* 28 (1987): 457–82. The practices of identity maintenance are the focus of George's analysis of headhunting rituals in K. George, *Showing Signs of Violence: The Cultural Politics of a Twentieth-Century Headhunting Ritual* (Berkley: University of California Press, 1996).

40 M. Herzfeld, *Anthropology through the Looking-glass: Critical Ethnography in the Margins of Europe* (Cambridge: CUP, 1987), 154.

both 'togetherness' and 'otherness' not just at the level of national boundaries but in everyday interaction.

In his study of genocide Alex Hinton proposes that the construction of 'the other' is the first 'grammatical rule' of genocidal practice. This entails 'local construction of group boundaries, a marking off of similarity from difference, of an "us" from a "them" '.[41]

> To facilitate violence against such newly marked enemies, perpetrator regimes usually initiate a series of institutional, legal, social, and political changes that transform the conditions under which the target victim groups live and, ultimately, perish. The structural changes that underlie this 'organization of difference' create mechanisms, disciplines, and social spaces for distinguishing, dividing, confining, and regulating the target group . . . [although] [e]ven as they are asserted with conviction, the categories that perpetrators manufacture are arbitrary constructions imposed from above that never fully accord with the more fluid and less rigid realities existing on the ground.[42]

If life is 'chaotic and contradictory', as Rapport suggests, these constructions can never correspond with some ontological essence possessed by 'the other',[43] which leads to the second grammatical rule, viz., the bodily inscription of signs in order to overcome the uncertainty that 'threatens to shatter the crystallization of difference'.[44] Thus 'perpetrator regimes organize difference in ways that create mechanisms for sorting and institutions for confining people in spaces that demarcate and affirm (by "their" very location in a place like a ghetto or concentration camp) alleged identities'.[45] The bodily inscription of difference is especially important when other markers are absent: one must look for clues

41 A. Hinton, 'The Poetics of Genocidal Practice: Violence under the Khmer Rouge', in *Violence* (SARASS; ed. N. L. Whitehead; Oxford: James Curry, 2004), 157–84, quote 162.

42 Hinton, 'Genocidal Practice', 162–63.

43 Cf. M. Aguilar, *The Rwanda Genocide and the Call to Deepen Christianity in Africa* (Eldoret: AMECEA Gaba Publications Spearhead, 1998), 24.

44 Hinton, 'Genocidal Practice', 163. Simon Harrison observes that the construction of the Japanese enemy as sub-human meant their body parts were 'traded' in ways that would have been deemed inappropriate with European enemies, S. Harrison, 'Skull Trophies of the Pacific War: transgressive objects of remembrance', *JRAI* 12 (2006): 817–36, especially 826.

45 Hinton, 'Genocidal Practice', 163.

for who is 'one of us' from actions or opinions. A third grammatical rule of genocidal violence is that 'violence always contains an immediate, experiential component that even the most powerful poetry, memoir, or analysis cannot convey'.[46] That is, it is a concrete, physical action causing harm to others, which at the same time possesses a performative aspect in the creation of 'the other'.

The performative element of violence has been observed in non-genocide studies. Laurie Taylor's ethnography of the London underworld linked the moral assessment that something or someone was 'out of order' with consequent violence to enforce 'proper respect'. Being 'out of order' described diverse anti-social acts, as defined by the criminal 'micro-society' that employed the phrase. 'The violent acts themselves, matter-of-fact and routine, were simply the instrumental means by which departures-from-order were socio-culturally inscribed and overcome'.[47] Note that the norms were also inscribed upon the enforcer as he embodied the socially acceptable values.

The values to be embodied and inscribed in any given situation will be local products, highlighting the importance of context. Maria Olujic observes that 'war rapes in the former Yugoslavia would not be such an effective weapon of torture and terror if it were not for concepts of honor, shame, and sexuality that are attached to women's bodies in peacetime'.[48] Thus the meaning of this sort of violence is predictable; it is not simply explosive rage, but a strategy for human relationships of domination. Rapport and Overing label this 'democratic violence', because its significance is understood by perpetrator, victim and observers. They contrast the shared comprehension of democratic violence with 'nihilistic violence' that 'negates common forms of exchange'.[49] In his ethnography of the Lebanese province of Akkar, Michael Gilsenan notes that cultural practice may often demand violence.[50] In Rapport and Overing's terms the actions he discusses are clearly 'democratic', and largely understood

46 Hinton, 'Genocidal Practice', 172.

47 Rapport and Overing, *Anthropology*, 382–83; cf. L. Taylor, *In the Underworld* (Oxford: Blackwell, 1984).

48 M. Olujic, 'Embodiment of Terror: Gendered Violence in Peacetime and Wartime in Croatia and Bosnia-Herzegovina', *MAQ* NS 12 (1998): 31–50, quote 31–32.

49 Rapport and Overing, *Anthropology*, 383–86, quote 386.

50 M. Gilsenan, *Lords of the Lebanese Marches: Violence & Narrative in an Arab Society* (London: I. B. Tauris, 1996).

in terms of ordinary practice as responses to challenges to a man's honour. Bourdieu observes that the

> point of honour is the ethic appropriate to an individual who always sees himself through the eyes of others, who has need of others in order to exist, because his self-image is inseparable from the image of himself that he receives back from others. Respectability . . . is essentially defined by its social dimension, and so must be won and defended in the face of everyone.[51]

Defence of honour is something that a man must prosecute himself, since appeal to a higher authority would be a sign of weakness. Julian Pitt-Rivers notes that the 'ultimate vindication of honour lies in physical violence'.[52] While the *act* of fighting is deprecated as signifying lack of self control the *potential* for violence is frequently communicated, because, as in the Spanish bullfight, it is important that a man 'confront, withstand and direct the physical force of his opponent'.[53] The extreme form of violence is killing another. Campbell contends that '[a]lthough aimless violence is dishonourable there is no missing the pleasure it gives when a man is forced to kill; nor the prestige which it brings him. For there is no more conclusive way of showing that you are stronger than by taking away the other man's life'.[54] Gilsenan, however, presents a more nuanced picture of the consequences of murder and the very long-term difficulties it brings in its wake. In some cases status is gained. In

51 P. Bourdieu, *Algeria 1960: Essays by Pierre Bourdieu* (Cambridge: CUP, 1979), 113. One of the most well-known anthropological resources employed in biblical studies is the 'model' of 'honour and shame'. The relevant scholarly literature is substantial, which precludes a detailed discussion here, although it will be obvious from the discussion above that I think such 'models' should be used with caution.

52 J. Pitt-Rivers, 'Honour and Social Status', in *Honour and Shame: The Values of Mediterranean Society* (ed. J. G. Peristiany; London: Weidenfeld and Nicolson, 1965), 19–77, quote 29.

53 G. Marvin, 'Honour, Integrity and the Problem of Violence in the Spanish Bullfight', in *The Anthropology of Violence* (ed. D. Riches; Oxford: Basil Blackwell, 1986), 118–35, quote 127. Marvin contends that the bull is in a similar structural position as other males and that the 'fact that one of the contestants is an animal allows for the incorporation of acts of violence which would be intolerable in a contest between men', Marvin, 'Spanish Bullfight', 129. It is the matador's performance rather than the death of the animal that is the focus of attention.

54 J. K. Campbell, *Honour, Family, and Patronage: A Study of Institutions and Moral Values in a Greek Mountain Community* (New York: OUP, 1964), 318.

others the killer may be lauded for a time, perhaps because the murder was almost akin to an initiation rite into manhood, but then becomes increasingly sidelined. By virtue of having shed blood he becomes dangerous to others. Most obviously, he and his family are now a potential target for retaliation. But the killer, having stepped outside the normal means of defending honour at a less definitive level of violence, is also considered less predictable and controllable by his own family. In Gilsenan's narrative this frequently leads to social marginalization and an exclusion of the individual from the demands of the honour code, in particular the demand for kin to respond to a slight to his honour, or even his killing, with violence.

The avoidance of violence is an important theme in anthropological studies of honour, although often overlooked by biblical scholars. That is, the application of violent measures *and* the avoidance of violence are *both* properly considered as part of the honour code.[55] This ambiguity means that 'challenge-riposte' is not a mechanistic scheme that can be used to interpret all practice; attention must be paid to individual agency. At a fundamental level the reason for avoiding violence is that there are multiple cultural goods – honour is *not* the only desirable object of existence; life itself is another, for example – and these goods frequently conflict. But even at the level of the honour code the avoidance of violence is a sign of honourable self control, and a desire to present oneself appropriately is a curb upon violent excess.[56] Instead, alternative strategies, for example, joking and other ostensibly positive social activities, are laced with an undercurrent of competition.[57] This antagonism occurs between rivals, which points to another key restraint upon violence: it is opponents who are the audience for displays of honour as affirmations of self identity. '[S]ince social prestige requires the favourable response of the community to a man's qualities and actions after these have been evaluated in terms of the accepted system of values, it depends overwhelmingly on the opinions of *enemies*'.[58] According to Campbell, there is a symbiotic relationship with

55 Cf. M. Herzfeld, *The Poetics of Manhood: Contest and Identity in a Cretan Mountain Village* (Princeton: Princeton University Press, 1985), 76.

56 Banfield labels this 'vanity', in E. C. Banfield, *The Moral Basis of a Backward Society* (New York: Free Press, 1958), 137. Abstaining from violence can also allow the stronger side to demonstrate moral superiority, see Herzfeld, *Looking-glass*, 159.

57 See Gilsenan, *Lords*, 206–30.

58 Campbell, *Honour, Family and Patronage*, 264. My emphasis.

enemies in all areas of life. 'The position [any family] is able to occupy in public life, the quality of the marriage alliances it establishes, depend entirely on its social prestige, that is, they depend on the favourable response of enemies; or more accurately, on the inability of enemies effectively to denigrate a family's reputation'.[59] In his ethnography Campbell observes that competitive behaviour such as reciprocal trespass for grazing sheep is preferred to outright violence. Thus 'in grazing disputes shepherds are careful to fight with weapons which may cause unpleasant wounds but are unlikely to kill. Wanton murders are discouraged through removal of the killer by imprisonment, voluntary exile, or vengeance'.[60]

Gilsenan also observes that individuals' violent acts are often part of wider competition for control. So a powerful *bey* may oblige his client *aghas* and *fellahin* to violate others' property or persons as part of his claim to honour and power.[61] And, of course, other *beys* may respond not by direct personal retaliation but by ordering their clients to perpetrate violent acts. The ability to order and control violence by others is a sign of high social status. In 1 Samuel 19, the fact that Saul sends messengers is significant. He is king and he acts accordingly – as another biblical text said he would (1 Sam. 8:11-16; cf. 1 Sam. 25:5) – ordering others to execute violent acts on his behalf, not for their own ends but for those of their patron.

All these sorts of violence are 'democratic' in that they are understood by people as part of the flow of ordinary practice. Nihilistic violence, on the other hand, is unpredictable: it does not conform to established patterns of violent behaviour so disturbs social relations by disorientating others. In general, it is not tolerated by authority figures when practised by inferiors, for it threatens the established order in which they have a vested interest. Thus when individuals engage in non-democratic nihilistic violence it is necessarily conceived as extraordinary praxis, that is, based upon a culturally alternative logic not shared by others. While nihilistic violence is usually perceived as (undesirable) extraordinary praxis, if it is executed by the *very* powerful or old it *can* be construed as intentional action. This is because by engaging in unpredictable

59 Campbell, *Honour, Family and Patronage*, 265.

60 Campbell, *Honour, Family and Patronage*, 264.

61 For an explanation of these terms see Gilsenan, *Lords*, xi. Briefly, a *bey* is a large landowner, an *agha* a smallholder and *fellahin* landless labourers.

violence they affirm their personal transcendence of the ordinary code, which is acceptable because their negation of democratic violence affirms their ability to impose accepted norms upon others. For this reason it is only those who are clearly superior because of age or acquired status that are allowed to act thus: pretension to this status by those who are perceived as still needing to compete for honour and power will receive a rapid riposte.[62]

C. UNDERSTANDING DAVID AS 'MY ENEMY'

It is now possible to consider Saul's actions towards David as his enemy. I reiterate that I do not seek an essentialist understanding of 'biblical culture' with respect to enemies, for the plurality of social and moral goods, and the complex, sometimes contradictory and contested, nature of social life militates against such homogenizing conceptions. For this reason I have followed Aguilar's injunction to consider the context of particular interpretations, that is, wider anthropological work relating to enemies and violence. Instead of seeking confirmation of a particular model of violent acts I use the resources discussed above to suggest new interpretations of 1 Sam. 19:10-18a.

According to 1 Samuel, Saul does not always consider David as his enemy. At first unknown (1 Sam. 17:58 – the author probably wishes to make a theological point, cf. 1 Sam. 2:7-8), David is conscripted into Saul's service where he enjoys notable success, eventually being appointed leader of the fighting men (1 Sam. 18:2, 5).[63] His loyalty to Saul is tested and proven, and

62 James Watson posits another reason for accepting extreme violence. If aggression is both a fact of sociality and key attribute of manhood then the demonstration of violence by the very powerful without the constraints felt by others can mean that they are more fully men than others. Referring to the violent Tairora despot, Matoto, Watson observes that he 'is a fuller embodiment of the emphases of the male cult than most apprentices can ever become. Hence he is logically a *better* man. He is no bizarre phenomenon outside the system, but fulfils in unusual degree the teachings and exhortations given to Tairora youths', J. Watson, 'Tairora: The Politics of Despotism in a Small Society', in *Politics in New Guinea* (ed. R. Berndt and P. Lawrence; Nedlands: University of Western Australia Press, 1971), 224–75, quote 268. Emphasis original.

63 LXX^B omits 17:55-18:6a although remnants of 18:4-5 have been identified at Qumran, cf. McCarter, *1 Samuel*, 303–305; DJD 17.80. 1 Sam. 17:1-18:5 has appeared to many critics 'impossible' (Driver, *Notes*, 149) to harmonize with 1 Sam. 16:14-23, even if one opts exclusively for LXX^B (which omits 1 Sam. 17:12-31, 41, 50, 55–18:5): compare 1 Sam. 17:33, 38-39 with 1 Sam. 16:18, 21. Modern literary approaches have suggested a way of reconciling chronological difficulties by conceiving these chapters as 'a binocular

'all the people, even the servants of Saul, approved' (1 Sam. 18:5). David is portrayed as an individual properly incorporated into Saul's service, someone who is personally powerful, yet in a client relationship with the king. Despite this rosy picture the text alludes to friction between the two men from the very beginning. Although there is no suggestion that the victory parade upon returning from killing Goliath was anything other than a celebration, Saul takes umbrage at the women's exuberant singing of 'Saul has killed his thousands and David his ten thousands' (1 Sam. 18:7-8).[64] Saul perceives a slight to his honour, which leads him to eye, עוין, David suspiciously from that day on (1 Sam.18:9).[65] No other motive than jealousy and fear for his throne is provided for Saul's anxiety (cf. 1 Sam. 18:8). Within the narrative he has known himself to have been rejected as king by God since ch. 15, but is unaware of his replacement's identity. Fokkelman proposes that Saul has been tormented by continually looking around for his rival.

> He has now reached the stage where he identifies him as David, and that is correct despite the fact that he reaches this interpretation via false contact with the poem. This moment is a milestone to Saul's process: on the one hand it denotes the start of a drastic reduction of tormenting uncertainty . . . on the other hand

vision by montage', J. P. Fokkelman, *Narrative Art and Poetry in the Books for Samuel. A full interpretation based on stylistic and structural analyses. Vol. II: The Crossing Fates (1 Sam. 13–31 and II Sam 1)* (SSN 23; Assen: Van Gorcum, 1986), 203; for the original idea see R. Alter, *The Art of Biblical Narrative* (New York: Basic Books, 1981), 147–54. That is, the various sources are presented a-chronically in order to offer various perspectives upon the important event of David's introduction to Saul's court. I am sympathetic to the literary resolutions of this problem; in any case I wish to affirm that David is, at different times, both Saul's friend and enemy. It is the construction of each status that is important for my interpretation.

64 Gevirtz notes that the parallelism of אלף and רבבה is not antithetical. He maintains it is very unlikely the welcoming party of women should insult Saul on his return from victory, concluding the song is lavish praise of both Saul and David, see S. Gevirtz, *Patterns in the Early Poetry of Israel* (Chicago: Chicago University Press, 1963), 24. The interpretation of their eulogy as an insult is thus Saul's alone. For a detailed analysis of the pericope and Saul's 'paranoia' see Fokkelman, *Crossing*, 210–21.

65 Following the *Qere*; for discussion see Driver who argues ויהי with participle 'expresses at once origin and continuance', Driver, *Notes*, 151–52; cf. Gen. 4:17; 21:20; Judg. 16:21; 2 Kgs 15:5, something made explicit by the phrase מהיום ההוא והלאה. Esler thinks the 'eying' is related to the evil eye, see P. Esler, 'The Madness of Saul: A Cultural Reading of 1 Samuel 8–31', in *Biblical Studies/Cultural Studies* (JSOTSup 266; ed. J. C. Exum and S. D. Moore; Sheffield: Sheffield Academic Press, 1998), 220–62, especially 240.

> the identification gives his jealous aggression which has concentrated all the time without finding a way out, an object at which to direct itself.[66]

Thus the following narrative details an attempt to place David closer to the firing line by demoting him to commander and enticing him to take extreme risks by offering his daughter's hand in marriage.[67] At this time Saul seeks to prejudice David alone and covertly, perhaps because of the people's adulation (cf. 1 Sam. 18:16, 30).

The text lends support to the view that Saul appreciated multiple cultural goods, not just the death of a personal foe. Indeed, these are the basis for Jonathan's petition in 1 Sam. 19:4-5. He does not argue that Saul acts unreasonably if David is his enemy, but offers a two-pronged argument: that David has not harmed Saul, and that David has been useful. He contends kings need competent military commanders, and should maintain order by reciprocating respect and service. In other words, Jonathan argues for democratic violence and the tangible good of military prowess. Saul recognizes the logic of Jonathan's petition, of the need for these cultural goods even though they competed with his desire to eliminate someone he considered as a competitor for the throne, and restores David to court (1 Sam. 19:7).

I noted above that the existence of multiple cultural goods means that 'the other', the differentiated individual or group, is a social construct, not an ontological description. Saul constructs David as 'the other' when he speaks 'with his son Jonathan and with all his servants about killing David' (1 Sam. 19:1). The point is that as the king's enemy David was deserving of death, regardless of whether Saul practices democratic or nihilistic violence (cf. 1 Sam. 18:29; 19:1). There are two ways in which the inscription of David's otherness occurs in 1 Sam. 19:10-18a. First, Saul sends messengers to corral David in his house. Although a temporary location, David's 'otherness' is visible as one hemmed in by the king's forces and subject to his majesty's pleasure. Second, Saul's purpose throughout is the ultimate inscription of power upon a body: David's death. This observation enables us to shed new light on the question of why

66 Fokkelman, *Crossing*, 221.

67 This interpretation of 1 Sam. 18:17-27 is well defended by D. Clines, 'Michal Observed: An Introduction to Reading Her Story', in *Telling Queen Michal's Story: An Experiment in Comparative Interpretation* (JSOTSup 119; ed. D. J. A. Clines and T. C. Eskenazi; Sheffield: Sheffield Academic Press, 1991), 24–63, especially 27–32.

Saul *wanted* to wait until the morning in order to kill David. At a literary level the delay both creates tension – what *will* happen in the morning? – and facilitates to the author the time his characters need to make the subsequent moves in the story. But I suggest that this is not a forced device. To date those commentators who speculate upon this 'delay' have made two suggestions. First, Bressen argues that 'for the ancient Semite the night was sacred: it was unlawful to kill someone in their sleep'.[68] However, while the Philistines waited until morning to attack and kill Samson (Judg. 16:2), the law allowing the killing of nocturnal thieves indicates that the practice of breaking and entering certainly occurred, and darkness would have been no impediment to Saul's thugs. Furthermore, killing at night is nowhere condemned in the Old Testament, indeed, Jael probably kills Sisera during the hours of darkness (Judg. 4:21). Second, Erdmann cites Kitto, a nineteenth-century source unavailable to me, who maintained that '[w]e may guess that only the fear of alarming the town, and of rousing the populace to rescue their favourite hero, prevented him from directing them to break into the house and slay David there'.[69] But this does not solve the problem, for presumably 'rescue of their favourite hero' could be accomplished even more easily by daylight.

The supposition of these exegetes is that Saul's action is an aberration: he has become a 'brazen murderer' or a 'mad king'. They assume that the 'correct' moral behaviour is that sanctioned by the modern state, with its emphasis upon due process and 'impartiality'. I propose, however, that this supposition is unlikely and that Saul's action can be explained as culturally expected – not for everyone but certainly for a powerful leader. I noted above that rulers exercise nihilistic violence in order to demonstrate their superiority over others: as the guardians of order they show that they can do as they please. Indeed, it is their ability to do so that reveals they are able to impose order on others. So Gilsenan notes that 'Abboud fulfilled the "character" of the "great *bey*", of the "one who goes to excess" and becomes the supreme figure of order in negating the order through which others imagine existence'.[70] This excess can be wanton – Abboud smashes a man's head against a wall 'for nothing', and

68 Bressan, *Samuele*, 317. My translation.

69 Erdmann, *Samuel*, 251. As an aside, Erdmann also suggests that the fear of harming Michal could have been a motive.

70 Gilsenan, *Lords*, 35.

shoots a boy to test his new rifle – or by ignoring the 'rules' of honour and shame. In the biblical narrative, for example, the latter occurs when Saul is magnanimous to 'the worthless fellows' who initially refused to support him (1 Sam. 10:27; 11:12-13).[71] This was only possible because overwhelming violence was a potential option. While modern Westerners tend to read this as 'the right thing to do', 'the people' were expressing the cultural expectation of vengeance upon those who attempt to dishonour a powerful figure. In fact, the appeal to 'the right thing' is an appeal beyond the person of the king. That God and not the monarch is the ultimate authority is a constant Old Testament theme precisely because it was counter-cultural (see especially Deut. 17:14-20). When visible authority resides in a person and not a bureaucratic state, however, that individual must continually reassert his right to exercise power. Michael Foucault addresses this issue in *Discipline and Punish* by contrasting medieval and modern economies of power with reference to penal styles. He argues nineteenth-century prison discipline aimed to control individuals, objectifying and observing their 'docile bodies'. In monarchical law, however, both process and punishment was simultaneously a restoration of order *and* a reaffirmation of the regal claim *to* order. Thus a (perceived) crime against the monarch was defiance towards sovereignty itself, requiring a kingly response to the personal affront in the form of revenge. Furthermore, '[i]ts aim is not so much to re-establish a balance as to bring into play, at its extreme point, the dissymmetry between the subject who has dared to violate the law and the all-powerful sovereign who displays his strength'.[72] Foucault makes much of the spectacle of torture and public execution:

> punishment is a ceremonial of sovereignty; it uses the ritual marks of the vengeance that it applies to the body of the condemned man; and it deploys before

71 On בני בליעל see J. Burnside, *The Signs of Sin: Seriousness of Offence in Biblical Law* (JSOTSup 364; Sheffield: Sheffield Academic Press, 2002), 55–58; Fokkelman, *Reading*, 151–53. Saul's was also a shrewd political move: ruthless leaders always have uses for 'worthless fellows'.

72 M. Foucault, *Discipline and Punish: The Birth of the Prison* (trans. A. Sheridan; London: Penguin, 1977), 48–49. On the basis of works like Gilsenan's I think it is unnecessary to speculate that the transgression need always be against 'law'. Any violation of the king's will would in principle be adequate, although conflicting demands upon him, e.g. the need for the transgressor's services against the violation of his desires, will mean the king will not always burn everyone who crosses him at the stake.

> the eyes of the spectators an effect of terror as intense as it is discontinuous, irregular and always above its own laws, the physical presence of the sovereign and of his power.[73]

I do not suggest that ancient Israelite monarchy shared the baroque execution practices of medieval Europe. Nevertheless, it is possible to relativize the assumption that Saul's actions in seeking to detain David in his house at night, yet kill him 'in the morning', that is, *publicly*, were somehow strangely inexplicable. The point of David's house arrest was to demonstrate that Saul dominated his enemy: he was *able* to restrict his movements for as long as he pleased. His death, the ultimate inscription of regal power upon the body of a subject, would have proclaimed the same thing. That no reason for Saul's enmity towards David is given in the text is, of course, significant – the books of Samuel are an apology for David's kingship[74] – but besides the point for ancient implied readers with respect to Saul's violence. Gilsenan and Foucault help us see that while Saul's behaviour could have been erratic in that David had *not* done anything wrong, it could still have been, and perceived to have been, typical for kings and other very senior authority figures in a context where the modern state apparatus of violence did not exist.[75] In this case Saul's actions could be considered as acceptable practice for a king.

The final aspect of Saul's inscription of his power upon his subjects is the performative obligations imposed upon his messengers to act violently in specific situations. He commands them to go and watch David's house: they obey. He sends them to fetch David: they go. He resends them to check Michal's story that David is ill: they do so. At each point Saul reasserts his power to order. The messengers' lack of success will be discussed later, but it is not significant with respect to the performative aspect of Saul's inscription of his authority upon the *messengers*. This aids translation of להמתו in v. 15, which many authorities render 'so I can kill him'.[76] A more literal translation

73 Foucault, *Discipline*, 130.

74 K. McCarter, 'The Apology of David', *JBL* 99 (1980): 489–504.

75 Here I do not fall into the evolutionary trap of defining the past with reference to the *absence* of some facet of modern society, simply couch my argument in terms that contrast the suppositions of some exegetes with my contention; cf. Michael Herzfeld, *Anthropology: Theoretical Practice in Culture and Society* (Oxford: Blackwell, 2001), 118.

76 For example, Klein, de Vaux, Smith, NRSV, NIV.

is 'in order to kill him',[77] but this begs the question as to *who* would do so. It is possible to suppose that Saul wished to slaughter David personally, much as Samuel executed Agag (1 Sam. 15:33). There are two reasons, however, for thinking the messengers were to be responsible for the killing. First, the identical verb, with the messengers as the implied subjects, is found in v. 11. Second, the anthropology of violence and in particular the performative aspect of 'corrective' violence suggests it would have only been a failure of the messengers, that is an inability of Saul to oblige them to act as he wished, that could have induced Saul to kill David directly. A more exemplary form of violence, one that inscribed Saul's authority in the messengers themselves, would have been to command them to kill David in Saul's presence. This is what seems to be envisaged in v. 15.

An interesting comparison can be made with Judg. 8:20-22, where Jether's reluctance to kill Zebah and Zalmunna obliges Gideon to kill them himself. In these verses the author portrays Gideon as a powerful figure, accustomed to oblige others to do his bidding, then questions the reality of this authority by having his son prevaricate. This failure of Jether *and* Gideon is excused כי ירא כי עודנו נער. Then, however, the writer has the kings of Midian further question Gideon's authority by challenging him to kill them himself כי כאיש גבורתו – to demonstrate that he, too, is not simply a lad, but a 'real man'. The resolution, Gideon's execution of his adversaries, reconfirms his authority, something reiterated by the Israelites inviting him to rule over them in the next verse. To return to Saul, it is obvious that he also intends that David should be affected by these acts of violence. That he is not, beyond being forced to escape, is thanks to Michal, who does not acquiesce to Saul's attempt to impose regal power, but urges David to flee. At the end of the scene when confronted by Saul she excuses her actions with the words הוא־אמר אלי שלחני למה אמיתך. They constitute Michal's reply to Saul's aggrieved query למה ככה רמיתני ותשלחי את־איבי, and, as readers are aware, are no less a creative invention than the *teraphim* dummy.[78] I highlight

77 Cf. Fokkelman, *Crossing*, 267; D. Alter, *The David Story*: *A Translation with Commentary of 1 and 2 Samuel* (New York: W. W. Norton, 1999), 120. McCarter, *1 Samuel*, 324, has 'so that he can be put to death'.

78 This despite Edelman's opinion that Michal's words introduce the possibility that David *did* take the initiative; the *text* says that Michal was the active agent, and a reading *of the text* must therefore contrast the two statements and assume that the second is a lie. See

two elements of Michal's excuse. First, in the Masoretic tradition Michal underscores the fact that two moral agents are acting and that David's position is distinct from hers: '*he* said, *to me*'.[79] She thus distinguishes and separates herself from her husband by emphasizing the individual identity of them both. Second, Michal claims that David threatened her, forcing her to facilitate his escape, with the words 'Why should I kill you?'. Most commentators reduce the significance of Michal's utterance to a last ditch attempt at saving her own skin. Thus Campbell argues that the 'exchange with Saul is important less for Michal's lame excuse than for Saul's characterization of David as "my enemy" '.[80] In fact, Michal's words carry more freight, and are successful – Saul does not punish Michal[81] – precisely because of what they signify. We have seen that biblical narratives present the killing of enemies as normal. That is what Saul has been attempting to effect throughout the passage. The reason for his actions is disclosed by Saul himself in his accusing question to Michal in the first half of the verse: David is 'my enemy'. By having David threaten to kill her, therefore, Michal takes up Saul's perspective and presents him not only as a violent husband but, much more importantly, as *her enemy*. That is, Michal construes herself as having been construed by David as an opponent, and herself as on Saul's side. For the implied readers, Saul could be understood to interpret the fact David did not kill her but sought to avoid violence not as sage discretion but a sign of weakness. That is why he attempts to press home his advantage in the following verses, pursuing David to Naioth and beyond.

Michal's words suggest that she is in a similar position to Saul. They invite him to believe, despite doubts about her loyalty to him in the matter of the *teraphim*, that she remains a faithful daughter. This excuse often sounds hollow to modern Western readers who assume that Michal's natural loyalty would have been to her husband and that Saul was demanding the unreasonable, namely,

D. Edelman, *King Saul in the Historiography of Judah* (JSOTSup 121; Sheffield: Sheffield University Press, 1991), 148.

79 LXX^B omits 'to me', cf. McCarter, *1 Samuel*, 325; Klein, *1 Samuel*, 193.

80 Campbell, *Samuel*, 205.

81 Although he does inscribe his power in her body by giving her to another husband, Paltiel, cf. 1 Sam. 25:44. This helps explain *David's* claim for her restitution in 2 Sam. 3:13-14, which is also an inscription of royal power in Paltiel himself and, performatively, in Abner and Ishbaal. See also Z. Ben-Barak, 'The Legal Background to the Restoration of Michal to David', in *Studies in the Historical Books* (VTSup 30; ed. J. A. Emerton; Leiden: Brill, 1979), 15–29.

his daughter's prioritization of loyalty to him over that towards her spouse. Fokkelman comments that Saul 'maintained the illusion that the bond of blood would be the decisive factor for her, and not the bond of marriage'. That Saul appears to accept her explanation, however, indicates implied readers could have been expected to view her excuse as entirely plausible. At the same time it means Michal's actions were problematic not just in terms of obedience to the monarch but also in the context of the family. In order to justify such an interpretation I now consider their relationship in more detail.

3. Fathers and Daughters

Michal is introduced to readers in a list of Saul's relations in 1 Sam. 14:49,[82] but her 'voice' is heard for the first time four chapters later when the narrator reports that 'Saul's daughter Michal loved David' (1 Sam. 18:20). Michal's textual relationships are almost entirely limited to those with her father and (future) husband, or their proxies (cf. 1 Sam. 18:20-28; 19:11-17; 25:44; 2 Sam. 3:13-16; 6:16-23). The task of this section is to examine how Michal might have been expected to behave as Saul's daughter and David's wife.

A. MICHAL: SAUL'S DAUGHTER/DAVID'S WIFE

In the books of Samuel being given or taken as a bride is a daughter's most important social role.[83] Perhaps the most obvious difference between modern Western marriages and those described in the Old Testament is that the latter are arranged by fathers or their representatives (see Genesis 26, cf. Deut. 7:2-3). Raphael Patai asserts that '[o]nly the disobedient son, the recalcitrant and rebellious one, would marry a woman of his own choice without the prior consent of his father'.[84] Although love may influence a parent's decision, as it does

82 MT and 4QSam[a]; LXX reads Μελχολ, cf. McCarter, *1 Samuel*, 254.

83 See 1 Sam. 17:25; 18:17, 19, 27; 1 Sam. 25:44. Other roles include being perfumers, cooks, bakers (1 Sam. 8:13), and a prized prisoner of war (1 Sam. 30:3, 6; rescued 1 Sam. 30:19), mourning the death of her father (2 Sam. 1:24), celebrating military victories (2 Sam. 1:20), and of being a mother in a genealogy in order to specify a relationship between men (1 Sam. 14:49-50; 2 Sam. 17:25; 21:8. The identity of a woman is sometimes established in relation to her male relatives, e.g. 2 Sam. 3:3, 7; 21:10-11; and, especially, 'Saul's daughter Michal' 2 Sam. 3:13; 6:16, 20, 23; 11:3).

84 R. Patai, *Family, Love and the Bible* (London: MacGibbon & Kee, 1960), 44, citing

when Michal is the object of Saul's matrimonial strategies,[85] the institution of marriage fundamentally involved the transfer of rights between families. The bridegroom's family paid the 'bride price' to her relations, while the bride and the right to any children of the union went in the opposite direction.[86] A bride price of several years wages may have been distributed among kin, perhaps explaining why Rebekah's brother negotiated eagerly with Eliezer.[87] The bride herself could receive a portion of the bride price as dowry. 'Only the stingy father keeps all the bride price for himself and uses it for his own purposes – "eats it up", as both the modern Arabic and Biblical phrases (Gen. 31:15) have it'.[88] The dowry comprised moveable possessions, possibly including slave girls (Gen. 29:24, 29), and remained the property of wives not the husband.[89]

There are several indications that the preferred Old Testament marriage is endogamous to the kin group (Gen. 11:27-29; 28:9; 29; 36:3; 50:23; Exod. 6:20; Num. 26:59; 1 Chron. 2:4-5, 21). Leaders, however, often marry exogamously, especially from the time of the monarchy.[90] The advantage of endogamous marriage is patrimonial cohesion (cf. Num. 27:1-11; 36:1-12), while exogamous alliances facilitate political cooperation between kin groups,

Gen. 26:34-35 where Esau's taking of Judith and Basemath 'makes life bitter' for Isaac and Rebekah.

85 See also Gen. 29:20; 34:3; Judg. 14:1-3; the further examples of David and Bathsheba, and Adonijah and Abishag proposed by Patai, *Family*, 42, are debatable. That the woman had the right of refusal may be indicated in Gen. 29:51, 57-58.

86 See R. Wakely, 'מֹהַר', *NIDOTTE* 2.859–63. Wright demonstrates that neither the bride nor children were 'property', see C. Wright, *God's People in God's Land: Family, Land and Property in the Old Testament* (Grand Rapids: Eerdmans, 1990), 183–238. Instead, the issue concerns the group with which they will live, and thus the family that will benefit from their presence.

87 So Patai, *Family*, 54; cf. Gen. 24:29, 31–50, 55.

88 Patai, *Family*, 54. For detailed discussion of dowry see R. Westbrook, *Property and the Family in Biblical Law* (JSOTSup 113; Sheffield: Sheffield Academic Press, 1991), 142–64.

89 See J. Paradise, 'A Daughter and her Father's Property at Nuzi', *JCS* 32 (1980): 189–207. Although there is no biblical evidence of the practice, note Patai's contention that the bride price is not normally paid in full, so that about a third remains to be paid upon divorce, a powerful disincentive to overly precipitous action, see Patai, *Family*, 52.

90 See H. Neimann, 'Choosing Brides for the Crown-Prince. Matrimonial Politics in the Davidic Dynasty', *VT* 56 (2006): 226–38. Exogamous, alliance orientated union is characteristic of 'חתן-type' marriages according to A. Guenther, 'A Typology of Israelite Marriage: Kinship, Socio-Economic, and Religious Factors', *JSOT* 29 (2005): 387–407, especially 390–96.

tribes or nations. Thus, affirms Deist, the 'choice of marriage partners depends, among other things, on whether, given the environment and economic system, intra- or inter- group relations are more important for a group's survival'.[91] The books of Samuel contain data about Saul and David's families' marriages only. Sometimes details are scanty, for example, readers know only that Saul's wife Ahinoam was daughter of Ahimaaz (1 Sam. 14:50), and his concubine, Rizpah, daughter of Aiah (2 Sam. 3:7). Other passages provide clues that he married his daughters to notables of strategic towns within Gibeah's sphere of influence. The father of Merab's husband, Adriel, was Barzillai the Gileadite from Rogelim. Barzillai was a local notable, a 'very wealthy man' (2 Sam. 19:32 [33]; Heb: איש גדול הוא מאד). His town was a dependency of Abel Meholah, in Gilead (2 Sam. 17:27; 19:32; 21:8 – 'Gilead' is used as a geographical reference to the (Israelite) Transjordan not simply the Gileadite clan of the tribe of Manasseh), and the marriage was designed to cement an alliance with towns to the east of Gibeah.[92] David's marriages also appear to be contracted with political alliances in mind. Ahinoam, his first wife, is from Jezreel, a town to the south of Hebron.[93] According to the chronology of the text David resided in the Wilderness of Ziph at this time and took advantage of the death of one Nabal, a leading Carmelite farmer, to establish another alliance with his widow, Abigail. It is possible that David's fourth, fifth and sixth wives, Haggith, Abital and Eglah, also hailed from towns to the south of Hebron. The text describes David settling the families of him and his men בערי חברון,[94]

91 F. Deist, *The Material Culture of the Bible: An Introduction* (BS 70; ed. R. P. Carroll; London: Sheffield Academic Press, 2000), 239. He argues that the 'amount of attention devoted to Jacob's marriage and his relation to Laban in the patriarchal narratives holds up *this* kind of marriage [mother's brother's daughter] as the ideal solution for marriages in "Israelite" society', Deist, *Material Culture*, 246. Emphasis original. Cf. R. Oden Jr, 'Jacob as Father, Husband, and Nephew: Kinship Studies and the Patriarchal Narratives', *JBL* 102 (1983): 189–205.

92 2 Sam. 17:27; 19:31-9 record that these territories shifted their loyalties to David. Baruch Halpern concludes that David's war against Israel and the eclipse of Jabesh Gilead, which 'vastly enhanced the status of Abel Meholad', outweighed a marriage alliance with Saul and compensated for the massacre of his grandsons (2 Sam. 21), B. Halpern, *David's Secret Demons: Messiah, Murderer, Traitor, King* (Grand Rapids: Eerdmans, 2001), 301–302.

93 Josh. 15:56. The exact site is unknown, although Kh. Terrama has been accepted by some, e.g. L. Grollenberg, *Atlas de la Bible* (trans. R. Beaupère; Brussels: Elsevier, 1954), 60; *pace* Melvin Hunt, 'Jezreel', *ABD* 3.850.

94 For discussion of the phrase and rejection of possible emendations see A. Anderson,

obviously extant towns. It is likely that David married the daughters of local notables to strengthen ties with nearby population centres, a strategy that may be inferred in 2 Sam. 3:2-6 where David's wives and their sons are listed followed by the editorial note 'These were born to David in Hebron'. Indeed, the strengthening of Judean alliances coheres with the placing of this biographical note directly after the comment about war between the houses of David and Saul, and that David gradually gained the upper hand.[95] David's third wife was the daughter of King Talmai of Geshur, a town to the north of Israel on the Golan Heights. Here, David formed an alliance with another king who shared antipathy towards Saulide regional hegemony.

It appears that residence following marriage was usually patrilocal, although there are biblical examples of residence with the wife's kin (Genesis 29–30; Judg. 8:31; 14; 15:1; 2 Sam. 17:25; Ezra 2:61; 1 Chron. 2:16-17; 34–35). von Rad thought there was a discrepancy between patriarchy and יעזב־איש את־אביו ואת־אמו in Gen. 2:24.[96] Those unwilling to postulate, with von Rad, an original 'matriarchal culture' interpret this text as speaking of interpersonal priorities. Wenham, for example, argues that 'leave'

> was not meant so much literally as emotionally. In traditional societies, the most important social obligation is to one's parents. 'Honor your father and mother' is the first of the commands in the Decalogue regarding obligations to other people. But Genesis is saying that when a man marries, his order of responsibilities changes: though his parent's needs are still important, his wife's needs are even more important. Responsibility for her welfare now must take priority even over care for his parents.[97]

I doubt that this text enjoins such a psychological *volte-face* at marriage. von Rad himself notes that it is aetiological, an explanation for the mutual attraction

2 Samuel (WBC 11; Dallas: Word Books, 1989), 24.

95 On the villages around Hebron as a '80%-endogenous' grouping see G. Lehmann, 'Reconstructing the Social Landscape of Early Israel: Rural Marriage Alliances in the Central Hill Country', *Tel Aviv* 31 (2004): 141–93, especially 164–67.

96 Cf. G. von Rad, *Genesis: A Commentary* (OTL; trans. J. H. Marks; Philadelphia: Westminster Press, 1961), 82–83.

97 G. Wenham, 'Family in the Pentateuch', in *Family in the Bible: Exploring Customs, Culture, and Context* (ed. R. S. Hess and M. D. Carroll R.; Grand Rapids: Baker Academic, 2003), 17–31, quote 18.

of the sexes, and, in my view, there is no reason to suppose that Gen. 2:24 affirms anything other than that the man leaves his parents' house upon marriage in order to live in another dwelling within the compound of the בית אב.

Very few clues are available as to the social role of wives in the books of Samuel, which restrict themselves to references to 'knowing' or lying with a wife (1 Sam. 1:19; 2 Sam. 11:11), specifying the relationship of a woman to a man in order to identify the woman (e.g. 'his daughter-in-law, the wife of Phinehas' or 'Saul's wife was Ahinoam' 1 Sam. 1:4; 4:19; 14:50; 19:11; 25:3, 14, 37; 25:44; 2 Sam. 3:5, 14; 11:3; 12:9-10, 15, 24; 17:19), and being given to a man as a wife (1 Sam. 18:17, 19, 27; 25:39-40, 42; 2 Sam. 11:27). The regulations in Numbers 30, however, seem to have been conceived for a situation in which the status of wife comes into conflict with that of daughter since the teaching assigns the right to determine the ongoing validity of a woman's vow to *either* her father or husband.[98] This guidance is surprising if one simply assumes a husband's authority over his wife, and points to the ongoing influence of a father in the life of a married woman. Indeed, a new residence at marriage does not seem to have been the end of a wife's links with her natal kin, and widows or divorcees usually returned to their original בית אב (Gen. 31:30; 38:11; Lev. 22:13; Judg. 19:2 – Ruth was a *rare* case of a woman cleaving to her husband's family rather than to her own). A view from the husband's perspective is reflected in Samson's objection to telling his wife the secret of his strength. It suggests caginess towards the newcomer, a sign that she was not yet considered a full member of the family (Judg. 14:16).

Marriage also has implications for relationship between a woman's father and her husband, his son-in-law. Early anthropological kinship studies focused upon the classification of relatives through kinship terms. Radcliffe-Brown asserts that the

> general rule is that the inclusion of two relatives in the same terminological category implies that there is some significant similarity in the customary behaviour due to both of them, or in the social relation in which one stands to each of them.[99]

98 For the distinction between legal and personal responsibility, and the view that this text does not signify personal oppression of women see G. Emmerson, 'Women in Ancient Israel', in *The World of Ancient Israel: Sociological, Anthropological and Political Perspectives* (ed. R. E. Clements; Cambridge: CUP, 1991), 371–94, especially 380–82.

99 A. Radcliffe-Brown, 'Introduction', in *African Systems of Kinship and Marriage* (ed.

In biblical Hebrew, a daughter's husband refers to her father with a word that has the same root, חתן, as that which the latter employs to address his son-in-law. In other words, the term is used for male relationships of affinity like those of Saul and David.[100] The most likely explanation for their being classificatory kin is their obligation to protect the same woman, and possibly the duty of the father-in-law to protect the son-in-law.[101] If this is the case, both men failed to fulfil the stereotype. In any case I have argued that social structure is an insufficient guide to individuals' actual practice. It is essential, therefore, to examine marriage and its implications in more detail.

B. MARRIAGE – ANTHROPOLOGICAL PERSPECTIVES

Constructing a universal definition of marriage is problematic. Stone comments that '[e]very society in the world has something we might roughly recognize as "marriage". But beyond this, little can be said of marriage that holds cross-culturally'.[102] Barnard suggests it is usually considered 'the mechanism which provides for the legitimation of children and defines their status in relation to the conjugal family and the wider kin group'.[103] That is, marriage is a rearrangement of social structure, a new relationship between families – not merely individuals – that confers rights and establishes duties.

A. R. Radcliffe-Brown and D. Forde; Oxford: OUP, 1950), 1–85, quote 9.

100 And thus also indicates brother-in-law, certainly in other Semitic languages and possibly Hebrew, cf. E. Kutsch, 'חתן *ḥtn*', *TDOT* 5.270–77; R. H. O'Connell 'חתן', *NIDOTTE* 2.325–28; Deist, *Material Culture*, 246–47.

101 O'Connell outlines the debate about whether the Hebrew has a semantic connection to the Akkadian *hatānu*, 'to protect'. Although Kutsch rejected a link some studies adduce Old Testament examples that appear to support it, e.g. S. Rattray, 'Marriage Rules, Kinship Terms and Family Structure in the Bible', SBLSP 26 (1987): 537–44.

102 L. Stone, *Kinship and Gender: An Introduction* (3rd ed.; Boulder: Westview, 2006), 191.

103 A. Barnard, 'Rules and Prohibitions: The Form and Content of Human Kinship', in *Companion Encyclopedia of Anthropology* (2nd ed.; ed. T. Ingold; London: Routledge, 2002), 783–812, quote 798. Fox notes that the bride price is often conceived as giving the man's family rights over any children, citing a Bantu proverb: 'Cattle beget children', R. Fox, *Kinship and Marriage* (London: Penguin, 1967), 119. See also Radcliffe-Brown: 'Marriage is a social arrangement by which a child is given a legitimate position in the society, determined by parenthood in the social sense', Radcliffe-Brown, 'Introduction', 5. For difficulties of this definition in polyandrous societies see E. Leach, 'Polyandry, Inheritance and the Definition of Marriage', *Man* 55 (1955): 182–86. On the practice of ghost and woman marriage among the Nuer see Evans-Pritchard, *Nuer*, 29–123.

Stone remarks upon the 'basic tension between marriage as a social, political, or economic strategy and marriage as an institution involving individuals in intimate interpersonal relations'.[104] Although the emotive element of the union is not normally neglected, different contexts treat it differently. In particular, it may not be the basis for either the coming together of the couple or of their personal loyalty to each other.[105] In some cases 'love' is perceived as a threat to the family's control of female sexuality. Abu-Lughod argues that among the Egyptian Bedouin the acceptance of love matches 'would be to legitimate as a force in social life passion that does not derive from relationships of kinship'.[106] This does not obliterate pre-matrimonial 'love'. Instead, the emotion is expressed in ways that do not directly challenge the social *status quo*, such as poetry. The fact that marriages are arranged enhances the authority of the family. Indeed, the girl's paternal first cousin can be understood to have the 'right' to marry her should the wider kin group need to arbitrate in the matter. The existence of such 'norms', however, is evidence for a father's discretion to negotiate with the families of other potential partners. It is this freedom of choice that undermines the use of *categories* in alliance theory. According to Trawick, the exclusion of real people draws attention to the fact that it is the *idea* of affinity rather than affinity itself that is at stake: 'the cultural relationship linking this pair of individuals is a matter of the categories they belong to and has nothing to do with the relationship of each . . . to the other'.[107] For this reason she prefers Bourdieu's portrayal of marriage practices as relating to, but not determined by, dominant preferences. He recognizes that although the preferred match for a man might be his Mother's Brother's Daughter (MBD), actual marriage contracts can be very different, while being associated with, or even justified by, this scheme.[108] Trawick notes that in South India there is a distinct preference for known non-kin or close cross-cousins

104 Stone, *Kinship and Gender*, 203.

105 The latter may be a function of social identity, for example, 'husband', see S. Yanagisako, 'Variance in American Kinship: Implications for Cultural Analysis', *AE* 5 (1978): 15–29, especially 21.

106 L. Abu-Lughod, *Veiled Sentiments: Honor and Poetry in a Bedouin Society* (2nd ed.; Berkley: University of California Press, 1999), 210.

107 M. Trawick, *Notes on Love in a Tamil Family* (Berkeley: University of California Press, 1990), 129.

108 P. Bourdieu, *Outline of a Theory of Practice* (Cambridge: CUP, 1977), 58–71.

over distant cross-cousins in actual marriage practice. She claims this 'hints at the way in which the institution of cross-cousin marriage is taken as an affirmation of personal ties, more than just a reproduction of categorical affinities'.[109] Indeed, she continues, if 'you marry a stranger that stranger *becomes* your cross-cousin. The kinship system, unlike caste, bends to accommodate the heart's desire, or seems so to bend, promises the hope of joy, or seems so to promise'.[110]

The father's strategies are illuminated by Martha Roth's study of age at marriage in ancient societies. She adduces three models. In the Western model marriage is late, there is a narrow age difference, a low proportion of people marrying ever, and a low proportion of multi-generational households. Eastern marriage practices entail early unions, narrow age difference, a high proportion of people marrying ever, and a high proportion of multi-generational households. In the Mediterranean, however, marriage is late for men but early for women, with a correspondingly wide age difference, a high proportion of people marry, and there is a high proportion of multi-generational households. Roth concludes that the typical model of marriage in Neo-Assyria and Neo-Babylonia approximated to that of 'Mediterranean marriage' in which husbands married aged 26–32 and new wives were aged 14–20. According to this model a man marries at about the same time as he receives his patrimony. Roth remarks:

> When the new husband begins his economic independence and sets up his own household he will have the economic and social advantages of his association with his father-in-law. The father-in-law in turn can utilize his son-in-law in the economic arena in ways in which his own, younger, sons cannot be utilized.[111]

109 Trawick, *Notes on Love*, 151.

110 Trawick, *Notes on Love*, 151. Emphasis original. She discusses cross-cousin marriage as a romantic ideal.

111 See M. Roth, 'Age at Marriage and the Household: A Study of Neo-Babylonian and Neo-Assyrian Forms', *CSSH* 29 (1987): 715–47, quote 747. The wife, aged mid-teens, will have a mother aged 40 and father about 50; the husband, aged late 20s, will have mother aged 50 and father either in his 60s or deceased. Roth continues: 'Many wives will outlive their husbands, and society will have a high number of widows, relatively young and economically independent. As a widow, such a woman might live in her son's house along with his young bride, just as her own mother-in-law had done'.

The father's 'use' of his daughter for his chosen purposes can result in a certain conditionality in their relationship. I will discuss the woman's perspective shortly, but regarding the father Campbell's comments are instructive of an extreme possibility: 'If the girl's reputation for virtue remains unblemished, she receives his favour; if it does not, she may suffer the ultimate sanction of death at the hands of her own father'.[112]

Although many matches may conform to the parallel or cross-cousin ideal (where this exists), this is less likely to hold for higher-ranking families. Bourdieu states:

> In accordance with the general law of exchanges, the higher a group is placed in the social hierarchy, and hence the richer it is in official relationships, the greater the proportion of its work of reproduction that is devoted to reproducing such relationships. It follows that the poor, who have little to spend on solemnities, tend to settle for the ordinary marriages that practical kinship provides for them, whereas the rich, that is, those richest in kinsmen, expect more from – and sacrifice more to – all the more or less institutionalized strategies aimed at maintaining social capital, the most important of which is undoubtedly the extra-ordinary marriage with prestigious 'strangers'.[113]

The prestige of marriage with a stranger is a function of the difficulty of its arrangement: assessing distant families over a long period is costly, involving 'payment' of intermediaries, for example, of a priest by gifts at major religious feasts, and the expenditure of symbolic capital in the form of marshalling notable kinsmen of affines as guarantors. Bourdieu claims that prestige marriages are high-risk adventures aimed at turning strangers into relatives for political ends. Because of this the dowry is transformed from a means of passing on the daughter's share of the family's wealth into a statement of honour.[114] There is a similar inflation of the bride price. Abu-Lughod mentions the case of Fāyga

112 Campbell, *Honour, Family, and Patronage*, 172.

113 P. Bourdieu, *The Logic of Practice* (trans. R. Nice; Stanford: Stanford University Press, 1990), 180.

114 The dowry, as an indication of the bride's value to her natal family, may be means of acquiring honour – even a lower status son-in-law can enhance his father-in-law's status by enlisting his family as clients, see A. Schlegel and R. Eloul, 'Marriage Transactions: Labor, Property, Status', *AA* 90 (1988): 291–309, especially 301.

and Rashīd: because both were from 'high-status families that were unrelated, the negotiations had been long and the bride price was high. There was a big wedding'.[115]

Residence patterns after marriage can take a number of forms.[116] When residence is patrilocal and descent patrilineal there is a convergence of authority structures. However, even in this situation a new wife inevitably disturbs established familial practices, for marriage gives younger men a domain of their own. Indeed, incoming wives may be catalyst for younger brothers to split from the father's or elder brother's household. In such cases the wife is then more independent, nearer the top of the familial hierarchy. Abu-Lughod records wedding songs that recognize these conflicting bonds.

> When he shuts the door behind him
> he forgets the father who raised him.
>
> He reached your arms stretched on the pillow
> forgot his father, and then his grandfather.[117]

Abu-Lughod concludes that the 'challenge to the hierarchical relationship between providers and dependents, or elders and juniors, is at the heart of Bedouin attitudes about sexuality'.[118] The need to secure descendents conflicts with the desire to maintain control, one reason why senior men arrange but refrain from celebrating young men's weddings. This perception, however, is not the only point of view. Many ethnographies of Mediterranean societies note that a wife is only gradually accepted into her husband's family. Campbell argues that conjugal solidarity on the part of the husband is subordinate to sibling solidarity until the birth of the first child. Nadia Abu-Zahra thinks progression is even more protracted: the 'social incorporation of a married woman into her husband's *dār* is a very slow process . . . only completed when the wife has grown-up sons'.[119] Kathey-Lee Galvin's theoretical work shows why this

115 Abu-Lughod, *Veiled Sentiments*, 216; cf. Bourdieu, *Logic*, 183–84.
116 For a typology see Barnard, 'Human Kinship', 795.
117 Abu-Lughod, *Veiled Sentiments*, 147.
118 Abu-Lughod, *Veiled Sentiments*, 147.
119 Nadia Abu-Zahra, 'Family and Kinship in a Tunisian Peasant Community', in *Mediterranean Family Structures* (ed. J. G. Peristiany; Cambridge: CUP, 1976), 157–71, quote 165.

is so. While Schneider argued that the orders of law and nature were uniquely American and thus not cross-culturally valid, Galvin enlarges the categories. On the basis of case studies from places as diverse as Ecuador, Nepal and Malaysia she contends that there are two orders: of sharing and ratification. She further distinguishes between tangible and intangible sharing, and explicit and implicit ratification.[120] Figure 4 shows how the orders are related.[121]

Employing these insights to elucidate the ethnographic data one can see that a new wife is incorporated into her husband's family by explicit ratification (the formal or legal aspect of marriage) and implicit ratification over time. Yet, full assimilation also depends upon sharing, for example, food or pollution, and progeny. Until this combination of orders is effected husbands are likely to champion their mothers in preference to spouses, since brides remain outsiders, 'worms within the apple of a patrilocal domestic group'.[122]

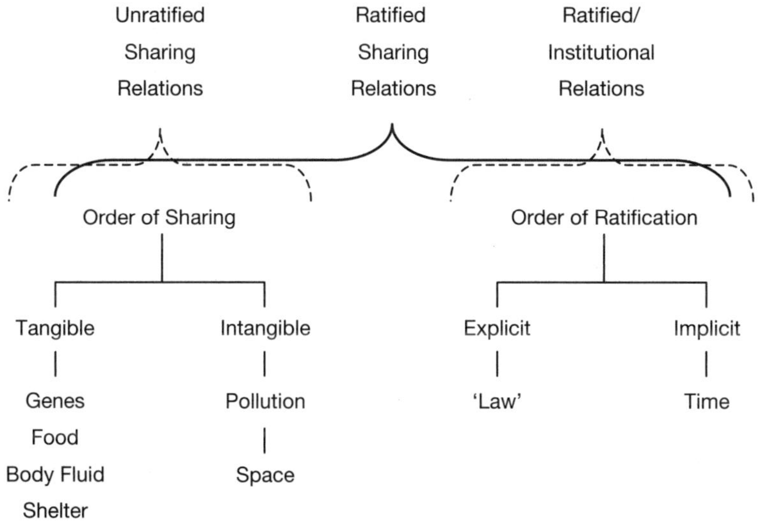

Figure 4 A Cross-Cultural Model of Relatedness

120 Ratification 'refers to processes that legitimize relationships through social convention (which might be codified in written language and law) rather than the sharing of substances', K. Galvin, 'Schneider Revisited: Sharing and Ratification in the Construction of Kinship', in *New Directions in Anthropological Kinship* (ed. L. Stone; Lanham: Rowman & Littlefield, 2001), 109–24, quote 121.

121 From Galvin, 'Schneider Revisited', 119.

122 Abu-Lughod, *Veiled Sentiments*, 148, quoting J. Collier, 'Women in Politics', in *Women, Culture, and Society* (ed. M. Z. Rosaldo and L. Lamphere; Stanford: Stanford University Press, 1974), 89–96, quote 92.

The gradual incorporation of a wife into their husband's family also affects the woman's view of to whom she should naturally be loyal. Rudolph Bell argues that although modern people start with an ancient paterfamilias and work down, this is the opposite to the perception of the family held by the Italian peasants that he studied. They started with ego and conceived of the family as four spirals emanating towards parents, siblings, spouse and children.[123] Since the woman is an independent ego it is important to consider where her loyalties might lie. Several ethnographies record contingency in the relationship between father and daughter. The attitude of a daughter can depend upon her assessment of her father's choice of husband. Is he, for example, a good man from an honourable family? Campbell comments upon one woman who disparaged her father's selection:

> The daughter of a rich and powerful family, forced against her will to marry her second cousin, swore to her father as she left her home that she would never set foot in it again. Such a case of complete breach of trust and mutual esteem between father and daughter is rare; but there are also women who harbour resentment against their fathers because, as they allege, they were given to indifferent husbands in order to avoid the payment of a substantial dowry.[124]

Lloyd and Margaret Fallers comment that since the responsibility for finding a husband lies with others, the woman does not accept full responsibility for the outcome of her marriage.[125] 'She has a sense of fate about it – and

123 R. Bell, *Fate and Honor, Family and Village: Demographic and Cultural Change in Rural Italy since 1800* (Chicago: University of Chicago Press, 1979), 76. This is a slightly different, although related, point to that which Caroline Brettell argues: 'once male and female roles are given equal analytical focus, the multidimensional meanings of kinship, family, and descent are revealed', C. Brettell, 'Not That Lineage Stuff: Teaching Kinship into the Twenty-First Century', in *New Directions in Anthropological Kinship* (Lanham: Rowman & Littlefield, 2001), 48–70, quote 59. Not that doing so is without its problems, cf. Karen Field on Ivan Illich's thesis regarding the differences between ancient and modern family roles: 'while it is true that women in preindustrial societies enjoyed forms of power and prestige denied them in the modern West, they also encountered some very real restrictions, to which Illich, in his enthusiasm for a *temps perdu*, seems blind', K. Field, 'Review of Ivan Illich's *Gender*', *JMF* 45 (1983): 710.

124 Campbell, *Honour, Family and Patronage*, 172.

125 Although it is often the father's obligation to find a spouse for his daughters, to *whom* this is an obligation is not necessarily obvious. It could be to his daughter, the wider family,

resignation'.[126] Instead, she identifies with her patrikin, especially her brothers. The expectation that a woman will take this view can be shared by her husband's family. Abu-Lughod comments that a

> woman retains her tribal affiliation throughout her life and should side with her own kin in their disputes with her husband's kin; I heard many stories of women who left for their natal homes, abandoning children, under such conditions. In her marital camp people refer to her by her tribal affiliation, and she may refer to herself as an outsider even after twenty years of marriage.[127]

The identification of the woman with her patrikin provides her with some backing during the years of integration, and protection against abuse by her husband's family. 'When mistreated or wronged, she argues that she need not put up with such treatment because "behind me are men" '.[128] On the other hand the woman remains responsible to her agnates for her behaviour. In particular, 'they, and not her husband, kill her if she commits adultery, in order to preserve *their* honour'.[129] The ambivalence of the husband–wife relationship contrasts with the close ties between brother and sister highlighted in many studies. Women, peripheral to their husband's father's household, depend upon brothers for assistance. Peristiany observes that this 'permits the brother of a marginally–integrated woman to meddle in her affairs. A man wishing to be in full control of his home should be careful to choose a wife whose father and/or brother are not powerful and overbearing enough to interfere in its administration'.[130]

the descent line, or even himself, cf. the Kabyle proverb 'He who has a daughter and does not marry her off must bear the shame of it', Bourdieu, *Logic*, 177.

126 L. Fallers and M. Fallers, 'Sex Roles in Edremit', in *Mediterranean Family Structures* (CSSA 13; ed. J. G. Peristiany; Cambridge: CUP, 1976), 243–60, quote 253.

127 Abu-Lughod, *Veiled Sentiments*, 54.

128 Abu-Lughod, *Veiled Sentiments*, 54. Note also the tale of a woman who justified her threat to leave her husband after the latter had slurred her father with the appeal: 'Would you stay if anyone said that about your father?', Abu-Lughod, *Veiled Sentiments*, 65.

129 L. Holy, *Kinship, Honour and Solidarity: Cousin marriage in the Middle East* (Manchester: Manchester University Press, 1989), 123. My emphasis. Holy argues that the practice of bride capture also symbolizes a woman's continuing attachment to her natal relations.

130 J. Peristiany, 'Introduction', in *Mediterranean Family Structures* (CSSA 13; ed. J. G. Peristiany; Cambridge: CUP, 1976), 1–23, quote 9.

This discussion leads us to conclude, with Michael Peletz, that '[t]otal assimilation of women into their husband's kin groups (like the notion of their complete severance from natal kin) is . . . a Western fiction informed by market metaphors and economistic thinking'.[131] It also explains why the preferred partner for a man in many Middle Eastern societies is his Father's Brother's Daughter (FBD), because there is a coincidence of interests. As one of Abu-Lughod's informants declares, 'a father's brother's daughter cares about you and your things because they are hers'.[132] And, from woman's perspective, a common patrimony means a FBD has the right to support from the patriline independent of her ability to bear children. An example of emotional aspect of the parallel-cousin marriage ideal may be found in 2 Chron. 11:20-21, where one reads that 'Rehoboam loved Maacha the daughter of Absalom above all his wives and concubines' – a total of 78 women![133] It is worth repeating that the

> bond between generations, the bond between siblings, and the bond between spouses, are likely to come in conflict with each other in any kin-based society . . . The trick is to have as many bonds as possible and keep them all in harmony with each other, not let any of them break.[134]

Did Michal (and for that matter Saul and David) manage to achieve this? It is time for a conversation between biblical text and ethnographic data.

131 M. Peletz, 'Kinship Studies in Late Twentieth-Century Anthropology', *ARA* 24 (1995): 343–72, quote 356–57.

132 Abu-Lughod, *Veiled Sentiments*, 58, quoting an informant. For the argument that FBD is not primarily a means of protecting family property interests but a statement of family solidarity see Holy, *Kinship*, especially ch. 5 'Preference for FBD marriage in context'.

133 Further examples of romance are listed in V. Matthews and D. Benjamin (eds.), *Social World of Ancient Israel 1250–587 BCE* (Peabody: Hendrickson, 1993), 13; *pace* Blenkinsopp, who opines that a whole battery of factors 'discouraged emotional warmth and intimacy', J. Blenkinsopp, 'The Family in First Temple Israel', in *Families in Ancient Israel* (ed. L. G. Perdue *et al.*; Louisville: Westminster John Knox, 1997), 48–103, quote 77. On romantic emotion in the Old Testament and its relationship to other values see L. Lawrence, *Reading with Anthropology: Exhibiting Aspects of New Testament Religion* (Carlisle: Paternoster, 2005), 131–51; for comparison with other ANE literature see Hennie Marsman, *Women in Ugarit and Israel: Their Social and Religious Position in the Context of the Ancient Near East* (OS 44; Leiden: Brill, 2003), 73–84.

134 Trawick, *Notes on Love*, 157.

C. UNDERSTANDING MICHAL'S EXCUSE

The context for Michal's excuse in 1 Sam. 19:17 is Saul's arrangement of her marriage to David. This tale commences when, having promised his first daughter, Merab, to the vanquisher of Goliath, Saul instead gives her to Adriel.[135] David Clines summarizes a number of interpretations of 1 Sam. 18:17-27, concluding that virtually all commentators fail to produce a coherent reading *of the text* without making unwarranted suppositions.[136] A satisfactory account must explain *all* the following points *and* their interrelations:

(i) Saul's offer of Merab to David (v. 17)
(ii) David's protestation of his 'unworthiness' to be Saul's son-in-law (v. 18)
(iii) Saul's decision to give Merab to Adriel (v. 19)
(iv) Saul's subsequent decision to offer Michal to David (v. 21)
(v) Why Michal's love for David pleased Saul (v. 20)
(vi) The persuasion required to convince David to accept Michal (vv. 22-26)
(vii) The nature of the bride price (vv. 25, 27)
(viii) David's pleasure at becoming Saul's son-in-law (v. 26)
(ix) Saul's decision to give Michal to David despite not having given Merab (v. 27)

The verses immediately preceding the pericope portray Saul being offended by the praise heaped upon David by the people, and his attempts against David's life, both personally and by placing him in the line of fire as a battle commander. The end of v. 17 makes it clear that Saul's offer of Merab is a continuation of this quest. He is motivated by the desire to encourage David to take military risks with the hope that he fall in battle. David's answer is entirely conventional in that he came from a perfectly suitable family. Although Saul used the prospect of marriage to his daughters as a trap, it would have been entirely natural for Saul to seek an alliance with someone like 'Jesse the

135 The text of 1 Sam. 18:17-19 is found in MT and LXX^{AL} but not LXX^{B}, leading some commentators to suppose the account has been interpolated with 'a minimum of redactional harmonization', see McCarter, *1 Samuel*, 306–9, quote 308. I follow MT because, *pace* McCarter, there are both lexical and thematic links between these verses and the ongoing narrative.

136 See Clines, 'Michal Observed', 27–32.

Bethlehemite'. To judge from the size of his family Jesse was the head of a significant house in a potentially strategic border region and, further, one that had already provided Saul with military assistance (1 Sam. 17:13). Indeed, Saul probably follows the same strategy in marrying Michal to Paltiel of Gallim (1 Sam. 25:44).[137] Nevertheless, within this narrative the expression 'Who am I and who are my kinfolk?' is a form of refusal.[138] It is possible that David is negotiating. Fokkelman suggests he enquires after advantages for his family, for example, exemption from taxes, if he agreed to become Saul's son-in-law (cf. 1 Sam. 17:25).[139] If so, the reason why David did not marry Merab was because *Saul* decided not to give her to David rather than because of the latter's refusal. This interpretation is defended by Clines, who argues, correctly, that Saul *never* intended to marry Merab to David – he planned that he should die before the time came.[140] However, David's words *do* constitute a refusal, whether as the first stage in a process of negotiation cut off by Saul's decision, or not, is impossible to say. That David repudiates Saul's offer in this way explains why he has to be persuaded to accept Michal's hand in marriage in v. 25 when he makes a similar protestation. The NRSV translates v. 19, 'But at the time when Saul's daughter Merab should have been given to David, she was given to Adriel the Meholathite as a wife'. Taking David's words as a conventional expression of refusal means this rendering is problematic. The difficulty with the adversative is that Saul's action is cast adrift from its narrative context. It is preferable to translate ויהי, 'and so', thus McCarter: 'So at the time to give'.[141] This temporal reference presumably refers to the promise of his daughter's hand in marriage to the slayer of Goliath. Avoiding the adversative also answers the question raised by Clines concerning why

137 1 Sam. 25:44 reads Palti for Paltiel. Gallim: MT; LXX^{B} reads Ρομμα, which McCarter explains as a corruption of the Greek majuscules; LXX^{L} and the Old Latin read 'Goliath', a gloss dismissed by McCarter with an exclamation mark, McCarter, *1 Samuel*, 369. The location of Gallim is unknown, although probably north of Jerusalem, possibly 1km west of Anatoth, see Isa. 10:30; D. Christenson, 'The March of Conquest in Isaiah X 27c-34', *VT* 26 (1976): 385–99; J. Hamilton, 'Gallim', *ABD* 2.901.

138 MT חַיָּי, 'my life', a gloss for the original חַיִּי, 'my kinsfolk', subsequently explicated by the addition of משפחת אבי, cf. Driver, *Notes*, 153; McCarter, *1 Samuel*, 303; *pace* Smith, *Samuel*, 172, who follows LXX^{L} in omitting the explanation and reads ומי חי אבי. See also G. Coats, 'Self-Abasement and Insult Formulas', *JBL* 89 (1970): 14–26.

139 See Fokkelman, *Crossing*, 232.

140 See Clines, 'Michal Observed', 30.

141 McCarter, *1 Samuel*, 301; cf. MNK 333.

Saul had to marry Merab to Adriel for, he supposes, David could have been sent on missions against the Philistines even as the king's son-in-law.[142] My interpretation, however, does not create this problem because it recognizes that Merab had to be married to *someone*; and since David refused Saul's offer, or, at least, was taken to have refused it, another marriage had to be arranged.

Verse 21 states Saul wanted to offer Michal in marriage for the same reason he offered Merab, to entrap David. This time, however, the opportunity Saul sees to use his daughter as bait arises because 'Michal loved David'. Fokkelman attends to the 'theological' importance of her love, claiming that its repeated mention 'occurs almost as a foreign body or disturbance between the lines concerning Saul's misery. This repetition makes her love something worth mentioning as an independent entity'.[143] I concur that mention of Michal's love only makes sense if it *is* a 'foreign body', a factor which explains the otherwise inexplicable. The ethnographic data presented above shows why this could be so. First, love is not normally the basis for marriage. Indeed, taking it into account, as Saul does, could be interpreted as a risky move that potentially damages kin relations and undermines social hierarchy. Second, a family with a stock of symbolic capital would be expected to arrange prestige marriages. It is instructive to consider the effect upon daughters of this sort of union. Bernard Batto's study shows that becoming the wife of an ancient Near Eastern king for diplomatic purposes could be risky. He describes how one Inib-šarri bewails her condition as a 'political' wife. Treatment of another's daughter married to cement a treaty was a proxy for the current status of the

142 See Clines, 'Michal Observed', 27.

143 Fokkelman, *Crossing*, 243. There is a debate about whether political or romantic love is in view in 1 Samuel, see P. Ackroyd, 'The Verb Love – *'āhēb* in the David-Jonathan Narratives – A Footnote', *VT* 25 (1975): 213–14; Ada Taggar-Cohen, 'Political Loyalty in the Biblical Account of 1 Samuel XX-XXII in the Light of Hittite Texts', *VT* 55 (2005): 251–68; J. A. Thompson, 'The Significance of the Verb *Love* in the David-Jonathan Narratives in Samuel', *VT* 24 (1974): 334–38; idem, 'Israel's Lovers', *VT* 27 (1977): 475–81. I see no reason why both aspects should not be present, even though the political seems to dominate, see S. Ackerman, 'The Personal is Political: Covenantal and Affectionate Love (*'āhēb*, *'ahăbâ*) in the Hebrew Bible', *VT* 52 (2002): 437–58; P. J. J. S. Els, 'אהב', *NIDOTTE* 1.277–99. The moral issue lies in the fact that love implies partiality, which can lead to 'moral danger', see D. Cocking and J. Kennett, 'Friendship and Moral Danger', *JP* 97 (2000): 278–96. My argument for the priority of the good means, *pace* Cocking and Kennett, that this risk should not be framed in terms of a conflict between abstract principle and personal loyalty, but between the moral goods of loyalty to different people.

alliance, and Inib-šarri complains that she is not properly respected because her husband wishes to assert his political independence.[144] Sarah Melville states that despite 'lively communication via messengers and embassies, once a woman married a foreign king, she was not able to remain in close contact with her original family'.[145] It is probable, therefore, that royal daughters were wary of consenting to matrimony with foreigners.[146] This may explain the attraction of someone in a position like David's. Cyrus Gordon discusses the Egyptian romance of Sinuhe, concluding it was

> not uncommon to welcome desirable foreigners (like Sinhue) as sons-in-law. But in such cases, the husband joined the bride's family; and, if he eventually returned to his homeland, he could not force his wife to leave her father's domain. Such a marriage gave the groom practical opportunities, but socially the wife was protected; for she, her children and property could not be removed.[147]

Removed, that is, without her family's consent: Sinhue eventually turns his property over to his sons and leaves. In this connection it is probably significant that following their marriage David and Michal lived near *her* father's house (1 Sam. 19:11). It is possible to observe that David was a potentially sound choice of husband both for a 'princess' like Michal and a father-in-law like Saul, despite the fact the latter did not envisage David being able to survive the ordeal of providing 100 Philistine foreskins. Thus regardless of what prompted her love – something about which the text is profoundly silent[148] – Saul could easily have surmised that Michal would be prepared to be married to David: *she*, at least, would not create an insurmountable hurdle to his stratagem.

144 See B. Batto, *Studies on Women at Mari* (Baltimore: John Hopkins University Press, 1974), 37–40, 42. Further discussion of Zimri-Lim's daughters can be found in D. Bodi, *The Michal Affair: From Zimri-Lim to the Rabbis* (Sheffield: Sheffield Phoenix Press, 2005), 64–87.

145 S. Melville, 'Royal Women and the Exercise of Power in the Ancient Near East', in *A Companion to the Ancient Near East* (ed. D. C. Snell; Oxford: Blackwell, 2005), 219–28, quote 225.

146 On the necessity of consent see Marsman, *Women in Ugarit and Israel*, 52–53, 70–72.

147 C. Gordon, 'The Marriage and Death of Sinuhe', in *Love and Death in the Ancient Near East: Essays in Honor of Marvin H. Pope* (ed. J. H. Marks and R. M. Good; Guilford: Four Quarters, 1987), 43–44, quote 44.

148 Cf. Clines, 'Michal Observed', 32–37.

Saul's negotiations with David once again produce a conventional excuse, but this time he is not dissuaded. Using intermediaries, which, as we have seen, is standard practice in the arrangement of prestige marriages, Saul rejoins that 100 Philistine foreskins will suffice as bride price, with the intention that David be killed in the process of collecting them. David's opinion of the matter is a little less clear. The fact that Michal loved David was told to Saul וישר הדבר בעינו, is mirrored by the phrase וישר הדבר בעיני דוד (1 Sam. 17:20, 26).[149] The contrast is the motivation for the men's satisfaction: Saul was pleased he had thought of a way of disposing of David, David of becoming the king's son-in-law.

Many scholars note that David's enthusiasm has nothing to do with Michal. While concern with marriage in the books of Samuel is not limited to political alliances it is certainly connected to monarchical legitimacy. Matitiahu Tsevat's study of non-descendents succeeding to thrones in Ugarit and Israel leads him to conclude that 'the temporal, protological, and quasi-legal order is: marriage – kingship . . . and not kingship – marriage, which would merely be a special case of inheritance'.[150] This may lie behind Ishbaal's challenge to Abner (2 Sam. 3:7), Nathan's affirmation that David had received his master's wives (2 Sam. 12:8; Tsevat understands 'and *thus* gave you the house of Israel and Judah', but whether David did marry any of Saul's wives is debated), Ahithophel's advice to Absalom (2 Sam. 16:21),[151] and Adonijah's request for Abishag (1 Kgs 2:13-25). Thus, without undermining the role of Jonathan in the 'transfer' of kingship to David, and without necessarily concluding that Michal was merely instrumental to David's political ambitions, the fact that

149 This expression is idiomatic, see H. Olivier, 'ישׁר', *NIDOTTE* 2.563–8, especially 565; *pace* Bodi, *Michal Affair*, 16–22.

150 M. Tsevat, 'Marriage and Monarchical Legitimacy in Ugarit and Israel', *JSS* 3 (1958): 237–43, quote 242.

151 Ahithophel advises Absalom to enter his father's concubines 'and all Israel will hear כי־נבאשת את־אביך'. Since, according to Tsevat, all other cases of the verb באש in Samuel (1 Sam. 13:4; 27:12; 2 Sam. 10:6) epitomize political challenge, he translates this that 'you have challenged your father', concluding that reading 'נבאשת as what it is, a term in the field of government and politics, we recognize that it is precisely the public appropriation by Absalom of part of David's harem that is the decisive act in the plot and the fanfare to rally and reassure his followers', see Tsevat, 'Monarchical Legitimacy', 242–3 for discussion and comparison with ancient sources. There are exceptions to the conferment of kingship through marriage, e.g. Gen. 36:31-9.

they were married gives David's claim to the Northern throne a validity it would otherwise have lacked.

Nevertheless, the *text* links David's pleasure to the prospect of avenging the king's enemies; any other interpretation is a secondary elaboration beyond the text. And while Saul failed to fulfil his obligations by the appointed time (18:19), David completes his mission to deliver the bloody tokens before time (1 Sam. 18:26-27). That 200 was twice Saul's demand demonstrates David's valour – or that of his friends.[152] The theological point is clear: while Saul intended that David be harmed, actually he is doubly successful because, as the next verse makes explicit, 'the LORD was with David' (1 Sam. 18:28).

This reading of Saul's marrying of Michal to David accounts for all the textual data enumerated above and, importantly, enables similar elements to be interpreted in the same way. Throughout 1 Samuel 18, though, Michal is mute. It is Saul's voice that is heard as he uses the opportunities afforded by his daughters' marriages to pursue his own ends. Saul's agency, however, receives a sharp riposte from the narrator in v. 28, when he records that 'the LORD was with David, and that Saul's daughter Michal loved him'.[153] What this means for the relationship between father and daughter becomes clear in 1 Samuel 19.

The discussion of anthropological evidence concerning a daughter's loyalty leads one to suppose that she would normally be loyal to her father and his house for many years after her marriage. Many commentators, assuming modern Western notions of family dynamics, fail to perceive that Michal's

152 On the number in 1 Sam. 18:27 MT reads 200; LXX 100. Although NRSV; McCarter, *1 Samuel*, 316 follow LXX the harder reading is to be preferred, so Fokkelman, *Crossing*, 242 (who discusses a number of duplications in the passage); H. W. Hertzberg, *I & II Samuel* (OTL; London: SCM, 1964), 162. I disagree with Driver that וימלאום supports reading 100 foreskins since the author could simply be emphasizing the fact that a full set of 200 was presented to Saul and not that David '*completed* the tale of them [i.e. the 100 in verse 25] to the king', Driver, *Notes*, 154; cf. NRSV 'were given in full number'.

153 NRSV, following MT; LXX^{B} reads καὶ πᾶς Ισραηλ ἠγάπα αὐτόν; LXX^{L} reads that both Michal and all Israel love David, see B. Grillet and M. Lestienne, *Premier Livre des Règnes* (Bd'A 9.1; Paris: Les Éditions du Cerf, 1997), 316; McCarter, *1 Samuel*, 321. Driver posits that LXX 'states the *ground* for Saul's greater dread', while the MT merely repeats v. 20, Driver, *Notes*, 155. Emphasis original. Similarly, Clines suggests that it is 'virtually certain' ומיכל בת־שאול is an orthographical error for וכי כל־ישראל because otherwise the emphatic 'saw and knew' is redundant, since Saul already knew Michal loved David, D. Clines, 'X, X *BEN* Y, *BEN* Y: Personal Names in Hebrew Narrative Style', *VT* 22 (1972): 266–87, especially 270. However, the MT yields exegetical results unavailable to those who emend according to LXX^{B}, so also Fokkelman, *Crossing*, 243.

fidelity to her husband would be very unlikely in any clash of obligations. Even Philbeck's assertion that 'Michal's support of her husband is not to be taken for granted. Marriages in important families were often arranged for political purposes in ancient Israel, and intrigue was commonplace', only moves part of the way towards my interpretation.[154] I propose that implied readers would assume that normal practice for a woman like Michal faced with the dilemma of facilitating her husband's escape or siding with his father-in-law would be to opt for her father. Any other course of action would leave her, already isolated in her husband's household, without support from her natal kin. Additional intra-textual evidence for my interpretation includes Ps. 45:10 [11]. Pedersen asserts that it 'is only at a royal wedding that it can be said to a bride: Forget also thine own people and thy father's house',[155] but it is much better to take the phrase as an exhortation directed towards the bride *precisely because* the father's house was where her loyalties would have laid. The continuing importance of the *mother's* בית אב is also discernable in 2 Sam. 14:9 (cf. Judg. 9:1). Bendor suggests that the 'reason for the wording of the exoneration is that the *beit 'ab* into which she married will no longer exist, and she therefore swears by the *beit 'ab* from which she came',[156] but it is preferable to suppose that the woman's protestation is evidence for her continued loyalty was to *her* father's house: that is what gives her words their force.

At this point one could ask whether Michal is in fact an agent in her own right – *can* she act on her own account?; *must* she adhere to the cultural schema? Cheryl Exum opines that Michal is always 'acted upon' and that the text never allows her an agency of her own. She is 'hemmed in' by the narrative because 'the scenes where she is a subject are surrounded by scenes in which she is "acted upon"'.[157] Exum supposes that it is her gender that inhibits her choosing between conflicting loyalties. In Bakhtinian terms she has no voice. But, regardless of other scenes, this view contradicts the emphasis

154 B. Philbeck, '1–2 Samuel', in *1 Samuel-Nehemiah* (BBC 3; ed. C. J. Allen; Nashville: Broadman Press, 1970), 13–145, quote 60.

155 Pedersen, *Israel*, I–II.68.

156 S. Bendor, *The Social Structure in Ancient Israel: The Institution of the Family (*Beit 'ab*) from the Settlement to the End of the Monarchy* (JBS 7; Jerusalem: Simor, 1996), 79.

157 J. C. Exum, *Tragedy and Biblical Narrative: Arrows of the Almighty* (Cambridge: CUP, 1992), 84. See also E. Fuchs, *Sexual Politics in the Biblical Narrative: Reading the Hebrew Bible as a Woman* (JSOTSup 310; Sheffield: Sheffield University Press, 2000), 140.

upon Michal's agency in 1 Sam. 19:11-17. Rather than hemming Michal in by writing out her agency it is essential to investigate the meaning of her actions.

In the final form of the narrative the conjunction of spear throwing, and David's evasion, flight and escape is deliberate. The slightly breathless nature of the narrative may reflect David's own state as he arrives home with Saul's henchmen hot on his heels. The house surrounded, v. 11b states that 'David's wife Michal told him'. This simple introductory phrase contains two pieces of information. First, Michal is described as David's wife. David Clines analyses the use of biblical name styles, concluding that some forms have particular significance for narrative meaning. With respect to this text, however, I cannot agree with Clines that styling Michal 'David's wife' indicates to readers that she is behaving as they would have expected her to do *as* his wife.[158] Quite the contrary, the author titles her thus because Michal's warning to David is startling: as *David's wife* she would *not* be expected to warn him of *Saul's* actions. Readers are now learning what 'loving David' means, and why Saul had good grounds for being afraid. Second, 'Michal told David'. 'Telling', נגד, is important for the development of the plot in ch. 19 (see vv. 2, 3, 7, 11, 18, 19, 21). When Saul speaks with his son about killing David, Jonathan tells, נגד, David to be on his guard. The same verb is used when he promises to obtain further details of Saul's intentions and, having negotiated David's return to court, when Jonathan tells him of Saul's decision. In the context of our passage, therefore, 'telling' has echoes of the conflict between David and Saul. How will Michal respond?

In complete contrast to those who see a hemming in of Michal, the author repeatedly highlights Michal's agency in the next verses. Her actions are given prominence by her being the subject of a string of verbs: Michal tells, lets down, takes, lays, puts and covers. Patently, the writer employs literary repetition to underscore Michal's status as an acting subject. Given the context I suggest her actions are not trivial but momentous; and her initiative is

158 Cf. Clines, 'Personal Names', 269, 272. Clines argues that the normal form of identification for a married woman was 'X wife of Y'. Marsman's assessment of literary and epigraphic evidence from Israel and Ugarit, however, shows that kings married their daughters to both other regents and high-ranking officials within their own courts, and that if a woman's father was more powerful than her husband she sometimes used the style X *bt* Y for formal identification, see Marsman, *Women in Ugarit and Israel*, 643–58, 702, 717, 722.

important theologically because it is unexpected: another sign that God is on David's side.

When Saul discovers that David has escaped he confronts his daughter, asking why Michal has contravened father–daughter solidarity. But in another twist to the tale Michal uses this very conception as the basis for her excuse. At the beginning of this chapter, I asked whether Saul might have had grounds for supposing that Michal should not have deceived him. An affirmative answer to this question is suggested by the anthropological resources surveyed above. On the basis of the narrator's evaluation in 1 Sam. 18:28-29 and his dialogue with Jonathan in 1 Sam. 19:1-7, however, one may surmise that Saul's suspicions have been aroused. But although Michal's deception is patent to readers it is important to recognize Saul's view of the matter could not be so categorical. The genius of Michal's use of the *teraphim* is that its role in healing rituals means both her ruse with the dummy and reply to the messengers were ambiguous; indeed, the messengers' credulity is evidence for this ambiguity.

Despite the absence of detail in the Samuel narrative a plausible scenario is: (1) the *teraphim* were employed in healing rituals; (2) the first time they were sent the messengers saw them from a distance, at which point Michal told them David was sick (if they did not see the dummy, or if Michal did not expect them to want to see it, it would have been unnecessary); (3) the messengers believed Michal because it appeared she was telling the truth; so (4) they returned to Saul empty handed, possibly because of sensibilities about disturbing a ritual in progress; but (5) Saul had no such qualms and resends the messengers לראות את־דוד, the sick man rather than the *teraphim* (the Hebrew emphasizes *David* not the messengers' seeing, *pace* NRSV 'to see David for themselves'); so (6) the real situation is discovered.

Michal plays upon multiple ways of interpreting her action. While Saul charges Michal with responsibility for David's escape and of violating the cultural schema, Michal shifts the blame onto David, alleging that he threatened to kill her. In doing so she *uses* shared understandings of familial loyalty, specifically, the schema of father–daughter loyalty, and the perception that women, regardless of their marital status, form part of a family's symbolic capital. Bourdieu elaborates upon the latter point:

> The patrimony of the lineage, symbolized by its name, is defined not only by possession of its land and its house, precious and therefore vulnerable assets,

> but also by possession of the means of protecting them, that is, its men, because land and women are never regarded as simple instruments of production or reproduction, still less as chattels or 'property'. An attack on these material and symbolic assets is an attack on their master, on his *nif*, his potency, his very *being* as defined by the group.[159]

Her construction of David as threatening Saul's בית אב is an attempt to bring accepted norms onto her side of the argument. Using social-science enables one to comprehend how she does this since family solidarity for a newly married woman means loyalty towards her father's house, for she is hardly a member of her husband's household.[160] Thus it is entirely plausible to implied readers that Saul believes Michal's assertion of unwilling complicity, and that her husband could act against her. Any such action would also be construed as an attack of her father's household, specifically its honour. Michal, therefore, cleverly manipulates received understandings of acceptable social practice in order to change Saul's conception of her actions from betrayal to innocent, wounded party. And in doing so she puts the ball back in Saul's court for, she asserts, it is *his* failure to protect *her* that left her with no choice. Michal's excuse, therefore, is an example of the employment of cultural categories to (re)construct kin relations for individual ends.

Saul's voice in 1 Sam. 19:11-17 is consistent. He starts with a strategy to eliminate David and does not deviate from this objective. His direct speech to Michal asks why she has deceived him and thwarted his plans. Against those who argue Michal is 'hemmed in' I assert that she *has* a voice. It comprises positive support of David and deception of Saul. Because it is unexpected within the social milieu that forms the background to implied readers' understandings her voice is prominent. The author presents a richly portrayed narrative: in the dark of the night he directs a spotlight onto Michal and holds it upon her as she 'speaks' in favour of David. However, while readers are

159 Bourdieu, *Logic*, 189. Emphasis original.

160 David Jobling argues that David did not love Michal, and asks: 'If David had gone about the court behaving like an ecstatic newly wed would Saul have been prepared to believe that David would threaten Michal's life under any circumstances?', D. Jobling, *1 Samuel* (Berit Olam; Collegeville: Liturgical Press, 1998), 152. I agree with Jobling that David did not waltz about as a star-struck lover, but this is beside the point, since he would never have been expected to.

allowed to observe all the action, Saul possesses only partial insight, and to him the meaning of her agency is uncertain. His inability to perceive correctly in the half-light of ambiguity makes it possible for the author to have Michal manipulate cultural categories to produce a new interpretation of her actions for Saul's consumption. I will argue later that this move enables the writer to make a theological point regarding moral choices in situations of value conflict. However, Michal's mendacity is itself a moral problem for many commentators. Given that readers of the Old Testament usually suppose that lying falls short of morally upright behaviour it is necessary to consider further the ethics of lying and deception.

4. Lying and Deception

I have argued that the moral dilemma facing Michal is most appropriately understood in terms of conflicting moral goods. Abraham Cowley anticipated modern interpretations that suppose the clash is between Michal's untruth and Saul's intention to kill David:

> To unjuſt Force ſhe oppoſes juſt deceit.
> She meets the Murd'erers with a *vertuous Ly*,
> And good deſſembling Tears; May he not *Dy*.[161]

The interpretation of Saul's violence, however, suggests such an understanding may be challenged, for if the force is not unjust, then one can also question where that leaves the contrast with the lie. In this section, I will approach the issue by looking first at the Old Testament's prohibition upon telling untruths.

A. 'YOU SHALL NOT BEAR FALSE WITNESS'

The ninth commandment is an obvious place to start.[162] It is widely thought that it is not a blanket interdiction of lying, but that the noun עד, 'witness', and verb ענה, 'testify', point to a prohibition of false charges against a neigh-

161 A. Cowley, *Davideis* (London: Henry Herringman, 1681), 15. Emphasis and spelling original.

162 According to the Jewish and Reformed order; the Roman Catholic tradition numbers it eighth.

bour in a judicial setting. We may follow Anthony Phillips in supposing that there is no material difference between the versions of the commandment in Exod. 20:16, which reads שקר, 'deception', and Deut. 5:20, which reads שוא, 'vanity'. Phillips rejects the attempt to identify a wider prohibition in the latter and a stricter indictment limited to lying as 'much too subtle', since the Exodus text 'simply refers to what the witness does, namely causes deception . . . [while Deuteronomy] seeks to stress what the witness is, that is a worthless, empty man'.[163] Both, therefore, intend to cover both lying words and deception more widely. In line with the Old Testament's general concern for truthful testimony (Num. 35:30; Deut. 19:15; 1 Kgs 21; Ps. 27:12) the purpose of the commandment was to guard 'the basic right of the covenant member against the threat of false accusation'.[164] In his comments upon this stipulation, however, Allan Harman speaks of 'the sanctity of truth', arguing that the command commends a general prohibition upon lying.[165] Although I doubt that *this* text can carry quite so much freight, other references do condemn lying and commend its avoidance. Kirkpatrick claims that 'Scripture affirms the universal duty of Truth without any exception . . . nor can it be understood to sanction breaches of this general law by recording them without disapproval. It is left to the casuist to justify a falsehood or an act of deception'.[166]

Evidence for a general prohibition upon lies might be found, for example, in Lev. 19:11, which states 'you shall not steal, nor deal falsely, nor lie to one another', a prohibition that can be properly interpreted as referring to deception in general, not just judicial contexts,[167] and Lev. 19:16, which refers to lying in contexts beyond the legal setting. Furthermore, Job, as a model of moral behaviour, protests that he has not practiced falsehood and deceit (Job 31:5).[168]

163 A. Phillips, *Ancient Israel's Criminal Law: A New Approach to the Decalogue* (Oxford: Blackwell, 1970), 142.

164 B. Childs, *The Book of Exodus: A Critical, Theological Commentary* (OTL; Louisville: Westminster, 1974), 424. Note that since evidence in judicial proceedings was not given under oath the ninth commandment is not concerned with perjury, cf. Phillips, *Criminal Law*, 147–48.

165 A. Harman, 'Decalogue (Ten Commandments)', *NIDOTTE* 5.513–19, especially 518.

166 Kirkpatrick, *Samuel*, 173

167 M. A. Klopfenstein, 'שקר *šqr* Engañar', *DTMAT* 2.1265–76, especially 1269.

168 G. Fohrer, 'The Righteous Man in Job 31', in *Essays in Old Testament Ethics* (ed. J. L. Crenshaw and J. T. Willis; New York: Ktav, 1974), 1–22, especially 14. On individual

And Prov. 12:19 contrasts truthful lips that endure forever with the transience of a lying tongue, a difference echoed in other parts of the Old Testament: note, for example, the strong contrasts between truth and lies (Ps. 52:1-7; Isa. 59:12-15; Jer. 7:9; Hos. 7:3), God's law and lies (Ps. 119:29, 64, 104, 128, 163; Prov. 30:8; Isa. 59:12-15; Hos. 4:2; 10:12-13; Mic. 6:12; Amos 2:4), and the identification of idols with falsehood (Isa. 44:20; Jer. 13:25; 16:19; 51:17; Hab. 2:18). Finally, Prov. 6:16-19 makes it quite clear that God abhors lies; and various psalms are unequivocal that lying is something done by evil people (Pss. 5:9; 58:3; 109:2; 144:8, 11; cf. Isa. 32:7).

Scholars of an earlier generation contended Old Testament truth is not propositional but relational; not to do with adhering to an abstract principle, but about being dependable and steadfast.[169] The basis for this claim was etymological: both אמת and אמונה are derived from אמן, 'which in its simple stem means to be steady, to be firm'.[170] Although such arguments have been contested, most famously by James Barr, it does not necessarily mean it is any easier to justify deception.[171] Indeed, an imitative ethic must account for the Old Testament's view that YHWH is a God of truth (Ps. 31:6) and faithfulness (Deut. 32:4), that he is just and right (Deut. 32:4; Pss. 92:16; 119:137; 145:17) and without iniquity (Deut. 32:4; Ps. 92:16), as well as the explicit statements that God does not lie in Num. 23:19 and 1 Sam. 15:29. Kaiser concludes his survey with this polemical assertion:

> If truth telling was valued so highly in the courts that the perjurer was to be punished without pity, could it be esteemed any less in situations outside of the courtroom? Since truth ultimately was grounded in no one less than the God who was truth, all interpretations that would raise caveats and equivocations of one sort or another, outside a proper definition for truth or lying, must come to

moral exemplars in the Old Testament see also C. Wright, *Old Testament Ethics for the People of God* (Downers Grove: IVP, 2004), 368–78.

169 Jacob, for example, asserts that '*emunah* et '*emeth* définissent à la fois la fidélite et la véracité de Dieu et la foi de l'homme', E. Jacob, *Théologie de l'Ancien Testament* (Neuchatel: Éditions Delachaux et Niestlé, 1968), 141–42.

170 E. Ramsdell, 'The Old Testament Understanding of Truth', *JR* 31 (1951): 264–73, quote 264.

171 See J. Barr, *The Semantics of Biblical Language* (Oxford: OUP, 1961; repr. London: SCM Press, 1983), 161–205

> terms not with a system of God, but with a personal accounting to the true and living Lord.[172]

Kaiser's claim chimes with Augustine's influential treatise that lying is deviance from proper standards of truthful speech. According to Augustine, because the soul is worth more than the body lies are not permitted even to save a life.[173] Regardless of whether lies are rejected outright or otherwise justified, this tradition has proved enduring, so that truth and lying are mutually exclusive. Paul Horwich summarizes this position: 'if we can understand why truth is valuable, we can thereby explain why lying is wrong'.[174]

The Old Testament, however, contains a number of accounts of lying and deception that do not seem to condemn it as a deviant practice. John Ottwell lists cases of deception by men in the Old Testament, including Abraham's trickery (Genesis 12, 20, 26), Jacob and Laban's mutual deceit (Genesis 29–31), Saul's attempts to kill David (1 Samuel 18), the latter's murder of Uriah (2 Samuel 11), and Joab's ruse using the woman of Tekoa (2 Samuel 14).[175] Toni Craven points to female deceivers including Rebekah (Genesis 27–28), Tamar (Genesis 38), the Hebrew midwives (Exodus 1), Rahab (Joshua 2), Deborah (Judges 4–5) and Michal.[176] YHWH is occasionally implicated in deception, either personally or by approving those who engage in the practice (Exod. 3:18-20; 1 Sam. 16:1-5; 1 Kgs 22:2-23; Jer. 4:10; Ezek. 14:9).[177] In terms of lying as a specific case of deception, Erdmann uses Aquinas' typology

172 W. Kaiser, *Toward Old Testament Ethics* (Grand Rapids: Zondervan, 1983), 228.

173 *De mend.* 8.

174 Paul Horwich, 'The Value of Truth', *Noûs* 40 (2006): 347–60, quote 348.

175 J. Otwell, *And Sarah Laughed: The Status of Women in the Old Testament* (Philadelphia: Westminster Press, 1977), 108. Note the definition of deception provided by Williams: 'Deception takes place when an agent intentionally distorts, withholds, or otherwise manipulates information reaching some person(s) in order to stimulate in the person(s) a belief that the agent does not believe in order to serve the agent's purpose', M. Williams, *Deception in Genesis: an investigation into the morality of a unique Biblical phenomenon* (SBLit 32; New York: Peter Lang, 2001), 3. For other instances of deception in 1 Samuel see 10:15-16; 16:2-5; 18; 21; 23; 25.

176 T. Craven, 'Women who Lied for the Faith', in *Justice and the Holy* (ed. D. A. Knight and P. J. Paris; Atlanta: Scholars Press, 1989), 35–49.

177 On whether God is a liar see the exchange between Barr and Moberly: W. Moberly, 'Did the Serpent get it Right?' *JTS* 39 (1988): 1–27; J. Barr, 'Is God a Liar? (Genesis 2–3) – And Related Matters', *JTS* 57 (2006): 1–22; W. Moberly, 'Did the Interpreters get it Right? Genesis 2–3 Reconsidered', *JTS* 59 (2008): 22–40.

to identify instances of lies of necessity (Exod. 1:19; Gen. 20:2; 26:7; Josh. 2:6), lies of sport (Gen. 42:9; 27:15; Judg. 9:8), and shameful and hurtful lies.[178] However, it is one thing to identify cases of lying and deception, another to think that the Old Testament presents them as normative.

There are three typical approaches to this question. The first is to attempt to excuse the text, justifying the cases of lying as exceptions that do not undo or relativize what are supposed to be the proper standards of Old Testament morality. The most consistent proponent of this approach is Kaiser. He is concerned to protect the truthfulness of God, claiming that 'divine approval of an individual in one aspect or area of his life does not entail and must not be extended to mean that there is a divine approval of that individual in all aspects of his character or conduct'.[179] So although Rahab lied and is later commended she is not commended for lying per se, rather for protecting Israel's spies: it is her faith in YHWH that is in view. Augustine expresses it this way: 'God did good to the Hebrew midwives, and to Rahab the harlot of Jericho, this was not because they lied, but because they were merciful to God's people'.[180] He proceeds to assert that Rahab should be imitated in everything except her lying, but curiously omits mention of Michal.

A second approach, at the other end of the spectrum, posits that there is absolutely no theological difficulty with deceptive practices. Although he restricts his study to Genesis, Richard Freund perceives no attempt on the part of biblical authors to sanitize characters' actions with respect to lying and deception, concluding that 'a standard of absolute truthfulness does not seem to be a major issue in the Hebrew Bible'.[181] Similarly, Daniel Friedmann claims '[g]uile was regarded as a praiseworthy talent, legitimate in the attainment of just ends', arguing that only the slyness of the serpent is condemned and that all other cases are 'treated with tolerance and even admiration'.[182]

The first two approaches are relatively infrequent and most commentators seek reasons for occurrences of lying and deception in the Bible. A

178 Erdmann, *Samuel*, 256.

179 Kaiser, *Toward*, 270–71

180 *C. mend.* 34.

181 R. Freund, 'Lying and Deception in the Biblical and Post-Judaic Tradition', *SJOT* 5 (1991): 45–61, quote 45.

182 D. Friedmann, *To Kill and Take Possession: Law, Morality and Society in Biblical Stories* (Peabody: Hendrickson, 2002), 66.

source critical explanation is proposed by Caird, who supposes that Michal's 'untrustworthiness' is due to an early source.[183] More recent interpretations, however, posit theological explanations. Esther Fuchs, for instance, supposes the accounts of *women's* deception are included to smear their reputations and diminish the credibility of their perspectives.[184] Horn Prouser, though, carefully refutes Fuch's argument, showing that deception is not employed by women because they are presented as inherently more duplicitous, but because they are disadvantaged people. She avers that 'in biblical narrative lying is not considered a moral issue of absolutes. Rather, deception is considered an acceptable and generally praiseworthy means for a weaker party to succeed against a stronger power'.[185] An ancient audience, she argues, would have appreciated rather than condemned quick-thinking deception. Michael Williams rejects this conclusion, highlighting a number of different perspectives upon lying.[186] He finds that deceptive acts are positively evaluated in Genesis. In the Deuteronomistic History, however, the situation is more complicated, for deception against Israel is always viewed negatively; deception of Israelites by other Israelites is sometimes evaluated negatively (Josh. 7:19-21; 1 Sam. 28:3-12; 2 Sam. 3:27; 20:8-10; 4:5-12; 12:14; 13; 15:1-12; 1 Kgs 21:1-14), and at other times positively (1 Sam. 19:11-17; 2 Sam. 15:32-37; 16:15-17:16; 2 Kgs 9:22; 10:30);[187] and deception of others by Israelites is evaluated positively (Exod. 1:15-20; Josh. 2:1-21; 6:22-25; Judg. 3:12-30; 5:17-22; 5:24-27).[188] In short, it seems that within Genesis deception is acceptable to right a previous

183 Caird, *Samuel*, 987.

184 E. Fuchs, '"For I Have the Way of Women": Deception, Gender, and Ideology in Biblical Narrative", *Semeia* 42 (1988): 68–83; idem, 'Who Is Hiding the Truth? Deceptive Women and Biblical Androcentrism', in *Feminist Perspectives on Biblical Scholarship* (ed. A. Y. Collins; Missouls: Scholars Press, 1985), 137–44.

185 H. Prouser, 'The Truth about Women and Lying', *JSOT* 61 (1994): 15–28, 15.

186 Note also Wenham's remarks: 'Witty and perceptive as these observations may be about early Israelite attitudes, they do not represent those of the implied author of Genesis, who sets these episodes in contexts which may clear both his own and God's displeasure at these lies', G. Wenham, *Story as Torah: Reading the Old Testament Ethically* (OTS; Edinburgh: T & T Clark, 2000), 76. Regardless of the view one takes of Wenham's assertion regarding the Genesis stories, it is not the case that Michal's lie is undermined by a negative tenor in the narrative context.

187 Note, though, that Williams does not say *how* or *where* Michal's action is positively evaluated, cf. Williams, *Deception in Genesis*, 62.

188 A review of the ANE evidence of deception between the gods, between gods and people and between humans leads Williams to suggest that it is evaluated negatively when

wrong, and within the historical narratives if 'the deceptive behavior serves to protect, preserve, or restore the well-being of members of this group or the group as a whole, it is positively evaluated'.[189] Williams places this conclusion in cultural context by examining other ANE sources, concluding that intra-group deception is also negatively evaluated. Similarly, Craven's study supports the view that women's lies are endorsed because they are on the side of God and his people. These studies, though, beg the question of who constitutes the people of God; that is, of who is an 'insider' and who an 'outsider'. John Pilch thinks that it is not so much the people of God as the family that comprises the key group, and that individuals justifiably lie to protect 'family honour', positing the '*truth of the honor* of any family is much more important than *factual truth*'.[190]

The last two interpretations of Old Testament lies set them in the context of a clash of moral goods and commitments. Peter Barnes's careful assessment of Rahab's lie makes the same point: 'Truth-telling takes place in concrete situations, and can never be treated as though it occurs in a vacuum'.[191] He supposes that a commitment to YHWH means Rahab's lie was no sin. In order to understand whether Michal's deception can be similarly interpreted I turn now to consider anthropological perspectives upon lying.

B. LYING – ANTHROPOLOGICAL PERSPECTIVES

In a classic essay published at the beginning of the twentieth century Georg Simmel claimed that the important point about a lie is not that the other possesses false information – that is merely error – but that 'the person deceived is held in misconception about the true intention of the person who tells the lie. Veracity and mendacity are thus of the most far-reaching significance for the

between people but that there was an acceptance or even admiration of deception by gods, cf. Williams, *Deception in Genesis*, 151–91.

189 Williams, *Deception in Genesis*, 221.

190 J. Pilch, 'Lying and Deceit in the Letters to the Seven Churches: Perspectives from Cultural Anthropology', *BTB* 22 (1992): 126–35, quote 130. Emphasis original. He identifies seven kinds of deception and lies: concealment of failure; concealment of unintentional failures; false imputation; avoiding quarrels; attaining material gain; mischief; and defence of kin.

191 P. Barnes, 'Was Rahab's Lie a Sin?', *RTR* 54 (1995): 1–9, quote 9.

relations of persons with each other'.[192] Although the paucity of anthropological studies of lying and deception has been lamented,[193] those that exist differ from philosophical or theological appraisals in that they do not view lying as deviant but as a social phenomenon replete with meaning. Herzfeld explains that 'they may offend the moral sensibilities of some observers, but, when used consistently, they reflect moral valuations in which we may find explanations for what strike us, but do not strike our informants, as irrational practices'.[194]

Gilsenan argues that the practice of lying in the Lebanese community he studied was 'a fundamental element not only of specific situations and individual actions, but of the cultural universe as a whole'.[195] As such, lying has to be learnt. Julian Pitt-Rivers notes the importance of socialization. He calls the Andalusians 'accomplished liars', 'for it requires training and intelligence to distinguish rapidly when the truth is owed and when it is to be concealed'.[196] It is important to realize that the prevalence of lying does not indicate debased morality. The same author observes

> it is logical rather than paradoxical that the Andalusians should be people profoundly concerned with the truth and with the true state of the heart . . . When knowledge is something to give or to deny you become concerned with its exact worth.[197]

Gilsenan elaborates that the 'lie is a technique for the restriction of the social distribution of knowledge over time, and is thus ultimately woven into the system of power and control in society'.[198] Although this can be true in modern industrial societies, the most detailed ethnographies are from societies

192 G. Simmel, 'The Sociology of Secrecy and of Secret Societies', *AJS* 11 (1906): 441–98, quote 445. My emphasis.

193 J. Barnes, *A Pack of Lies: Towards a Sociology of Lying* (Cambridge: CUP, 1994), 8–9.

194 Herzfeld, *Anthropology*, 110.

195 M. Gilsenan, 'Lying, Honor, and Contradiction', in *Transaction & Meaning: Directions in the Anthropology of Exchange and Symbolic Behaviour* (ed. B. Kapferer; Philadelphia: American Anthropological Association, 1976), 191–219, quote 191.

196 J. Pitt-Rivers, *The People of the Sierra* (2nd ed.; Chicago: University of Chicago Press, 1971), xvi. Note the importance of embodiment: the quote continues 'and to acquire conscious control over facial expression is an ability which takes practice from childhood'.

197 Pitt-Rivers, *People of the Sierra*, xvii.

198 Gilsenan, 'Lying, Honor, and Contradiction', 191.

where people live very closely together so that there are few real secrets.[199] In such a community, claims Ursula Sharma, 'a sense of personal integrity and privacy is maintained less through the use of space than through the use of information'.[200] Because deception creates ambiguity and thus social distance Gilsenan is able to assert that lying 'is vital to the life of this society – indeed, lying *makes it possible*'.[201]

Lying can be used both to deceive and to reveal deeper truths. Jana Fortier describes how the Rāute adopt strategies of verbal evasion and deceit when in contact with Nepali agriculturalists in order to create social space for their nomadic practices. The main means by which this is achieved is through *uklān*, rhyming proverbs, which are performed in order both to entertain and mislead.[202] Similarly, in the psychiatric ward studied by van Dongen the very space and structure of the ward induced lying. Competition for staff time, disillusionment with years of care and no prospect of 'a cure', tensions between medical staff, psychologists and nurses, and the very art of the 'lying truths of psychiatry',[203] all provided an arena in which lying was a rational strategy for creating personal space. Lying is therefore a means of resisting the environment and even exaggerated lies, which are obviously false, may be admired

199 Cf. J. du Boulay, 'Lies, Mockery and Family Integrity', in *Mediterranean Family Structures* (CSSA 13; ed. J. G. Peristiany; Cambridge: CUP, 1976), 389–406; E. van Dongen, 'Theatres of the Lie: "Crazy" Deception and Lying as Drama', *A&M* 9 (2002): 135–51; J. Fortier, 'The Arts of Deception: Verbal Performances by the Rāute of Nepal', *JRAI* 8 (2002): 233–57; Gilsenan, 'Lying, Honor, and Contradiction'.

200 U. Sharma, 'Trust, Privacy, Deceit and the Quality of Interpersonal Relationships: "Peasant" Society Revisited,' in *An Anthropology of Indirect Communication* (ed. J. Hendry and C. W. Watson; London: Routledge, 2001) 115–27, quote 122. Note, *pace* Sharma, that this need not be linked to ideas of limited good.

201 Gilsenan, 'Lying, Honor and Contradiction', 211. Emphasis original. Cf. J. du Boulay, *Portrait of a Greek Mountain Village* (Oxford: Clarendon Press, 1974), 405–6; J. Hendry, 'To Wrap or Not to Wrap: Politeness and Penetration in Ethnographic Inquiry', *Man* NS 24 (1989): 620–35.

202 Cf. Fortier, 'Arts of Deception', 233–34. Fortier (or rather, as she acknowledges, her 'research assistant', Bishnu) recognizes that most proverbs were used to disguise the situation of the Rāute, these were 'fake' proverbs, since they 'did not describe Rāute experiential knowledge'. Other proverbs were revelatory of Rāute perspectives. ' "Real" proverbs are voiced only during moments of exceptional conversational conflict, effectively pulling off the elegant mask of the performance to reveal the sweating actor underneath', Fortier, 'Arts of Deception', 237.

203 T. Sasz, 'The Lying Truths of Psychiatry', *JLS* 3 (1986): 121–39.

because they show a person is unwilling to succumb to reality.[204] On the other hand, sometimes lies can be told in order to ascertain the truth, for example, to catch another liar. Gilsenan recounts how a particularly depraved member of the community pretended to become a disciple of a visiting sheikh in order to test whether he possessed the powers he claimed. The whole group, normally warily suspicious of this individual, went along with the deception, thus exposing the visitor's assertion of supernatural insight as a lie.[205]

The relationship between truth and deception can be complex. Van Dongen asserts that in the context of a mental health ward, 'it did not make sense to look for the truth . . . nobody would make a deep search for the truth, simply because all were aware that there was more at stake than simple truth'.[206] Part of what is at stake is ongoing relations between people as autonomous individuals. Bella DePaulo and Deborah Kashy conclude their empirical study of the differences in patterns of lying between close and more distant relationships by suggesting that truth can be more prejudicial than lies, with the result that 'close relationships may be breeding grounds for deceit'.[207] This conclusion appears to clash with the notion that marriages and friendships, for example, are arenas of trust and transparency. Barnes' comments, however, are instructive:

> An absence of mutual trust may lead to an abundance of lies, each party trying to deceive the other, but the presence of trust does not necessarily result in an absence of lies. In intimate face-to-face relations the shared expectation of mutual trust may lead to collaboration between, or more likely connivance by, liars and dupes in order to maintain the plausibility of a lie, as well as the plausibility of

204 Cf. van Dongen, 'Theatres of the Lie', 145–46. Such lies are 'grotesque' in Bakhtin's sense of ridiculous and world reversing. Note also Abu-Lughod's accounts of women maintaining the socially expected stance that they had no interest in their husbands and had thus fought him off on their wedding night, even though the tent walls had told a different story, Abu-Lughod, *Veiled Sentiments*, 48. Van Dongen points to other uses of the lie: to joke, be polite, or because of a feeling of affection.

205 Gilsenan, 'Lying, Honor and Contradiction', 206–10.

206 Van Dongen, 'Theatres of the Lie', 141. He notes the exception of when a patient harmed another.

207 B. DePaulo and D. Kashy, 'Everyday Lies in Close and Casual Relationships', *JPSP* 74 (1998): 63–79, quote 77. Overall, people more often lied to those in casual rather than close relationships. See also C. Palmer, 'When to Bear False Witness: An Evolutionary Approach to the Social Context of Honesty and Deceit Among Commercial Fishers', *Zygon* 28 (1993): 455–68.

> continuing trust. When this happens it is no longer obvious who is deceiving whom.[208]

In any case, when people live in close proximity, promoting misinformation by lying, or attempting to control access to information through secrecy, can only have the effect of delaying people's eventual understanding. The hope is that by the time all are appraised of an event and the lie 'uncovered' it is sufficiently overshadowed by the individuals' entanglement in other, more immediate considerations.[209] That this is so indicates people know they should not lie or, to express the matter more precisely, that 'truth' is also a moral good. Campbell states that a 'head of family who was sincere (εἰλικρινής), or without cunning words (ντόμπρος), would be considered foolish and neglectful of his duty. This is not to say that the Sarakatsani fail to understand the virtues of truth and sincerity'.[210]

Edward Banfield glossed the prioritization of family interest as 'amoral familism', asserting that 'most people of Montegrano have no morality except, perhaps, that which requires service to the family'.[211] Herzfeld refrains from nuancing his rejection of Banfield's thesis: 'Lies . . . may be a legitimate defense of a kin group's interests, and dismissing such a perspective as "amoral familism" . . . is a piece of self-contradictory nonsense that blithely ignores its fundamentally ethical focus'.[212] Herzfeld's point is that Banfield only looks to deceptive behaviour in isolation, failing to include in his appraisal the social and moral good of 'the family' itself. This good is protected both by lying, and

208 Barnes, *Pack of Lies*, 23. There may be 'norms' of cooperation in deception. For example, a lie told only once or twice may not be considered as such: 'Among the Navajo the fourth time a lie is repeated it becomes deceitful', Barnes, *Pack of Lies*, 67.

209 Cf. Sharma, 'Trust, Privacy, Deceit', 122. Brandes' cynicism may be typical: 'It is simply assumed that if a person can get away with it, he will engage in almost any activity to further his own well-being regardless of how his actions affect others', S. Brandes, *Migration, Kinship and Community: Tradition and Transition in a Spanish Village* (New York: Academic Press, 1975), 149. On the other hand, Argenti-Pillen describes the how deception can be *immediately* followed by disclosure, both to flirt and to avoid conflict with more the powerful by 'a type of trial-and-error communication', A. Argenti-Pillen, 'Obvious Pretence: For Fun or For Real? Cross-Cousin and International Relationships in Sri Lanka', *JRAI* NS 13 (2007): 313–29, quote 321.

210 Campbell, *Honour, Family, and Patronage*, 283.

211 Banfield, *Moral Basis*, 134.

212 Herzfeld, *Anthropology*, 110.

maintaining a reputation for lying and dirty tricks.[213] Du Boulay's typology of lies distinguishes between defensive and offensive mendacity. Defensive lies conceal a person's deficiencies with respect to social norms and thus are prevalent in situations of competing obligations in which it is impossible to meet all expectations, to conceal family behaviour, or to defend kin or friends. Offensive lies, for example, false accusations, are told in order to smear another's character and to create mischief.[214] All of these strategies can be employed to draw a veil around family activities.

Many early ethnographies constructed a sharp divide between those who could be trusted and those who could not; between those to whom the truth might be disclosed and outsiders from whom family secrets should be concealed.

> Secrecy erects a barrier around the members of the family and their intimate relations. The family secrets, whether they have significant content or not, are relevant, simply because they represent something which is denied to other people who are not members of the group.[215]

The act of lying itself helps create group identity. Pitt-Rivers' monograph shows how lying to outsiders both hides divisions within the community and performatively reduces these divisions as those on the 'inside' are able to 'read' the lie more easily than those on the 'outside'.[216] Fissures within the family group, however, point to the weakness of a simple 'them' versus 'us' view of the matter. People lie to family group members in order not to offend or to avoid appearing not to fulfil obligations to kin, thus demonstrating that individual social goals are as important as group concerns, although these may often coincide. Pitt-Rivers describes 'a kaleidoscope of changing relationships' that depend upon context. He continues by observing that the individuals he studied 'faced choices of allegiance and *defined themselves* by

213 Cf. Sharma, 'Trust, Privacy, Deceit', 121.

214 Du Boulay, *Portrait*, 399–404. Peristiany speaks of 'the defensive use of deception and the offensive use of ridicule', Peristiany, 'Introduction', 23.

215 Campbell, *Honour, Family, and Patronage*, 192.

216 Cf. Pitt-Rivers, *People of the Sierra*, 8–10, 29–30; A. P. Cohen, *The Symbolic Construction of Community* (London: Routledge, 1985), 89, 110–11.

the attitudes they adopted. They were not simply members of a given tribe and tribal segment'.[217]

In Chapter 3 I used Rapport's work to highlight both the importance of individual agency for practice, and the ubiquity of ambiguity in social interaction. The latter causes problems, for people cannot be certain that their trust and confidence is rightly placed, a situation only exacerbated when lying and deception are common features of social intercourse. To ameliorate uncertainly, when an interlocutor wishes to be taken seriously, explicit markers are employed to warrant veracity; for example, 'on my honour'. The latter is a type of oath, an appeal to a higher good or god to guarantee the truthfulness of the affirmation. Although oaths can form part of ordinary speech, more formal oath-taking in sacred places can be used to validate protestations of innocence. Herzfeld's study of oath taking among Cretan shepherds involved in cycles of reciprocal sheep rustling illustrates its social function.

> The practice of resolution by oath permits a face-saving avoidance of further conflict in the name of higher truths, but this implies precisely the opposite of ingenuous trust: it furnishes a ritualised means of letting a rival escape further retributions without necessarily changing one's mind about his guilt. The invitation to take the oath comes invested with a guarantee that the matter will end there. The very sanctity of the process is what protects the lie that it may – and, in general estimation, often does – conceal.[218]

And even if the truth should come to light, '[m]ere evidence cannot gainsay an oath's holy authority and it is both blasphemous and a heinous solecism to suggest that it might'.[219] This does not lead to easy demands that others swear, for obliging another to do so means one cannot refuse to take an oath in return as a gesture of one's own commitment to restoring goodwill. The accuser, for example, may have to swear that the animals *are* missing.

We have seen that attention to the social dynamics of lying does not preclude

217 Pitt-Rivers, *People of the Sierra*, xix. My emphasis. Cf. Sharma, 'Trust, Privacy, Deceit', 121: 'Family honour is not irrelevant in Ghanyari, but personal reputation can be distinguished from it to a large extent'.

218 M. Herzfeld, 'Pride and Perjury: Time and the Oath in the Mountain Villages of Crete', *Man* NS 25 (1990): 305–22, quote 311.

219 Herzfeld, 'Pride and Perjury', 312.

appreciation of truthfulness. But nor is it the case that family well-being and truth are the only moral goods. Many studies of the Mediterranean identify 'honour' as another, perhaps the key, value. Although space precludes extensive discussion of 'honour and shame', it is necessary to ask how 'honour' relates to the ostensively dishonourable practice of lying. Bourdieu comments that the 'ethos of honour is fundamentally opposed to a universal and formal morality which affirms the equality in dignity of all men and consequently the equality of their rights and duties'.[220] The reason for this is that a universal duty to be truthful curtails a person's autonomy, which is the essence of honour. For a person who adheres to the 'honour code', therefore, the obligation to speak truthfully is situational: deception is perfectly acceptable as long as one deals with people to whom there are no duties of honour. Strangers would be such individuals. Thus to 'lie is to deny the truth to someone who has the right to be told it and this right exists only where respect is due'.[221] The moral obligation to tell the truth, then, derives from a prior commitment to individuals. This explains how an honourable man may be faithful and truthful to some, yet not be dishonoured by practising deceit. Of course, omnipresent ambiguity means a person's intentions are never transparent, so it is always possible to question whether a statement did in fact commit the honour of the speaker. Where no oath or other marker removes this doubt and the intentions of the interlocutor were misinterpreted the dupe, and not the deceiver, is humiliated. Pitt-Rivers concludes that according to the 'honour code', 'it is lack of steadfastness in intentions which is dishonouring, not misrepresentation of them'.[222] The implications for someone who sticks doggedly to the truth, the 'pathologically honest',[223] are patent: '*Adami*, "a good man", is a term of moral approval but not of prestige. It relates to personal characteristics but not to social rank, save insofar as it is frequently followed by *mishin*, "poor chap" '.[224] In a similar vein Sharma notes that truthful 'simplicity' is only advantageous 'when allied to a

220 P. Bourdieu, 'The Sentiment of Honour in Kabyle Society', in *Honour and Shame: The Values of Mediterranean Society* (ed. J. G. Peristiany; Chicago: University of Chicago Press, 1966), 191–242, quote 228.

221 Pitt-Rivers, 'Honour', 33.

222 Pitt-Rivers, 'Honour', 32; cf. Phillip Esler, 'Making and Breaking an Agreement Mediterranean Style: A New Reading of Galatians 2:1-14', *BI* 3 (1995): 285–314.

223 Barnes, *Pack of Lies*, 21.

224 Gilsenan, 'Lying, Honor and Contradiction', 215.

genuine otherworldly piousness [*sic*], a reputation for utter moral rectitude'.[225] If this is unattainable then a tendency towards truthfulness will probably result in others taking advantage.

A final area of anthropological research into the lie is the literature on 'tricksters'. Robert Pelton's description of the African trickster Ananse points to the essence of these characters: 'Tricksterlike, Ananse speaks the truth by dissembling'.[226] Lawrence Sullivan summarizes a trickster as 'a type of mythic figure distinguished by his skill at trickery and deceit as well as by his prodigious biological drives and exaggerated bodily parts'.[227] He or she is both comic and amoral, occasionally human, but often animal. Above all the trickster parodies pretension. Cristiano Grottanelli identifies essential traits of lowliness, rule breaking in tragic yet comical ways, and sacredness.[228] Pelton cautions against two prominent approaches to tricksters: splitting the trickster's contradictions up into different beings, and accepting the ambiguities but explaining them away. Similarly, Ellen Basso argues against the common approach of *distinguishing* tricksters from ordinary people, instead proposing that they are 'flawed cultural heroes' with whom people identify, at least in part. She comments that

> the very attributes that make such tricksters inventive heroes and clownish fools in the first place are, after all, natural necessities of human intelligence, operating in practical concrete, face-to-face relations that people negotiate all the time, sometimes with considerable immediacy.[229]

She records numerous Kalapalo oral narratives, concluding that these 'stories

225 Sharma, 'Trust, Privacy, Deceit', 121.

226 R. Pelton, *The Trickster in West Africa: A Study of Mythic Irony and Sacred Delight* (Berkeley: University of California Press, 1980), 2.

227 L. Sullivan, 'Tricksters', *ER* 15.45–46, quote 45. See also P. Radin, *The Trickster: A Study in American Indian Mythology* (New York: Schocken Books, 1976).

228 Cf. C. Grottanelli, 'Tricksters, Scape-Goats, Champions, Saviors', *HR* 23 (1983): 117–39, especially 120.

229 E. Basso, *In Favor of Deceit: A Study of Tricksters in an Amazonian Society* (Tuscon: University of Arizona Press, 1987), 8. Diamond contrasts the trickster with Job in S. Diamond, 'Introductory Essay: Job and the Trickster', in *The Trickster: A Study in American Indian Mythology* (ed. P. Radin; New York: Schocken Books, 1976), xi–xxii. Diamond contrasts Job's possession of clearly demarcated conceptions of good and evil with the trickster's embrace of the ambivalence and tragedy of real life.

about deceit are especially concerned with people's action qualified by feelings: about how enacted emotions give meaning to particular contexts, relationships, and goals'.[230] The tales examine issues from various points of view, for example, the consequences of being either too sceptical or overly trusting, and seek to stimulate and engage the emotions. A key theme is how the trickster uses duplicity in the context of unequal power relations to reverse socially expected outcomes. Thus Basso states that 'Kalapalo deceit has less to do with truth or falsehood than with enactment of an illusionary relationship'.[231] It is this reversal of the social order that Grottanelli highlights as the social 'meaning' of tricksters, since they demonstrate 'the power of breaking boundaries, of getting away with it, and of achieving salvation through sin'.[232]

The trickster motif views lying very differently from the Augustinian tradition that has informed much European thinking. It points to the truth of Barnes' comment that '[s]ocieties vary not only in their recognition of the ubiquity of lying and other modes of deceit but also in the way in which they evaluate different kinds of lies'.[233] The account of Michal's lie hails from a very different social setting to that of contemporary Western readers; how might it be understood?

C. UNDERSTANDING MICHAL'S LIE

So far I have not attempted to *define* lying. This apparent lacuna has enabled me to refrain from excluding material pertinent to this study on the basis of a potentially erroneous classification. Nevertheless, an adequate definition will aid interpretation of Michal's actions and words. Augustine's definition of lying views it as the stating of one thing while thinking another, with the intent to deceive.[234] Many commentators follow him in distinguishing between deception and the narrower practice of lying. Sissela Bok describes deception as communicating messages that are intended to lead others to believe what we ourselves do not hold. A lie is a subset of deception, 'an intentionally deceptive

230 Basso, *In Favor of Deceit*, 351.
231 Basso, *In Favor of Deceit*, 3.
232 Grottanelli, 'Tricksters', 139.
233 Barnes, *Pack of lies*, 66.
234 *C. mend.* 23.

message in the form of a *statement*'.[235] According to this definition there are two important components to a lie: the *intention* to deceive, and the *verbal* statement. Regarding the first element there is little discussion, although it is important to highlight that the veracity of the statement is not an issue, i.e. it is possible to lie yet state a fact, or not lie yet communicate a falsehood: the matter concerns *intention*. About the necessity of 'stating' the lie, however, there is considerable debate. In their typology of deceit Roderick Chisholm and Thomas Feehan maintain that 'stating' or 'saying' should not be interpreted narrowly to mean only something that is verbally asserted, but that it should also include a nod or other conventional sign.

> What distinguishes lying as such from the other types of intended deception is the fact that, in telling the lie, the liar 'gives an indication that he is expressing his own opinion.' And he does this in a special way – by getting his victim to place his faith in him. The sense of to 'say', therefore, in which the liar may be said to 'intend to say what is false' is that of 'to *assert*'.[236]

An assertion is confirming the truth of what is communicated in spite of actually communicating what one believes to be false. Thus lies are frequently considered worse than other forms of deception because 'is assumed that, if a person *L asserts* a proposition *p* to another person *D*, then *D* has the *right to expect* that *L* himself believes *p*'.[237]

This moves the question on, for now the issue is not simply whether someone intends to deceive and does so by saying something, but whether in any specific case they do, or do not, assert the truth of what they communicate. Thomas Carson supposes that the use of language involves an implicit promise to tell the truth, affirming that 'making a statement (ordinarily) involves warranting that what one says is true'.[238] However, Maria Bettetini correctly observes that this 'confuses the implicit commitment to use words and phrases

235 S. Bok, *Lying: Moral Choice in Public and Private Life* (2nd ed.; New York: Vintage, 1999), 13–15, quote 15. Emphasis original.

236 R. Chisholm and T. Feehan, 'The Intent to Deceive', *JP* 74 (1977): 143–59, quote 149. Emphasis original. In their typology Chisholm and Feehan classify lying as '*always* involv[ing] the intent of what we have called "positive deception *simpliciter*" [i.e. to *add* to another's beliefs something false]', Chishom and Feehan, 'Intent to Deceive', 153. Emphasis original.

237 Chisholm and Feehan, 'Intent to Deceive', 153. Emphasis original.

238 T. Carson, 'The Definition of Lying', *Noûs* 40 (2006): 284–306, quote 292.

according to a shared grammar and lexicon, with the convention to tell the truth and not deceive'.[239] Although the ethnographic data above leads one to be sceptical of Carson's claims that the default situation of most intercourse is that statements will be true, his emphasis upon the importance of the liar 'warranting' the lie is helpful.[240] Carson commends a definition of lying as involving a warrant because it explains why there is often dispute about whether a statement is a lie. Furthermore,

> it makes sense of the common view that lying involves a breach of trust. To lie . . . is to invite others to trust and rely on what one says by warranting its truth, but, at the same time, to betray that trust by making false statements that one does not believe.[241]

In courtrooms witnesses are required explicitly to state that they warrant the truth of what they affirm. In everyday interaction the warranting of an affirmation is usually implicit, which means it can be ambiguous and open to manipulation. We have seen that in societies in which people assume others' statements will quite often *not* be true, especially when dealing with unknown or casual acquaintances, there is tremendous ambiguity, requiring special speech markers explicitly to warrant veracity, although even then truthfulness does not *necessarily* follow. Furthermore, interlocutors are not obliged to recognize a warrant, indeed they may manipulate expectations for their own idiosyncratic ends. Nevertheless, it does seem to be reasonable to suppose that the 'wrongness or culpability of a lie is determined, in part, by the strength with which it is warranted to be true'.[242]

There are two instances of lying in 1 Sam. 19:10-17. In the first case Michal precedes her lie by disguising a *teraphim*. Regardless of the significance of

239 M. Bettetini, *Breve historia de la mentira: De Ulises a Pinocho* (CT; trans P. Linares; Madrid: Ediciones Cátedra, 2002), 52. My translation.

240 Cf. Carson, 'Definition of Lying', 295–98. In a footnote Carson recognizes that the presumption of implicit warranty is not universal, quoting Barnes, *Pack of Lies*, 70, who in turn cites Gilsenan, 'Lying, Honor, and Contradiction'. I do not accept Carson's assertion that the 'villagers Barnes describes have different understandings about when statements are warranted to be true than people in most other societies', Carson, 'Definition of Lying', 305.

241 Carson, 'Definition of Lying', 302.

242 Carson, 'Definition of Lying', 302

this item[243] it is essential to the efficacy of her lie. The anthropological material pointed to the ubiquity of lying as a defensive measure in societies where the family is central. Given the importance of kin in the Old Testament, attention to how mendacity functions in ethnographic accounts can suggest a new interpretation of Michal's words and actions. It was observed that because people are sceptical of the claims of others, they tend not to have confidence in their affirmations unless accompanied by a marker of intention. The data surveyed indicated that oaths were one way in which an individual's true purposes can be revealed. In our text, though, Michal does not warrant her assertion that David is ill in this way. Instead, the narrative takes great pains to describe her preparation of a dummy comprising *teraphim* and pillow of goat's hair.[244] I will argue below that there is a theological motive for prolonging the focus upon the *teraphim*, but the ruse itself also serves as a warrant for Michal's words. The messengers may have thought that Saul's daughter would 'naturally' have sided with her father against David, yet readers may suspect that the very fact they have been sent on this mission could have sown seeds of doubt in their minds so that they distrusted Michal's assertion. Yet, a dummy purporting to be David or one associated with a healing ritual – it is not necessary to choose between these options – pointed to the truth of her claim that David was sick: she warranted her assertion. On the definition above, Michal lied.

To readers, Michal's other statement, in 1 Sam. 19:17, is obviously a lie; but Saul cannot be so certain. Although her claim that David threatened to kill her is not explicitly warranted one may suppose that the context of Michal and Saul's relationship as father and daughter constitutes a type of implicit

243 See n. 3, above.

244 The translation of כביר העזים is contested. LXX reads כבד, 'liver', for כביר, and Josephus subsequently portrays Michal as putting a throbbing goat's liver into the bed to give the impression that David was gasping in his illness, *Ant.* 6.217. Since העזים signifies goats' hair (Exod. 25:4) and the cognates כברה, 'sieve' (Amos 9:9), and מכבר, 'network' (Exod. 27:4; 38:4; 2 Kgs 8:15), it is probable that כביר העזים is something woven from goat's hair. Thus, 'un tresse en poils de chèvre', de Vaux *Samuel*, 103, cf. Rouillard and Tropper, '*TRPYM*', 343–46. Smith, however, contends that מראשתיו means 'at his head' (cf. 1 Sam. 26:7; 1 Kgs 19:6), which 'would not naturally be used of a net put over the head', Smith, *Samuel*, 180; thus a pillow or blanket, *pace* McCarter, *1 Samuel*, 326, who suggests the article indicates '*a certain* tangle', cf. GKC 125r. Caird strikes the right note: 'The phrase *pillow of goat's hair* is a conjectural translation of unintelligible Hebrew. We have accordingly to accept with resignation the fact that we do not know the nature of either of the objects which Michal used for her deception', Caird, *Samuel*, 987. Emphasis original.

warrant. Indeed, I argued above that the very nature of Michal's affirmation plays upon this supposition. One could ask why Saul, who obviously considers himself deceived in the matter of the *teraphim*, should think that her words are any more reliable. Jonathan Adler comments that when people betray another by lying, 'although full trust may have been sacrificed sufficient trust may remain'.[245] The ambiguity of the situation and his understanding of 'natural' loyalties mean Saul's apparent acceptance of Michal's second lie is understandable. In any case, drawing upon the anthropological data, one could surmise that both he and she may be viewed as not desiring to validate the truth of the matter for the sake of their continuing relationship.

On the definition above it is clear that Michal does indeed lie, twice. However, it is one matter to analyse whether Michal dissembles, another to think that there are cases in which lies are acceptable or, specifically, that Michal's deception might be justified. On the rigorist view, they are not, since even the prospect of David's death would not justify her dissembling as she stated David's infirmity. Given that the author does not indicate any sort of mental reservation, it is appropriate to think that her lie is justified only if Michal did not have the obligation to reveal the truth to either the messengers or Saul. The accounts of deception in the Old Testament would tend to indicate that lying occurs to those outside the 'in-group'. The commentators noted previously assume that the group is both static and known, namely, either Israel or the family. Although many ethnographies also point to lying in service of the family or village, they also highlight that groups are not fixed but fluid, and that individuals use situational ambiguity to define and redefine their relationships with others.[246] For this reason truthfulness is not expected unless *explicitly* warranted, and *even then* lying is only condemned if a person's intentions are unambiguous. Although I have argued that Michal's lie to the messengers was warranted by the *teraphim* dummy, the polysemous nature of symbols means that the warrant could be misinterpreted. By resending the messengers, Saul indicates that he suspects as much, and when the matter is laid bare these suspicions are confirmed. The anthropological perspectives adduced above suggest that the issue for them would not have been the lie as such, but her choice of David. This is confirmed in the text, where both Saul and Michal

245 Adler, 'Lying', 441.
246 Cf. Herzfeld, *Poetics of Manhood*, 76.

assume that the fundamental question is one of loyalty not mendacity, for it is *not* the lie but the *change in loyalty* that is challenged. Both father and daughter understand that Michal's loyalty is *revealed* by her lie. But then, as I explained above, Michal lies again. This time she uses cultural categories to redefine her loyalty as being to Saul. Only readers, however, know this is what she does: while Saul can accept her words as a reaffirmation of his daughter's loyalty to the family, readers can perceive her true allegiance.

A final consideration is whether Michal's lying and disloyalty to Saul signifies that she is a trickster figure. Ann Engar claims that many Old Testament women demonstrate their faith in God by engaging in trickery. 'Though deceit has connotations of wrong doing, the trickery of each woman is seemingly blessed by God and brings about his will'.[247] Michal certainly fulfils the criteria for a trickster adduced by Naomi Steinberg: she is socially disruptive and operates from a position of comparative weakness.[248] However, Michal is not a comic figure, a defining feature of virtually all tricksters. This is important, for not every liar is a trickster.[249] Furthermore, although Michal does appear to resist expectations of loyalty to her father, she is not a model of resistance to David; indeed, if she were, the author's theological point would be undermined.[250] Given the absence of a number of defining attributes of tricksters it seems best to view Michal simply as a woman who lied to her father. By doing so Michal crosses from the category of loyal family member to outsider or, at

247 A. Engar, 'Old Testament Women as Tricksters', in *Mapping of the Biblical Terrain: The Bible as Text* (BR 33; ed. V. L. Tollers and J. Maier; Lewisberg: Bucknell University Press, 1990), 143–157, quote 143. The purpose of women's trickery is defence of Israel or family.

248 N. Steinberg, 'Israelite Tricksters, Their Analogues and Cross-cultural Study', *Semeia* 42 (1988): 1–13; cf. S. Niditch, 'Samson as Culture Hero, Trickster, and Bandit: The Empowerment of the Weak', *CBQ* 52 (1990): 608–24; idem, *Tricksters and Underdogs: A Prelude to Biblical Folklore* (San Francisco: Harper and Row, 1987); M. Jackson, 'Lot's Daughters and Tamar as Tricksters', *JSOT* 26 (2002): 29–46. Steinberg also notes, however, that biblical tricksters are human, not demigod or animal; and that while non-biblical trickster tales deal with macrocosmic issues of human boundaries the Bible's stories touch upon the microcosm of daily life, see Steinberg, 'Israelite Tricksters', 9.

249 Cf. Edwin Good, 'Deception and Women: A Response', *Semeia* 42 (1988): 117–32, especially 120–21.

250 For the view that David himself is a trickster see Raymond-Jean Frontain, 'The Trickster Tricked: Strategies of Deception and Survival in the David Narrative', in *Mapping of the Biblical Terrain: The Bible as Text* (BR 33; ed. V. L. Tollers and J. Maier; Lewisberg: Bucknell University Press, 1990), 170–92.

least, to some sort of ambiguous, indeterminate state 'between' categories, a place where she remains for the remainder of her textual life.

To conclude, Michal's 'voice' tells lies. But by lying she reveals that she has chosen loyalty to David over Saul. Although modern interpreters are scandalized more by her mendacity than her choice of allegiance, I have suggested that ancient implied readers would have viewed the matter the other way around. Her lie was merely an incidental consequence of her prior choice to be loyal to David. Michal's voice, then, speaks of the priority of loyalty to God's anointed. Saul's question, the only time he utters anything in this pericope, speaks of the priority of family loyalty. The key theological question concerns which of the text's voices is affirmed by the author.

5. Michal's Voice Approved

I have suggested that Saul's voice would have resonated with cultural mores and that despite his murderous intentions readers would have expected Michal to remain loyal to her father. Right from the very beginning of the pericope, however, readers are led to mistrust Saul's voice. The narrative uses a variety of devices to undermine his perspective and promote an alternative ethic.

A. A HOUSE, IN THE NIGHT

One of Mikhail Bakhtin's central concepts for literary interpretation is the chronotope, an intersection of time and place that cannot be reduced to either. According to Bakhtin

> [i]n the literary artistic chronotope, spatial and temporal indicators are fused into one carefully thought-out, concrete whole. Time, as it were, thickens, takes on flesh, becomes artistically visible; likewise space becomes charged and responsive to the movements of time, plot and history.[251]

The significance of this for narrative is that events are organized by the

251 M. Bakhtin, 'Forms of Time and of the Chronotope in the Novel', in *The Dialogic Imagination: Four Essays* (ed. M. Holquist; trans. C. Emerson and M. Holquist; Austin: Texas University Press, 1981), 84–258, quote 84.

chronotope, 'it is the place where the knots of narrative are tied and untied',[252] an image that readers utilize in their interpretation.

The initial action in our passage occurs at night. In biblical narratives the night is an occasion of danger and uncertainty, a time to attack (Josh. 8:3; Judg. 7:9; 9:32-34; 16:2; 1 Sam. 14:36; 2 Kgs 6:14; 8:21), when protection is required (Exod. 13:22; 1 Sam. 25:16), when death may visit (Exod. 11:4; 12:29-30; 2 Kgs 19:35) and when a negative assessment of even righteous acts is expected (Gen. 19:34; Judg. 6:27; 1 Sam. 15:11, 16; 28:8). In short, the night is the archetypal time for wickedness.[253] But these allusions by no means exhaust the significance of Saul's sending messengers to the house at night. This particular space – time combination or chronotope is pregnant with negative associations that count against Saul's voice. Apart from Joshua's spies' sojourn at Rahab's house, mentioned below, the two other Old Testament instances of people laying siege to a house at night compromise Saul's voice by alluding to the most depraved iniquity. Lot's invitation to the angels in Sodom and Gomorrah presents the house as a place of refuge and succour in contrast to the dangers of spending the night in the village square (Gen. 19:1-8).[254] But even before the family and guests had retired to sleep Lot's house was surrounded by agitating townsmen, and only divine intervention saved Lot and his visitors from being abused. The parallels with 1 Samuel 19 are patent, as Figure 5 reveals.

	Genesis 19	*1 Samuel 19*
A man in his house:	Lot	David
Accompanied by:	Lot's family and angels	Michal
House besieged by:	Townsmen of Sodom	Saul's Messengers
Deliverance by:	Angels	Michal

Figure 5 Parallels between Genesis 19 and 1 Samuel 19

252 Bakhtin, 'Chronotope', 250.

253 Cf. Ps. 17:3: 'If you try my heart, if you visit me by night, if you test me, you will find no wickedness in me; my mouth does not transgress'. The night can also be the time for provision (Num. 11:9) and visions from God (Gen. 20:3; 26:24; 40:5; 46:2).

254 Two interpretations that compare day and night in this passage are R. Letellier, *Day in Mamre, Night in Sodom: Abraham and Lot in Genesis 18 and 19* (Leiden: Brill, 1995) and B. Doyle, '"Knock, Knock, Knockin' on Sodom's Door": the Function of פתח/דלת in Genesis 18–19', *JSOT* 28 (2004): 431–48.

In both cases the threat to the house and its occupants is removed by someone else in the man's house, the angels in Genesis 19 and Michal in our passage. The comparison between the men of Sodom and Saul's messengers, who fulfil exactly the same role in each case, clearly portray Saul in a negative light, and partly assuage doubts concerning Michal's behaviour.

The second instance of the chronotope occurs in Judges 19. A man of Gibeah invites a Levite stranger to spend the night in his house rather than in the square (Judg. 19:20). Again, the house was surrounded by 'wicked men' demanding that the man be handed over to them for sexual gratification, and once again the owner of the house confronted them, offering his virgin daughter in lieu.[255] This time there are no structural parallels to the angels in Genesis 19 to strike the assailants blind; and the Levite expelled his concubine to endure their abuse. Although the text does not say that the men of Gibeah wanted to kill the host or Levite stranger (though see Judg. 20:5 where the Levite embellishes the narrative report in Judges 19 by suggesting that he was threatened with death), Judges 19 displays the same chronotope of the house at night. Their perversities are not attributed to Saul, but the fact that his hometown was Gibeah, and that the concubine's, like David's, was Bethlehem, directly links his actions in 1 Samuel 19 and the men of Gibeah in the Judges account.

To conclude, by setting David's escape from Saul in a house, in the night, the author undermines Saul's voice, however much it may have chimed with contemporary morals.

B. SENDING AND BEING SENT

Another way in which the writer of Samuel subverts Saul's voice is by highlighting the decreasing efficacy of Saul's commands as the narrative progresses. This is particularly true of his sending. While Saul is the subject of שלח in vv. 11, 14 and 15, his messengers' mandate 'shrinks into an anticlimax'.[256] At first Saul sends messengers to *kill* David. Even before Michal's ruse has

255 This horrifying thought is probably meant to signify that the host was beyond reproach with respect to fulfilling his duties of hospitality, since there is no reason to assume this offer would not have been equally as shocking to ancient readers as modern ones. For a detailed exegesis of this passage see P. Trible, *Texts of Terror* (OBT; Minneapolis: Fortress, 1984), 65–91.

256 Fokkelman, *Crossing*, 265.

been discovered, however, the narrative hints at a diminution of Saul's kingly power: וישלח . . . לקחת את־דוד, he sends messengers to *fetch* David.[257] Nor is this the end of the process. The messengers, thinking Michal remained loyal to Saul, as discussed above, accepted her lie as an adequate excuse. Saul, not so easily deflected – and possibility alerted by his prior apprehensions concerning Michal and Jonathan's advocacy of David – sends again. This time, however, וישלח . . . לראות את־דוד, he merely sends messengers to *see* David. Ironically, David is absent during most of Saul's decreasingly efficacious sending – to kill, then to fetch, and finally to see. Only the reader, with Michal and the narrator, knows this; Saul remains in not so blissful ignorance, a sardonic comment upon the pretensions to kingly control symbolized by his sending messengers.[258] Furthermore, some commentators suggest that 'brought up' indicates Saul's house was on the height of Gibeah.[259] This supposition can be juxtaposed with an observation by Gilsenan to intensify Saul's bathos. Gilsenan refers to a powerful lord whose

> domain lies beneath his gaze and he is the focus of men's regard; he is the centre of a landscape formed and given meaning by the controlling force of his possession. This visual/spatial perspective is crucial both to the fantasy and the actualities of power, to the fantasy as part of the actualities of power.[260]

The lord both sees and is seen to see, a construction of reality represented by the location and design of his palace: an imposing edifice high upon the hill overlooking his domains, and with large windows in which he can sit in order to be observed by others as he fulfils the obligations of his position, including that of appearing to take his ease. If Saul's palace is indeed on the hill it, too, could reflect a construal of his kingship as 'feudal' control, not only by Saul himself but his subjects. They would observe the sending of messengers and

257 The differences in vocabulary are one reason for rejecting David Tsumura's proposal that there was only one sending, i.e. v. 11 = v. 14, David Tsumura, *The First Book of Samuel* (NICOT; Grand Rapids: Eerdmans, 2007), 494.

258 Cf. Fokkelman, *Crossing*, 258. That it is typical of kings to oblige others to do their bidding is further evidenced by David's sending, שלח, of messengers to inquire about and then fetch Bathsheba (2 Sam. 11:1-3).

259 Erdmann, *Samuel*, 252; Kirkpatrick, *Samuel*, 172.

260 Gilsenan, *Lords*, 34; cf. also 3–22, which imagines how a great lord seated in his palace fits into a wider narrative concerning the exercise of power.

interpret this action as an indication of his authority. By doing so, of course, they inscribe Saul's authority in themselves.

By v. 16, however, David has vanished from sight. Saul is wholly thwarted and left to ponder his political impotence. His only recourse is to challenge his daughter, although even then his vocabulary implicitly recognizes that he has failed: he accuses Michal both of deceiving him ותשלחי את־איבי. The NRSV translates the phrase 'and let my enemy go', which, while a perfectly good translation, disguises the fact that the root is שלח. The author has Michal rub more salt into his wounds with her reply: 'He said', with the emphatic pronoun, הוא, שלחני. There is no direct speech by David in the pericope, yet even his 'reported' discourse, in his absence, is utterly effective. While Saul struggles yet fails to effect his commands employing significant military resources, David's single word and the assistance of a woman[261] achieve his objective.

The following verses hint at divine working behind David's escape, since when Saul once again sends messengers to capture David in Naioth in Ramah they fall into a prophetic frenzy. After sending messengers three times with the same result he himself travels to Naioth. Yet, Saul is not only unable to control the messengers but is also subject to a similar experience (1 Sam. 19:18-24). This is a far cry from Saul's initial experience of sending. In 1 Sam. 11:7 and 13:2, for example, his command was devastatingly effective. The turning point seems to come in 1 Sam. 15:20, where Saul's view is that he has walked in the ways God has sent him.[262] Samuel, however, hears not obedience but the bleating of sheep and rejects Saul as king.[263] From this point Saul's sending is ineffective, except when it is to promote David (1 Sam. 16:19-20, 22; 18:5). In contrast, David's sending is successful (1 Sam. 25:14; 26:4; 2 Sam. 2:5; 3:14; 9:5; 10:2, 7; 11:1, 3–4, 6, 14, 27; 13:7; 18:12; 19:11). In the Bathsheba episode, which uses שלח extensively, the problem is not with his ability to command, rather the view that he himself is above moral norms. Although I suggested above that some ethnographies point to an expectation that 'great lords' will 'abuse' their position, as a sign of their power, the Old Testament's view of such excesses is uniformly negative (Deut. 17:14-20; 1 Sam. 8:6-18;

261 NB this is simply a comment upon the mores of ancient manly honour.
262 Note the use of the verb שלח: ואלך בדרך אשר־שלחני יהוה.
263 1 Sam. 15:26. Note the irony: קול יהוה (what Saul hears, 1 Sam. 15:20) with קול־הצאן . . . וקול הבקר (what Samuel hears in v. 14).

2 Samuel 12). The latter perspective is clear also in 1 Sam. 22:11, Saul's only 'successful' post-rejection sending – for the priests of Nob in order to have them massacred. The contrast between the two men could not be sharper, and points to the writer's subversion of Saul's voice.

An intra-textual allusion to שלח in Josh. 2:1-22 supports this interpretation. The parallels between the passages are remarkable and I think it probable that the author of 1 Sam. 19:10-17 had access either to the Rahab text or the underlying traditions, which he used to inform the Michal narrative. Although the events described in each passage are distinctive, the structural and verbal connections are obvious. First, both start with a woman in a house, who is accompanied by men that she will eventually lead to safety. Second, the threat to Joshua's spies commences when the king of Jericho sends (the same verbal root, שלח, as when Saul sends) for Rahab (Josh. 2:3). Third, the time of the subsequent action is night; and, fourth, the initiative comes from the women. Fifth, both Rahab and Michal lie to their king's messengers.[264] Sixth, as Michal takes, תקח, the *teraphim* in order to simulate David's sleeping body (1 Sam. 19:13), Rahab takes, תקח, the men in order to hide them (Josh. 2:4). Seventh, the means of escape is through the window. The author of Joshua concludes the account of the spies' escape with the phrase ותשלחם וילכו. Thus, eighth, just as the king of Jericho sent in vain but Rahab sent successfully, so with king Saul and Michal; and, finally, the verb הלך is employed by the writer of Samuel to conclude the 'David's escape' portion of the narrative in v. 12.[265]

What do these intra-textual allusions mean for the interpretation of 1 Samuel 19? Obviously, the meaning of the Rahab text is quite different, yet the close parallels point to the real possibility that readers were meant to connect the two narratives. The King of Jericho represents the land to be conquered and Joshua's spies the precursors of the rightful heirs to the territory, which will be given by God.[266] The king is duped by Rahab, despite his best attempts at 'sending', and she lowers the escapees through a window so that they are able

264 The imperative at the end of her speech (Josh. 2:5), רדפו (third-person masculine plural), indicates that she speaks to the king's messengers rather than him personally – like Saul he does not deign to visit himself.

265 The whole phrase reads: וילך ויברח וימלט. The additional words function as a bridge between the statement in v. 10, וימלט, and the conclusion in v. 18 that employs the identical phrase, ויברח וימלט.

266 See the dialogue between Rahab and the spies in vv. 9-14. For discussion of the

to get away. In the Samuel narrative Michal replaces Rahab as the cunning woman who deceives a king. It is probably significant that the allusion is to the king of Jericho for it portrays Saul as the king to be defeated by miraculous means; and David, like the spies, the inheritor of the king's kingdom.

To conclude, Saul's voice is further undermined by his inability efficaciously to send, something highlighted in 1 Samuel 19. It is a reminder of a theological point made repeatedly in the books of Samuel that exercise of power depends not on human will alone but divine providence.

C. *TERAPHIM*

The most commentated topic in our passage is the identity of the *teraphim*. Despite the stalwart efforts of exegetes, however, the meaning of both התרפים and כביר העזים remain opaque.[267] In short, there is little to profit in discussing the precise identity of the objects Michal employed for her ruse. Nevertheless, I suggest that the author highlights her use of *teraphim* to subvert Saul's voice.

The *teraphim* appear to link Michal with Rachel, both daughters loyal to their husbands over their fathers. Bodner elaborates that Genesis 31 and 1 Samuel 19 'feature *angry father-in-laws* (Saul and Laban), *younger daughters* (Michal and Rachel), *fugitive husbands* (David and Jacob) and *deceptive idols*'.[268] Although these texts may constitute a common type-scene, and the similarity of structure is suggestive, since Saul takes the role of Laban, this does not seem to me to be the key to understanding the writer's emphasis upon Michal's use of *teraphim*.[269] The only other reference to this object in the books of Samuel is in 1 Sam. 15:23, a chapter central to the author's whole thesis. The narrative commences when Saul is charged to attack and utterly destroy, חרם, Amalek (1 Sam. 15:3). The text highlights the partial fulfilment of his commission: 'Saul and the people spared Agag, and the best of the sheep and of the cattle and of the fatlings, and the lambs, and all that was valuable, and would

differences between the two passages see A. Caquot and P. du Robert, *Les Livres de Samuel* (CAT VI; Genève: Labor et Fides, 1994), 233.

267 See notes 3 and 244, above.

268 K. Bodner, *National Insecurity: A Primer on the First Book of Samuel* (Toronto: Clements, 2003), 140. Emphasis original.

269 Furthermore, I doubt whether one text is a commentary on the other, as claimed by Craig Y. S. Ho, 'The Stories of the Family Troubles of Judah and David: A Study of their Literary Links', *VT* 44 (1999): 514–31.

not utterly destroy, חרם, them; all that was despised and worthless they utterly destroyed, חרם' (1 Sam. 15:10). In the next verse YHWH himself declares to Samuel that Saul's disobedience means he regrets making him king; and Samuel journeys to confront Saul. The latter protests that he has been obedient, and that the spoil was brought back 'to sacrifice, זבח, to the LORD your God in Gilgal' (1 Sam. 15:21). Niditch notes, however, that from '*zĕbāḥîm*, sacrifices of the sort Saul mentions[,] one makes a feast and enjoys eating meat from the sanctified flesh. That devoted to destruction is not to be shared with God in any sense'.[270] Thus Saul's response provokes Samuel to pronounce (in succinct verse, highlighting the climatic nature of the declamation):

> Has the LORD as great delight in burnt offerings and sacrifices (זבח),
> as in obeying the voice of the LORD?
> Surely, to obey is better than sacrifice (זבח)
> and to heed than the fat of rams.

Then comes an explicit reference to *teraphim*: כי הטאת־קסם מרי ואון ותרפים הפצר, 'for rebellion [is] [the] sin of divination, presumption [is] vanity and *teraphim*' (1 Sam. 15:23).[271] Here Saul's disobedience is classified as rebellion, in turn described as the sin of divination. It is juxtaposed with presumption,[272]

270 Niditch, *War*, 62.

271 Smith comments that this 'verse is obscure, and the versions do not give much help', Smith, *Samuel*, 138. I follow the MT; for discussion of the LXX see Grillet and Lestienne, *1 Règnes*, 279–80. Regarding the first clause: NRSV, on the basis of presumed parallelism with v. 22, *compares* the seriousness of rebellion and divination. Others *define* rebellion as the sin of divination (e.g. Smith, McCarter), or suggest rebellion 'is *like*' (Klein), 'is *as*' (Erdmann) divination. On the order of subject and predicate in nominal clauses see WO'C 130, and the literature cited there. Regarding the second clause: I take the subject to be הפצר, cf. WO'C 591. Driver proposes that 'the fundamental idea of און is apparently what is *valueless and disappointing*', Driver, *Notes*, 127. Emphasis original. It denotes, according to context, either calamity, naughtiness or worthlessness, the latter in reference to idols, cf. Isa. 66:3; Zech. 10:2, where התרפים דברו־און. I translate it 'vanity', see also Klein, *1 Samuel*, 145. On the meaning of הפצר see below.

272 הפצר is the pausal form of an absolute hiphil infinitive with substantival force, cf. Driver, *Notes*, 127. פצר means to urge or press upon (Gen. 19:3, 9; 33:11; Judg. 19:7; 2 Kgs 2:17; 5:16); the hiphil, which is unique, appears to mean 'display pushing' or, in the nominal infinitive, 'forwardness', 'presumption', cf. Klein, *1 Samuel*, 145; McCarter, *1 Samuel*, 263; *pace* Smith who translates it 'obstinacy' on the basis that a 'too insistent [en]treaty of God was not Saul's fault', Smith, *Samuel*, 139. He overlooks the fact that there is no need for God to be involved here: the charge is that Saul was too insistent or presumptuous *on*

Saul's pushiness to get things done his way.[273] The piling up of the negative characterizations of rebellion, idolatry and presumption, all associated with the concrete, physical *teraphim*, produces the sensation of a wave whose crest tips over and crashes down as Samuel declares God's rejection of Saul in the next verse: 'Because you have rejected the word of the LORD, he has also rejected you from being king'.

Many commentators, obviously at a loss to explain the significance of the *teraphim*, think that they cast a negative shadow over Michal. Bergen declaims that in 'the present compelling scene and without the intrusion of a didactic commentary, the writer suggests that Michal was as much a spiritual rebel as her father' and that 'whereas Michal trusted in a teraphim to save David, David trusted in the Lord'.[274] I doubt that this is the issue. Bergen's citation of Psalm 59 does not inform the first element of his contention; and the more moderate positions of others, for example, Klein's suggestion that the *teraphim* were Michal's, not David's, are without textual support.[275] Instead I propose that the *teraphim* symbolize both Saul's rejection of God and God's rejection of him as ruler. Observing that the *teraphim* of 1 Sam. 15:23 form the link between Samuel's declaration that God prefers obedience to sacrifice, precisely in contradistinction to Saul's priorities, and the final rejection of Saul as king, has tremendously important ramifications for their significance in Michal's ruse. In the drama of ch. 19 the *teraphim* remind readers that although Saul appears to act as king, the days of his reign are numbered. Their prominence in the narrative is clearly intended to subvert the authority of Saul's voice: however acceptable it may have seemed to his contemporaries, it is a vain rebellion against God.

his own account. Smith attempts to find an alternative reading that could be parallel to מרי yet corrupted to הפצר. LXX reads ἐπάγουσιν, 'they urge on', leading him to suggest הפיצו, but McCarter doubts if this is original, being a change 'which could have arisen from the reading of MT in the third century BC when *r* and *w* were especially easily confused', McCarter, *1 Samuel*, 263.

273 On the latter as a good characterization of Saul see 1 Sam. 14:24-46; 15:13, 15, 20. I think it is pushiness rather than a concern with 'ritual action without obedience', as claimed by Fokkelman, *Crossing*, 100. Cf. Mary Evans who notes that one of Samuel's central themes is the contrast between 'grasping' after power and offering support from a position of weakness, M. Evans, *1 and 2 Samuel* (NIBC 6; Carlisle: Paternoster, 2000), 9–10.

274 R. Bergen, *1, 2 Samuel* (NAC 7; Nashville: Broadman and Holman, 1996), 208.

275 Klein, *1 Samuel*, 197.

D. MICHAL'S CHARACTERIZATION

At *this stage* in the narrative Michal is a presented by the author as a reliable character.[276] Although her literary persona is flat rather than rounded two 'character traits' can be identified.[277] First, Michal is Saul's 'youngest daughter' (1 Sam. 14:49). In Old Testament narrative such brief descriptors are significant. Sternberg explains that in general 'the epithet is a ticking bomb, sure to explode into action in the narrator's (and God's) own good time'.[278] He observes that 'a woman described as good-looking will sooner or later become an object of love or lust'.[279] This may well explain why Michal is *not* described in these terms, for her role in the narrative is to exercise decisive agency, for good or ill, not simply to be an object of desire.[280] That Michal is described as the youngest, therefore, is theologically important since it is a sign of favour (see Genesis 44–45; Judg. 9:5; 1 Sam. 16:11). A second feature of Michal's character is revealed by the author's description of her inner thoughts in the repeated statement that 'Michal loved David' (1 Sam. 18:20, 28). Robert Lawton argues that the Merob – Leah parallelism highlights David's lack of love for Michal.[281] Similarly, Jobling comments that '[o]minously . . . there is no mention of any reciprocating love on David's side . . . A reader who pursues the story of Michal to its end will doubt that David ever had any love for her'.[282] These authors make much of David's supposed emotional detachment, concluding that he views his marriage to Michal as merely instrumental – which is viewed as a bad thing. However, I do not think it is especially significant that Michal's love is not recorded as being requited, since my discussion of

276 So also E. White, 'Michal the Misinterpreted', *JSOT* 31 (2007): 451–64, especially 456.

277 For this distinction see S. Bar-Efrat, *Narrative Art in the Bible* (JSOTSup 70; Sheffield: Almond Press, 1989), 90. Bar-Efrat identifies the following methods of characterization in Biblical narrative: outward appearance, inner personality, and indirect characterization by speech. Alter suggests characterization is revealed by a scale from actions or appearance through direct speech to the narrator's explicit statement, see R. Alter, *The Art of Biblical Narrative* (New York: Basic Books, 1981), 117.

278 M. Sternberg, *The Poetics of Biblical Narrative: Ideological Literature and the Drama of Reading* (Bloomington: Indiana University Press, 1987), 339.

279 Sternberg, *Poetics*, 339.

280 While, for example, Abigail is, cf. 1 Sam. 25:3; A. Berlin, 'Characterization in Biblical Narrative: David's Wives', *JSOT* 23 (1982): 69–85.

281 R. Lawton, 'David, Merob, and Michal', *CBQ* 51 (1989): 423–25.

282 Jobling, *Samuel*, 151.

marriage, above, points to the inappropriateness of conceiving of ancient Near Eastern political marriages in primarily emotional terms; and if the love here is essentially political, then the ideological nature of the history of David's rise means it is obvious that only love for the Davidic dynasty will be highlighted. In short, regardless of whether Michal's love refers to political allegiance or an emotional disposition the author highlights that she is on David's side. By doing so, the author prepares readers to listen to Michal's voice rather than Saul's.

The interesting and theologically important facets of Michal's characterization, however, do not lie in her 'character traits' but in the way she is used. In the words of David McCracken, '[c]haracter is something that the author tends toward speaking *with* rather than speaking *about*'.[283] This Bakhtinian mode of thinking views characterization as occurring on the boundaries of interaction, and since characters' voices engage in dialogue their characterization is not fixed but changeable. Michal is a good example of changing characterization, although the way in which it occurs safeguards the author's preference for Michal's voice over Saul's in 1 Samuel 19 and David's over Michal's in 2 Samuel 6. This is crucial, for when Michal acts in the latter passage she is not portrayed positively but as a despiser of David's antics before the ark of God (2 Sam. 6:12-23 – the notes about her marriage to David [1 Sam. 25:43-44] and enforced remarriage [2 Sam. 3:12-16] do not refer to Michal's agency). What, then, to do with the final negative verdict upon Michal expressed in the damning phrase 'and Michal the daughter of Saul had no child to the day of her death'? Alter remarks that 'by suppressing any causal explanation in his initial statement of Michal's scorn [the author] beautifully suggests the "overdetermined" nature of her contemptuous ire, how it bears the weight of everything that has not been said but obliquely intimated about the relations between Michal and David'.[284] I cannot agree, however, that 2 Sam. 6:23 should be viewed as encapsulating the whole of Michal's characterization, for

283 D. McCracken, 'Character in the Boundary: Bakhtin's Interdividuality in Biblical Narratives', *Semeia* 63 (1993): 29–42, quote 36. Emphasis original. McCracken identifies five features of the Bakhtinian interdividual character: (1) character is relatively free from objective authorial determination; (2) character exists in relation with others; (3) character is presently real to readers, thus forming a dialogic with them; (4) characterization aims to provoke a response, not merely describe; and (5) character exists in discourse, it is not simply described by an omniscient narrator.

284 Alter, *Art*, 123.

the reason that Michal ends her textual days in barren disgrace for despising David (2 Sam. 6:16). As Alter himself notes, a 'theologically minded reader, and certainly any advocate of the divine right of the Davidic dynasty, is invited to read this statement [about her barrenness] as a declaration that Michal was punished by God for her presumption in rebuking His anointed king'.[285] The narrative has stressed the holiness of the ark and the logistical steps taken by the king to placate God following the death of Uzzah (2 Sam. 6:1-15). This is the context for the presentation of David and Michal according to their reactions to the entrance of YHWH's ark into Jerusalem. David dances, shouts, sacrifices, blesses and distributes food. Liturgically correct and bountifully generous he contrasts with Saul, who could not seem to sacrifice properly, and took rather than gave – as king, Saul is the quintessential 'taker', as Samuel threatened he would be (1 Sam. 8:11-17, cf. 1 Sam. 12:3). But Michal 'daughter of Saul' – it is highly significant that her lineage is highlighted every single time her name is mentioned in this passage (2 Sam. 6:16, 20-21, 23; in v. 21 David contrasts himself and 'your father') – is said to despise David in her heart. This is ominous not only because David was worshipping YHWH but also because readers may hear intra-textual resonances within the books of Samuel. The word despise, בזה, is used by God to make the theologically important point that 'those who honour me I will honour, and those who despise me shall be treated with contempt' (1 Sam. 2.30). Furthermore, Michal is in the same category as the 'worthless fellows' who despised Israel's first king, and the Philistine who despised David (1 Sam. 10:27; 17:42). All of these despisers receive a riposte, by being rejected, shown to be wrong, or killed. Michal is condemned to die without having produced life. In all these examples the pairing despiser – opponent is a proxy for the pairing despiser – YHWH: Eli's sons – YHWH; worthless fellows – Saul (who was chosen by God); Philistine – David (who comes in the name of the living God). But this is *not* the case in 1 Samuel 19. There she is on God's side, as 1 Sam. 18:28 makes explicit: 'for the LORD was with David and Saul's daughter Michal loved him' (my translation). Following Bakhtin, we can see that it is the interaction of David and Michal that determines her characterization: Michal is portrayed positively when she supports

285 Alter, *Art*, 123.

David, and negatively when she despises him. In 1 Sam. 19:11-17, therefore, her voice is to be preferred over Saul's.

It is suggestive to interpret Michal's characterization as a process of being stripped of agency. In her analysis of Grimm's fairy tales Ortner discerns a difference between the portrayal of men and women, boys and girls. She argues that 'female characters had to be *made* passive, weak and timorous, that is a recognition that agency in girls had to be *unmade*'.[286] Thus girls who exercise agency are punished, either by not maturing into adults or by passing through trials to undo learned agency.

> If any sort of agency must be punished, even for 'good' girls, the punishment is even worse for 'bad' female characters, witches, and wicked stepmothers. These women are highly agentic – they have projects, plans, plots. Needless to say, they all come to terrible ends.[287]

It is important to observe, however, that Michal's lot derives not from her agency with respect to letting David go, but because she despises him for his conduct at the parade. Whereas she acts contrary to societal expectations in her loyalty to David and deception of Saul, in 2 Samuel 6 she is concerned to uphold proper standards of decency, protesting that David has acted shamefully in full view of the maids. It is precisely the concern for such 'norms' that receives David's heated reply that he will degrade himself yet further because he was dancing 'before the LORD'. The condemnation of her defence of societal values where they conflict with honouring YHWH lends further support to her counter-cultural action in letting David go. The final snuffing out of Michal's agency, which would seem to fit Ortner's appraisal of other morality tales, is given a theological rationale in David's retort. He declares that he danced 'before the LORD, who chose me in place of your father and all his household, to appoint me as prince of Israel, the people of the LORD' (2 Sam. 6:21). David makes explicit that Michal pertains to the rejected house of Saul. And the narrator makes sure that the legitimacy of David's claim to

286 Ortner, *Making Gender*, 9. Emphasis original.

287 Ortner, *Making Gender*, 10. One difference between these fairy tales and the Old Testament, therefore, would seem to be that in the latter not *every* woman comes to a sticky end, e.g. Deborah (Judges 4–5), Ruth, Hannah (1 Sam. 1:1-2:10), Abigail (1 Samuel 25).

the kingship is unquestioned by observing that 'Michal the daughter of Saul had no child to the day of her death'.[288] To conclude, both Michal's characterization in 1 Samuel and the contrast with the more negative presentation in her final appearance show that her voice as she facilitates David's escape is approved by the author.

6. Understanding Michal's Moral Dilemma

In the introduction, I observed that the concerns of the author in 1 Sam. 19:10-18a are sharply focused upon ethical questions, including lying and loyalty. In this chapter, I have employed the interpretative approach outlined in the first half of this book carefully to examine Michal's moral dilemma using anthropology. Starting from a consideration of Saul's question to Michal 'Why did you let my enemy go?', I have examined the passage from various angles. First was the angle of violence against enemies. Considering the passage in the light of anthropology suggested new interpretations that explain both Saul and Michal's actions in the narrative, and how implied readers may have comprehended the text. Thus although Saul's behaviour may not have been condoned, it can be understood as having been acceptable, even 'logical', for a powerful leader. Second, I considered family relations, in particular thinking about the implications of marriage for a daughter's loyalties towards both her father and new husband. It became clear that in a society like that of ancient Israel a woman's 'natural' inclination would have been to support her father against her spouse. That Michal did not would have surprised readers, obliging them to think about the theological significance of her choice. Third, I focused upon lying and truth-telling in social context, finding that lying is a dynamic practice that is both influenced by social relations, yet also helps establish them. In the case of Michal, her lie would not have been intrinsically problematic for implied readers, but was intended to reveal her loyalties.

288 2 Sam. 6:23. In the absence of male heirs transmission of the patrimony to the grandsons was through daughters, cf. the daughters of Zelophedad (Num. 27:1-7; 36:1-11). Both biblical and ANE sources point to the desirability of the daughter's husband having some relationship to the patriarch. Ben-Barak notes an adoption certificate from Nuzi obliging the adopted son to marry one Gilimninu, see Z. Ben-Barak, 'Inheritance by Daughters in the Ancient Near East', *JSS* 25 (1980): 22–33, especially 23. Since the adopted son was to receive the adopted father's estate the interest was clearly in *her* descendants, thus the scheme of inheritance is: father–daughter–inheriting grandsons.

While these studies have enabled a new interpretation of Michal and Saul's interactions, the crucial question is which narrative 'voice', if any, is endorsed by the author. Via a consideration of the 'chronotope' of a house in the night, Saul's decreasingly efficacious sending, the author's references to *teraphim*, and the characterization of Michal at this stage in the narrative, I have shown that Michal's voice is preferred to Saul's. However, both Michal's choice of David in preference to Saul and the author's endorsement of her choice would have been startingly unexpected, something that points to its theological significance.

Few commentators remark upon 1 Sam. 19:10-18a in detail, perhaps because they consider it to be an insignificant element of the overall narrative. Those that do deal with Michal's moral dilemma tend to concentrate on exculpating her lie. Very few indeed notice a conflict of values involving a decision concerning family loyalty. Juxtaposing the passage with anthropological data, however, has offered a new way of reading this text that shows it to be surprisingly 'heavy' with meaning. In the final chapter I sketch some implications of my interpretation.

Chapter 6

Contradicting Values

'Who is the greatest Italian painter?'
'Leonardo da Vinci, Miss Brodie.'
'That is incorrect. The answer is Giotto,
he is my favourite.'

Muriel Spark, *The Prime of Miss Jean Brodie*[1]

In this book I have constructed an interdisciplinary conversation between Old Testament studies, anthropology and ethics in order to elucidate the significance of the moral dilemma facing Michal. I have argued that her conundrum is best explicated by attending to the moral goods that feature in the biblical narrative, but that these can only be adequately comprehended when the social world of authors and implied readers is understood. To achieve this, I have examined anthropological resources relating to practices of enmity, affinity and mendacity, asking how these might inform the interpretation of characters' narrative voices. The approval of some voices as they present particular configurations of moral goods reveals the author's theological affirmations. In adopting this innovative methodology, I have refrained from simply assuming the superiority of my interpretation à la Miss Brodie. Instead, I have sought to commend my interpretative understandings with discussion of how they account for the textual data and why they would have resonated with ancient implied readers.

At the end of Chapter 3, I identified three key aspects of the practice of the

1 The epigraph is from M. Spark, *The Prime of Miss Jean Brodie* (London: Penguin, 1961), 11.

ethics of kinship, viz. the existence of multiple, contradicting and potentially mutually exclusive moral goods in the text, the variety of perception of any particular situation or action, and the necessarily personal, and thus open, nature of practice, which nevertheless can exhibit regularity. By way of conclusion I shall outline how each of these facets of practice may be observed in 1 Sam. 19:10-18a.

The textual voices of Michal, David and Saul point to several moral goods, not all of which can be achieved in the situation described by the author. The good of life is prominent because of the threat to David. Yet the good of family loyalty, with all that this implies in terms of continuance of the father's house and lineage, which itself is a guarantor of life and a source of protection, is also present. Truth telling, which for modern commentators is the moral good most obviously betrayed, also competes with the need to protect the family, and the benefits of dominating or eliminating enemies. And among these moral goods, unknown to characters but revealed to readers, is God. He has spoken his rejection of Saul and already arranged for the anointing of David. It is noteworthy that the author does in fact construct a conflict of values and does not simply assert the hegemonic schema. However, rather than assume the appropriateness of intuitive responses to the dilemma by modern Western readers, I have demonstrated that reading with anthropology reveals the multifaceted nature of the conundrum confronting Michal. Attention to the contested nature of anthropology has served as a caution against importing the supposedly 'assured results' of ethnographic investigation into biblical studies in the form of models of social or moral action. The attention to particularity as well as generality has revealed that the truth of Michal's utterances is neither the only, nor most important, moral issue. In this particular case, I have argued, family loyalty is more prominent. Furthermore, it has been possible to observe that habitual constructions of moral goods are not simply accepted, but *used* by both Michal and Saul to justify their choices – my interpretation of characters' practices demonstrates how cultural 'norms' can be manipulated in ambiguous situations.

As one may expect given my discussion of variety of perception, these goods and the appropriate way of resolving their conflict are viewed differently by each character. Furthermore, the perceptions themselves are sometimes opaque and uncertain. David seems not to appreciate his situation until Michal informs him that unless he saves himself he will be killed. Perhaps he cannot envisage Saul actually prosecuting nihilistic violence. I have suggested that it was quite logical that the king, meanwhile, would *not* have assumed that husband and wife were 'one flesh' with a natural tendency to act together against the wife's father should the situation demand, but that Michal would turn David over at first light. Readers perceive that Saul acts in line with societal expectations in terms of the practice of violence, his marriage strategies and in his assumption that Michal should tell him the truth. When Saul acts within the narrative his agency conforms to the cultural schema regarding the moral goods in conflict. Michal, however, acts in extraordinary ways, bucking the expectations of 'structure'.

It is in the description of Michal's perceptions that the theology of the books of Samuel takes over. In the programmatic hymn of praise at the beginning of the composition (1 Sam. 2:8-10) Hannah declares that

> the pillars of the earth are the LORD's,
> and on them he has set the world.
> He will guard the feet of his faithful ones,
> but the wicked shall be cut off in darkness;
> for not by might does one prevail.
> The LORD! His adversaries shall be shattered;
> the Most High will thunder in heaven.
> The LORD will judge the ends of the earth;
> he will give strength to his king,
> and exalt the power of his anointed.

Hannah attributes to YHWH the power to turn the world upside down, to reverse the status of the powerful but wicked, and the poor but faithful. For that reason, she declaims, God's anointed will be protected. Against all probability as far as implied readers are concerned – and this is the crucial point – Michal perceives the clash of moral goods in culturally unexpected ways, and prioritizes David's life over loyalty to her father. The epigraph to Chapter 5, in which I offered my interpretation of this narrative, points to such an understanding: the author told 'the truth' that the pillars of the earth, the way the world works, are subject to God's rule.[2] But he did so using the unpalatable truth of a lie.

2 In this light, some scholars have portrayed Saul's fighting against his destiny as

In the case of modern readers this is the point that causes ethical problems; to ancient implied readers, I have argued, the lie was merely symptomatic of Michal's (dis)loyalty.

Walter Brueggeman claims that this narrative is devoid of God. 'We are treated to calculating human actions that do not conform to our expectations. Something is deeply awry when a future king must crawl through a window, when the wife of a coming king must lie to the father who is still king'.[3] Yet this pessimistic evaluation is not quite correct. 1 Sam. 19:10-18a constitutes a key moment for David, Saul and Michal. For David, because he is in a corner and his life is threatened. For Michal, because she must decide, perhaps unwittingly, between two anointed kings. For Saul, because he is about to eliminate his rival. And for God, because his anointed is in mortal danger. At this moment, Michal lets David down through a window, thus thwarting Saul's attempt to have him brought up to death.[4] Some commentators are unhappy with her actions, arguing that '[a]lthough imperfect moral conduct may subserve the interests of God's servants, it nevertheless is dishonouring to them'.[5] However, if the moral dilemma which faces Michal is conceived in terms of contradicting voices that conflict, then *her* voice, which contradicts societal norms unexpectedly to assert fidelity to David, YHWH's anointed, is endorsed by the author.

This conclusion has implications for ethics. McCarter outlines seven ways in which the 'History of David's Rise' justifies the political legitimacy of David's kingship in theological terms.[6] The incidents involving Michal fit into

'tragic', e.g. D. Gunn, *The Fate of King Saul: An Interpretation of a Biblical Story* (JSOTSup 14; Sheffield: Sheffield University Press, 1980), 78–83; C. Exum, *Tragedy and Biblical Narrative. Arrows of the Almighty* (Cambridge: CUP, 1992), 16–42; E. Good, *Irony in the Old Testament* (Sheffield: Almond Press, 1981), 56–80. For a detailed response see P. Williams, 'Is God Moral? on the Saul Narratives as Tragedy', in *The God of Israel* (UCOP 64; ed. R. P. Gordon; Cambridge: CUP, 2007), 175–89. Note especially William's observation that Saul is an agent: he is not simply trapped by fate.

3 W. Brueggemann, *First and Second Samuel* (Interpretation; Louisville: John Knox, 1990), 144

4 Cf. J. P. Fokkelman, *Narrative Art and Poetry in the Books for Samuel. A full interpretation based on stylistic and structural analyses. Vol. II: The Crossing Fates (I Sam 13–31 and II Sam 1)* (SSN 23; Assen: Van Gorcum, 1986), 267.

5 R. Payne Smith and C. Chapman, *1 Samuel* (PC; ed. H. D. M. Spence and J. S. Snell; London: Kegan Paul & Co, 1881), 366.

6 K. McCarter, 'The Apology of David', *JBL* 99 (1980): 489–504, especially 499–502.

this apology by showing how power comes to him: David does not grasp it. While David's marriage to Michal does not confer the kingship upon David, her choice to facilitate David's escape speaks of loyalty to *this* king: if Michal chose David, so should readers. The other side of the coin is the 'negative' assertion concerning the validity of societal norms when these conflict with loyalty to David's house. Just as Michal in preferring David also *rejected* not only Saul but also the dominant schema of a morality that prioritized family loyalty and filial obedience, so readers should remember that loyalty to YHWH's anointed – and his successors – is paramount. *This* is the central concern of the narrative.

These 'political' affirmations are set in the context of a wider assertion concerning YHWH's agency. As Fokkelman remarks, 'it is not at all self-evident that the hero's career will terminate in succession to the throne', or that 'power falls into David's lap like a ripe apple'.[7] That David does become king is the result of God's work, a theological assertion that leads us from questions about why these narratives *did* matter, to another: why *do* they matter?

Some commentators are troubled that the books of Samuel fail explicitly to condemn 'questionable' morality. Gordon observes that 'they often stop short just where we might expect a word of censure or a moralizing tailpiece', and he feels compelled to exculpate *his* lack of attention to their present relevance by assuring readers that he, too, is '"against" murder, duplicity and all their evil cronies'.[8] When considered in the context of competing moral goods, however, the matter is not so black and white, for the interpretative issues concern which goods are preferred in cases when attaining them all is impossible. In such situations narratives can play an important role in moral formation. They can certainly do so by exemplifying virtues or principles. However, a more significant way is by engaging readers in the moral dilemma itself, thus training the moral faculties of readers, both by analogy ('this is what to do, or not do, if you find yourself in a similar situation') and by refining appreciation of moral goods and their relations to each other.[9] In the case of 1 Sam. 19:10-18a the

See also Frank Frick, '*Cui Bono*? – History in the Service of Political Nationalism: The Deuteronomistic History as Political Propaganda', *Semeia* 66 (1994): 79–92.

7 Fokkleman, *Crossing*, 313.

8 R. Gordon, *1 and 2 Samuel: A Commentary* (Exeter: Paternoster Press, 1986), 9. See also T. W. Cartledge, *1 & 2 Samuel* (SHBC 7; Macon: Smyth & Helwys, 2001), 248–49.

9 Cf. R. Parry, *Old Testament Story and Christian Ethics: The Rape of Dinah as a*

author wishes to justify a novel solution to the moral dilemma itself, one that the implied readers would have found counter-intuitive, so this is an essential didactic move.

Augustine supposed that a moral community is one that shares common objects of love.[10] As texts shared by today's readers the relevance of the Samuel narratives extends beyond their initial audience to the formation of contemporary reading communities. Perhaps it will be helpful to give an example using what is often considered to be the central moral problem of my chosen text: lying. I noted above that Augustine held that lying was always impermissible. He thought it was worse than other forms of deception because it involves asserting something that one knows to be false and, because the soul is worth more than the body, did not permit lying even to save a life.[11] Nor, maintained Augustine, is it justified even if more certain of success than simply hiding the truth. A rigorist posture against lies was also maintained by Immanuel Kant, who asserted that truthfulness 'is the formal duty of an individual to everyone, however great may be the disadvantage accruing to himself or to another'.[12] Kant's duty, though, is an unconditional duty to humanity, not towards the individual with whom one is relating, and although he calls truth-telling 'sacred', his view of the deity is not that of the Old Testament. It is unsurprising that the rigorist position has been challenged. In the words of Duns Scotus, it is 'less bad to take away true opinion from one's neighbor, or to be the occasion of generating false opinion in him, than to take away his bodily life. Indeed, there is scarcely a comparison'.[13] Yet the problem remains: what should one

Case Study (PBM; Milton Keynes: Paternoster, 2004), 4; John Barton, 'Introduction', in *Understanding Old Testament Ethics: Approaches and Explorations* (Louisville: Westminster John Knox Press, 2003), 1–11, especially 10.

10 Cf. *Civ.* 19.24. For discussion see O. O'Donovan, *The Common Objects of Love: Moral Reflection and the Shaping of Community* (Grand Rapids: Eerdmans, 2002), 20–24.

11 *De mend.* 8; *C. mend.* 23; cf. Jonathan Adler, 'Lying, Deceiving, or Falsely Implicating', *JP* 94 (1997): 435–52. For an exposition of Augustine and representative later authorities see P. Griffiths, *Lying: An Augustinian Theology of Duplicity* (Grand Rapids: Brazos, 2004). For Aquinas on lies see *Summa* II–II q.109–110; it is merely a venial sin.

12 I. Kant, 'On a Supposed Right to Lie from Altruistic Motives', in *Critique of Practical Reason and Other Writings in Moral Philosophy* (ed. and trans L. W. Beck; Chicago: University of Chicago Press, 1949; repr. in Sissela Bok, *Lying: Moral Choice in Public and Private Life* 2nd ed.; New York: Vintage, 1999), 267–72, quote 268.

13 Quoted in T. Williams, 'Lying, Deception, and the Virtue of Truthfulness: A Reply to Garcia', *FP* 17 (2000): 242–48, quote 245.

do when one recognizes the moral imperative to tell the truth at the same time as observing that this may bring about or be evil? An approach commended by some is the 'mental reservation', in which deception is effected by omitting some of the truth. Another, which does not cause the same disquiet about the ethics of manipulating the message, is to assert that a lie is only such if the recipient has the right to the truth. Originally adopted by Grotius, the major twentieth-century exponent of this position was Paul Ramsey.[14] Ramsey maintains that rules prohibiting lying are *always* to be obeyed, but defines a lie as 'withholding the truth from someone to whom the truth is due'. Bok, however, protests that Ramsey's definition ignores the question of what it means to have a right to truthful information, a fundamental lacuna.[15] Perhaps the problem is viewing truth and lying as mutually exclusive. The reflections of Dietrich Bonhoeffer are illuminating. He distinguishes between God's truth, grounded in love, and Satan's truth, which hates creation.

> It is only the cynic who claims 'to speak the truth' at all times and in all places to all men in the same way, but who, in fact, displays nothing but a lifeless image of the truth . . . He wounds shame, desecrates mystery, breaks confidence, [and] betrays [the] community in which he lives.[16]

Interestingly, Bonhoeffer considered that when things that belong to one 'order' or sphere of life are used in another – he provides the example of a child being asked about private family matters in a public classroom – then lying is inevitable. Thus truth-telling, according to Bonhoeffer, must account for a person's relationships in order to identify to whom one is obliged to reveal 'the truth'. Bonhoeffer's observations lead us straight back to the narrative that we have studied so carefully in this book. The story of Michal's lying to Saul, as I have interpreted it, also highlights the centrality of relationships when considering truth-telling, and points to the Bible's concern with truth understood

14 Cf. T. Grotius, *On the Law of War and Peace* (trans. A. C. Campbell; Kitchener: Batoche Books, 2001), 258–61; P. Ramsey, 'The Case of the Curious Exception', in *Norm and Context in Christian Ethics* (ed. P. Ramsey and G. H. Outka; London: SCM, 1968), 67–135.

15 See S. Bok, *Lying: Moral Choice in Public and Private Life* (2nd ed.; New York: Vintage, 1999), 15.

16 D. Bonhoeffer, *Ethics* (ed. E. Bethge; trans. N. H. Smith; New York: MacMillan, 1955), 328.

in this context. The fact that this text offers readers different voices promoting different answers to the moral question forces readers, both ancient and modern, to grapple with it, a process in which their own moral faculties are trained and sharpened. This training highlights the importance of perception, for even if a rule relating to specific people (e.g. 'do not lie to your family') is to be followed, moral action 'depends upon seeing truthfully those relationships for what they are'.[17] All this, though, takes us a very long way from 'fetishising [verbal] assertion' in our consideration of lies.[18] Instead, we are invited to consider both the simplicity *and* complexity of the moral life informed by the Church's Scriptures and tradition.

There are undoubtedly many more lessons for contemporary moral reflection that can be learnt from the story of Michal. For the present I would only hope that studies such as this one, whose methodology is in principle transferable to any other biblical narrative, might provide new interpretative understandings that help bridge the 'troublesome gap'[19] between biblical scholarship and ethics.

17 C. Hovey, 'Putting Truth To Practice: MacIntyre's Unexpected Rule', *SCE* 19 (2006): 169–86, quote 183; cf. A. MacIntyre, 'Truthfulness, Lies, and Moral Philosophers: What Can We Learn from Mill and Kant?' Tanner Lectures on Human Values, 1994.

18 See B. Williams, *Truth and Truthfulness: An Essay in Genealogy* (Princeton: Princeton University Press, 2002), 107–10.

19 T. Ogletree, *The Use of the Bible in Christian Ethics* (Oxford: Blackwell, 1984), xi.

APPENDIX A

Crime and Punishment in the Book of the Covenant (Exod. 20:1-23:33)

Punishment	*Crime*	
Death	Exod. 21:12	Mortal assault
	Exod. 21:15	Striking parents
	Exod. 21:16	Kidnap
	Exod. 21:17	Cursing father or mother
	Exod. 21:29	Of ox owner if ox has a history of goring and kills man or woman (plus stoning of ox)
	Exod. 22:18	Of female sorcerer
	Exod. 22:19	Bestiality
'Devoted to destruction'	Exod. 22:20	Idolatry
Ransom	Exod. 21:30	Of ox owner's life (in lieu of capital punishment) if ox has a history of goring and kills man or woman / boy or girl (plus stoning of ox)
Release of slave as a free person	Exod. 21:11	Denying first (slave) wife marital rights
	Exod. 21:26	Assault of slave leading to loss of eye, as compensation
Payment of bride price, marriage to virgin	Exod. 22:16	Seduction of unengaged virgin

Compensatory fine / Restitution	Exod. 21:19	Assault leading to loss of productive time while recuperating
	Exod. 21:22	Miscarriage as result of injury to third party with no further injury
	Exod. 21:33	If animal falls into uncovered pit
	Exod. 22:12	Animal stolen while in safekeeping
Fixed fine	Exod. 21:32	Payment of 30 shekels of silver by ox owner if ox has a history of goring and kills a male or female slave (plus stoning of ox)
Deterrent fine	Exod. 22:1	Theft of livestock subsequently killed or sold: 5 oxen per stolen ox; 4 sheep per stolen sheep; thief sold into slavery if unable to pay
	Exod. 22:7	Theft of livestock subsequently found in thief's possession: double value of theft
	Exod. 22:9	Theft in case of disputed ownership determined by 'coming before God' [some sort of lot?]; double value of disputed item
'Eye for eye, etc.'	Exod. 21:22	Miscarriage as result of injury to third party with further injury
Stoning of ox, with prohibition on sale of meat	Exod. 21:28	Goring to death of man or woman
Bloodguilt	Exod. 22:3	Bludgeoning to death of thief caught breaking and entering after sunrise (no bloodguilt if killed before sunrise)
No punishment specified	Exod. 21:20	Slave-owner killing slave (Capital punishment assumed from context?)
No punishment	Exod. 22:11	Animal killed, injured or carried off unseen while in safekeeping, provided guardian makes oath before the LORD

APPENDIX B

Crime and Punishment in the Holiness Code (Lev. 17:1-26:46)

Punishment	*Crime*	
Death through burning	Lev. 21:9	For prostitute who is daughter of priest
	Lev. 20:13	Marrying a woman and her mother (punishment for all parties)
Death	Lev. 20:2	Giving offspring to Molech
	Lev. 20:9	Cursing father or mother
	Lev. 20:10	Adultery (punishment for both parties)
	Lev. 20:11	Sex with father's wife (punishment for both parties)
	Lev. 20:12	Sex with daughter-in-law (punishment for both parties)
	Lev. 20:13	Homosexual sex (punishment for both parties)
	Lev. 20:16	Woman who practises bestiality (punishment for both parties)
	Lev. 20:27	For male or female medium or wizard
	Lev. 24:16, 23	Blasphemy (punishment for both Israelite and alien)
	Lev. 24:17	Murder
Cut off from God's presence	Lev. 22:3	If any of Aaron's priestly descendents approach sacred donations while in state of uncleanness

Cut off from the people	Lev. 17:4, 9	Sacrifice not at entrance to tent of meeting
	Lev. 18:29	Sexual relations prohibited in Lev. 18.6–19.23
	Lev. 19:8	Eating sacrificed meat on third day
	Lev. 20:17	Incest (punishment for both parties)
	Lev. 20:18	Sleeping with a woman during her menstruation (punishment for both parties)
'Bear their guilt'	Lev. 17:15	Not cleansing themselves after eating animal with blood
Guilt offering of ram	Lev. 19:21	Sexual relations with slave woman
Restitution	Lev. 24:18, 21	Killing of animal
'Eye for eye, etc.'	Lev. 24:19-20	Maiming of person
20% fine	Lev. 22:14	If person eats sacred food destined for priests

APPENDIX C

Crime and Punishment in the Deuteronomic Code (Deut. 12:1-26:19)

Punishment	*Crime*	
Total destruction of town	Deut. 13:15	Idolatry (punishment for whole town)
Death	Deut. 17:5	Idolatry
	Deut. 17:12	Disobeying judicial decision
	Deut. 18:20	False prophet
	Deut. 21:18	Rebellious son
	Deut. 22:21	Non-virgin bride
	Deut. 22:22	Adultery (punishment for both parties)
	Deut. 22:24	Seduction of engaged woman in city (punishment for both parties)
	Deut. 22:25	Seduction / rape of engaged woman in countryside (punishment for man only)
	Deut. 24:7	Kidnap
'Eye for eye, etc'.'	Deut. 19:19	False witness
Freedom for slave wife	Deut. 21:14	Dishonouring unwanted slave wife
100 shekels to father / forfeit right to divorce	Deut. 22:19	Slandering woman's presumed virginity
50 shekels to father / enforced marriage without right to divorce	Deut. 22:29	Seduction / rape of unengaged woman if caught *in flagrante*
Shaming	Deut. 25:9	Refusal to perform Levirate duties
Removal of hand	Deut. 25:12	Woman who defends husband in fight by grabbing his opponent's genitals

BIBLIOGRAPHY

Abu-Lughod, Lila. *Veiled Sentiments: Honor and Poetry in a Bedouin Society*. 2nd ed. Berkley: University of California Press, 1999.

Abu-Zahra, Nadia. 'Family and Kinship in a Tunisian Peasant Community'. Pages 157–71 in *Mediterranean Family Structures*. Cambridge Studies in Social Anthropology 13. Edited by J. G. Peristiany. Cambridge: CUP, 1976.

Ackerman, Susan. 'The Personal is Political: Covenantal and Affectionate Love (*'āhēb, 'ahăbâ*) in the Hebrew Bible'. *Vetus Testamentum* 52 (2002): 437–58.

Ackroyd, Peter R. 'The Verb Love – *'āhēb* in the David-Jonathan Narratives – A Footnote'. *Vetus Testamentum* 25 (1975): 213–14.

Adler, Jonathan E. 'Lying, Deceiving, or Falsely Implicating'. *The Journal of Philosophy* 94 (1997): 435–52.

Aguilar, Mario. 'Changing Models and the Death of Culture'. Pages 299–313 in *Anthropology and Biblical Studies: Avenues of Approach*. Edited by L. J. Lawrence and M. I. Aguilar. Leiden: Deo Publishing, 2004.

—*The Rwanda Genocide and the Call to Deepen Christianity in Africa*. Eldoret: AMECEA Gaba Publications Spearhead, 1998.

Ahearn, Laura M. *Invitations to Love: Literacy, Love Letters, and Social Change in Nepal*. Ann Arbor: University of Michigan Press, 2001.

Alkire, Sabina. 'The Basic Dimensions of Human Flourishing: A Comparison of Accounts'. Pages 73–110 in *The Revival of Natural Law: Philosophical, Theological and Ethical Responses to the Finnis-Grisez School*. Edited by N. Biggar and R. Black. Aldershot: Ashgate, 2001.

Alonso Schökel, Luis. 'טוֹב'. Pages 291–93 in *Diccionario Bíblico Hebreo-Español*. Madrid: Trotta, 1994.

Alter, Robert. *The Art of Biblical Narrative*. New York: Basic Books, 1981.

—*The David Story: A Translation with Commentary of 1 and 2 Samuel*. New York: W. W. Norton, 1999.

Amadi, Elechi. *Ethics in Nigerian Culture*. Ibadan: Heinemann, 1982.

Andersen, Francis I. 'Israelite Kinship Terminology and Social Structure'. *The Bible Translator* 20 (1969): 29–39.

Anderson, Arnold A. *2 Samuel*. Word Biblical Commentary 11. Dallas: Word Books, 1989.

—*Psalms (73–150)*. New Century Bible Commentary. London: Marshal, Morgan & Scott, 1972.

Aquinas, Thomas. *Summa Theologica*. 2nd ed. Translated by the Fathers of the English Dominican Province. London: Burns, Oates and Washbourne, 1920.

Argenti-Pillen, Alexandra. 'Obvious Pretence: For Fun or For Real? Cross-Cousin and International Relationships in Sri Lanka'. *Journal of the Royal Anthropological Institute* NS 13 (2007): 313–29.

Aristotle. *Nicomachean Ethics*. 2nd ed. Translated by T. Irwin. Indianapolis: Hackett, 1999.

Attwood, David. *Changing Values: How to Find Moral Truth in Modern Times*. Carlisle: Paternoster, 1998.
Augustine. 'City of God'. Pages 1–512 in vol. 2 of *The Nicene and Post-Nicene Fathers*. Edited by Philip Schaff. 1886–89. 14 vols. Repr. Peabody: Hendrickson, 1994.
— 'On Lying'. Pages 457–77 in vol. 3 of *The Nicene and Post-Nicene Fathers*. Edited by Philip Schaff. 1886–89. 14 vols. Repr. Peabody: Hendrickson, 1994.
—'To Consentius: Against Lying'. Pages 481–500 in vol. 3 of *The Nicene and Post-Nicene Fathers*. Edited by Philip Schaff. 1886–89. 14 vols. Repr. Peabody: Hendrickson, 1994.
Bakhtin, Mikhail. 'Discourse in the Novel'. Pages 259–401 in *The Dialogic Imagination: Four Essays*. Edited by M. Holquist. Translated by C. Emerson and M. Holquist. Austin: Texas University Press, 1981.
—'Forms of Time and of the Chronotope in the Novel'. Pages 84–258 in *The Dialogical Imagination: Four Essays*. Edited by M. Holquist. Translated by C. Emerson and M. Holquist. Austin: Texas University Press, 1981.
—*Problems of Dostoevsky's Poetics*. Translated by C. Emerson. Minneapolis: University of Minnesota Press, 1984.
Banfield, E. C. *The Moral Basis of a Backward Society*. New York: Free Press, 1958.
Banner, Michael. *Christian Ethics and Contemporary Moral Problems*. Cambridge: CUP, 1999.
Bar-Efrat, Shimon. *Narrative Art in the Bible*. Journal for the Study of the Old Testament Supplement Series 70 / Bible and Literature Series 17. Translated by D. Shefer-Vanson. Sheffield: Almond Press, 1989.
Barmash, Pamela. 'The Narrative Quandary Cases of Law in Literature'. *Vetus Testamentum* 54 (2004): 1–16.
Barnard, Alan. 'Rules and Prohibitions: The Form and Content of Human Kinship'. Pages 783–812 in *Companion Encyclopedia of Anthropology*. 2nd ed. Edited by T. Ingold. London: Routledge, 2002.
Barnard, Alan and Jonathan Spencer. *Encyclopedia of Cultural and Social Anthropology*. 3rd ed. Edited by J. Spencer and A. Barnard. London: Routledge, 2002.
Barnes, J. A. *A Pack of Lies: Towards a Sociology of Lying*. Cambridge: CUP, 1994.
Barnes, Peter. 'Was Rahab's Lie a Sin?'. *Reformed Theological Review* 54 (1995): 1–9.
Barr, James. *Biblical Faith and Natural Theology – The Gifford Lectures for 1991*. Oxford: OUP, 1994.
—'Is God a Liar? (Genesis 2–3) – And Related Matters'. *Journal of Theological Studies* 57 (2006): 1–22.
—*The Semantics of Biblical Language*. 1961. Repr. London: SCM Press, 1983.
—'Why? in Biblical Hebrew'. *Journal of Theological Studies* 36 (1985): 1–33.
Barré, Michael L. 'The Formulaic Pair טוב (ו)חסד in the Psalter'. *Zeitschrift für die alttestamentliche Wissenschaft* 98 (1986): 100–105.
Barrett, Stanley. *Anthropology: A Student's Guide to Theory and Method*. Toronto: University of Toronto Press, 1996.
Barton, John. 'Amos's Oracles against the Nations'. Pages 77–129 in *Understanding Old Testament Ethics: Approaches and Explorations*. Louisville: Westminster John Knox Press, 2003.
—'Disclosing Human Possibilities: Revelation and Biblical Stories'. Pages 53–60 in *Revelation and Story: Narrative Theology and the Centrality of Story*. Edited by J. Barton and G. Sauter. Burlington: Ashgate, 2000.
—*Ethics and the Old Testament*. London: SCM, 1998.

—'Imitation of God in the Old Testament'. Pages 35–46 in *The God of Israel*. University of Cambridge Oriental Publications 64. Edited by R. P. Gordon. Cambridge: CUP, 2007.
—'Introduction'. Pages 1–11 in *Understanding Old Testament Ethics: Approaches and Explorations*. Louisville: Westminster John Knox Press, 2003.
—'Natural Law and Poetic Justice in the Old Testament'. Pages 32–44 in *Understanding Old Testament Ethics: Approaches and Explorations*. Louisville: Westminster John Knox Press, 2003.
—'Reading for Life: The Use of the Bible in Ethics'. Pages 55–64 in *Understanding Old Testament Ethics: Approaches and Explorations*. Louisville: Westminster John Knox Press, 2003.
—'The Basis of Ethics in the Hebrew Bible'. Pages 45–54 in *Understanding Old Testament Ethics: Approaches and Explorations*. Louisville: Westminster John Knox Press, 2003.
—'Understanding Old Testament Ethics'. Pages 15–31 in *Understanding Old Testament Ethics: Approaches and Explorations*. Louisville: Westminster John Knox Press, 2003.
—*Understanding Old Testament Ethics: Approaches and Explorations*. Louisville: Westminster John Knox Press, 2003.
—'Virtue in the Bible'. Pages 65–74 in *Understanding Old Testament Ethics: Approaches and Explorations*. Louisville: Westminster John Knox Press, 2003.
Barton, Stephen. C. 'Historical Criticism and Social-Scientific Perspectives in New Testament Study'. Pages 61–89 in *Hearing the New Testament: Strategies for Interpretation*. Edited by J. B. Green. Grand Rapids: Eerdmans, 1995.
Basso, Ellen. *In Favor of Deceit: A Study of Tricksters in an Amazonian Society*. Tuscon: University of Arizona Press, 1987.
Batto, Bernard F. *Studies on Women at Mari*. Baltimore: John Hopkins University Press, 1974.
Bell, Rudolph M. *Fate and Honor, Family and Village: Demographic and Cultural Change in Rural Italy since 1800*. Chicago: University of Chicago Press, 1979.
Ben-Barak, Zafrira. 'The Legal Background to the Restoration of Michal to David'. Pages 15–29 in *Studies in the Historical Books of the Old Testament*. Vetus Testamentum Supplement Series 30. Leiden: Brill, 1979.
—'Inheritance by Daughters in the Ancient Near East'. *Journal of Semitic Studies* 25 (1980): 22–33.
Bendor, S. *The Social Structure in Ancient Israel: The Institution of the Family (Beit 'ab) from the Settlement to the End of the Monarchy*. Jerusalem Biblical Studies 7. Jerusalem: Simor, 1996.
Bergen, Robert D. *1, 2 Samuel*. The New American Commentary 7. Nashville: Broadman and Holman, 1996.
Berger, John. *A Fortunate Man: The Story of a Country Doctor*. New York: Holt, Rinehart and Winston, 1967.
Berlin, Adel. 'Characterization in Biblical Narrative: David's Wives'. *Journal for the Study of the Old Testament* 23 (1982): 69–85.
Berry, George R. 'The Ethical Teaching of the Old Testament'. *The Biblical World* 21 (1903): 108–18.
Betchel, Lynn M. 'Shame as a Sanction of Social Control in Biblical Israel: Judicial, Political, and Social Shaming'. Pages 232–58 in *Social-Scientific Old Testament Criticism. A Sheffield Reader*. The Biblical Seminar 47. Edited by D. J. Chalcraft. Sheffield: Sheffield University Press, 1997. Repr. from *Journal for the Study of the Old Testament* 49 (1991): 47–76.

Bettetini, Maria. *Breve historia de la mentira: De Ulises a Pinocho*. Colección Teorema. Translated by P. Linares. Madrid: Ediciones Cátedra, 2002.

Birch, Bruce C. 'Divine Character and the Formation of Moral Community in the Book of Exodus'. Pages 119–35 in *The Bible in Ethics: The Second Sheffield Colloquium*. Journal for the Study of the Old Testament Supplement Series 207. Edited by J. W. Rogerson, M. Davies and M. D. Carroll R. Sheffield: Sheffield Academic Press, 1995.

—*Let Justice Roll Down: The Old Testament, Ethics, and the Christian Life*. Louisville: Westminster John Knox Press, 1991.

—'Moral Agency, Community, and the Character of God in the Hebrew Bible'. *Semeia* 66 (1994): 23–41.

—'Old Testament Narrative and Moral Address'. Pages 75–95 in *Canon, Theology and Old Testament Interpretation*. Edited by G. M. Tucker, D. L. Petersen and R. R. Wilson. Philadelphia: Fortress, 1988.

Blenkinsopp, Joseph. 'The Family in First Temple Israel'. Pages 48–103 in *Families in Ancient Israel*. Edited by L. G. Perdue *et al*. Louisville: Westminster John Knox, 1997.

Bloch, Maurice, and Dan Sperber. 'Kinship and Evolved Psychological Dispositions: the Mother's Brother Controversy Reconsidered'. *Current Anthropology* 43 (2002): 723–48.

Blum, Lawrence A. *Moral Perception and Particularity*. Cambridge: CUP, 1994.

Bockmuehl, Markus. 'Natural Law in Second Temple Judaism'. *Vetus Testamentum* 45 (1995): 17–44.

Bodi, Daniel. *The Michal Affair: From Zimri-Lim to the Rabbis*. Sheffield: Sheffield Phoenix Press, 2005.

Bodner, Keith. *National Insecurity: A Primer on the First Book of Samuel*. Toronto: Clements, 2003.

Boehm, Christopher. 'Exposing the Moral Self in Montenegro: The Use of Natural Definitions to Keep Ethnography Descriptive'. *American Ethnologist* 7 (1980): 1–26.

Bok, Sissela. *Lying: Moral Choice in Public and Private Life*. 2nd ed. New York: Vintage, 1999.

Bonhoeffer, Dietrich. *Ethics*. Edited by E. Bethge. Translated by N. H. Smith. New York: MacMillan, 1955.

Booth, Wayne. *The Company We Keep: An Ethics of Fiction*. Berkley: University of California Press, 1988.

Boulay, Juliet du. 'Lies, Mockery and Family Integrity'. Pages 389–406 in *Mediterranean Family Structures*. Cambridge Studies in Social Anthropology 13. Edited by J. G. Peristiany. Cambridge: CUP, 1976.

—*Portrait of a Greek Mountain Village*. Oxford: Clarendon Press, 1974.

Bourdieu, Pierre. *Algeria 1960: Essays by Peirre Bourdieu*. Cambridge: CUP, 1979.

—*Outline of a Theory of Practice*. Cambridge: CUP, 1977.

—*Pascalian Meditations*. Translated by R. Nice. Cambridge: Polity, 2000.

—*The Logic of Practice*. Translated by R. Nice. Stanford: Stanford University Press, 1990.

—'The Sentiment of Honour in Kabyle Society'. Pages 191–242 in *Honour and Shame: The Values of Mediterranean Society*. Edited by J. G. Peristiany. Chicago: University of Chicago Press, 1965.

Bowman, Richard G. 'The Complexity of Character and the Ethics of Complexity: The Case of King David'. Pages 73–97 in *Character and Scripture: Moral Formation, Community and Biblical Interpretation*. Edited by W. P. Brown. Grand Rapids: Eerdmans, 2002.

Brandes, Stanley H. *Migration, Kinship and Community: Tradition and Transition in a Spanish Village*. New York: Academic Press, 1975.

Bressan, Gino. *Samuele*. Rome: Marietti, 1960.

Brettell, Caroline B. 'Not That Lineage Stuff: Teaching Kinship into the Twenty-First Century'. Pages 48–70 in *New Directions in Anthropological Kinship*. Edited by L. Stone. Lanham: Rowman & Littlefield, 2001.

—'The Individual/Agent and Culture/Structure in the History of the Social Sciences'. *Social Science History* 26 (2002): 429–45.

Brontë, Anne. *The Tenant of Wildfell Hall*. 2nd ed. Harmondsworth: Penguin, 1979 [1848].

Brown, Francis, S. R. Driver and Charles A. Briggs. *A Hebrew and English Lexicon of the Old Testament*. 2nd ed. Oxford: Clarendon, 1952.

Brown, William P. *Structure, Role, and Ideology in the Hebrew and Greek Texts of Genesis 1:1-2:3*. Society of Biblical Literature Dissertation Series 132. Atlanta: Scholars Press, 1993.

Bruckner, James K. *Implied Law in the Abraham Narrative: A Literary and Theological Analysis*. Journal for the Study of the Old Testament Supplement Series 335. London: Sheffield, 2001.

Brueggemann, Walter. *First and Second Samuel*. Interpretation: A Bible Commentary for Teaching and Preaching. Louisville: John Knox, 1990.

Burnside, Jonathan P. *The Signs of Sin: Seriousness of Offence in Biblical Law*. Journal for the Study of the Old Testament Supplement Series 364. Sheffield: Sheffield Academic Press, 2003.

Byrne, Peter. *The Philosophical and Theological Foundations of Ethics: An Introduction to Moral Theory and its Relation to Religious Beliefs*. 2nd ed. Basingstoke: MacMillan, 1999.

Caird, George B. 'The First and Second Books of Samuel'. Pages 853–1176 in vol. 2 of *The Interpreter's Bible*. 12 vols. New York: Abingdon, 1953.

Campbell, Anthony F. *1 Samuel*. The Forms of Old Testament Literature 7. Grand Rapids: Eerdmans, 2003.

Campbell, J. K. *Honour, Family, and Patronage: A Study of Institutions and Moral Values in a Greek Mountain Community*. New York: OUP, 1964.

Caplan, Pat. 'Introduction: Anthropology and Ethics'. Pages 1–33 in *Ethics and Anthropology: Debates and Dilemmas*. Edited by P. Caplan. London: Routledge, 2003.

Caquot, André and Philippe de Robert. *Les Livres de Samuel*. Commentaire de l'Ancien Testament 4. Genève: Labor et Fides, 1994.

Carroll R, Daniel. *Contexts for Amos: Prophetic Poetics in Latin American Perspective*. Journal for the Study of the Old Testament Supplement Series 132. Sheffield: JSOT Press, 1992.

—'La ética de los profetas y su relevancia para América Latina hoy: La contribución de la ética filosófica'. *Kairós* 35 (2005): 7–30.

Carroll R, Daniel, and Jacqueline E. Lapsely (eds.). *Character Ethics and the Old Testament*. Lousiville: Westminster John Knox, 2007.

Carroll, Robert P. 'Prophecy and Society'. Pages 203–25 in *The World of Ancient Israel: Sociological, Anthropological and Political Perspectives*. Edited by R. E. Clements. Cambridge: CUP, 1989.

Carson, Thomas L. 'The Definition of Lying'. *Noûs* 40 (2006): 284–306.

Carsten, Janet. *After Kinship*. Cambridge: CUP, 2004.

—'Introduction: Cultures of Relatedness'. Pages 1–36 in *Cultures of Relatedness: New Approaches to the Study of Kinship*. Edited by J. Carsten. Cambridge: CUP, 2000.

—'The Substance of Kinship and the Heat of the Hearth: Feeding, Personhood, and Relatedness among Malyans in Pulau Langkawi'. *American Ethnologist* 22 (1995): 223–42.

Carsten, Janet and Stephen Hugh-Jones. 'Introduction: About the House – Levi-Strauss and Beyond'. Pages 1–46 in *About the House: Lévi-Strauss and Beyond*. Edited by J. Carsten and S. Hugh-Jones. Cambridge: CUP, 1995.

Carter, Stephen and Carol Meyers. 'Editors' Preface'. Pages xiii–xv in *Community, Identity and Ideology: Social Science Approaches to the Hebrew Bible*. Sources for Biblical and Theological Study 6. Edited by S. Carter and C. Meyers. Winona Lake: Eisenbrauns, 1996.

Cartledge, Tony W. *1 & 2 Samuel*. Smyth & Helwys Bible Commentary 7. Macon: Smyth & Helwys, 2001.

Chagnon, Napoleon. 'Life Histories, Blood Revenge, and Warfare in a Tribal Population'. *Science* 239 (1988): 985–92.

—*Yanomamo: The Fierce People*. New York: Holt, Reinhardt and Winston, 1977.

Childs, Brevard S. *The Book of Exodus: A Critical, Theological Commentary*. Old Testament Library. Louisville: Westminster, 1974.

Chisholm, Roderick M. and Thomas D. Feehan. 'The Intent to Deceive'. *The Journal of Philosophy* 74 (1977): 143–59.

Christenson, Duane A. 'The March of Conquest in Isaiah X 27c-34'. *Vetus Testamentum* 26 (1976): 385–99.

Clark, Katerina and Michael Holquist. *Mikhail Bakhtin*. London: Belknap, 1984.

Clines, David J. A. 'Michal Observed: An Introduction to Reading Her Story'. Pages 24–63 in *Telling Queen Michal's Story: An Experiment in Comparative Interpretation*. Journal for the Study of the Old Testament Supplement Series 119. Edited by D. J. A. Clines and T. C. Eskenazi. Sheffield: Sheffield Academic Press, 1991.

—'X, X *BEN* Y, *BEN* Y: Personal Names in Hebrew Narrative Style'. *Vetus Testamentum* 22 (1972): 266–87.

Clines, David J. A. and Tamara C. Eskenazi (eds.). *Telling Queen Michal's Story: An Experiment in Comparative Interpretation*. Journal for the Study of the Old Testament Supplement Series 119. Sheffield: Sheffield Academic Press, 1991.

Coats, George. 'Self-Abasement and Insult Formulas'. *Journal of Biblical Literature* 89 (1970): 14–26.

Cocking, Dean and Jeanette Kennett. 'Friendship and Moral Danger'. *The Journal of Philosophy* 97 (2000): 278–96.

Cohen, A. P. *The Symbolic Construction of Community*. London: Routledge, 1985.

Collier, Jane. 'Women in Politics'. Pages 89–96 in *Women, Culture, and Society*. Edited by M. Z. Rosaldo and L. Lamphere. Stanford: Stanford University Press, 1974.

Cowley, Abraham. *Davideis*. London: Henry Herringman, 1681.

Craigie, Peter C. *Deuteronomy*. New International Commentary on the Old Testament. Grand Rapids: Eerdmans, 1976.

Craven, Toni. 'Women Who Lied for the Faith'. Pages 35–49 in *Justice and the Holy*. Edited by D. A. Knight and P. J. Paris. Atlanta: Scholars Press, 1989.

Crenshaw, James L. *Old Testament Wisdom: An Introduction*. London: SCM, 1982.

Crites, Stephen. 'The Narrative Quality of Experience'. *Journal of the American Academy of Religion* 39 (1971): 291–319.

Cross, Frank Moore. 'The Oldest Manuscripts from Qumran'. *Journal of Biblical Literature* 74 (1955): 147–72.

Cross, Frank Moore *et al*. *Qumran Cave 4.XII: 1–2 Samuel*. Discoveries in the Judean Desert 17. Oxford: Clarendon, 2005.

Darwall, Stephen, ed. *Virtue Ethics*. Oxford: Blackwell, 2003.

Davies, Douglas J. *Anthropology and Theology*. Oxford: Berg, 2002.

Davies, Eryl W. 'The Morally Dubious Passages of the Hebrew Bible: An Examination of Some Proposed Solutions'. *Currents in Biblical Research* 3 (2005): 197–28.

—'Walking in God's Ways: The Concept of *Imitatio Dei* in the Old Testament'. Pages 99–115 in *In Search of True Wisdom: Essays in Old Testament Interpretation in Honour of Ronald E. Clements*. Journal for the Study of the Old Testament Supplement Series 300. Edited by E. Ball. Sheffield: Sheffield Academic Press, 1999.

de Certeau, Michel. *The Practice of Everyday Life*. Translated by S. Rendall. Berkley: University of California Press, 1984.

Deist, Ferdinand E. *The Material Culture of the Bible: An Introduction*. The Biblical Seminar 70. Edited by R. P. Carroll. London: Sheffield Academic Press, 2000.

DePaulo, Bella M. and Deborah A. Kashy. 'Everyday Lies in Close and Casual Relationships'. *Journal of Personality and Social Psychology* 74 (1998): 63–79.

Diamond, Stanley. 'Introductory Essay: Job and the Trickster'. Pages xi–xxii in *The Trickster: A Study in American Indian Mythology*. Edited by P. Radin. New York: Schocken Books, 1976.

Douglas, Mary. *Purity and Danger: An Analysis of Concept of Pollution and Taboo*. London: Routledge, 2002 [1966].

Doyle, Brian. '"Knock, Knock, Knockin" on Sodom's Door': the Function of פתח/דלת in Genesis 18–19'. *Journal for the Study of the Old Testament* 28 (2004): 431–48.

Driver, S. R. *Deuteronomy*. 3rd ed. International Critical Commentary. Edinburgh: T&T Clark, 1901.

—*Notes of the Hebrew Text and the Topography of the Books of Samuel.* 2nd ed. Oxford: OUP, 1913.

Dutcher-Walls, Patricia. 'The Clarity of Double Vision: Seeing the Family in Sociological and Archaeological Perspective'. Pages 1–15 in *The Family in Life and in Death: The Family in Ancient Israel.* Library of Hebrew Bible / Old Testament Studies 504. Edited by P. Dutcher-Walls. New York: T&T Clark, 2009.

Edel, May and Abraham Edel. *Anthropology & Ethics: The Quest for Moral Understanding*. 1968. Repr. New Brunswick: Transaction Press, 2000.

Edelman, Diana V. *King Saul in the Historiography of Judah*. Journal for the Study of the Old Testament Supplement Series 121. Sheffield: Sheffield University Press, 1991.

Erdmann, David. *The Books of Samuel*. Lange's Commentary 5. Translated by C. H. Toy and J. A. Broadus. New York: Scribner, Armstrong & Co., 1877.

Elliott, John H. *What is Social-Scientific Criticism?* Guides to Biblical Scholarship. Minneapolis: Fortress, 1993.

Emerson, Caryl. *The First Hundred Years of Mikhail Bakhtin*. Princeton: Princeton University Press, 1997.

—'Theory'. Pages 271–92 in *The Cambridge Companion to the Classic Russian Novel*. Edited by M. V. Jones and R. F. Miller. Cambridge: CUP, 1998.

Emmerson, Grace I. 'Women in Ancient Israel'. Pages 371–94 in *The World of Ancient Israel*. Edited by R. E. Clements. Cambridge: CUP, 1989.

Engar, Ann W. 'Old Testament Women as Tricksters'. Pages 143–57 in *Mappings of the Biblical Terrain: The Bible as Text*. Bucknell Review 33. Edited by V. L. Tollers and J. Maier. Lewisberg: Bucknell University Press, 1990.

Esler, Phillip F. 'Introduction: Models, Context and Kerygma in New Testament interpretation'. Pages 1–20 in *Modelling Early Christianity: Social-scientific studies of the New Testament in its context*. Edited by P. F. Esler. London: Routledge, 1995.

—'Making and Breaking an Agreement Mediterranean Style: A New Reading of Galatians 2:1-14'. *Biblical Interpretation* 3 (1995): 285–314.

—'Models in New Testament Interpretation: A Reply to David Horrell'. *Journal for the Study of the New Testament* 78 (2000): 107–13.
—'Review of D.G. Horrell, *The Social Ethos of the Corinthian Correspondence*'. *Journal of Theological Studies* 49 (1998): 253–60.
—'Social Identity, the Virtues, and the Good Life: A New Approach to Romans 12:1-15:13'. *Biblical Theology Bulletin* 33 (2003): 51–63.
—'Social-Scientific Models in Biblical Interpretation'. Pages 3–4 in *Ancient Israel: The Old Testament in Its Social Context*. Edited by P. F. Esler. Minneapolis: Fortress, 2006.
—*The First Christians in their Social Worlds: Social-scientific Approaches to New Testament Interpretation*. London: Routledge, 1994.
—'The Madness of Saul: A Cultural Reading of 1 Samuel 8–31'. Pages 220–62 in *Biblical Studies / Cultural Studies*. Journal for the Study of the Old Testament Supplement Series 266. Edited by J. C. Exum and S. D. Moore. Sheffield: Sheffield Academic Press, 1998.
—'The Role of Hannah in 1 Samuel 1:1-2:21: Understanding a Biblical Narrative in its Ancient Context'. Pages 15–36 in *Kontexte der Schrift. Band II: Kultur, Politik, Religion, Sprache. Festschrift fur Wolfgang Stegemann*. Edited by C. Strecker. Stuttgart: Kohlhammer, 2005.
Esler, Philip F. and Anselm C. Hagedorn. 'Social-Scientific Analysis of the Old Testament: A Brief History and Overview'. Pages 15–32 in *Ancient Israel: The Old Testament in its Social Context*. Edited by P. F. Esler. Minneapolis: Fortress, 2006.
Evans, Mary J. *1 and 2 Samuel*. New International Bible Commentary 6. Carlisle: Paternoster, 2000.
Evans-Pritchard, Edward E. *The Nuer: A Description of the Modes of Livelihood and Political Institutions of a Nilotic People*. Oxford: Clarendon Press, 1940.
Exum, J. Cheryl. *Tragedy and Biblical Narrative. Arrows of the Almighty*. Cambridge: CUP, 1992.
Falk, Ze'ev. 'Law and Ethics in the Hebrew Bible'. Pages 82–90 in *Justice and Righteousness: Biblical Themes and their Influence*. Journal for the Study of the Old Testament Supplement Series 137. Edited by H. G. Reventlow and Y. Hoffman. Sheffield: JSOT Press, 1992.
Fallers, Lloyd A. and Margaret C. Fallers. 'Sex Roles in Edremit'. Pages 243–60 in *Mediterranean Family Structures*. Cambridge Studies in Social Anthropology 13. Edited by J. G. Peristiany. Cambridge: CUP, 1976.
Faubion, James D. 'Introduction: Toward an Anthropology of the Ethics of Kinship'. Pages 1–28 in *The Ethics of Kinship: Ethnographic Inquiries*. Edited by J. D. Faubion. Lanham: Rowman & Littlefield, 2001.
—'Toward an Anthropology of Ethics: Foucault and the Pedagogies of Autopoiesis'. *Representations* 74 (2001): 83–104.
Ferguson, Brian. 'Explaining War'. Pages 26–55 in *The Anthropology of War*. Edited by J. Haas. Cambridge: CUP, 1990.
—'Introduction: Studying War'. Pages 1–79 in *Warfare, Culture and Environment*. Edited by B. Ferguson. London: Academic Press, 1984.
—*Warfare, Culture and Environment*. New York: Academic Press, 1984.
Field, Karen. 'Review of Ivan Illich's *Gender*'. *Journal of Marriage and the Family* 45 (1983): 710.
Finnis, John. *Fundamentals of Ethics*. Washington, DC: Georgetown University Press, 1983.
Fletcher, V. 'The Shape of Old Testament Ethics'. *Scottish Journal of Theology* 24 (1959): 47–73.

Fohrer, Georg. 'The Righteous Man in Job 31'. Pages 1–22 in *Essays in Old Testament Ethics*. Edited by J. L. Crenshaw and J. T. Willis. New York: Ktav, 1974.

Fokkelman, J. P. *Narrative Art and Poetry in the Books for Samuel. A Full Interpretation Based on Stylistic and Structural Analyses. Vol. II: The Crossing Fates (1 Sam. 13–31 and II Sam 1)*. Studia Semitica Neerlandica 23. Assen: Van Gorcum, 1986.

—*Reading Biblical Narrative: An Introductory Guide*. Louisville: Westminster John Knox, 1999.

Foot, Philippa. 'Moral Realism and Moral Dilemma'. Pages 250–70 in *Moral Dilemmas*. Edited by C. W. Gowans. New York: OUP, 1987.

—'Utilitarianism and the Virtues'. *Mind* NS 94 (1985): 196–209.

—*Virtues and Vices – And Other Essays in Moral Philosophy*. Oxford: OUP, 2002.

Fortes, Meyer. *The Web of Kinship Among the Tallensi*. Oxford: OUP, 1949.

Fortier, Jana. 'The Arts of Deception: Verbal Performances by the Rāute of Nepal'. *Journal of the Royal Anthropological Institute* NS 8 (2002): 233–57.

Foucault, Michael. *Discipline and Punish: The Birth of the Prison*. Translated by A. Sheridan. London: Penguin, 1977.

Fox, Michael. 'Tôb as Covenant Terminology'. *Bulletin of the American Schools of Oriental Research* 209 (1973): 41–42.

Fox, Robin. *Kinship and Marriage*. London: Penguin, 1967.

Franklin, Sarah. 'Re-thinking Nature-Culture: Anthropology and the New Genetics'. *Anthropological Theory* 3 (2003): 65–85.

Fretheim, Terence E. *God and the World in the Old Testament: A Relational Theology of Creation*. Nashville: Abingdon, 2005.

Freund, Richard A. 'Lying and Deception in the Biblical and Post-Judaic Tradition'. *Scandinavian Journal of the Old Testament* 5 (1991): 45–61.

Frick, Frank S. '*Cui Bono*? – History in the Service of Political Nationalism: The Deuteronomistic History as Political Propaganda'. *Semeia* 66 (1994): 79–92.

Friedmann, Daniel. *To Kill and Take Possession: Law, Morality and Society in Biblical Stories*. Peabody: Hendrickson, 2002.

Frontain, Raymond-Jean. 'The Trickster Tricked: Strategies of Deception and Survival in the David Narrative'. Pages 170–92 in *Mapping of the Biblical Terrain: The Bible as Text*. Bucknell Review 33. Edited by V. L. Tollers and J. Maier. Lewisberg: Bucknell University Press, 1990.

Fuchs, Esther. '"For I Have the Way of Women": Deception, Gender, and Ideology in Biblical Narrative'. *Semeia* 42 (1988): 68–83.

—*Sexual Politics in the Biblical Narrative: Reading the Hebrew Bible as a Woman*. Journal for the Study of the Old Testament Supplement Series 310. Sheffield: Sheffield Academic Press, 2000.

—'Who is Hiding the Truth? Deceptive Women and Biblical Androcentrism'. Pages 137–44 in *Feminist Perspectives on Biblical Scholarship*. Edited by A. Y. Collins. Missouls: Scholars Press, 1985.

Galvin, Kathey-Lee. 'Schneider Revisited: Sharing and Ratification in the Construction of Kinship'. Pages 109–24 in *New Directions in Anthropological Kinship*. Edited by L. Stone. Lanham: Rowman & Littlefield, 2001.

Gammie, John G. *Holiness in Israel*. Overtures to Biblical Theology. Minneapolis: Fortress Press, 1989.

Garcia, J. L. A. 'Lies and the Vices of Deception'. *Faith and Philosophy* 15 (1998): 514–37.

Geertz, Clifford. *Available Light: Anthropological Reflections on Philosophical Topics*. Princeton: Princeton University Press, 2000.

Geisler, Norman L. *Christian Ethics*. Leicester: Apollos, 1989.
Gemser, Berend. 'The Importance of the Motive Clause in Old Testament Law'. Pages 50–66 in *Congress Volume: Copenhagen 1952*. Vetus Testamentum Supplement Series 1. Edited by G. W. Anderson *et al*. Leiden: Brill, 1953.
George, Kenneth M. *Showing Signs of Violence: The Cultural Politics of a Twentieth-Century Headhunting Ritual*. Berkley: University of California Press, 1996.
Gerstenberger, Erhard S. *Theologies in the Old Testament*. Translated by J. Bowden. Edinburgh: T&T Clark, 2002.
Gesenius, W. *Genesius' Hebrew Grammar*. 2nd English Edition. Edited by E. Kautzsch. Translated by A. E. Cowley. Oxford: Clarendon, 1910.
Gevirtz, Stanley. *Patterns in the Early Poetry of Israel*. Chicago: Chicago University Press, 1963.
Gewirth, Alan. 'Is Cultural Pluralism Relevant to Moral Knowledge?'. Pages 180–90 in *Moral Disagreements: Classic & Contemporary Readings*. Edited by C. W. Gowans. London: Routledge, 2000.
Giddens, Anthony. *Central Problems in Social Theory: Action, Structure and Contradiction in Social Analysis*. Berkeley: University of Los Angeles Press, 1979.
Gilsenan, Michael. *Lords of the Lebanese Marches: Violence & Narrative in an Arab Society*. London: I. B. Tauris, 1996.
—'Lying, Honor, and Contradiction'. Pages 191–219 in *Transaction & Meaning: Directions in the Anthropology of Exchange and Symbolic Behaviour*. Edited by B. Kapferer. Philadelphia: American Anthropological Association, 1976.
Gluckman, Max. *Custom and Conflict in Africa*. Oxford: Blackwell, 1959.
Goffman, Erving. 'The Interaction Order'. *American Sociological Review* 48 (1983): 1–17.
Golding, William. *Lord of the Flies*. London: Faber & Faber, 1954.
González Lamadrid, Antonio. 'Apuntes sobre יטב/טוב y su traducción en las Biblias modernas'. *Estudios Bíblicos* 50 (1992): 443–56.
—'Pax et Bonum: «*Shalôm*» y «*ṭôb*» en relación con «*berit*»'. *Estudios Bíblicos* 28 (1969): 61–77.
Good, Edwin M. 'Deception and Women: A Response'. *Semeia* 42 (1988): 117–32.
—*Irony in the Old Testament*. Sheffield: Almond Press, 1981.
Gordon, Cyrus H. 'The Marriage and Death of Sinuhe'. Pages 43–44 in *Love and Death in the Ancient Near East: Essays in Honor of Marvin H. Pope*. Edited by J. H. Marks and R. M. Good. Guilford: Four Quarters Publishing Company, 1987.
Gordon, Robert P. *1 and 2 Samuel: A Commentary*. Exeter: Paternoster Press, 1986.
—'טוב'. Pages 353–57. in vol. 2 of *New International Dictionary of Old Testament Theology and Exegesis*. Edited by W. A. VanGemeren. 5 vols. Carlisle: Paternoster, 1997.
Gottwald, Norman K. *The Tribes of Yahweh: A Sociology of the Religion of Liberated Israel 1250–1050 B.C.E.* London: SCM, 1979.
Gowans, Christopher W. 'The Debate on Moral Dilemmas'. Pages 250–70 in *Moral Dilemmas*. Edited by C. W. Gowans. New York: OUP, 1987.
Green, Barbara. *How are the Mighty Fallen?: A Dialogical Study of King Saul in 1 Samuel*. Journal for the Study of the Old Testament Supplement Series 365. London: Sheffield Academic Press, 2003.
—*Mikhail Bakhtin and Biblical Scholarship: An Introduction*. Atlanta: Society of Biblical Literature Press, 2000.
Griffiths, Paul J. *Lying: An Augustinian Theology of Duplicity*. Grand Rapids: Brazos, 2004.

Grillet, Bernard and Michel Lestienne. *Premier Livre des Règnes*. La Bible d'Alexandrie 9.1. Paris: Les Éditions du Cerf, 1997.
Grollenberg, Luc. *Atlas de la Bible*. Translated by R. Beaupère. Brussels: Elsevier, 1954.
Grotius, Thomas. *On the Law of War and Peace*. Translated by A. C. Campbell. Kitchener: Batoche Books, 2001.
Grottanelli, Cristiano. 'Tricksters, Scape-Goats, Champions, Saviors'. *History of Religions* 23 (1983): 117–39.
Guenther, Allen. 'A Typology of Israelite Marriage: Kinship, Socio-economic, and Religious Factors'. *Journal for the Study of the Old Testament* 29 (2005): 387–407.
Gunn, David M. *The Fate of King Saul: An Interpretation of a Biblical Story*. Journal for the Study of the Old Testament Supplement Series 14. Sheffield: Sheffield University Press, 1980.
Hall, Pamela. 'Limits of the Story: Tragedy in Recent Virtue Ethics'. *Studies in Christian Ethics* 17 (2004): 8–9.
Halpern, Baruch. *David's Secret Demons: Messiah, Murderer, Traitor, King*. Grand Rapids: Eerdmans, 2001.
Hamilton, Jefferies A. 'Gallim'. Page 901 in vol. 2 of *Anchor Bible Dictionary*. Edited by D. N. Freedman. 6 vols. New York: Doubleday, 1992.
Hamilton, Victor P. *The Book of Genesis: Chapters 1–17*. New International Commentary on the Old Testament. Grand Rapids: Eerdmans, 1990.
Hare, R. M. *The Language of Morals*. 2nd ed. Oxford: OUP, 1960.
Harman, Allan M. 'Decalogue (Ten Commandments)'. Pages 513–19 in vol. 4 of *New International Dictionary of Old Testament Theology and Exegesis*. Edited by W. A. VanGemeren. 5 vols. Carlisle: Paternoster, 1997.
Harrison, Simon. *The Mask of War: Violence, Ritual and Self in Melanesia*. Manchester: Manchester University Press, 1993.
—'Skull Trophies of the Pacific War: Transgressive Objects of Remembrance'. *Journal of the Royal Anthropological Institute* NS 12 (2006): 817–36.
—'The Symbolic Construction of Aggression and War in a Sepik River Society'. *Man* NS 24 (1989): 583–99.
—'Warfare'. Pages 561–62 in *Encyclopaedia of Social and Cultural Anthropology*. Edited by A. Barnard and J. Spencer. London: Routledge, 2002.
Hayden, Corinne P. 'Gender, Genetics, and Generation: Reformulating Biology in Lesbian Kinship'. *Cultural Anthropology* 10 (1995): 41–63.
Hebblethwaite, Brian. *Ethics and Religion in a Pluralistic Age*. Edinburgh: T&T Clark, 1997.
Hendry, Joy. 'To Wrap or Not to Wrap: Politeness and Penetration in Ethnographic Inquiry'. *Man* NS 24 (1989): 620–35.
Hertzberg, H. W. *I & II Samuel*. Old Testament Library. London: SCM, 1964.
Herzfeld, Michael. *Anthropology through the Looking-glass: Critical Ethnography in the Margins of Europe*. Cambridge: CUP, 1987.
—*Anthropology: Theoretical Practice in Culture and Society*. Oxford: Blackwell, 2001.
—'Disemia'. Pages 205–15 in *Semiotics*. Edited by M. Herzfeld and M. D. Lenhart. New York: Plenum, 1980.
—'Pride and Perjury: Time and the Oath in the Mountain Villages of Crete'. *Man* NS 25 (1990): 305–22.
—*The Poetics of Manhood: Contest and Identity in a Cretan Mountain Village*. Princeton: Princeton University Press, 1985.
Hinton, Alex. 'The Poetics of Genocidal Practice: Violence under the Khmer Rouge'. Pages

157–84 in *Violence*. School of American Research Advanced Seminar Series. Edited by N. L. Whitehead. Oxford: James Curry, 2004.

Hirschkop, Ken. 'Bakhtin, Discourse and Democracy'. *New Left Review* 160 (1986): 92–111.

—*Mikhail Bakhtin: An Aesthetic for Democracy*. Oxford: OUP, 1999.

Ho, Craig Y. S. 'The Stories of the Family Troubles of Judah and David: A Study of their Literary Links'. *Vetus Testamentum* 44 (1999): 514–31.

Hoeyer, Klaus. 'Ethics Wars: Reflections on the Antagonism between Bioethicists and Social Science Observers of Biomedicine'. *Human Studies* 29 (2006): 203–27.

Holquist, Michael. 'Introduction' and 'Glossary' to *The Dialogic Imagination*, by M. Bahktin. Edited by M. Holquist. Translated by C. Emerson and M. Holquist. Austin: Texas University Press, 1981.

Holy, Ladislav. *Kinship, Honour and Solidarity: Cousin Marriage in the Middle East*. Manchester: Manchester University Press, 1989.

Horrell, David G. *The Social Ethos of the Corinthian Correspondence: Interests and Ideology from 1 Corinthians to 1 Clement*. Edinburgh: T&T Clark, 1996.

—'Models and Methods in Social-Scientific Interpretation: A Response to Philip Esler'. *Journal for the Study of the New Testament* 78 (2000): 85–105.

Horwich, Paul. 'The Value of Truth'. *Noûs* 40 (2006): 347–60.

Houston, Walter J. *Contending for Justice: Ideologies and Theologies of Social Justice in the Old Testament*. Library of Hebrew Bible / Old Testament Studies 428. London: T&T Clark, 2006.

—*Purity and Monotheism: Clean and Unclean Animals in Biblical Law*. Journal for the Study of the Old Testament Supplement Series 140. Sheffield: Sheffield Academic Press, 1993.

—'The Character of YHWH and the Ethics of the Old Testament: Is *Imitatio Dei* Appropriate?' *Journal of Theological Studies* 58 (2007): 1–25.

Hovey, Craig. 'Putting Truth To Practice: MacIntyre's Unexpected Rule'. *Studies in Christian Ethics* 19 (2006): 169–86.

Höver-Johag, I. 'טוֹב *ṭôb*; טוּב *ṭûb*; יטב *yṭb*'. Pages 296–317 in vol. 5 of *Theological Dictionary of the Old Testament*. Edited by G. J. Botterweck, H. Ringgren and H-J Fabry. 15 vols. Grand Rapids: Eerdmans, 1974–2003.

Howell, Signe. 'Many Contexts, Many Meanings? Gendered Values among the Northern Lio of Flores, Indonesia'. *Journal of the Royal Anthropological Institute* NS 2 (1996): 253–69.

—'Introduction'. Pages 1–22 in *The Ethnography of Moralities*. Edited by S. Howell. London: Routledge, 1997.

Howell, Signe and Roy Willis. 'Introduction'. Pages 1–28 in *Societies at Peace: Anthropological Perspectives*. Edited by S. Howell and R. Willis. London: Routledge, 1989.

Hugenberger, Gordon P. 'Michal'. Page 348 in vol. 3 of *International Standard Bible Encyclopedia*. 2nd ed. Edited by G. W. Bromiley. 4 vols. Grand Rapids: Eerdmans, 1982.

Humphrey, Caroline. 'Exemplars and Rules: Aspects of the Discourse of Moralities in Mongolia'. Pages 25–47 in *The Ethnography of Moralities*. Edited by S. Howell. London: Routledge, 1997.

Hunt, Melvin. 'Jezreel'. Page 850 in vol. 3 of *Anchor Bible Dictionary*. Edited by D. N. Freedman. 6 vols. New York: Doubleday, 1992.

Hursthouse, Rosalind. *On Virtue Ethics*. Oxford: OUP, 1999.

Irwin, Terence. Introduction, Notes and Glossary to *Nicomahcean Ethics* by Aristotle. Translated by T. Irwin. 2nd ed. Indianapolis: Hackett, 1999.
Jacob, Edmond. *Théologie de l'Ancien Testament*. Neuchatel: Éditions Delachaux et Niestlé, 1968.
Jacobs, Mignon R. 'The Conceptual Dynamics of Good and Evil in the Joseph Story: An Exegetical and Hermeneutical Inquiry'. *Journal for the Study of the Old Testament* 27 (2003): 309–38.
Jackson, Bernard S. 'Ideas of Law and Legal Administration: a Semiotic Approach'. Pages 185–202 in *The World of Ancient Israel: Sociological, Anthropological and Political Perspectives*. Edited by R. E. Clements. Cambridge: CUP, 1989.
—'Models in Legal History: The Case of Biblical Law'. *Journal of Law and Religion* 18 (2002–2003): 1–30.
—*Wisdom – Laws: The Mishpatim of Exodus 21:1-22:16*. Oxford: OUP, 2007.
Jackson, Melissa. 'Lot's Daughters and Tamar as Tricksters'. *Journal for the Study of the Old Testament* 26 (2002): 29–46.
Janzen, J. Gerald. 'Kugel's Adverbial *kî ṭôb*: An Assessment'. *Journal of Biblical Literature* 102 (1983): 99–106.
Janzen, Waldemar. *Old Testament Ethics: A Paradigmatic Approach*. Louisville: Westminster John Knox, 1994.
Jenson, Philip. 'Holiness in the Priestly Writings of the Old Testament'. Pages 93–121 in *Holiness: Past & Present*. Edited by S. C. Barton. London: Continuum, 2003.
Jobling, David. *1 Samuel*. Berit Olam Studies in Hebrew Narrative & Poetry. Collegeville: Liturgical, 1998.
Johnson, Alan F. 'Is There a Biblical Warrant for Natural-Law Theories?' *Journal of the Evangelical Theological Society* 25 (1982): 185–99.
Kaiser, Walter C. *Toward Old Testament Ethics*. Grand Rapids: Zondervan, 1983.
Kant, Immanuel. *Groundwork of the Metaphysics of Morals*. New York: Harper & Row, 1948 [1785].
—'On a Supposed Right to Lie from Altruistic Motives'. Pages 346–50 in *Critique of Practical Reason and Other Writings in Moral Philosophy*. Edited and Translated by L. W. Beck. Chicago: University of Chicago Press, 1949. Repr. Pages 267–72 in Sissela Bok, *Lying: Moral Choice in Public and Private Life*. 2nd ed. New York: Vintage, 1999.
Keck, Leander E. 'Rethinking "New Testament Ethics"'. *Journal of Biblical Literature* 115 (1996): 3–16.
Keil, C. F. and F. Delitzsch. *Joshua, Judges, Ruth, I & II Samuel*. Vol. 2 of *Commentary on the Old Testament in Ten Volumes*. Translated by J. Martin. Grand Rapids, Eerdmans, 1980.
Kidner, Derek. *Psalms 73–150*. Tyndale Old Testament Commentary. Leicester: IVP, 1975.
Kirkpatrick, A. F. *The Book of Psalms*. Cambridge: CUP, 1902.
—*The First Book of Samuel with Map, Notes and Introduction*. Cambridge Bible. Cambridge: CUP, 1890.
Klein, R. W. *1 Samuel*. Word Biblical Commentary 10. Waco: Word Books, 1983.
Klopfenstein, Martin A. 'שׁקר *šqr* Engañar'. Pages 1265–76 in vol. 2 of *Diccionario Teológico Manual del Antiguo Testamento*. Edited by E. Jenni and C. Westermann. Translated by J. A. Múgica. Madrid: Ediciones Cristiandad, 1978.
Kluckhohn, Clyde. 'Ethical Relativity: Sic et Non'. *The Journal of Philosophy* 52 (1955): 663–77.
—'Some Navaho Value Terms in Behavioural Context'. *Language* 32 (1956): 140–45.

Knauft, B. M. 'Reconsidering Violence in Simple Human Societies: Homicide among the Gebusi of New Guinea'. *Cultural Anthropology* 28 (1987): 457–82

Koch, Klaus -F. *War and Peace in Jalemo*. Cambridge: Harvard University Press, 1974.

Kraus, Hans-Joachim. *Los Salmos II: Salmos 60–150*. Translated by C. Ruiz-Garrido. Salamanca: Sígueme, 1995.

Kraut, Richard. *What is Good and Why: The Ethics of Well-Being*. Cambridge: Harvard University Press, 2007.

Kugel, James L. 'The Adverbial Use of *KÎ ṬÔB*'. *Journal of Biblical Literature* 99 (1980): 433–35.

Kutsch, E. 'חתן *ḥtn*'. Pages 270–77 in vol. 5 of *Theological Dictionary of the Old Testament*. Edited by G. J. Botterweck, H. Ringgren and H-J Fabry. 15 vols. Grand Rapids: Eerdmans, 1974–2003.

Laidlaw, James. 'For an Anthropology of Ethics and Freedom'. *Journal of the Royal Anthropological Institute* NS 8 (2002): 311–32.

Lawrence, Louise J. *An Ethnography of the Gospel of Matthew: A Critical Assessment of the Use of the Honour and Shame Model in New Testament Studies*. Wissenschaftliche Untersuchungen zum Neuen Testament 2 Reiche 165. Tübingen: Mohr Siebeck, 2003.

—*Reading with Anthropology: Exhibiting Aspects of New Testament Religion*. Carlisle: Paternoster, 2005.

Lawson, Thomas and Robert McCauley. *Rethinking Religion: Connecting Cognition and Culture*. Cambridge: CUP, 1990.

Lawton, Robert B. '1 Samuel 18: David, Merob, and Michal'. *Catholic Biblical Quarterly* 51 (1989): 423–25.

Leach, Edmund. 'Anthropological Approaches to the Study of the Bible During the Twentieth Century'. Pages 18–49 in *Structuralist Interpretations of Biblical Myth*. Edited by E. Leach and D. A. Aycock. Cambridge: CUP, 1983.

—'Brain Teaser'. *NY Review of Books* October (1967): 10.

—'Polyandry, Inheritance and the Definition of Marriage'. *Man* 55 (1955): 182–86.

Lehmann, Gunnar. 'Reconstructing the Social Landscape of Early Israel: Rural Marriage Alliances in the Central Hill Country'. *Tel Aviv* 31 (2004): 141–93.

Lemche, Niels P. *Early Israel: Anthropological and Historical Studies on the Israelite Society Before the Monarchy*. Vetus Testamentum Supplement Series 37. Leiden: Brill, 1985.

—'From Patronage Society to Patronage Society'. Pages 106–20 in *The Origins of the Ancient Israelite States*. Journal for the Study of the Old Testament Supplement Series 228. Edited by V. Fritz and P. R. Davies. Sheffield: Sheffield Academic Press, 1996.

Lepri, Isabella. 'The Meanings of Kinship among the Ese Ejja of Northern Bolivia'. *Journal of the Royal Anthropological Institute* 11 (2005): 703–24.

Letellier, Robert. *Day in Mamre, Night in Sodom: Abraham and Lot in Genesis 18 and 19*. Leiden: Brill, 1995.

Levenson, Jon D. 'The Theologies of Commandment in Biblical Israel'. *Harvard Theological Review* 73 (1980): 17–33.

Lévi-Strauss, Claude. 'Guerre et commerce chez les Indiens de l'Amérique du Sud'. *Renaisance* 1 (1943): 122–39.

—*The Elementary Structures of Kinship*. London: Eyre & Spottiswoode, 1969.

—*The Way of Masks*. Translated by S. Modelski. London: Jonathan Cape, 1983.

Lisón-Tolosana, Carmelo. 'The Ethics of Inheritance'. Pages 305–15 in *Mediterranean Family Structures*. Cambridge Studies in Social Anthropology 13. Edited by J. G. Peristiany. Cambridge: CUP, 1976.

Lohfink, Norbert. 'God the Creator and the Stability of Heaven and Earth'. Pages 116–35 in *Theology of the Pentateuch: Themes of the Priestly Narrative and Deuteronomy*. Translated by L. M. Maloney. Minneapolis: Fortress, 1994.

MacIntyre, Alasdair. *After Virtue: A Study in Moral Theory*. 3rd ed. London: Duckworth, 2007.

—*A Short History of Ethics: A History of Moral Philosophy from the Homeric Age to the Twentieth Century*. 2nd ed. London: Routledge, 1998.

—'Moral Dilemmas'. *Philosophy and Phenomenological Research* 50 (1990): 367–82.

—'Truthfulness, Lies, and Moral Philosophers: What Can We Learn from Mill and Kant?' Tanner Lectures on Human Values. 1994.

Malina, Bruce J. 'The Social Sciences and Biblical Interpretation'. *Interpretation* 36 (1981): 229–42.

Malinowski, Bronislaw. *A Diary in the Strict Sense of the Term*. New York: Harcourt, 1967.

—*Argonauts of the Western Pacific*. London: Routledge, 1922.

—'Kinship'. *Man* 30 (1939): 19–29.

Marsman, Hennie J. *Women in Ugarit and Israel: Their Social and Religious Position in the Context of the Ancient Near East*. Oudtestamentische Studiën 44. Leiden: Brill, 2003.

Marvin, Garry. 'Honour, Integrity and the Problem of Violence in the Spanish Bullfight'. Pages 118–35 in *The Anthropology of Violence*. Edited by D. Riches. Oxford: Basil Blackwell, 1986.

Matthews, Victor H. and Don C. Benjamin (eds.). *Social World of Ancient Israel 1250–587 BCE*. Peabody: Hendrickson, 1993.

Mazar, Amihai. 'Three Israelite Sites in the Hills of Judah and Ephraim'. *Biblical Archaeologist* 45 (1982): 167–78.

McCarter, P. Kyle. *1 Samuel: A New Translation with Introduction, Notes and Commentary*. The Anchor Bible 8. Garden City: Doubleday, 1980.

—'The Apology of David'. *Journal of Biblical Literature* 99 (1980): 489–504.

McConville, J. Gordon. *Deuteronomy*. Apollos Old Testament Commentary 5. Leicester: Apollos, 2002.

McCracken, David. 'Character in the Boundary: Bakhtin's Interdividuality in Biblical Narratives'. *Semeia* 63 (1993): 29–42.

McKeating, Henry. 'Sanctions against Adultery in Ancient Israelite Society, with Some Reflections on Methodology in the Study of Old Testament Ethics'. *Journal for the Study of the Old Testament* 11 (1979): 57–72.

McNutt, Paula. *Reconstructing the Society of Ancient Israel*. Library of Ancient Israel. London: SPCK, 1999.

Melville, Sarah C. 'Royal Women and the Exercise of Power in the Ancient Near East'. Pages 219–28 in *A Companion to the Ancient Near East*. Edited by D. C. Snell. Oxford: Blackwell, 2005.

Meyers, Carol. 'The Family in Early Israel'. Pages 1–47 in *Families in Ancient Israel*. Edited by L. G. Perdue *et al*. Louisville: Westminster John Knox, 1997.

Millar, J. Gary. *Now Choose Life: Theology and ethics in Deuteronomy*. New Studies in Biblical Theology 6. Leicester: Apollos, 1998.

Miller, Robert D. II. *Chieftains of the Highland Clans: A History of Israel in the Twelfth and Eleventh Centuries B.C.* Grand Rapids: Eerdmans, 2005.

Mills, David. '"Like a Horse in Blinkers"?: A Political History of Anthropology's Research Ethics'. Pages 35–55 in *Ethics and Anthropology: Debates and Dilemmas*. Edited by P. Caplan. London: Routledge, 2003.

Moberly, R. and Walter L. *Bible, Theology and Faith*. Cambridge Studies in Christian Doctrine. Cambridge: CUP, 2000.
—'Did the Interpreters get it Right? Genesis 2–3 Reconsidered'. *Journal of Theological Studies* 59 (2008): 22–40.
—'Did the Serpent get it Right?' *Journal of Theological Studies* 39 (1988): 1–27.
Moore, George E. *Principia Ethica*. Cambridge: CUP, 1959 [1907].
Muilenburg, James. *The Way of Israel: Biblical Faith and Ethics*. New York: Harper & Row, 1961.
Nagel, Thomas. 'The Fragmentation of Value'. Pages 174–187 in *Moral Dilemmas*. Edited by C. W. Gowans. New York: OUP, 1987.
Naudé, Jackie A. 'קָדֹשׁ'. Pages 877–87 in vol. 3 of *New International Dictionary of Old Testament Theology and Exegesis*. Edited by W. A. VanGemeren. 5 vols. Carlisle: Paternoster, 1997.
Needham, Rodney. 'Prescription'. *Oceania* 42 (1973): 166–81.
Neimann, Hermann M. 'Choosing Brides for the Crown-Prince. Matrimonial Politics in the Davidic Dynasty'. *Vetus Testamentum* 56 (2006): 226–38.
Newsom, Carol A. 'Bakhtin, the Bible, and Dialogic Truth'. *Journal of Religion* 76 (1996): 290–306.
Niditch, Susan. 'Samson as Culture Hero, Trickster, and Bandit: The Empowerment of the Weak'. *Catholic Biblical Quarterly* 52 (1990): 608–24.
—*Tricksters and Underdogs: A Prelude to Biblical Folklore*. San Francisco: Harper and Row, 1987.
—*War in the Hebrew Bible: A Study in the Ethics of Violence*. Oxford: OUP, 1993.
Nietzsche, Friedrich. *On the Genealogy of Morality: A Polemic*. Translated by M. Clark and A. J. Swensen. Indianapolis: Hackett, 1998 [1887].
Nussbaum, Martha. *Love's Knowledge: Essays on Philosophy and Literature*. Oxford: OUP, 1990.
—'Non-Relative Virtues: An Aristotelian Approach'. Pages 242–69 in *The Quality of Life*. Edited by M. Nussbaum and A. Sen. Oxford: Clarendon Press, 1993.
—*The Fragility of Goodness: Luck and Ethics in Greek Tragedy and Philosophy*. 2nd ed. Cambridge: CUP, 2001.
Obeyesekere, Gannath. *Medusa's Hair*. Chicago: University of Chicago Press, 1981.
O'Connell, Robert H. 'עַם'. Pages 429–32 in vol. 3 of *New International Dictionary of Old Testament Theology and Exegesis*. Edited by W. A. VanGemeren. 5 vols. Carlisle: Paternoster, 1997.
Oden, Robert A. Jr. 'Jacob as Father, Husband, and Nephew: Kinship Studies and the Patriarchal Narratives'. *Journal of Biblical Literature* 102 (1983): 189–205.
O'Donovan, Oliver. *Common Objects of Love: Moral Reflection and the Shaping of Community*. The 2001 Stob Lectures. Grand Rapids: Eerdmans, 2002.
—*Resurrection and Moral Order: An Outline for Evangelical Ethics*. 2nd ed. Leicester: Apollos, 1994.
Ogletree, Thomas W. *The Use of the Bible in Christian Ethics*. Oxford: Blackwell, 1984.
Olivier, Hannes. 'יָשׁר'. Pages 563–68 in vol. 2 of *New International Dictionary of Old Testament Theology and Exegesis*. Edited by W. A. VanGemeren. 5 vols. Carlisle: Paternoster, 1997.
Olson, Robert G. 'Good, The'. Pages 367–70 in vol 3 of *The Encyclopedia of Philosophy*. Edited by P. Edwards. 4 vols. New York: Macmillan / Free Press, 1967.
Olujic, Maria B. 'Embodiment of Terror: Gendered Violence in Peacetime and Wartime

in Croatia and Bosnia-Herzegovina'. *Medical Anthropology Quarterly* NS 12 (1998): 31–50.

Ortner, Sherry B. *High Religion: A Cultural and Political History of Sherpa Buddhism*. Princeton: Princeton University Press, 1989.

—*Making Gender: The Politics and Erotics of Culture*. Boston: Beacon Press, 1996.

Otto, Eckhart. 'Of Aims and Methods in Hebrew Bible Ethics'. *Semeia* 66 (1994): 161–72.

—*Theologische Ethik des Alten Testaments*. Stuttgart: Kohlhammer, 1994.

Otto, Rudolf. *The Idea of the Holy: An Inquiry into the Non-Rational Factor in the Idea of the Divine and its Relation to the Rational*. 2nd ed. Translated by J. W. Harvey. New York: OUP, 1950.

Otwell, John H. *And Sarah Laughed: The Status of Women in the Old Testament*. Philadelphia: Westminster Press, 1977.

Outka, Gene. *Agape: An Ethical Analysis*. New Haven: Yale University Press, 1972.

Palmer, Craig T. 'When to Bear False Witness: An Evolutionary Approach to the Social Context of Honesty and Deceit Among Commercial Fishers'. *Zygon* 28 (1993): 455–680.

Paradise, Jonathan. 'A Daughter and her Father's Property at Nuzi'. *Journal of Cuneiform Studies* 32 (1980): 189–207

Pardo, Italo. *Managing Existence in Naples: Morality, Action and Structure*. Cambridge Studies in Social and Cultural Anthropology 104. Cambridge: CUP, 1996.

Paris, Peter J. 'An Ethicist's Concerns about Biblical Ethics'. *Semeia* 66 (1995): 173–79.

Parish, Steven M. *Moral Knowing in a Hindu Sacred City: An Exploration of Mind, Emotion, and Self*. New York: Columbia University Press, 1994.

Parkin, David. 'Introduction'. Pages 1–25 in *The Anthropology of Evil*. Edited by D. Parkin. Oxford: Basil Blackwell, 1985.

—'Introduction: Terminology and Affinal Alliance'. Pages 121–35 in *Kinship and Family: An Anthropological Reader*. Edited by R. Parkin and L. Stone. Oxford: Blackwell, 2004.

Parry, Robin. *Old Testament Story and Christian Ethics: The Rape of Dinah as a Case Study*. Paternoster Biblical Monographs. Milton Keynes: Paternoster, 2004.

Pascal, Blaise. *Pensées et opuscules*. 20th ed. Paris: Librairie Hachette, nd.

Patai, Raphael. *Family, Love and the Bible*. London: MacGibbon & Kee, 1960.

Payne Smith, R. and C. Chapman. *1 Samuel*. Pulpit Commentary. Edited by H. D. M. Spence and J. S. Snell. London: C. Kegan Paul & Co, 1881.

Pedersen, Johannes. *Israel: Its Life and Culture*. 4 vols. Oxford: OUP, 1926.

Peletz, Michael G. 'Kinship Studies in Late Twentieth-century Anthropology'. *Annual Review of Anthropology* 24 (1995): 343–72.

Pelton, Robert D. *The Trickster in West Africa: A Study of Mythic Irony and Sacred Delight*. Berkeley: University of California Press, 1980.

Peristiany, John G. 'Introduction'. Pages 1–23 in *Mediterranean Family Structures*. Cambridge Studies in Social Anthropology 13. Edited by J. G. Peristiany. Cambridge: CUP, 1976.

Philbeck, Ben F. '1–2 Samuel'. Pages 13–145 in *1 Samuel-Nehemiah*. The Broadman Bible Commentary 3. Edited by C. J. Allen. Nashville: Broadman Press, 1970.

Phillips, Anthony. *Ancient Israel's Criminal Law: A New Approach to the Decalogue*. Oxford: Blackwell, 1970.

Pilch, John J. 'Lying and Deceit in the Letters to the Seven Churches: Perspectives from Cultural Anthropology'. *Biblical Theology Bulletin* 22 (1992): 126–35.

Pitt-Rivers, Julian A. 'Honour and Social Status'. Pages 19–77 in *Honour and Shame: The*

Values of Mediterranean Society. Edited by J. G. Peristiany. London: Weidenfeld & Nicholson, 1965.
—'The Moral Foundations of the Family'. Pages 71–93 in *The Fate of Shechem, or the Politics of Sex: Essays in the Anthropology of the Mediterranean*. Cambridge Studies in Social Anthropology 19. Cambridge: CUP, 1977.
—*The People of the Sierra*. 2nd ed. Chicago: University of Chicago Press, 1971.
Plato. *Republic*. Translated by R. Waterfield. Oxford: OUP, 1993.
Pocock, D. F. 'The Ethnography of Morals'. *International Journal of Moral and Social Studies* 1 (1986): 3–20.
Polzin, Robert. *Moses and the Deuteronomist*. Bloomington: Indiana University Press, 1980.
Pontara, Giulliano. 'Violencia'. Pages 1659–64 in vol. 2 of *Diccionario de Ética y de Filosofía Moral*. Edited by M. Canto-Sperber. 2 vols. México: Fondo de Cultura Económica, 2001.
Porter, Jean. *The Recovery of Virtue. The Relevance of Aquinas for Christian Ethics*. Louisville: Westminster John Knox Press, 1990.
Prouser, Ora Horn. 'The Truth about Women and Lying'. *Journal for the Study of the Old Tesatment* 61 (1994): 15–28.
Provan, Iain W. *1 and 2 Kings*. New International Biblical Commentary 7. Peabody: Hendrickson, 1995.
Putnam, Hilary. 'Taking Rules Seriously: A Response to Martha Nussbaum'. *New Literary History* 15 (1983): 193–200.
Quigley, Declan. 'Anthropology in Disneyworld: Rapport, Gardner, and the 'Discipline' of Social Anthropology'. *Australian Journal of Anthropology* 12 (2001): 182–89.
Quinn, Philip L. 'Divine Command Theory'. Pages 53–73 in *The Blackwell Guide to Ethical Theory*. Edited by H. LaFollette. Oxford: Blackwell, 1999.
Rad, Gerhard von. *Deuteronomy: A Commentary*. Old Testament Library. Translated by D. Barton. London: SCM, 1966.
—*Genesis: A Commentary*. Old Testament Library. Translated by J. H. Marks. Philadelphia: Westminster Press, 1961.
—*Old Testament Theology*. 2 vols. Traslated by D. M. G. Stalker. New York: Harper & Row, 1962–65.
Radcliffe-Brown, Alfred R. 'Introduction'. Pages 1–85 in *African Systems of Kinship and Marriage*. Edited by A. R. Radcliffe-Brown and D. Forde. Oxford: OUP, 1950.
Radin, Paul. *The Trickster: A Study in American Indian Mythology*. New York: Schocken Books, 1976.
Ramsdell, Edward T. 'The Old Testament Understanding of Truth'. *Journal of Religion* 31 (1951): 264–73.
Ramsey, Paul. 'Incommensurability and Indeterminacy in Moral Choice'. Pages 69–145 in *Doing Evil to Achieve Good: Moral Choice in Conflict Situations*. Edited by R. McCormick and P. Ramsey. Chicago: Loyola University Press, 1978.
—'The Case of the Curious Exception'. Pages 67–135 in *Norm and Context in Christian Ethics*. Edited by P. Ramsey and G. H. Outka. London: SCM, 1968.
Rapport, Nigel. 'Context as an Act of Personal Externalisation: Gregory Bateson and the Harvey Family in the English Village of Wanet'. Pages 187–211 in *The Problem of Context*. Edited by R. Dilley. New York: Berghahn Books, 1999.
—*Diverse World-Views in an English Village*. Edinburgh: Edinburgh University Press, 1993.

—'Envisioned, Intentioned: A Painter Informs an Anthropologist about Social Relations'. *Journal of the Royal Anthropological Institute* NS 10 (2004): 861–81.
—'Random Mind: Towards an Appreciation of Openness in Individual, Society and Anthropology'. *Australian Journal of Anthropology* 12 (2001): 190–208.
—'The "Contrarieties" of Israel: An Essay on the Cognitive Importance and the Creative Promise of Both/And'. *Journal of the Royal Anthropological Institute* NS 3 (1997): 653–72.
—*The Prose and the Passion: Anthropology, Literature and the Writing of E. M. Forster*. Manchester: Manchester University Press, 1994.
—*Transcendent Individual: Towards a Literary and Liberal Anthropology*. London: Routledge, 1997.
Rapport Nigel and Joanna Overing. *Social and Cultural Anthropology: The Key Concepts*. London: Routledge, 2000.
Rasanayagam, Johan and Monica Heintz. 'An Anthropology of Morality'. Pages 51–60 in *Max Plank Institute for Social Anthropology Report 2004–2005*. Halle: Max Plank Institute for Social Anthropology, 2005.
Rashkow, Illona N. 'Daughters and Fathers in Genesis . . . Or, What is Wrong with This Picture?' Pages 22–36 in *A Feminist Companion to Exodus to Deuteronomy*. Edited by A. Brenner. Sheffield: Sheffield Academic Press, 1994.
Ratner, Carl. 'Agency and Culture'. *Journal for The Theory of Social Behavior* 30 (2000): 413–34.
Rattray, S. 'Marriage Rules, Kinship Terms and Family Structure in the Bible'. Society of Biblical Literature Seminar Papers 26 (1987): 537–44.
Read, K. E. 'Morality and the Concept of the Person Among the Gahuku-Gama'. *Oceania* 25 (1955): 233–82.
Reckwitz, Andreas. 'Toward a Theory of Social Practices: A Development in Culturalist Theorizing'. *European Journal of Social Theory* 5 (2005): 243–63.
Reed, Esther D. *The Genesis of Ethics: On the Authority of God as the Origin of Christian Ethics*. London: Darton, Longman & Todd, 2000.
Richards, Paul. 'New War: An Ethnographic Approach'. Pages 1–21 in *No Peace No War: An Anthropology of Contemporary Armed Conflicts*. Edited by P. Richards. Oxford: James Curry, 2005.
Riches, David. 'Aggression, War, Violence: Space/Time and Paradigm'. *Man* NS 26 (1991): 281–97.
Robbins, Derek. *Bourdieu and Culture*. London: SAGE, 2000.
Roberts, Jimmy J. M. *The Bible and the Ancient Near East: Collected Essays*. Winona Lake: Eisenbrauns, 2002.
Rodd, Cyril S. *Glimpses of a Strange Land: Studies in Old Testament Ethics*. Old Testament Studies. Edinburgh: T&T Clark, 2001.
—'On Applying a Sociological Theory to Biblical Studies'. Pages 22–33 in *Social-Scientific Old Testament Criticism. A Sheffield Reader*. The Biblical Seminar 47. Edited by D. J. Chalcraft. Sheffield: Sheffield University Press, 1997. Repr. from *Journal for the Study of the Old Testament* 19 (1981): 95–106.
Rogerson, John W. 'Old Testament Ethics'. Pages 116–37 in *Text in Context: Essays by Members of the Society for Old Testament Study*. Edited by A. D. H. Mayes. Oxford: OUP, 2000.

Rosengren, Dan. 'Matsigenka Myth and Morality: Notions of the Social and the Asocial'. *Ethnos* 63 (1998): 249–72.
Ross, William. *The Right and the Good*. Edited by P. Stratton-Lake. Oxford: OUP, 2002.
Roth, Martha T. 'Age at Marriage and the Household: A Study of Neo-Babylonian and Neo-Assyrian Forms'. *Comparative Studies in Society and History* 29 (1987): 715–47.
Rouillard, H. and J. Tropper. '*TRPYM*, Rituels de guérison et Culte des Ancêtres d'après 1 Samuel XIX 11–17 et les Textes Parallèles d'Assur et de Nuzi'. *Vetus Testamentum* 37 (1987): 340–61.
Routledge, Bruce. 'Average Families?: House Size Variability in the Southern Levantine Iron Age'. Pages 42–60 in *The Family in Life and in Death: The Family in Ancient Israel*. Library of Hebrew Bible / Old Testament Studies 504. Edited by P. Dutcher-Walls. New York: T&T Clark, 2009.
Rydstrøm, Helle. *Embodying Morality: Growing Up in Rural Vietnam*. Honolulu: University of Hawai'i Press, 2003.
—'Like a White Piece of Paper. Embodiment and the Moral Upbringing of Vietnamese Children'. *Ethnos* 66 (2001): 394–413.
Sahlins, Marshall. *Historical Metaphors and Mythical Realities: Structure in the Early History of the Sandwich Islands Kingdom*. Association for Social Anthropology in Oceania Special Publications 1. Ann Arbor: University of Michigan Press, 1981.
Sasz, T. 'The Lying Truths of Psychiatry'. *Journal of Libertarian Studies* 3 (1986): 121–39.
Scheffler, Harold W. 'Sexism and Naturalism in the Study of Kinship'. Pages 361–82 in *Gender at the Crossroads of Knowledge: Feminist Anthropology in the Postmodern Era*. Edited by M. di Leonardo. Berkeley: University of California Press, 1991.
Scheper-Hughes, Nancy. 'The Primacy of the Ethical: Propositions for a Militant Anthropology'. *Current Anthropology* 36 (1995): 409–40.
Schlegel, Alice, and Rohn Eloul. 'Marriage Transactions: Labor, Property, Status'. *American Anthropologist* 90 (1988): 291–309.
Schneider, David M. *A Critique of the Study of Kinship*. Ann Arbor: University of Michigan Press, 1984.
—*American Kinship*. Englewood Cliffs: Prentice Hall, 1968.
—'What is kinship all about?' Pages 257–74 in *Kinship and Family: An Anthropological Reader*. Edited by R. Parkin and L. Stone. Oxford: Blackwell, 2004. Repr. from pages 32–63 in *Kinship Studies in the Morgan Centennial Year*. Edited by P. Reining. Washington DC: Anthropological Society of Washington, 1972.
Schröder, Ingo W. and Bettina E. Schmidt. 'Introduction: Violent Imaginaries and Violent Practices'. Pages 1–24 in *Anthropology of Violence and Conflict*. Edited by Bettina E. Schmidt and Ingo W. Schröder. London: Routledge, 2001.
Schweitzer, Peter P. 'Introduction'. Pages 1–32 in *Dividends of Kinship: Meanings and Uses of Social Relatedness*. Edited by P. P. Schweitzer. London: Routledge, 2000.
Sharma, Ursula. 'Trust, Privacy, Deceit and the Quality of Interpersonal Relationships: "Peasant" Society Revisited'. Pages 115–27 in *An Anthropology of Indirect Communication*. Edited by J. Hendry and C. W. Watson. London: Routledge, 2001.
Shilling, Chris. 'Towards an Embodied Understanding of the Structure / Agency Relationship'. *British Journal of Sociology* 50 (1999): 543–62.
Shore, Bradd. 'Human Ambivalence and the Structuring of Moral Values'. *Ethos* 18 (1990): 165–79.
Shweder, Richard A. 'Ethical Relativism: Is There a Defensible Version?' *Ethos* 18 (1990): 205–18.
Sidgwick, Henry. *The Methods of Ethics*. 7th ed. London: Macmillan, 1907.

Simons, Anna. 'War: Back to the Future'. *Annual Review of Anthropology* 28 (1999): 73–108.
Simmel, Georg. 'The Sociology of Secrecy and of Secret Societies'. *American Journal of Sociology* 11 (1906): 441–98.
Smith, Daniel J. 'Kinship and Corruption in Contemporary Nigeria'. *Ethnos* 66 (2001): 344–64.
Smith, Henry P. *Samuel*. International Critical Commentary. Edinburgh: T&T Clark, 1899.
Smyth, Newman. *Christian Ethics*. 3rd ed. Edinburgh: T&T Clark, 1892.
Sonsino, Rifat. *Motive Clauses in Hebrew Law: Biblical Forms and Near Eastern Parallels*. Society of Biblical Literature Dissertation Series 45. Chico: Scholars Press, 1980.
Soskice, Janet M. 'The Truth Looks Different from Here or On Seeking the Unity of Truth from a Diversity of Perspectives'. Pages 43–59 in *Christ and Context: The Confrontation between Gospel and Culture*. Edited by H. D. Regan and A. J. Torrance with A. Wood. Edinburgh: T&T Clark, 1993.
Spark, Muriel. *The Prime of Miss Jean Brodie*. London: Penguin, 1961.
Speiser, E.A. *Genesis*. Anchor Bible 1. New York: Doubleday, 1964.
Spencer, Jonathan. 'Violence'. Pages 559–60 in *Encyclopaedia of Social and Cultural Anthropology*. Edited by A. Barnard and J. Spencer. London and New York: Routledge, 2002.
Stager, Lawrence E. 'The Archaeology of the Family in Ancient Israel'. *Bulletin of the American Schools of Oriental Research* 260 (1985): 1–35.
Steinberg, Naomi. 'Israelite Tricksters, Their Analogues and Cross-cultural Study'. *Semeia* 42 (1988): 1–13.
Sternberg, Meir. *The Poetics of Biblical Narrative: Ideological Literature and the Drama of Reading*. Bloomington: Indiana University Press, 1987.
Stiebert, Johanna. *The Construction of Shame in the Hebrew Bible: The Prophetic Contribution*. Journal for the Study of the Old Testament Supplement Series 346. Sheffield: Sheffield Academic Press, 2002.
Stoebe, Hans Joachim. 'טוֹב *ṭôb Bueno*'. Pages 902–918 in vol. 1 of *Diccionario Teológico Manual del Antiguo Testamento*. Edited by E. Jenni and C. Westermann. Translated by J. A. Múgica. Madrid: Ediciones Cristiandad, 1978.
Stone, Ken. *Sex, Honor, and Power in the Deuteronomistic History*. Journal for the Study of the Old Testament Supplement Series 234. Sheffield. Sheffield Academic Press, 1996.
Stone, Linda. 'Introduction: The Demise and Revival of Kinship'. Pages 241–56 in *Kinship and Family: An Anthropological Reader*. Edited by R. Parkin and L. Stone. Oxford: Blackwell, 2004.
—*Kinship and Gender: An Introduction*. 3rd ed. Boulder: Westview, 2006.
Stone, Linda, ed. *New Directions in Anthropological Kinship*. Lanham: Rowman & Littlefield, 2001.
Sullivan, Lawrence E. 'Tricksters'. Pages 45–46 in vol. 15 of *Encyclopaedia of Religion*. Edited by M. Eliade. 16 vols. New York: MacMillan, 1987.
Swanton, Christine. 'A Virtue Ethical Account of Right Action'. *Ethics* 112 (2001): 32–52.
—*Virtue Ethics: A Pluralistic View*. Oxford: OUP, 2003.
Taggar-Cohen, Ada. 'Political Loyalty in the Biblical Account of 1 Samuel XX-XXII in the Light of Hittite Texts'. *Vetus Testamentum* 55 (2005): 251–68.
Tate, Marvin E. *Psalms 51–100*. Word Biblical Commentary 20. Waco: Word, 1990.
Taylor, Laurie. *In the Underworld*. Oxford: Blackwell, 1984.
Thompson, J. A. 'Israel's Lovers'. *Vetus Testmentum* 27 (1977): 475–81.

—'The Significance of the Verb *Love* in the David-Jonathan Narratives in Samuel'. *Vetus Testamentum* 24 (1974): 334–38.

Throop, C. Jason and Keith M. Murphy. 'Bourdieu and Phenomenology'. *Anthropological Theory* 2 (2002): 185–207.

Trappolet, Christine. 'Dilemas Morales'. Pages 437–42 in vol. 1 of *Diccionario de Ética y de Filosofía Moral*. Edited by M. Canto-Sperber. 2 vols. México: Fondo de Cultura Económica, 2001.

Trawick, Margaret. *Notes on Love in a Tamil Family*. Berkeley: University of California Press, 1990.

Trible, Phyllis. *Texts of Terror*. Overtures to Biblical Theology. Minneapolis: Fortress, 1984.

Tsevat, Matitiahu. 'Marriage and Monarchical Legitimacy in Ugarit and Israel'. *Journal of Semitic Studies* 3 (1958): 237–43.

Tsumura, David T. *The First Book of Samuel*. New International Commentary on the Old Testament. Grand Rapids: Eerdmans, 2007.

van der Merwe, C. H. J., J. A. Naudé and J. H. Kroeze. *A Biblical Hebrew Reference Grammar*. Biblical Languages: Hebrew 3. London: Sheffield Academic Press, 2002.

van der Toorn, Karel. *Family Religion in Babylonia, Syria and Israel: Continuity and Change in the Forms of the Religious Life*. Leiden: Brill, 1996.

van Dongen, Els. 'Theatres of the Lie: "Crazy" Deception and Lying as Drama'. *Anthropology and Medicine* 9 (2002): 135–51.

Vaux, Roland de. *Les Livres de Samuel*. 2nd ed. Paris: Les Éditions du Cerf, 1961.

Vice, Sue. *Introducing Bakhtin*. Manchester: Manchester University Press, 1997.

Wacquant, Loïc J. D. 'Habitus'. Pages 315–19 in *International Encyclopedia of Economic Sociology*. Edited by M. Zafirovski. London: Routledge, 2005.

Wakely, Robin. 'מֹהַר'. Pages 859–63 in vol. 2 of *New International Dictionary of Old Testament Theology and Exegesis*. Edited by W. A. VanGemeren. 5 vols. Carlisle: Paternoster, 1997.

Walsh, Andrew. 'Responsibility, Taboos and "The Freedom to do Otherwise" in Ankarana, Northern Madagascar'. *Journal of the Royal Anthropological Institute* NS 8 (2002): 451–68.

Waltke, Bruce K. and M. O'Connor. *An Introduction to Biblical Hebrew Syntax*. Winona Lake: Eisenbrauns, 1990.

Watson, James B. 'Tairora: The Politics of Despotism in a Small Society'. Pages 224–75 in *Politics in New Guinea*. Edited by R. Berndt and P. Lawrence. Nedlands: University of Western Australia Press, 1971.

Watts, James W. *Reading Law: The Rhetorical Shaping of the Pentateuch*. The Biblical Seminar 59. Sheffield: Sheffield Academic Press, 1999.

Wellhausen, Julius. *Der Text der Bücher Samuelis*. Göttingen: Vandenhoeck und Ruprecht, 1871.

Wenham, Gordon J. 'Family in the Pentateuch'. Pages 17–31 in *Family in the Bible: Exploring Customs, Culture, and Context*. Edited by R. S. Hess and M. D. Carroll R. Grand Rapids: Baker Academic, 2003.

—*Genesis 1–15*. Word Biblical Commentary 1. Waco: Word, 1987.

—'Law and the legal system in the Old Testament'. Pages 24–52 in *Law, Morality and the Bible*. Edited by B. Kaye and G. Wenham. Downers Grove: IVP, 1978.

—*Leviticus*. New International Commentary on the Old Testament. Grand Rapids: Eerdmans, 1979.

—'The Gap between Law and Ethics in the Bible'. *Journal of Jewish Studies* 48 (1997): 17–29.

—*Story as Torah: Reading the Old Testament Ethically*. Old Testament Studies. Edinburgh: T&T Clark, 2000.

Westbrook, Raymond. *Property and the Family in Biblical Law*. Journal for the Study of the Old Testament Supplement Series 113. Sheffield: Sheffield Academic Press, 1991.

White, Ellen. 'Michal the Misinterpreted'. *Journal for the Study of the Old Testament* 31 (2007): 451–64.

Whitehead, Neil L. 'Introduction'. Pages 3–24 in *Violence*. School of American Research Advanced Seminar Series. Edited by N. L. Whitehead. Oxford: James Curry, 2004.

Whybray, R. Norman. 'Genesis'. Pages 38–66 in *The Oxford Bible Commentary*. Edited by J. Barton and J. Muddiman. Oxford: OUP, 2001.

—*The Good Life in the Old Testament*. Edinburgh: T&T Clark, 2002.

Widlock, Thomas. 'Sharing by Default?: Outline of an Anthropology of Virtue'. *Anthropological Theory* 4 (2004): 53–70.

Wikan, Unni. *Managing Turbulent Hearts: A Balinese Formula for Living*. Chicago: University of Chicago Press, 1990.

Williams, Bernard. *Truth and Truthfulness: An Essay in Genealogy*. Princeton: Princeton University Press, 2002.

Williams, Michael J. *Deception in Genesis: An Investigation into the Morality of a Unique Biblical Phenomenon*. Studies in Biblical Literature 32. New York: Peter Lang, 2001.

Williams, Peter J. 'Is God Moral?: on the Saul Narratives as Tragedy'. Pages 175–89 in *The God of Israel*. University of Cambridge Oriental Publications 64. Edited by R. P. Gordon. Cambridge: CUP, 2007.

Williams, Thomas. 'Lying, Deception, and the Virtue of Truthfulness: A Reply to Garcia'. *Faith and Philosophy* 17 (2000): 242–48.

Wolfram, Sybil. 'Anthropology and Morality'. *Journal of the Anthropological Society of Oxford* 13 (1982): 262–74.

Wright, Christopher J. H. *Deuteronomy*. New International Bible Commentary 4. Carlisle: Paternoster, 1995.

—'Ethics'. Pages 585–94 in vol. 4 of *New International Dictionary of Old Testament Theology and Exegesis*. Edited by W. A. VanGemeren. 5 vols. Carlisle: Paternoster, 1997.

—'Family'. Pages 761–69 in vol. 2 of *Anchor Bible Dictionary*. Edited by D. N. Freedman. 6 vols. New York: Doubleday, 1992.

—*God's People in God's Land: Family, Land and Property in the Old Testament*. Grand Rapids: Eerdmans, 1990.

—*Living as the People of God: The Relevance of Old Testament Ethics*. Leicester: IVP, 1983.

—'Old Testament Ethics'. Pages 48–55 in *New Dictionary of Christian Ethics and Pastoral Theology*. Edited by D. J. Atkinson and D. H. Field. Leicester: IVP, 1995.

—*Old Testament Ethics for the People of God*. Downers Grove: IVP, 2004.

—*Walking in the Ways of the Lord: The Ethical Authority of the Old Testament*. Leicester: Apollos, 1995.

Yanagisako, Sylvia J. 'Variance in American Kinship: Implications for Cultural Analysis'. *American Ethnologist* 5 (1978): 15–29.

Yanagisako, Sylvia J. and Janet F. Collier. 'Towards a Unified Analysis of Gender and Kinship'. Pages 14–50 in *Gender and Kinship: Essays towards a Unified Analysis*. Stanford: Stanford University Press, 1987.

Yanagisako, Sylvia and Carol Delaney. 'Naturalizing Power'. Pages 1–22 in *Naturalizing*

Power: Essays in Feminist Cultural Analysis. Edited by S. Yanagisako and C. Delany. London: Routledge, 1995.

Zappen, James. 'Mikhail Bakhtin (1895–1975)'. Pages 7–20 in *Twentieth-Century Rhetoric and Rhetoricians: Critical Studies and Sources*. Edited by M. G. Moran and M. Ballif. Westport: Greenwood Press, 2000.

Zigon, Jarrett. 'Moral Breakdown and the Ethical Demand: A Theoretical Framework for an Anthropology of Moralities'. *Anthropological Theory* 7 (2007): 131–50.

—*Morality: An Anthropological Perspective*. Oxford: Berg, 2008.

Zonabend, Françoise. 'An Anthropological Perspective on Kinship and the Family'. Pages 8–68 in *A History of the Family: Volume One: Distant Worlds, Ancient Worlds*. Edited by A. Burguière *et al*. Translated by S. H. Tenison, R. Morris and A. Wilson. London: Polity Press, 1996.

Zorn, Jeffrey R. 'Estimating the Population Size of Ancient Settlements: Methods, Problems, Solutions, and a Case Study'. *Bulletin of the American Schools of Oriental Research* 295 (1994): 31–38.

Author and Subject Index

Scripture Index

Old Testament

Other Ancient Sources